To Moira and Maggie.

With thanks for your patience, understanding and more.

There are a set of religious, or rather moral writers, who teach that virtue is the certain road to happiness, and vice to misery, in this world. A very wholesome and comfortable doctrine, and to which we have but one objection, namely, that it is not true.

Henry Fielding, *Tom Jones*

Contents

PART ONE: Out With The Old … 5

1. THE GIRL IN THE LIFT 6

2. A CALL FROM WHITEHALL 8

3. BODKIN AND LOGGER 12

4. THE TUTORIAL 18

5. A VISIT TO CAMBRIDGE 22

6. READING FROM DIFFERENT MENUS 29

7. HURLY BURLEY 33

8. A DIFFERENT KETTLE OF SUIT 37

9. SOUNDS MADE BY TOP BRASS 42

10. ARS LONGA, PATIENTIA BREVIS 49

11. BRENDA'S LITTLE SECRET 61

12. TROUSER TROUBLE 64

13. ED DINES A DINOSAUR 68

14. BRIAN GOES TO WORK 72

15. SHAKING THE TREE 76

16. BRIAN FIXES IT 80

17. LET'S RUN OVER LALIQUE 83

18. PILLOW TALK 87

19. THE SECRET LIFE OF BRIAN 91

20. UTOPIA COMES TO MIXTON 96

21. GARY MAKES AN OFFER 103

22. A SPLIFFING IDEA 105

23. STORMING THE BASTILLE 108

24. DARLINGS OF THE MEDIA 111

25. 'WHAT'S THIS MALARKEY ABOUT?' 118

26. DEMOS FOR DUMMIES 119

27. AFFECTING ME, AFFECTING YOU 124

28. LET'S CALL THE WHOLE THING OFF 130

29. THE BOMBSHELL 139

30. A CHANCE ENCOUNTER 145

31. OBSTACLES – CLEARED AND CREATED 148

PART TWO:... In With The New 154

32. INQUEST, DIGEST, PROGRESS 155

33. WINNERS OF THE ASHES 159

34. DISS-APPOINTMENT 163

35. MINDING THE GAP 167

36. PROFESSOR ABBOTT GOES ON-LINE – AND OFF-DESK 170

37. A DOUBLE WORK-OUT 174

38. UNTHANK TAKES SOUNDINGS 180

39. DAY TRIPPERS AND PHOTO BOMBERS 184

40. TWO CLOSE ENCOUNTERS 187

41. SOME OF THE EARTH HAD MOVED 193

42. ECO-WARRIORS UNITE! 195

43. CARDS ON THE TABLE 199

44. SHOCK, HORROR AND CAKE 203

45. THE GREEN GORILLAS 205

46. HOMES FIT FOR HEROES 207

47. CARBON FOOTPRINTS 209

48. GORILLA WARFARE 212

49. HOLLY'S LITTLE HELPER 216

50. BRIAN'S LIST 220

51. CAUGHT GREEN-HANDED 223

52. EROS AND THANATOS 228

53. THE POSTHUMOUS TECHNOPHILE 231

54. KEEPING AN EYE ON YOU 236

55. HAPPY BIRTHDAY, ASTRID 239

56. SPOT THE GOOSEBERRY 244

57. HOME DIAGNOSIS 250

58. CASTLES DECLARES WAR 255

59. THE LAUNCH OF MEDISKYPE 259

60. 'SOW A BIT OF DISCONTENT' 261

61. BEATING THE PANELS AND WINDING THE WIND
.... 264

62. HOLLY GETS A SHOCK 268

63. DESKTOP AVIATION 273

64. LEARN AND EARN – OR CRASH AND BURN? 276

65. GENTLEMAN WITH VERY FINE UNIFORM 279

66. GARY BLUFFS IT OUT 285

67. ONLY THE BOWL GOES BEGGING 289

68. BASTARD! 292

69. HEADING FOR A CELESTIAL STATE 297

70. FIT-ED UP 300

71. MORE THAN JUST DESSERTS 302

72. BEATEN TO THE PUNCH 308

73. THE SEARCH NARROWS 310

74. INSPECTOR FOREMAN IS BAFFLED 315

75. KATE'S PARTING GIFTS 316

76. FIT IS A FIDDLE 319

77. DARLING, I'LL NEVER LET YOU GO 321

78. GARY GROPES FOR THE RIP-CORD 326

79. OPEN SESAME! 330

80. ALL IS DECRYPTED 334

81. RAINING ON THE PARADE 342

82. SPIN WHILE YOU'RE LOSING 352

83. SHADES OF THE PRISON-HOUSE 355

84. IT'S NOT OVER TILL IT'S OVER 357

85. ASK ME NO QUESTIONS 358

86. MIXTON REDUX 361

87. NOT RESIGNED, SO RESIGNING 363

88. UNFINISHED BUSINESS 365

89. CRESTING THE WAVE 369

90. A CHILLY AUTUMN 371

PART ONE

Out with the old ...

·

1. THE GIRL IN THE LIFT

Richard Turpin, Vice Chancellor of the University of Mixton, swept his Director of Academic Development and their guest into the lift, pleased that the waiting throng acknowledged their collective eminence by allowing them sole occupancy.

'The doors are CLOSING!' said the disembodied voice as the vice chancellor pressed the button for the eighth floor. He cleared his throat, preparing to deliver a paean to the university which would nicely fill their ascent, when to his slight annoyance the lift immediately slowed for the first floor. The doors opened to reveal a young woman standing like a goddess in a temple. Majestically, she stepped into the lift, her scarlet lips slightly parted, and looked each of the three occupants steadily, smilingly and wantonly in the eye till they were forced to look away.

Except for a pair of bright red high-heeled shoes, she was naked.

Each man was transfixed. Each asked himself if he were hallucinating and if the apparition were visible to the others. Each struggled manfully with his own stirrings.

'Going UP!' affirmed the voice of the lift.

The woman pressed a button on the panel and continued her frank, amused appraisal of the men. The vice chancellor's eyes flicked everywhere, but mostly peered with what he hoped was a neutral, abstracted expression at the top left-hand corner of the lift. He had tried both to glance at the faces of his companions yet avoid eye contact. But the political animal within him was already busy. What the devil was this? Was someone trying to set him up? Had a member of staff learned about the occasion and decided to sabotage it? If so, he would wreak a vengeance of gruesome refinement . . . or was it a student stunt in protest against something? It could be that. Was it rents? Exams? Pass rates? Not the canteen food again? Would this damn lift never arrive? Save for its endless whirr, no sound was heard.

Fingering his cuff-links, Ed Prendergast, the Director of Academic Development looked straight at the woman without flinching. His first thought was 'Yes, please' but he suppressed it rapidly lest it show in his face. He knew that the Vice was keen to make the best of all possible impressions on this, the day of their guest's arrival at the university. Yet he still felt compelled to read what had been written just above the woman's breasts. 'Newfoundland' it said: 'I would be happy to settle there,' he thought. Despite his best endeavours his gaze slipped downwards and encountered, just below the navel, the legend 'Unexplored territory'. Made not of stone but flesh, he glanced lower and realised that the hair on her head was of the same natural colour. Moisture gathered under his collar. He was glad that after his shower that morning he had made free with the *eau de toilette*.

Their distinguished guest was a Cambridge classics don, the holder of a congratulatory first class degree, a doctor of philosophy and lauded author of *Prophetic Elements in the Cosmogenetic Theory of Empedocles*. Yet he couldn't fathom what on earth was going on. His two companions had not so much as raised an eyebrow, let alone uttered a word. Was this an everyday occurrence at the university? Was the campus populated by naked women? If so, what was one supposed to do? Would it seem naive to pass any kind of remark? Should he perhaps inquire what her course of study was? What was the social etiquette for this kind of occasion? The only thought that came to him was that surely 'territory' contained an *o* not an *a*, but somehow this didn't seem the time to offer spelling corrections.

At the sixth floor there was a *ting!* and the lift halted. Including them all in one last candid smile, the woman turned briskly, gave them a valedictory glimpse of her long back, sheer legs and tottering heels, and disappeared through the closing doors. The lift sighed and resumed its climb. Ed Prendergast hooked a finger inside his collar; Dr Robert Unthank, the distinguished guest, stared unseeingly at the doors. And still the silence reigned.

'This way please, gentlemen,' smiled the vice chancellor as the eighth floor arrived.

2. A CALL FROM WHITEHALL

Some months earlier Richard Turpin was looking out of the window, but only in so far as he was allowed to by the grime that had accumulated on the panes. He reflected for a moment that the bird droppings might be an avian version of the Rorschach ink tests, though what one would discern in them he couldn't imagine. One disadvantage of being on the eighth and top floor of the university building was that it hadn't been visited by the window cleaners for some time. As the winch on the cleaning cradle had jammed over the summer and not been repaired, it seemed he was in for an ever gloomier future. Not that the windows on the lower floors had got much attention, though some half-hearted attempts had been made to clean them using ladders and hoses on long telescopic arms. The economies in the maintenance budget might ensure that no windows above the fourth floor were ever cleaned again. Perhaps it was one of life's paradoxes that the higher you got, the better the view but the less able you were to see it. Was this what was meant by looking through a glass darkly?

His gaze returned to the papers on his desk from which even the murky view of the townscape provided respite. He looked at the summary of the university's student recruitment figures, the dropout rates, the numbers gaining firsts or higher seconds, the student satisfaction rating and the staff turnover figures. Beneath these papers, and already pondered, were those advising of the increasing costs of the university's estate, the massive fall in revenue from the government, the ever-rising running, maintenance and administrative costs per head of student and, seemingly added as some kind of bitter financial dessert, last year's takings from the student and staff canteens. The hope of increasing income from the first was dashed by the rising costs of consumables associated with the second.

'What's been going on?' he cried aloud as he looked at the figures again, 'Have they been serving *pâté de foie gras*?'

8

Marian Bussell, his secretary and personal assistant, walked in with coffee in a percolator, cream and sugar, a plate of amoretti biscuits and a large folder. She placed the tray on the desk and poured some coffee.

'I suspect you'll want to drink this before you open this.'

'This being what?' inquired the vice chancellor.

'This being coffee and this being the league tables for all establishments of higher education in the country. I wouldn't bother with the first five pages if I were you, just look at the last one.' Marian mimed passing a knife across her throat. He knew this was coming but had hoped it wouldn't arrive until next week. The folder meant an impending call from the Department, almost certainly Brenda Hodges the Permanent Under-Secretary.

'Has she phoned yet?' It was more of a sigh than a question.

'First thing this morning, such an early bird. I told her you had to take your sick mother to hospital very unexpectedly and that I'd ask you to ring as soon as you got in.'

'Thank you, very helpful.' He wondered, as he often did, why it was that Marian mixed the casually callous, the mimed knife gesture, with the considerate, holding Brenda at bay. He'd inherited her from his predecessor, but because his predecessor had been removed from the building on a stretcher and had never returned, he hadn't had the benefit of a briefing. For a long time he'd assumed she was married. She wore a wedding ring and sometimes referred to someone called Derek in that combination of warmish familiarity and enduring impatience that he took to be the classic demeanour of a wife. But after she mentioned Derek's involvement in a car accident and he had, he thought kindly, inquired after her husband's health she brusquely told him she was not married.

'I'm so sorry. I'd supposed Derek was your husband.'

'Derek supposes the same thing on occasions but I always put him straight.'

It wasn't until late one evening, while he was checking for a missing letter in Marian's office, that more of her relationship emerged. Her phone rang, and picking it up absent-mindedly he had not declared who he was.

'No can do tonight, sweetheart. I've been put on the late shift at short notice. That shooting in Icklesham. Jenny's so worried she's

9

driven over to her parents' place with the kids. So how're you fixed for lunch on Thursday? Will Grumble Guts be out of the office?'

'Ms Bussell isn't here. Can I take a message?'

The caller swore and hung up. The next day Turpin remembered to tell her. 'Your gentleman friend, Derek, phoned for you yesterday evening. He seems to be a policeman.'

'He's certainly a policeman. Not sure about the gentleman.'

Their liaison had been going on for a number of years. In the police force his title was Detective Inspector Foreman, and the irregular hours, shift-work and unexpected incidents all provided ample cover for him to spend time with Marian. While his wife imagined he was lying low outside a seedy flat on one side of town, Foreman was lying comfortably in Marian's bed on the other. When she believed he was taking part in a training exercise so that he and his colleagues were readied against a major emergency, he was addressing the more modest emergency of a corked bottle of wine. Turpin wondered whether Marian had had a husband in the past. With her mannish haircut, angular jaw and strong shoulders, she could not be regarded as pretty but she was nevertheless attractive. What must have been a good figure in her youth had now rounded out, yet when she brought in the refreshments for his visitors their smiles went beyond the pleasure of noticing that the coffee wasn't instant and that some of the biscuits were chocolate.

He watched her top up his coffee and wondered again whether Grumble Guts was a name he truly deserved. The phone rang in the outer office and Marian went to answer it. As expected, he next heard her voice on the internal phone. 'It's Ms Hodges for you, Dr Turpin.' She muted the call and gave a strangled cry before putting it through.

'Good morning, Brenda, how are you?'

'Not good, not good at all, Richard. This is the ninth phone call this morning and none of the previous eight have been pleasant. It'd help me if universities actually got started before eleven in the morning. It's like trying to contact the dead.'

'Sorry I wasn't available earlier, I was – '

'Yes, yes, I know. I hope she's all right. Have you got the out-turn figures in front of you?'

'I have. I admit that they don't make the best sort of reading.'

'As my minister has pointed out in more colourful terms. We're supposed to be educating the nation, Richard, not generating drop-outs, debtors and graduates so poorly qualified they struggle to get jobs as road-sweepers. It's got to get better. We'll want a three-year strategy inside the next month setting out how you're going to turn the situation round., That means more students, fewer staff, an increase in firsts and upper seconds and a university that lives within its means.'

'Brenda, we've talked about these things before. The rationalisation and refurbishment programme's going through senate shortly. We're working on the drop-out rate. And we're always exploring ways to, er, recognise the latent merits of students who can't always do themselves justice in written exams.'

'Richard, you were appointed to solve the problems not explain them. The minister would like you to just get on with it. Remember, what's important is what works, and at Mixton University not a great deal does.'

'I'm going to have to appoint new people. What I inherited wasn't just clapped-out buildings but clapped-out staff.'

'Well, I'm not going to do your job for you, but here's a tip. Contact Bodkin and Logger. I'll email the details to your PA. You want someone with grit and iron. No time for pussy-footing. And Richard . . . do it fast. The target figures for next year will be with you by the end of the week. At the moment, you're below Bolton. I didn't know anywhere could be below Bolton. You're not delivering on the government's manifesto.'

'I can't recall the manifesto saying much about Bolton.'

'Bugger Bolton, Richard. Seventeen places up the league tables inside the next three years or carpet-bombing starts in Mixton.'

'I, I– ,' but the line had gone dead. The vice chancellor returned the phone to its cradle, tried to ignore the pain in his chest, and swivelled to face the window. While he'd been on phone, further bird droppings had streaked the glass. Their Rorschachian interpretation was all too obvious.

3. BODKIN AND LOGGER

Somewhat perversely, Turpin was looking forward to the meeting with the two individuals from Bodkin and Logger. It was a firm of management and recruitment consultants. Initial contacts had revealed that higher education, its ramifications, aspirations and challenges, was an area with which the firm was familiar. This was reassuring. He'd no wish to be talking to individuals who knew only about the problems associated with waste recycling.

Tamsin Ashwood and Katherine Dellacourt sounded young and appealing. He liked the prospect of setting out before them the issues that confronted him, the progress he had made, the hurdles that lay ahead, and the university's willingness to work with others to secure a better future for Mixton. When Marian announced their arrival he was just finishing an aide-memoire which would give a lucid exposition of the overall situation, accompanied by a frank recognition that the road was steep but that hard work leavened with flair and imagination would ensure a bright future. Tamsin and Katherine might wish to take notes and then depart to reflect on the senior appointments that would help turn vision into reality.

As the two women were shown in, he got to his feet but his welcome was almost ignored. Bearing a laptop, a portable screen, a document case and two bottles of expensive mineral water, Tamsin and Katherine politely but crisply refused coffee and requested two glasses. Tamsin placed the laptop on his desk and swiftly set up the screen. Katherine sat down and started talking.

'Thank you for the information your office forwarded. We got further details from the university website and Marian's been very helpful.'

'I'm delighted,' said Turpin.

'The trouble with academics is that they use ten words where one will do. So what Tamsin and I have done is distil the issues into a form we can present over the next forty minutes. Then we have some proposals to put to you. Is that OK?'

Turpin hoped that an airy manner would disguise his feeling that the rug had been pulled from under his feet. 'I'm sure that'll be most helpful but I thought you'd benefit from an overview from me first. Set the scene, so to speak, so that we can be sure that – '

'Of course, of course,' said Tamsin, 'but we do have to be in Wolverhampton by two, so would you mind if we set out our analysis and moved on from there?' Without waiting for a reply she switched on the laptop, pressed some keys and threw the first slide up on the screen.

Within the next quarter of an hour, Turpin's self-assurance drained away like water from a ruptured tank. The presentation was swift and brutal. Slide after slide whirled up, setting out the history of Mixton, its worsening finances, its ageing staff, its declining student numbers, its sclerotic management. Glowing extracts from the university's prospectus jostled with photos of the premises which appeared to have been taken by a paparazzo. The student canteen during what looked like a food riot, the shabby gymnasium, staff and students in scarves and coats because of a heating failure, and, beneath a large placard declaring 'Superfast Broadband for All', the image of a technician fiddling with the lead of an electric kettle.

'We have a number of recommendations,' advised Katherine. 'I'll set out the headlines and Tamsin will pick up the detail.' She then opened a notebook and proceeded to glance at it as she summarised the slide presentation and its implications.

'First, there's a lot of dead wood to get rid of. As you saw from the slides, there are subject areas which have almost as many staff as students. There are postgraduate courses which are taken up by very few students in one year, and then adjusted for the following year when they attract even fewer.'

'We've been anxious to retain the staff delivering these courses. In many cases they have an intellectual pedigree that benefits the university.'

'*Did* benefit, Dr. Turpin. Some of the pedigrees date back twenty years. If they were show-dogs they'd have been humanely destroyed long ago.'

'Resting on their laurels, you think.'

'No,' said Katherine, 'resting on their bottoms in armchairs and complaining about the rigours of teaching and the inadequate time for research.'

'We do have research students, you know: the MA in Product Engineering, for example.'

'Yes, we audited it. Six staff, an expensively equipped workshop, lots of visits to leading-edge companies, mainly in Barcelona, and six students.'

'Six very sun-tanned students,' interposed Tamsin.

'We're aware,' said Turpin, starting to bridle, 'that an inviting prospectus hasn't always attracted students in sufficient numbers. A cross-campus working party is looking at ways to rationalise.'

'Yes, we spoke to the working party's chair, the fourth in the last eighteen months, who seems frustrated at the lack of progress.'

Tamsin joined in again. '*Seems* frustrated, but actually he isn't. These working parties comprise turkeys who're not voting for Christmas but to adjourn it *sine die*. They've got their future to consider, including pension entitlements.'

'After all,' added Katherine, 'if you had a fifteen-hour teaching week, and twenty weeks 'non-contact time' a year, would you rush to bring it all to an end? I know, I know, there are the administrative duties, the planning of new courses and, of course, as you say . . .' Katherine paused for a moment and looked Turpin directly in the eye, 'the invaluable research.' She paused and read from a notebook in front of her, '"Dental Imagery in Contemporary Literature" by Dr. Eric Uggles; "Quiddity, Relativity and Numinosity in Scottish Empiricism" by Professor George Abbott. How would the world survive without it?'

Turpin opened his mouth to respond but sank back silent in his chair.

'On a cost-benefit analysis we believe the university should shed all foreign languages, all literature courses, anything and everything to do with mechanical engineering, electrical engineering, electronic engineering and production engineering. There are some pseudo-science courses that should either be shut down immediately or merged with something more comprehensible.'

'I thought you were here to advise on staffing, not destroy half the university's curriculum.'

'The two,' averred Tamsin, 'are related. Look, we know this is hard but it's unavoidable. There was a time – your time – when ten per cent of eighteen to twenty two year olds went to university. But

14

successive governments have set up a production line by conferring the title "university" on all sorts of places. In 1960 there were thirty universities, in 1970 fifty. Now there are over a hundred and thirty. Student numbers have gone up exponentially and average student attainment hasn't. But you know all this. The government now wants the able but unlettered to take apprenticeships, leaving the others to go to university and show that we can continue to be a well educated nation, able to compete with the best – '

' – which explains,' said Katherine, who had a talent for satirical asides, 'why our public utilities are run by foreign firms, our major London banks are controlled from overseas, the French run our nuclear industry, the high street is dominated by McDonald's and its ilk, and – '

' – and ,' resumed Tamsin, 'why our plumbers are Polish.'

Katherine leant forward in her chair. 'You know the Department for Education better than we do. They want higher numbers, bigger headlines and ever rising standards. We all know it can't be done, but what is needed are people of your, er, integrity to manage it as dextrously as possible so that the world of learning won't be taken over by . . . ' she paused, searching for a name.

'You're telling me that the Philistines are at the gate.'

'No,' said Katherine, 'not at the gate. In the entrance lobby and on their phones.'

'We're telling you,' said Tamsin, with sudden fervour, 'that there's an opportunity for Mixton to provide courses that will be useful. They'll allow young people to leave better educated than when they started, and be better fitted, even if not by a great deal, for the world of work. And that's what it's all about. You need someone to push through a tough agenda on the basis that there is no alternative."

'But what will we be teaching? You seem keen to eliminate everything that's academic,' protested Turpin.

'Mixton needs to focus on those things it does well, and those it can do better. All the creative arts stuff, especially the conceptual and interactive art, should stay. It's popular, eye-catching, engages with young people and pulls in the students. You must also develop the *para* agenda.'

'Para?'

15

'Para-medical, para-legal, para-clinical, para-pedagogy, para-veterinary. There's now no chance of offering courses without the prefix. You could give an academic gloss to a whole range of ancillary professions. Entry qualifications could be lower, the learning incline shallower, with lots of practical activities to make studying lighter and easier. And the courses could end in a qualification which, who knows, might even lead to a job.'

Katherine paused, but even before Turpin could think of responding Tamsin had taken up the theme. 'It's hardly surprising that as the NHS slides downhill, complementary health-care's on the rise. There's a growing industry in chiropractics, aromatherapy, acupuncture, mud-bathing, moxibustion, herbal medicine, rolfing, Alexander technique, and something even more esoteric which involves sticking hot glasses on people's bottoms.'

'You seem to have missed out voodoo.'

'We'd need to repackage it,' said Katherine without a pause. 'Then, as a separate major new development, there's the green agenda.' She threw up another slide.

'Spare me the BA in Composting,' sighed Turpin.

Katherine smiled, 'It's clear that global warming's moving out of the dry world of statistics and into the hearts and minds of the young. We must seize the opportunity and put on courses that are practical, relevant and even uplifting.'

'We've held focus groups,' said Tamsin, 'and young people really do want to save the planet.'

'Aren't they just the fickle followers of fashion? Put murder mysteries or spy movies on the telly and half the country's sixteen year-olds want to become pathologists or join MI6.'

'True. But if there's a ready-made enthusiasm like this, Mixton should exploit it under the slogan of "Mixton meets the moment. Get a degree, get a job, save the planet." This is one area where the government wants to try and demonstrate progress before the next election. You need a two-way tie-up with targeted funding from the government and from firms that are into solar power, water power, wind power, conservation, insulation, district heating and energy exchange. Couple all that, if you can, to a pilot development site for the lowest energy houses in Britain, and Mixton goes on the map. The green map.'

'So,' said Katherine, 'it's out with the Aga and in with the condensing-boiler. But you need to present as someone who's not afraid to take tough decisions because the alternatives are worse – closure or signing the whole university over to some pie manufacturer who wants to run a creationist college.'

'That's a poor joke,' said Turpin.

'We're not trying to be funny. Look at the growth of the academies, schools being run like mini-businesses by people who want to plant their logo in the middle of what used to be the public sphere. Universities are the next obvious target. There are rich folk who'd jump at the chance to have a uni named after them, and get even richer in the process. Once they've made their pile they grow hungry for public recognition, the baubles, the invitations to Downing Street, dinner at Chequers, invites to Buckingham Palace. They obsess about their legacy. We're fairly sure that discussions have already begun with some high street names. They'd blend nicely into the new ethos of higher education.'

'So do we get the "Toys R Us" University of Juvenile Leisure Technologies?'

Tamsin pretended to write it down.

'We think you need to move now and move fast,' said Katherine. 'We've looked at several universities and done a risk assessment of their chances of surviving the next three years. There are five categories: No Risk, Slight Risk, Medium Risk, Strong Risk.'

'That's four. What's the fifth and where is Mixton?'

'The fifth is Goodnight Vienna, and that's where Mixton will be without immediate action.'

Turpin looked mournfully up at the ceiling, 'I suppose that even in this context we should be grateful to be associated with Vienna.'

'Here's a draft advert for a Director of Academic Development along with the personal spec. And here,' Katherine reached inside her document case, 'are the four individuals we want you to talk to about putting their names forward.'

'But I don't know any of them.'

'They know about you. We've paved the way for your phone calls.'

'We must be off,' said Katherine, rising to her feet. 'We're leaving copies of the slides behind and the underlying analysis plus relevant names, contact phone numbers and email addresses. Look it all over and get back to us. We can run the recruitment exercise for you and get the right person in post within five weeks. But think,' and here she leant towards him almost seductively, 'Ed Prendergast.' Then, like a gambler playing a trump card, she flicked a photograph on to his desk.

For a long time Turpin stared gloomily at the door through which the two besuited women had left. He vaguely recognised two of the four names on the list and then his eye slid to the foot of the draft advertisement:

Mixton University is an Equal Opportunities employer which is keen to ensure that its staffing accurately reflects the communities and causes it serves. Its policy is that no person should be discriminated against by reason of their religious beliefs, ethnicity, gender, marital status, sexual orientation, age, hours of work, disability or membership/non-membership of a trade union.

He picked up the picture of Ed Prendergast and took in the bristly gelled hair, the fake tan and designer stubble. On the back were the words 'Available now!!'

4. THE TUTORIAL

'Come in!'

Gary Dorn answered the timid knock with a hint of petulance. A man of his leftward political views didn't wish to admit to himself that the students were getting in the way of his main preoccupation, which was to finish writing his new book. Entitled *Culture, Identity and the Postgendered Imaginary* it was already eighteen months overdue, and under their usual guise of genteel diffidence the publishers were growing importunate. Yet now it was his student consultation period, and before him lay a pile of essays he'd already spent several hours marking. They were the first assignment for the Level One module he taught on Media and Power, and they had to be returned to his umpteen tutees in a series of individual sessions. This would take up the best part of an afternoon.

There was something else he didn't wish to admit to himself. For the most part, and again for sound political reasons, he took a relaxed view of the way the students wrote their essays. Perhaps because his own style wasn't everything it might be, he felt that grammar, spelling and punctuation were trivial matters when weighed against the need to widen access to higher education and raise the kids' consciousness. Some of his colleagues, like that sad old fart George Abbott, were absurdly pedantic about these things, probably because they weren't up to speed on the more substantive stuff. Nevertheless, this latest batch of essays was pretty dispiriting. They seemed to be cobbled from a number of different idioms. Short stretches of adequate if wooden prose would suddenly veer into email and text-message lingo or bloom into purple passages artlessly plundered from library books or Wikipedia. Capital letters were missing when needed, present when not. A collective noun might meander between singular and plural verbs in the course of one unending sentence. You marked the essays not so much on what the students said as what you thought they were trying to say. It was fatiguing and time-consuming, and he had better things to do. His mood failed to improve when he noticed that the student who walked in was very pretty.

'Who are you?'

'Hi, Dr Dorn. I'm Holly. Holly Ainscough.'

She sat down in the empty chair at the side of his desk, and he pulled her essay out of the pile. He now remembered seeing her at his lectures. She always sat in one of the rows high up at the back, whispering and giggling with several other girls and a couple of youths. Throughout the lectures one of the youths chewed stolidly and wore earphones that were attached to an iPhone. Holly had long straw-coloured hair and a broad, ingenuous face with an ample mouth. She was wearing an embroidered T shirt with a scooped neck and a denim skirt that amounted to little more than a deep belt. Dorn tried not to notice.

He leafed through her essay, now remembering it as an especially illiterate and clueless travesty of several of his lectures. Those motifs that he'd carefully disentangled within the module's main theme and systematically expanded through week after luminous week she'd taken, and like some doltish machine operator in a car-breakers' yard, had compacted into a single, meaningless, lumpen mass. The essay was such a pig's breakfast that he didn't know where to begin. He re-read a line or two and looked wearily up at her. She gave him the smile of one who knows that all the world loves a pretty girl and will be kind to her. And then she shifted slightly in the chair and crossed one pert, sleek thigh over the other. Dorn felt less in control than he'd have liked and looking quickly back at the essay seized on the first thing that met his eye.

'Hedgemoney. Hedge money. What do you mean by this?' He slid the essay towards her and pointed and she picked up the page.

'Um . . .'

'I think you mean "hegemony", don't you? – the control exercised by a particular social group. And what you presumably have in mind here is the informal and to a degree paradoxical power relationships that exist between politicians and media professionals.'

She smiled at him winningly and didn't deny it. Dorn kindled to his subject. He pushed back his chair and pressed the tips of his fingers together. 'Of course, and in this case particularly, there are negotiated and conditional aspects to hegemonic control, and it's important to remember that . . . '

She continued to smile at him and he felt himself softening and smiling back too, and growing ever more eloquent and expansive. As a kid straight out of school perhaps she shouldn't be blamed too much for her naivety, and now that he was able to deconstruct for her the familiar world of radio and television, showing its organisational structures in a fresh and sophisticated light, she must be finding him very impressive. Yet as he finished his short disquisition, his irritation returned slightly. He'd relented rather more than he'd intended and now made another effort to restore the distance between them.

'So yes, Holly . . . hegemony, not hedge money. If you're not sure of the word, all you have to do is use the spell-checker.'

He was not being altogether reasonable. Part of being ignorant, he reflected, is not even to know when you're making a mistake, so why should it occur to you to check it? And in any event, the spell-checkers were often just as crass as those whose spellings they checked. In the senior common room Kate Huckerby told a story about one of her students who wished to cite the work of the distinguished feminist philosopher, Luce Irigaray. Unsure how to write the name, the student resorted to the spell-checker and in the course of an otherwise acceptable essay made references to the work of someone called Loose Urinary.

Dorn flicked through another page or two of Holly's essay and lighted on what passed for a sentence. *Because the bbc relys on the Goverment for it's License fee they cant critisise them to much the next time its up for grabs they could give some of it instead to channel Four says they could of had some of it, their a Broadcaster who's remit is pubic servise too*

'What do you mean by this?'

He swivelled the page towards her and she pushed her chair in a little and leaned forward to get a closer look. Dorn found himself staring at two plump, white breasts sitting neatly inside her scoop-top like tremulous eggs in a nest. A spasm of lust shot through him. She frowned at her own words with the total incomprehension of one who was reading something she'd never seen before – and which was written in a foreign language. Her lips worked slowly and silently as her eyes ran along the lines of the page. Dorn noticed the length of her neck and the way a dangly ear-ring lay across it like coins on satin. And again his eyes dropped to those perfect breasts. He grieved, not for the first time in his career, at the difference between how a student looked and what, if anything, she thought.

'Thing is, Dr Dorn – '

'Gary. We keep things informal in the Media team.'

' – Gary, I'm not used to writing essays and I find it really hard to say what I mean.' She spoke with a northern twang.

'Didn't you have to do them for your A levels?'

'I came in by the BTEC route.'

He already knew the answer to his next question.

'Didn't you write essays for the BTEC?'

Holly looked doubtful, as though the experience had happened to her a very long time ago. 'We mainly did practical projects and multiple choice stuff. I find essay writing *really* stressful.' And she drew in her lower lip with such a fetching show of dismay that Dorn began to think he'd been a bit hard on this, her first essay at the university, and with a casual twitch of his pen raised her mark from 42 per cent to 44.

'Look, tomorrow afternoon I've got a late window at five-thirty. Drop back then and I'll give you a short session on how to organise your ideas into an essay.'

'Oh thanks, Gary, I'd really appreciate that!' And she looked as gleeful as if he'd offered to buy her a nice top from Primark.

5. A VISIT TO CAMBRIDGE

The weekend in Cambridge had been in the diary for some time, and Turpin was glad of the break it would give him. The advert for the post of Director of Academic Development had gone out and he'd spent some time on the phone talking to prospective applicants who'd been invited to contact him 'for a confidential discussion'. Knowing the competition was a sham, he heard the boredom seeping into his voice as he repeatedly outlined to these already also-rans the strengths of Mixton and the challenges it faced. After concluding the chat with a sudden warm exhortation to the caller to apply, he always allowed himself some time for self-composure.

His escape from Mixton was sorely overdue, the more so because it would take him back to his old college and a reunion with friends and colleagues. As Turpin drove down, he was suffused with pleasurable anticipation. He knew how some of his old friends had fared in the years that followed: of others he was ignorant, since these reunions took place only once every ten years. The programme of events, which lay open on the front passenger seat, invited the guests to choose between options which were available throughout the weekend. As he came to some traffic lights and stopped, he glanced down at it.

FRIDAY AFTERNOON/EVENING
OPTION 1
For those arriving mid-afternoon there will be the opportunity to visit their old rooms and enjoy a chat with some of the staff.
OPTION 2
Those arriving from 6.00pm should secure their rooms and then come to the senior common room for cocktails at 7.00pm before dinner in the Grand Hall.

SATURDAY MORNING

OPTION 1: 10.00am to 12.00pm. Tour of the recent Cavendish Laboratory extension and an opportunity to learn about contemporary research in low temperature physics. Professor Francis Fitzgerald has kindly agreed to host the occasion.

OPTION 2: Punting on the Cam. A number of punts has already been reserved at the landing stage and it will be sufficient for you to give your name and show this invitation.

SATURDAY AFTERNOON: 2.30pm to 4.00pm

OPTION 1: A debate in Hall on the topic 'God *is* in the Quad'. The motion will be proposed by the Very Reverend Hugh Hopworth, seconded by the Chaplain for Jesus College, Prebendary Cressida Lessing, and opposed by Jeremiah Symon, Spasmodian Professor of Modern Philosophy, seconded by Peter Fong, Visiting Fellow in Eastern Religions.

OPTION 2: Walk across the meadows in the footsteps of Brooke, Russell, Keynes, Wittgenstein, and many others, to The Orchard in Grantchester for tea. Special arrangements have been made to ensure that even the jaded palate will be tempted.

SUNDAY MORNING:

OPTION 1:10.00am to 11.00am: Service in King's Chapel

OPTION 2: Lie-in with brunch served at 11.00am

12.00pm Depart

Turpin recognised himself as an Option 2 person.

The lights changed to green and his phone rang. It was a hands-free and he checked to see who the caller was: Ed Prendergast, the new Academic Development man. He let it ring and listened to the message being left, 'Vice, it's Ed. Good news. I can start sooner than I thought. Probably next week. Could you make sure my room, desk, computer and all that are sorted? Thanks. Speak later.'

The call served only to strengthen the unease Turpin already felt about his new colleague. Quite aside from the fact that the man whom he'd been bullied into appointing was now treating him like a valet, Turpin found a melancholy irony in the title of his post. In prospect was not so much academic development as academic destruction. Moreover, Prendergast himself seemed to have about as much academic gravitas as a salesman of pre-owned cars: he was no more, nor less, than a man wielding a hatchet, his object to salvage the institution without regard to the academic price that would be paid. After his appointment, Turpin had intended to brief him very particularly on what he saw as Prendergast's role, but before he could do so the latter dilated on the benefits of his impending arrival, the problems that faced them and his role in ensuring that 'positive outcomes' would be achieved. He spoke largely in slogans and advertising strap-lines. As Turpin moved to qualify his simplistic readings of complex situations, he was met with rejoinders intended to end debate rather than advance thought: 'No gain without pain', 'Close down swim lane communication', 'Promote the get-aheads over the thick heads'. Of analysis, tact, a wish to secure firm evidence, to persuade colleagues, to talk things through, there was no trace. Moreover, Prendergast reeked of *eau de toilette*, shot his cuffs, and with what he took to be a blend of the chummy and respectful, addressed Turpin as 'Vice'. Turpin shuddered, changed channels on the car radio and immersed himself in Haydn.

Grace was intoned in Latin and as they sat down for dinner Turpin was struck by the thought of where life had taken him. He looked round the Old Hall and compared the eighteenth century screens with the plastic partitions back at Mixton, the oriel windows with the jammed metal versions he had left behind, and the mosaic floor with those whose only decoration was impacted chewing gum. Such thoughts must be dismissed or the whole weekend would be painful rather than pleasant, and he concentrated on the potted grouse and quail's eggs before him.

The weekend was indeed pleasant. The cuisine was exquisite, the weather stayed fair, the programme of activities was relaxing, and Turpin pined happily for times that were irrevocable. Sensory delights were enhanced by animated conversations with those whom he'd not seen for ten years or more. Some had done better than he and some had not, but all, especially those in some way involved with higher education, voiced a sardonic view of the government, its practised ability to preach the preposterous with an air of great wisdom and extol the merits of 'education' when it was actually keen on nothing more than vocational training.

After dinner on the Saturday, a number had adjourned to the combination rooms where the conversation turned to the state of the

24

universities. Laurie Devlin, glass of scotch in hand and feet up on the chair opposite, began a tirade: 'The government wants equality of provision. It implies that all universities are equal at the same time as issuing league tables that put them in a hierarchical order. It wants the tired, the poor and the huddled masses, who are of course all yearning to be educated, to flock to the university portals, but is then astonished when they drop out to live off benefits and smoke pot. I think it's now time to abandon all pretence. What we need is the league structure that football enjoys. There'd be the Barclays Premier League consisting of Oxford and Cambridge. Then the Championship would consist of the Russell Group. League One would be the redbricks and the new universities from the sixties, and League Two the even newer universities from the eighties. And finally, there'd be the Freight-Rover Vans Relegation Conference to sweep up everything else. There'd be promotions and demotions between the leagues on an annual basis, along with "transfer windows" when prized academics would be permitted, via their agents, to move from one university to another. A "bung" culture could develop. Transfer fees would escalate, and prized academics, the Messis and Ronaldos of Astro Physics or European history or logical positivism, let us say, would command ever larger salaries.'

'Not sure it's going to work, Laurie,' intervened Erica Hopwood, the vice-chancellor of a London University college.

'Where's the weekly excitement of X playing Y? How are you going to determine what university goes into which league? Wouldn't the lower divisions collapse from lack of support?'

James Munro from Durham took up the challenge. 'We move from a narrow range of permitted student fees to market-driven ones. We remove this foolish cap which prevents us from charging the proper market rate. Harvard doesn't charge the same as Tombstone State, so why should we at Durham be charging the same as Mix-, er . . .' he caught Turpin's eye and decided not to embarrass his old friend, '. . . the Jaywick University of Performing Arts and Dancing Donkeys. Each university should charge the fees it thinks the punters would pay. £30,000 per annum at one end and £20 per month at the other.'

'Payable by the student or the university?' asked Devlin, with a self-satisfied snuffle into his whiskey.

Munro continued: 'Position in the league tables would be determined by a mix of degree results, staff-student ratios, entry qualifications and celebrity students.'

'Celebrity students?' queried Turpin.

'Yes, to help level the playing field. So a member of the royal family gives you one hundred points, any close relative of a TV presenter two hundred points, and the son or daughter of a recently convicted mass murderer, five hundred points. This is on the basis that it's not so much what or where you study as whom you are sitting next to.'

'I accept,' said Devlin, 'that we cannot replicate the uncertainty and drama of the weekly football matches. But I think we could spice things up by reviewing the league tables three times a year and getting William Hill to run a book on runners and riders, winners and losers. Five to one on Cleethorpes University getting into the Second Division. Bet now on Macclesfield's relegation.'

'Would we allow foreign imports?' queried Erica.

'Certainly!' replied Munro. 'Much effort'll be spent on luring the top players away from their *almae matres*. Plenty of brilliant minds are going to waste in places like Yale, Harvard, the Sorbonne and . . . the Bob Jones Theological College in Carolina. They'd be offered attractive packages of big salaries, book bonuses, loft apartments, return flights home five times a year, and membership of one of the more louche West End clubs.'

'Wouldn't we run the risk of having the top universities dominated by foreign players with little loyalty and less English?' asked a listener, 'Just like the Premiership?'

'Oh, I do hope so,' said Devlin, who liked foreign scholars and students of both sexes, especially if they were young and Chinese.

Turpin eased back into his large armchair and gave the nod to a waiter eager to replenish his glass of port. But something uneasy was developing at the back of his mind, and it wasn't just the knowledge of which league Mixton belonged to. He repressed the thought and resolved to enjoy the moment.

For the walk across the meadows to Grantchester, the late October sunshine was unusually warm. Only a few had braved the Cavendish to learn more about the problems posed by super fluids at temperatures close to zero. Most, dressed casually, assembled at the Backs for the gentlest of strolls in search of light refreshments on benches in a sheltered nook. Walking ahead and seemingly in their party yet not of it, was a fine looking man in his mid-thirties. He was tall and slim, with a full head of dark hair and a firm profile. He was immaculately dressed in an expensive open-necked shirt and well-fitting jacket, and as he strode firmly along he surveyed all around him with the pleasant countenance of a man who was confident, benign and at peace with the world. Suddenly Turpin thought that there was something familiar about him. He quickened his stride.

'Robert? Robert Unthank!'

'Uncle Richard!'

They shook hands warmly. The last time Turpin had seen him must have been some twenty or more years ago, when Unthank was a lad in his early teens at Winchester. The occasion might even have been the funeral of his father. The Reverend Doctor Charles Unthank had been a distant cousin and close boyhood friend of Turpin, and their friendship had continued through the years at Cambridge, where Charles, always intent on taking holy orders, had distinguished himself as a theological scholar. What had made him so attractive in the eyes of the world was that he combined a pleasant, charming and sociable disposition with great intellectual gifts, and, once ordained, a genuine zeal for his duties as a rural parish priest. Courteous and friendly to the least of his flock, he was universally loved and, on his death, grievously mourned. At his funeral Turpin was forced to reflect sadly on the vanity of human knowledge. For what a horrible irony it was that Charles Unthank, a man who had written a highly lauded doctoral thesis on the theme of human insights into divine providence, should then have fallen to his death while examining some dry rot in the roof of his church. He left behind him a wife, Laetitia, two beautiful daughters, and Robert, a handsome, clever little boy. Laetitia was a scion of nobility, so the children were well-provided for and promptly dispatched to public schools. Apart from the exchange of Christmas cards and a very occasional letter, Turpin had rather lost touch.

'What on earth are you doing in this party?'

'Here under false pretences. I've got rooms in college and was asked to act as a nanny for the weekend in case anyone got lost or confused. I'm pleased to say that nobody has.'

Further questions elicited details of an illustrious academic career that Laetitia, never one to gush about her children, had alluded to only briefly in her letters. After collecting a first in classics at Oxford, along with the highly competitive Makepeace Prize for Latin composition, Unthank had moved to Cambridge to study for his doctorate and written a thesis which formed the basis of his book on Empedoclean cosmogeny. 'But then my academic interests extended from the philosophical to the linguistic. I began to explore the diffusion of the Romance dialects and travelled round much of Central and South America. And that was when I noticed how poor and disadvantaged so much of the world is.'

'You're now a family man?'

Unthank smiled. 'I met Clare while she was reading English at Newnham, and we married soon after. We've got three kids – Severus, Dora and Joan. But what brings you here, Uncle Richard?'

'Oh, just chasing *le temps perdu*, dear boy. In another ten years we'll all be in wheel-chairs or clutching walking frames, so I thought I'd better get to this reunion before arthritis and anno domini got the better of us. At the moment I don't think there's an artificial hip in the entire bunch, but in another ten years we'll be fifty per cent spare parts.'

They laughed briefly and looked out over the haze of the meadows and the willows trailing their fronds in the water. It was a perfect scene, marred for Turpin only by the sudden thought of Prendergast gleefully honing his hatchet. He shook his head slightly in an effort to clear it. 'For a man still relatively young, you're a marvellous success story, Robert – on the threshold of a dazzling career as a scholar and with a flourishing family to go home to. Your father would have been proud of you.'

'I know, Uncle Richard, I know.' His young companion sighed and shook his head in a way that suggested, as well as gratitude, a hint of dissatisfaction or regret. 'In a way I've been far too lucky. I've seen just enough of the world to realise not only how wretched many of its people are but the limits of all our intellectual efforts to make sense of it. I really feel I should be putting something back.

28

Doing something else, at least for a while . . . something *practical.*'
They'd paused and Unthank stirred the ground meditatively with his
shoe. 'Perhaps I should do a spell of VSO. Or maybe help to turn
round some deprived, inner city school in Glasgow.'

A gleam appeared in Turpin's eye. 'I might have just the thing
for you, dear boy. But it would be a much, *much* tougher challenge
than any inner city school in Glasgow . . . '

6. READING FROM DIFFERENT MENUS

Ed Prendergast closed the menu and glanced round at his fellow
diners. They were all youngish couples talking with varying degrees
of intimacy. He cracked his knuckles one by one, played with his
untouched glass of mineral water, and thought about the guest who
would shortly join him. He'd arrived rather early but this would give
him time to marshal his thoughts.

Prendergast was a man of aggressive self-belief. He had a high
opinion of his own abilities and was willing to take on anyone who
doubted them or felt able to emulate them. He regarded those whom
he worked with less as colleagues than competitors, and though his
own academic background was modest he was not at all daunted by
the task of applying his managerial skills to the world of academia.
Indeed, he despised academics as a race, believing, no doubt
correctly, that he was more than a match for their naivety,
unworldliness and ineffectual theorisings. Yet he was irked by the
arrival at Mixton University of Robert Unthank, the man whom he'd
invited to lunch. He believed that Unthank would be a rival in his
efforts to steer Richard Turpin, and was determined to get the
measure of him.

Why on earth had Turpin hired him? When the appointment was
announced, Prendergast thumbed his phone and put the question to
Brenda Hodges at the Department for Education, whose protégé he
was. But he must have caught her at a bad moment, because she
claimed to know nothing of the matter and expressed uninterest.'Ed,
I've no idea who this Thankless is,' she purred. 'Richard Turpin is
his own man and appoints whom he wishes. But it doesn't alter the

fact that change must come to Mixton whether Richard and his new friend wish it or not, and I'm relying on you to drive it through.' And she hung up. Unthank had first appeared at Mixton University not long after Prendergast's own appointment – and as Turpin's VIP guest. Prendergast was summoned by Turpin to welcome him and accompany them both on a tour of the university buildings. He recalled that the occasion had almost been sabotaged when that naked woman had got into the lift with them, but stiff upper lips had carried them through. He reflected ruefully that he never had got to the, er, bottom of that young lady. But when the tour was over, Turpin dismissed Prendergast and swept Unthank off to a private lunch. The next thing was that an interview panel was convened, on which Prendergast was not invited to sit, and towards the end of the autumn term it was announced that Dr Robert Unthank had been appointed by the university as its Director of Outreach and Enterprise.

What on earth did that mean? 'Outreach' presumably had something to do with distance learning and widening student access, but 'enterprise' was business – selling – and aside from the fact that the university already had a marketing office, why appoint an academic to such a role? It was a well-known fact that academics couldn't sell hot crap to a hungry fly, and Unthank's rather gentle and donnish air suggested that he was unlikely to prove an exception. The conclusion was inescapable. Turpin had fabricated a job to get one of his Oxbridge cronies on board, though with what particular purpose remained to be seen.

Prendergast sipped some water and gazed once more round the restaurant. He regarded Unthank as a rival, but his feelings were complicated. As something of an inverted snob in his attitude to the values that Unthank embodied, he tried to dismiss him as a laughable toff. Yet they were values that were strangely enviable. And Prendergast's envy was aggravated by the fact that he had to admit to himself that Unthank came across as a very gracious toff. He was courteous without condescension, charming yet not unctuous. But before he took up his new post when the spring term began next week, Prendergast needed to learn more about what made him tick. Would he back the planned reforms or oppose them? And if he backed them, would he get more of the credit for their success than

Prendergast would? Prendergast was determined that when Mixton University was transformed, the achievement should be seen as his and his alone. And, by God, did the place need it! About a fortnight after he was appointed, he'd made a brief return to Mixton to finalise the terms of his job.

'I'm here to see Dr Turpin, but is there somewhere I can get a decent cup of coffee first?' The lady he had asked called over a rather scruffy individual in a uniform that struggled to fit him, and whose badge described him as Brian, an Estates Management Officer. Prendergast soon learned that this was the rather grand designation for those who worked as porters and caretakers, and was commonly abbreviated to 'ESMO'.

'This way, sir. Don't want you to get lost.'

As they walked along a corridor and descended a short flight of stairs, Prendergast asked whether the coffee bar was wireless-enabled.

'Yes, sir, but I'm afraid it's usually Radio One, which may not be your cup of tea – or even coffee,' he simpered. 'Here we are. Oh, no, sorry, wrong way. Just have to retrace our steps a bit.'

Prendergast saw Brian as personifying the organisation he was joining: flabby, shambolic, technologically backward, adrift. Later, the conversation with the Vice had gone much as he'd anticipated. He'd been obliged to cut through the pussy-footing and make it clear that he joined sinking ships only to raise them, and if it involved throwing people overboard, well and good. The Vice had responded with some pieties about collaborative endeavour, keeping staff onside, maintaining morale and not rocking the boat too much . . .

Prendergast's thoughts were interrupted by the arrival of his guest. Bestowing his overcoat with a smile on the waitress who hastened to take it, Unthank greeted him with a similar easy warmth and swiftly gave his order.

'Given the task ahead of us, I thought I should re-read Newman's *Idea of a University*. But you might agree that the lessons he offers us aren't wholly illuminating.'

Prendergast frowned at Unthank and chewing some smoked salmon, made no reply. Newman . . . the name rang a bell. Ah yes, he thought, I know the bloke.

'His idea that our role isn't to nurture talent or knowledge for its own sake but make students better members of society is clearly helpful. Instruction rather than research seems to be his theme. But then what are we to make of his assertion that we should be training minds rather than diffusing useful knowledge?'

'Frankly,' rejoined Prendergast, 'I don't think Newman has any right to sound off at us about what universities should and shouldn't be doing.'

'Really?' Unthank's fork stopped halfway to his mouth.

'No. He's only been vice chancellor at Bournemouth for six months, and before that he worked in the retail trade.'

Unthank threw back his head and laughed heartily. His new colleague evidently had a highly surreal sense of humour – and, he reflected, as Prendergast stared stonily at him, a brilliantly deadpan style of delivery.

'In any event,' continued Prendergast, 'I think we can leave the fancy theories to others. The way I see it is, we've been appointed to do a specific job to sort things out, put heads on blocks, shake things up, sort the dross from the chaff and hang on to the dr-, er, the cha- . . . whatever.'

Unthank felt the need to show a political realism that his new job would require. 'Of course, times have changed and the government approaches these matters from a different perspective. But I'm sure it'd be beneficial if the three of us, Richard, you and me, had a common view about what we thought we were doing.'

And for the rest of the meal, their conversation followed that familiar pattern in which each person talks past the other, and in such a way that he can take the other's remarks as a broad endorsement of his own. At the same time, both of them gradually sensed that they had rather little in common, and that any cooperation they achieved would arise from conscious effort rather than natural empathy. As coffee was being brought, Prendergast's phone rang. He punctuated a number of grunts and monosyllables with glances at a wrist-watch that appeared to have been designed for an astronaut.

'Sorry about this, Robert, but I've got to go. Great seeing you. I'm sure we can sort Mixton even if we have to climb over some dead bodies along the way. Can you settle the tab and I'll pick it up next time?' And with a perfunctory hand-shake he was gone, leaving Unthank groping for his credit cards.

Only as the waitress held the door open for him did it dawn on Unthank that his new colleague's joke about Cardinal Newman might not have been a joke at all.

7. HURLY BURLEY

Tom Burley leapt through the open doors and on to the dais at the front of Lecture Room ART 5. He wore what at first glance looked like a paint-spattered vest but which in fact expressed a pointillistic message, 'Keep A-breast of Art'. His long and unruly hair was tied to one side with a ribbon, and though clean-shaven, he sported sideburns that recalled the sixties. Built like a bricklayer rather than an artist, he had long arms that ended in calloused hands. On his left hand was tattooed the word 'RIGHT', and on his right one the word 'LEFT'. His face was an open one with smile wrinkles round the eyes and mouth, and his lips were often slightly parted as if in surprise. He raised both hands high and wide of his head.

'Hands up who loves Tracey Emin.'

A thicket of hands appeared.

'Hands up who loves Gilbert and George.'

The thicket became a forest.

'God, there's no hope for any of you.'

'Next: who was accused of throwing a pot of paint into the public's face?'

'My dad.'

'Your dad, Sunny?'

'Yeah, he dropped it when he was on a ladder painting the upstairs winders.'

'Well, he's in the exalted company of an artist called Whistler. What can you tell me about Whistler . . . Bobo? Angeline? Donny? Natcho? Ah, Shaun!'

'If it's the Mr Whistler who lives in the flat next door he's a grumpy old git.'

'Actually, so was the Whistler I had in mind. Here's the "pot of paint" he was accused of throwing.' *Nocturne in Black and Gold: the Rocket* by Whistler reared up on the screen. Never one to miss a chance to create some theatre, Burley put two fingers into his mouth and emitted a piercing whistle. 'Bring on the Whistler!'

Brian in his estates officer's uniform put his head round the door. 'You ready for the posh painting, sir?'

Burley turned back to the students. 'For this day only, and just for you, and under the strictest of security arrangements, I've borrowed the original from the National Gallery.' Through the swing doors, which were held open by Brian, edged two men carrying Whistler's framed masterpiece. They placed it carefully on an easel to one side of the dais. 'Thank you, gentlemen, you may wait outside now.'

'Look after it, sir, worth at least a million, you know,' said Brian, as he and the two men left the room.

Tom Burley bounced back and forth behind the picture with his arms flailing. 'Now, in Whistler's day there were no installations. Art wasn't interactive or dynamic. It just stood there, placid, sometimes flaccid, reified and often deified, hidden inside buildings, protected behind glass, a spectacle not for the people but the pretentious, not for the poor but the rich. Everyone had to be respectful. But here's a puzzle. This painting was seen to be so outrageous that it attracted the rude remark I've quoted. This picture was throwing a pot of paint into the public's face.' He walked off the dais and round to one side of the work that had caused such outrage. 'What do you think? Is it shocking?'

'Nah!'

'Boring, boring!'

'I 'spect he was, like, one of those sad geezers that collected engine numbers and then went and painted his favourite.'

'So are we provoked or offended or stimulated by this picture?' Tom Burley went back round the dais and reaching beneath it brought out a mallet which he brandished. 'Do we want to preserve it or get rid of it?'

'Get rid of it!' came the universal cry. Like a pantomime comic, Burley cupped his hand behind his ear and affected deafness.

'GET RID OF IT!'

'Too bloody right!' shouted Burley and to cries of mingled alarm and delight, swung the mallet into the glass. You could miss most of the lectures of the other staff but Burley was different. He was box office. Unpredictable, provocative, anarchic.

'And if someone throws a pot of paint at you, what do you do?'

'Throw one back,' came the chorus.

A two-and-a-half litre can of Dulux Peppermint Green appeared, along with a large screwdriver. Burley prised the lid from the can and flung the entire contents over Whistler's work. The whoops of delight mingled with gasps. This time Burley had gone too far. Hands went to mouths, there were cries of 'Oh, my God' and 'Fackin' 'ell'. Other mouths merely hung open. Peppermint green dripped to the floor. Students climbed up on the desks to get a better view of the shambles. The uproar had brought back the guards, who stood dumbstruck. 'You'd better come with us, sir,' said the larger of the two, and amid a buzz of apprehension Burley was bundled out of ART 5.

This was the kind of thing the students loved. Yet Burley had never before ventured to smash a framed picture. And he'd never hurled paint over something that was apparently worth a great deal of money. The silence was broken by a querulous voice: 'I know it wasn't much cop, but my mum would've liked it.' The class then broke into a fractious babble. Some deplored Burley's act, others applauded it. Some wondered whether he'd go to prison or whether he'd be bankrupted. Others asked if the class would be blamed.

'How do you mean, blamed?' asked an indignant Shaun.

'Well,' said Natcho, 'You know, like, accessorised after the fact.'

At this, a lot of voices protested that it was nothing to do with them. 'But if Tom gets done for this, we get stuffed, too. We'll all lose the credits we've got.'

The enjoyment of what had happened was now giving way to self-interest. Few students were doing well on the parallel module in the History of Art because it required the ability to write essays. But Burley's module asked little more of them than a willingness to enjoy his performances.

At this point, the doors at the back of ART 5 banged open and Tom Burley skipped down to the dais, waving his arms aloft like a triumphant boxer.

'All right, all right, don't panic. Nobody's going to blame you. It was just a reproduction. You're safe with replica rubbish, but if you demolish the rubbish that's real they'll send you to prison.'

The students cheered him loudly. 'Up the establishment!' 'Art for all!' 'Death to Sotheby's!' 'Burn down the National Gallery!'

'Now,' said Tom, 'there was a purpose behind that little piece of theatre. It should've got you thinking about your projects. Think bold. Think interactive. Think dynamic. And – ' he raised his eyes to heaven, ' – make sure you complete the risk assessment for the health and safety people or you'll only be allowed to fill in dot-to-dot drawings of Botticelli's *Birth of Venus*.'

'Botty who?' asked Sunny.

INVOICE NO. 45/895643
The DeepClean Company
'You splurge, we purge'
To specialist cleaning services undertaken at Mixton University on 23rd October.

To removing broken glass and carrying out thorough inspection to ensure area completely free of shards, splinters and fragments.

To clearing up quantity of imitation green paint, removing same from carpet, desk and other furnishings.

Undertaking the DeepClean Special Pristine Treatment employing proprietary cleaners and specialist carpet renovators.

TOTAL: £350.00 plus VAT
(Inclusive of materials and labour)
TERMS: 30 DAYS FROM DATE OF BILLING
'We keep it gleaming so you can keep beaming'
Send for illustrated brochure now!

RENTALUVVY
'All the world's our stage'
All theatrical activities, events, simulations, impromptu performances provided.

Fully trained actors available day and night to meet any requirement.

INVOICE
VENUE: Mixton University

EVENT: Delivering framed artefact to Lecture Theatre ART 5.
Retiring from Lecture Theatre
Apprehending individual who had undertaken destruction of artefact
Releasing same.
TOTAL: £300.00 inclusive of VAT and cleaning of uniforms.
TERMS: Within 7 days
Visit our website www.rentaluvvy@thegreenroom.com to see us in action.

MEMORANDUM
From: Bursar
To: Barry Powell, Head of Art and Design
I enclose two invoices.
I want Burley's head on a pike outside the staff canteen by tomorrow.

8. A DIFFERENT KETTLE OF SUIT

At the university's Fallowfields campus, tea was being taken in the 'senior common room', or SCR, an old-fashioned appellation that had survived hours of debate at academic board. But the SCR at Fallowfields was an anomaly in more than name. The university buildings elsewhere were provided with grim self-service canteens, but for the academics at Fallowfields afternoon tea was brought in to the SCR and served from a trolley by catering staff. The reason was simply that Fallowfields was an historic building under a preservation order, and owned not by the university but leased to it by Mr and Mrs Cyril Attwood, the last survivors of an ancient and once prosperous local family who owned several fine properties in the Mixton area.

Hence, when the university contemplated any alterations to Fallowfields or the uses to which it was put, it was obliged to consult with the Attwoods. In the incessant search for economies, the university's bursar determined to do away with both the SCR and the catering trolley and replace them with the standard university canteen, but the formidable Mrs Attwood, who possessed a strong sense of *noblesse oblige*, would have none of it: 'I don't understand how scholars can be expected to fulfil their duties if they are obliged to spend time queuing for refreshment at some . . . *serving hatch*!' She spat the last two words out. 'They should continue to be served with proper sandwiches and cakes, just as my brother was when he was at Cambridge.' Her views were so forcefully expressed that the bursar was too terrified to take the matter further.

Fallowfields housed two separate departments. The first was the Department of Art and Design, in which Tom Burley was only the most famous of the eccentrics who taught on degrees in both those subjects. The other was the Department of Media, Literature and Culture, which offered one degree in media studies and another in literature, both of them haphazardly covering that usefully nebulous category, 'culture'. Unlike the degrees in art and design, they were fighting a dogged rearguard against falling student numbers: if the university was planning to cut any of its courses, both would be highly vulnerable.

The media studies degree represented an opportunity it had bungled. During the 1990s such degrees became hugely popular, and Mixton University made an early attempt to clamber on to the bandwagon. The problem, however, was that the senior management had failed to appreciate the reasons for their popularity. For youngsters prone to fantasies about becoming news-readers, disc jockeys and film-makers, they involved relatively little book-learning and a great opportunity to play around with equipment, make programmes and shoot movies. But it was only halfway through the planning stage that the cost of this equipment – of building and fitting out radio and television studios and editing suites, and of buying portable cameras, sound recorders and countless more computers – became fully apparent. Appalled, the management got cold feet and decided to re-package the Mixton degree as one which was essentially about media theory rather than practice. But since most prospective media students were no more interested in theories of media than in theories of particle physics, recruitment was a severe disappointment – limited to the very few applicants who couldn't find places on media programmes elsewhere. Two things saved the degree from an early death. The first was the assiduous

38

way in which the university's marketing office misrepresented it by claiming that it was a ticket to a job in the media industries. The second was an early decision to enrich it with the cognate discipline of 'cultural studies', which at least allowed the students to spend a lot of time listening to pop music, watching TV and movies and reading comics, and thus remain undisturbed by any disjuncture between work and leisure. Nevertheless, the central problem remained, for the students were not only denied the chance to play with lots of glamorous equipment but expected to justify their consumption of the TV shows, movies and comics by providing critical reflections on them in the form of essays, dissertations and the like. Among aspiring students, the degree was acquiring a negative reputation, and admissions had gone into a steady decline.

The degree in literature was in scarcely better shape. In an era of computers and iPhones, fewer and fewer youngsters seemed to be interested in reading books. Indeed they looked on such behaviour as sad, even slightly morbid, and most of those who were interested could study at other, and better, universities than Mixton. The prospects for the entire department were not rosy.

It was tea-time in the SCR, and Professor George Abbott was leafing through a copy of *The London Review of Books*. Though Abbott taught on the media degree, he was a philosopher by training, an authority on the writings of the Scottish empiricist, David Hume. Eric Uggles, Senior Lecturer in Modern Literature, was academically less distinguished. He was hunched over a lap-top and writing in measured but pained terms to the editor of *Poetry Studies*. Beside him lay a letter with a compliments slip stapled to it on which someone had written 'Tell him his article is out-of-date Hoggart and up-to-date hogwash, but tell him nicely'. However, thanks to the administrative chaos that prevailed at *Poetry Studies*, the slip accompanied a letter describing Uggles's piece as 'very perceptive in many ways but one senses the too-long shadow of Raymond Williams's validating categories of culture'.

'Are they taking that article, Eric? I thought it was rather good. Not my field, of course.'

'They're having to hold it over,' replied Uggles, 'but I'm pressing the editor to make sure it gets into the next edition.'

Uggles was trying to balance his dislike of the editor with a recognition that he was in a weak position. The chief criteria by which universities were judged related to teaching, at which he was not good, and research and publication, at which he was worse. Academic managers kept talking about 'impact measurement', something which they claimed would show how influential someone would be in society at large. Uggles could see how it might apply in mechanical engineering, chemistry or biomedics but was unclear how Wittgenstein or Popper would have fared. He reflected that Wittgenstein's dictum, 'That of which we do not know, thereof we should not speak' wouldn't have earned him many impact marks. He'd decided that his best prospect lay in getting published in as wide a range of academic journals as he could. But his only recent success had been a letter in *The Mixton Chronicle* about the desecration of allotments. While he'd become inured to rejection slips over the years, he was dismayed by the fact that they now arrived almost by return of post, or even more dispiritingly, email, and worst of all, text message. But if he was to have a hope of promotion or even of hanging on to his job, he had to get something into print. His only hope was to fawn: 'I fully appreciate the very helpful points you make and am happy to revise the article in the way implicitly suggested. Indeed, I have already done so and hope that the accompanying re-draft will provoke the sort of debate in the journal that both of us are anxious to see.'

Silence descended, except for the pecking at the keyboard and a rhythmic, stentorian noise from Abbott, who was briefly resting his eyes. He and Uggles always arrived early for tea. They enjoyed listening out for the trolley, whose approaching clatter could now be heard. Abbott gave a start, closed *The London Review of Books* and dabbed at his lips. Yet what first burst through the doors was not the trolley but Gary Dorn.

'Enjoy the tea and cakes, gentlemen, because you won't be able to for much longer.'

'And why is that, Gary? Is the revolution going to sweep them away?' asked Abbott. 'Not, I trust' – as the trolley barged through the doors – 'before I can try the new carrot cake which I see we have today.'

'Are the anarchists going to banish the decadence of the cream puff?' inquired Uggles.

'The anarchists aren't going to do sod-all about anything,' said Gary, 'but I think change could be on the way, and we're in the line of fire.'

'Alas,' murmured Abbott, 'no more honey for tea, then.'

'No more nothing if we don't look sharp,' said Gary. He fished a sheet of paper out of his pocket and waved it at them. 'E-mail's just come through. I've printed it off. You've all been copied in. Consolidation, retrenchment, rationalisation; Mixton at the leading edge of change, updating and upgrading and all the rest of the management bollocks. Forget your furloughs, if we don't take action it's likely we'll have to pack up and ship out.'

'I am not,' pronounced Abbott, 'going to ship anywhere at my time of life.' He bit deeply into a scone on which he'd lavished much strawberry jam and a blob of cream.

'I thought the writing was on the wall when they didn't replace Ticker,' continued Gary gloomily. Jeff 'Ticker' Tait was their former head of department. He'd previously been news editor of a national daily paper, but suffering from a heart condition, which gave him his nickname, had entered academia in search of a quieter life and was appointed Head of Media, Literature and Culture some three years before. But the life had not proved quiet enough. After two years in the post, he'd left to become editor of the *Railway Modeller* and – ominously in Gary's view – had not been replaced.

'We've heard all this nonsense before,' rejoined Abbott, chewing busily and spraying bits of scone and jam down the front of his tie. 'Turpin will come down and huff and puff, we'll all sign indignant round robins that'll go to academic board, and the ship will sail on.'

'I know, I know, that's how it's been before. But this time it's not Turpin: it's Prendergast. A different kettle of suit, I think."

'Who is Prendergast?' inquired Uggles, who liked a spot of excitement over his tea. 'Sounds like the new head of office supplies.'

'If only,' said Gary. 'You remember the advert, "Wanted: a forward-thinking, innovative, cutting-edge academic manager of the highest calibre". And the subtext: "No previous experience of universities required but a knowledge of abattoirs would be invaluable". It's *that* Prendergast. Mr Scissorhands is coming to cut us up and feed us to the shredder. This time it's not going to be so easy. The word on the street is that they want to take this place over for two new departments. Install medical examination suites, consulting rooms, couches, diagnostic equipment and herbs and needles for wellness therapists. Solar panels, low-energy labs and, for all I know, compost heaps for the eco freaks. That is what we'll have to make way for.'

9. SOUNDS MADE BY TOP BRASS

Turpin, Prendergast and Unthank were sitting in the vice chancellor's office. The table was strewn with agenda papers and campus maps of various scales. The small-scale maps showed the disposition of the university's estate, while larger-scale ones contained just one or two sites and showed the distances and transport links between them. There was much handwriting on the maps, since each person had scrawled on them as the meeting had progressed, noting the age of the buildings, when they were acquired by the university, what upgrades and extensions there had been, what departments they now housed and how many students frequented each. On separate sheets were figures showing maintenance and running costs and imminent repairs of a capital kind that had been assessed at millions of pounds.

The meeting afforded Prendergast and Unthank a potted history of the university. One map showed two campuses which were once used but had now been sold off, one at Icklesham, the other at Swatchett. Turpin explained that the former had once been Icklesham College of Further Education, which was later proposed for a merger with what was then the Mixton College of Technology. Its purpose would be 'efficiencies through collaboration', as the local MP had put it. The principal of Icklesham College was new and realised that in any merger he would be the first casualty. Determined to oppose it in the local council and at the Department for Education, as well as by confronting the local MP and appealing to those whom the college served, he undertook a series of well-publicised activities which included all the staff lobbying the council and the MP, street demonstrations, and the recording of a song which was composed in support of the college and broadcast on local radio. The campaign was bearing fruit when the principal embarked on his most audacious publicity stunt, a bungee jump from the Lexley Viaduct. Unhappily, the anchoring point on the bridge gave way and the principal hit the ground at a speed in excess of thirty miles an hour. His funeral was well attended, he became known as the Icarus of Icklesham, and the college merger was ratified exactly a year later.

'The building we're in now used to be the college of technology. We moved out of Swatchett and Icklesham some years ago, and became first Mixton Polytechnic, then Mixton University. The label on the bottle changed from Lemonade to Cordial to Chateau Lafitte, though whether its contents have similarly evolved is, er, a moot point. Anyway, we're now approaching crunch time. The government want us to do seven amazing things, increase enrolment, reduce drop-out, crank up the number of upper seconds and firsts, widen participation, introduce innovative courses, either improve or kill off our research activity, and substantially modernise the buildings but with fifty per cent of the costs to be found from our present estate.'

Turpin picked up a biscuit and tapped it firmly on the table like a sailor trying to rid it of weevils. 'I used to tell them it couldn't be done, but was simply ordered to do it. I told Brenda Hodges at the Department for Education that it wasn't so much making bricks without straw as bricks without straw, clay or kiln. I said I'd rather be constructing tower blocks out of biscuits.'

'How did she respond?' inquired Unthank.

'Sent me a packet of ginger nuts. But by the grace of God we've had a stroke of luck. There's no question that the jewel in our crown is Fallowfields. The buildings are lovely and the whole site has huge potential. Only problem is that the university doesn't own it: it still belongs to the Attwoods. However, times are getting hard for them, and they've decided to sell up. The university has found itself in an auction against one other bidder, a gentleman from the Arab Emirates.'

'The Attwoods would surely prefer to sell to us than an Arab,' interposed Prendergast.

'Well, yes,' mused Turpin, "except that this gentleman holds a strong hand of cards. First, he's made clear to the Attwoods that he'll more than match any bid for the property that we can muster. He's already put a higher offer on the table. And there's a further problem. I've had to make clear to Cyril and Betty Attwood that the property would only be of value to us if we could develop it.'

'What scope for development is there?' asked Prendergast, making vigorous notes.

'We wouldn't wish to demolish the main group of buildings – they're in any case listed. But we would seek to enhance them. Make them part of what our architect terms "a dynamic visual cluster" of other structures. And we'd need to open up and build on the paddock and fields behind it. Even better, there's a fair chunk of farming land behind those. The Attwoods don't own that, but the farmer's desperate to sell, and the council are desperate to buy and build on it.'

'What's stopping them?'

'Neither the land behind Fallowfields nor Compton Farm, as it's called, are presently accessible by road. If we could acquire the Fallowfields estate and provide proper access to both it and Compton Farm, no end of things could happen. Planning approval from the council, which would allow us to raise several million pounds. Perhaps the joint development of a single large site. In any event, we'd get the campus we so desperately need.'

'I take it the Attwoods are opposed to any redevelopment of the property,' observed Unthank.

'That's certainly been true in the past,' grimaced Turpin.'They haven't been the easiest of landlords. A pair of nit-pickers. They can't see the world must change. Instead of looking at the bigger picture, they fuss about which way the lines on the bloody lawns run. And whether the stones edging the drive are whitewashed.'

As he delivered these remarks, Turpin had grown testier and testier until he looked down to find that he'd crushed the biscuit he was holding. He carefully tipped its powdered remains on to the table. 'This Arab gentleman, on the other hand, has recommended himself to the Attwoods because he wants to keep the property pretty much as it is. Says he's in love with the Fallowfields buildings and intends to alter them only internally – return them to the condition of a private residence for himself, his family and his entourage. In fact, he's stressed that without these buildings he wouldn't be interested in buying the property. He'd look elsewhere.'

'So the university's out of the running,' said Prendergast.

'Not quite. The Attwoods come from a long line of fervent Christians. They've always been keen for the estate to be used not only for education but Christian education. Was a time when they were pressing us to open a department of theology in Fallowfields. It was only when we persuaded them that this would result in an empty building that they accepted the agnostic state of the world. But they see their association with the university as having been long and happy, and remain religious enough to be uneasy about selling the property to someone of, ah, non-Christian – that is to say, Muslim – beliefs. Last month I got a call from Betty Attwood – she's the one who wears the trousers – and in return for a promise that we'd redevelop Fallowfields in a sensitive way announced she'd be willing to sell it lock, stock and minstrels' gallery to us. But it wasn't the easiest of phone calls. Mrs A does tend to ramble a bit. The call lasted nearly half an hour, with little breaks while she chatted with the dog walker, the postman and the cleaning lady. Then she started calling me Cyril.'

'Cyril?'

'Her husband. In the end, I said this was wonderful news and we'd want to move swiftly. She promised to contact her solicitors, a firm called Gardeners, and get them to provide me with more details.'

'Well, let's get on to them,' said Prendergast. 'Tell them to pull their finger out.'

'I've rung them and been advised that the matter's in hand. They added that Mrs Attwood is a valued client, but one who at her time of life is neither sharply focused nor expeditious.'

'In plain words,' returned Prendergast, 'one of those old biddies who struggles with the milk bill.'

There was a silence. It was Unthank who broke it. 'I think I know these Attwoods. The family was once fiercely Catholic but bent their principles during the Jacobean era so as to hang on to the estate. Emerged as Anglicans so high it would have been hard to slide a communion wafer between them and the pope.'

'I wouldn't know,' said Prendergast.

'They're the very same Attwoods,' said Turpin. 'How did you guess?'

'Relations on my mother's side are High Church, too. My own parents were much lower. But I heard one of the Attwoods deliver a sermon once. Inspiring stuff based on St John's Gospel – the bit about turning water into wine. Tremendous on the allegorical implications, what the French call *mise en abŷme*. Unhappily, it did go on a bit. A pervasive narcolepsy broke out.'

Prendergast raised his eyes upwards, swept a hand through his gelled hair and frowned. What was this sad toff banging on about?

'Why don't I pay them a visit?' said Unthank. 'I don't know them well but they'll certainly remember the family. I can tell her how grateful we are for their relationship with the university. Say we're keen to move forward and create better chances for young people.'

'Good idea. A different person, but still someone she knows. But leave it for a week or two. I understand Cyril's unwell, and it'd be better if you called when she was able to focus on what we want from her.'

Before resuming the meeting, they agreed to take a break. As Prendergast and Unthank left for their offices, Marian appeared. 'Sorry to disturb you, Dr Turpin, but Brian's here about the window cleaning cradle.'

'Who is Brian?'

'He's an ESMO.'

Brian shuffled nervously into the vice chancellor's office. 'Er, Marian, that is, Miss Bussell said that the cradle was still, you know, stuck. I think I might be able to help.'

'Why, are you a window cleaner?'

'I was once, but I've gone up in the world.' Brian showed his epaulette. 'Of course, I used to go *up* – but then down again.' He gave a nervous little laugh which a look from Marian silenced. 'Thing is, sir, and I don't want to intrude, but when it's convenient, if Marian could let me have a look at the winding gear from your window I might be able to sort it.'

'Would it be safe? I don't want any accidents.'

'Totally safe, sir. Very used to those things. Know all the safety drill.'

'Then it would be much appreciated. Maintenance can't seem to unblock a sink these days. I'm busy now but fix a time with Marian.'

Brian started to mumble something about worn carbon brushes and electric motors, but Marian put her hand in the middle of his back and propelled him out.

The trio resumed their deliberations. 'We've made a good start,' affirmed Turpin, selecting another biscuit. 'Securing Fallowfields would allow us to capitalise on a major asset. It's the home of the media, literature and culture department, while art and design are in the outbuildings. But if we located the new departments of ecology and complementary medicine there, we'd greatly improve our chances of getting first-class staff and lots of students. At the moment, Fallowfields is just a set of old buildings that's been altered in a makeshift way. But if we bought it we could give it a really good make-over so that it's suited to the new courses. Excellent!

'Right, now to the final item for this morning and totally crucial. What courses stay, what go? We've done some serious pruning already, but if we're to house the new degrees and keep our heads above water, it's got to go further. We've got to revisit courses, facilities, accommodation, student numbers. We've got to cleanse the Augean stables.'

Briefly wondering why toffs have to be so florid, Prendergast was ready to lead on the matter. Since his appointment, he'd worked his way through all the departments, categorising each of their courses on a four-point scale: 'Definitely Retain', 'Currently Viable', 'Candidate for Closure' and, his last category description, 'Triple D: Drop this Dead Donkey'. His analysis of Mixton's course provision – its unfitness for modern needs – was brisk and brutal. Because a degree subject had been around for a hundred years was no argument for preserving it during the next hundred. 'We have to scrutinise, prioritise, rationalise.'

Unthank heard the slogans with distaste. But his attempts to remind his colleagues of the virtues of a liberal education, of not binding intellectual inquiry too closely to the utilitarian, proved hard going. As he was developing with what he felt was some elegance an over-arching rationale for higher education, rock music began blasting from Prendergast's phone. Instead of muting it, he turned his head and took the call, barking just enough words into it to cause Unthank to lose his thread. And when he recovered it and began to dilate on the idea of the university as a classless, nurturing environment for civility and erudition, the biscuit that Turpin had been squeezing snapped and a fragment flew into Unthank's coffee.

Turpin nodded his sympathy at both his colleagues. He lamented the loss of a past more noble than the present, accepted that the enlargement of higher education came at a price, and wished that the autonomy of the universities was not being eroded. But he acknowledged, with Tennyson's King Arthur, that 'The old order changeth, yielding place to the new', evoking a resigned smile from Unthank and a blank stare from Prendergast.

It was the latter who once more seized the initiative, detailing the new degrees he planned. They would, he averred, professionalise the non-professionals, turning first-aiders, stretcher-bearers, masseurs and herbalists into complementary medics; gardeners, hedgers, ditchers and composters into environmental technologists. Unthank criticised, Turpin equivocated and ultimately Prendergast prevailed. Then the list of triple Ds was scrutinised, a few were given short reprieves, the rest condemned. Whatever the protests, staff would have to go, hours be switched from research to teaching, economies driven through. Prendergast had already created a PowerPoint sequence and planned to address all the university's departments. His talk would be called 'A Hard Message for Hard Times: Meeting Tomorrow's Challenges Today'.

'*O tempora, O mores,*' sighed Unthank.

'Won't they all go on strike?' sighed Turpin.

'I hope so,' replied Prendergast, 'because then they'll be signing their death warrants.'

10. ARS LONGA, PATIENTIA BREVIS

On the Glabthorpe-Mixton road traffic was at a standstill. Exhaust fumes thickened the chill winter mist. Ed Prendergast, always keen to be first through the door of any room in which a meeting was scheduled, was hitting the leather-bound steering wheel with rhythmic impatience. What the hell was causing this hold-up? He swore under his breath, then swore aloud softly, then aloud loudly.

Switching off the engine he got out of his car to join other drivers who were walking along the linc of vehicles. The cause lay at a zebra crossing. On one side of it, four folding desks had been positioned and at them sat well-dressed individuals with clip-boards. Above their desks was a banner proclaiming 'Crufties Dog Show – Judging Now'. Backwards and forwards across the crossing, the show's contestants were parading in a strange variety of dress. One wore a combat jacket and track-suit bottoms and was accompanied by a large dog on a lead. He was followed by someone in a suit who carried a white walking stick and trailed a lead with no dog at the end of it. Following him was a striking young woman in a two-piece swimsuit pulling a wheeled platform on which stood a stuffed badger. She, in turn, was followed by an individual carrying a large placard with 'WOOF WOOF' written on it. The last person was a young woman leading a semi-naked young man who wore over his face a cage-like construction of the kind used to muzzle fierce dogs. Alongside him were two girls in white coats. On the back of one was inscribed the words 'Rabies can kill' and on the other, 'Bite me to death darling'. The procession made its way to the far side of the crossing, there executed an elaborate winding loop and started back again.

'What's all this about,' Prendergast asked a bystander.

'Not sure. I think it's *students*.' He gave the word a disdainful sibilance.

'Why hasn't anyone told them to sod off?'

The man nodded towards the judges' desks and behind them Prendergast saw three burly, shaven-headed men in dark glasses and parkas. Each held up a placard in front of him. The first read 'DON'T', the second read 'MAKE', and the third 'TROUBLE'. All three were chewing gum and had the air of a night-club bouncer hoping for some action to enliven a quiet evening. Prendergast's intention of striding forward and telling the whole bloody bunch to get out of the bloody way faltered. With a snort of exasperation he swung round and almost collided with a bulky and familiar figure: wearing a shabby raincoat over his ESMO uniform, it was Brian.

'Hello, Mr Prendergast. I thought that was you sitting behind me in the Beamer. Bloody students, eh?' He nodded in the direction of the zebra crossing.

'What the hell are they up to?'

'It's what they call performance art, Mr Prendergast. They're Tom Burley's lot. They don't just paint pictures, they sort of act 'em out. Do it in strange places all over Mixton. Have to confess it's a bit beyond me.'

'Well, I'm in no mood for art appreciation. I've got an important meeting in Fallowfields in ten minutes, and I'm bloody well going to be late for it.'

They were now returning to their cars. In front of Prendergast's dark blue BMW was a battered and elderly Cavalier. With the exception of the front offside wing, which was an unpainted steel-grey, it was of a lurid orange. A year or two ago, Brian had had a bit of a shunt and bought the wing section from a scrapyard, but had never got round to spraying it. 'I think I might be able to help you out, Mr P. If we do a U-turn and go back about fifty yards, I know a nice little rat-run through to Fallowfields. Follow me.'

They swung into the car-park at Fallowfields with moments to spare. Brian ran the Cavalier into one of the few empty spaces and Prendergast, who had no time to find a space of his own, drove straight up to the main entrance, switched off the engine and began to mount the steps.

'Excuse me, Mr Prendergast,' Brian came panting up behind him. 'You won't be able to leave it there. Health and Safety won't wear it. Entrance has to be kept clear for emergency vehicles.'

'Then park it for me, Brian,' said Prendergast, tossing him the keys, 'and then drop those off in Reception.' As he made his way to the lecture theatre, the impending showdown began to excite him. In his view, most managers were feeble – those in higher education especially so. They bottled all the tough decisions because they hadn't got the balls to implement them. But this couldn't be said of him: far from ducking a challenge he relished it, and it was this quality that had caught the eye of Brenda Hodges. Fallowfields was the first port of call for his road-show, for, as Turpin put it, if Prendergast was obliged to enter a number of lions' dens it was best to begin at the one with the mangiest specimens. Its largest lecture room held just a hundred people, and when he stepped on to the rostrum it was packed. Though in no way daunted, Prendergast found the look of the audience dispiriting. He'd never accepted the fact that a suit and•tie and their smart feminine equivalents had been consigned to history. The ubiquity of open-necked shirts, vests, trainers, ripped jeans and bomber jackets set his teeth on edge. There were also some body piercings and tattoos. What a dingy bunch of plonkers, they deserved what was coming to them . . .

'Thank you all for coming here today. You'll know that we're enduring some testing times and facing a difficult future. However, I'm confident the commitment and hard work that have seen Mixton University this far will continue to serve it in the years ahead.' *Which is to say that you've had a cushy billet in even cushier surroundings for a long time. You have a less taxing job than a eunuch in a brothel and having ridden your luck for so long you think it'll last indefinitely. Think again.* 'Some particular challenges now face us. We haven't been very successful in attracting overseas students who pay enhanced fees, and that's unlikely to change. And the decision to remove the cap on numbers and allow universities to enrol as many students as they want may help Sussex University but won't do much for Mixton.

'The government's belief that a free market will produce a better health service also applies to the universities. We have to have student appeal, they have to want to come here, and once here they need to tell the world that Mixton's the place to be.' *Welcome to the real world. You've been out of it for too long and it's now not so much breathing down your neck as getting a hold of your sensitive parts.*

'But presently we're experiencing student flight from many of our academic specialisms. This may be regrettable and reflect a more, erm, consumerist approach to education, but it's a matter of undeniable fact. We've got to ensure that what we're offering is what students want. And we've got to get our nose ahead of the other uni's. Too often we've followed the crowd, not led it.' *If Mixton ever thought the dead weight of Eng Lit or that rag-bag called Modern European Studies was going to pull in the punters, it was kidding itself. And it was only by chance that it launched a degree in Sports Studies and Injuries.* (Prendergast had learned that it was a consequence of the bursar's brother-in-law being stretchered off at Preston North End. He'd suffered an acute groin injury that had put an end to his footballing career and other things besides.)

'You wouldn't want me to be less than honest with you about our present situation. The university's action plan involves immediate and difficult change. Some staff might have to redirect their expertise into new disciplines, some will have to re-train. Some might find the challenge of change too demanding and feel they'd be better able to serve the cause of education in another way . . . and in another place." *Several of you will have to stop poring over the poems of William Wirksworth and start teaching something useful like spelling, grammar and punctuation. And some'll have to take up bird watching or working for Meals on Wheels.*

'I must therefore tell you that Academic Board will authorise the closure of a number of degree courses with immediate effect. These will recruit no more students but those who are already enrolled on them will be allowed to complete their studies. In other words, the courses'll be wound down over the next two and a half years. Among them will be the degrees in English Literature and Media Studies, which for the rest of their duration will be taught in prefab-, er temporary, accommodation in the town centre.

'In their place, we'll be offering two new degrees here at Fallowfields. The first will cater to what we foresee as a growth in industries that seek to protect the planet, harness new forms of energy and conserve natural resources. Its students will explore the environment, ecology and clean and renewable energy systems. And the second is a response to the growing inability of the NHS to cope with the health needs of the population, particularly the growing numbers of elderly, and to concerns about the effectiveness of traditional forms of treatment. This will be a degree in complementary health-care covering chiropractics, aromatherapy, acupuncture, moxibustion, Pilates, the Alexander technique, and other fields that seek to restore health without pharmaceutical or surgical intervention. Together these degrees offer a synergy between the green and the renewable and the healthy and non-invasive.

'We're confident the degrees will be popular. They'll be innovative and the modes of assessment will be robust, flexible and transparent. Each will combine in a symbiotic way two strands of learning, that within the academy and that which is provided by the professional world. We want to demonstrate their relevance from the start so the students can see the point of what they're doing, and employers can see that those they wish to hire are the product of close contact with real life rather than with just lectures and book-learning – important, of course, as those are. Our longer-term aim is to implement the government's wish to introduce a scheme of work experience across all degrees at the university. This would be a spell of paid employment in which the students do jobs that are both challenging in themselves and directly relevant to the courses they're studying.' *We really do need to give the students a break from the monotony of your lectures, and how better than to get them out into the real world? It'll mean that many will lose the option of staying in bed till mid-day but, hey, welcome to the university of life.*

Prendergast paused to click the PowerPoint sequence and turn a page. The audience had been pinned back in its seats by the drive of his delivery and the shock of its content, but as he paused there grew an audible murmur, expressions of dismay, an exhalation of disbelief. Prendergast heard it, relished it, and resolved to push on.

'It'll take time to frame the courses and recruit the staff. At the same time we intend to develop the premises to ensure that they're fit for purpose, fit for the twenty-first century and fit for a new generation of committed and lively minds. It'll be a new and illustrious chapter in the university's history.' He paused and glanced up at the open mouths, horrified eyes and puckered foreheads. He had to suppress an urge to grin.

'For those of you who are willing to update your skills and work flexibly, there are exciting possibilities ahead. But we accept that there'll be some who will wish to take their talents elsewhere, and for them we'll offer a counselling service. For a few, hopefully a very few, there may be no other option but a termination of employment, albeit with due recognition of the distinguished service they've given. The university management will be willing to offer generous terms of severance wherever it can. Now . . . ' Prendergast looked at his watch, 'I have to announce these plans to the other university departments today, but I can stay for a little while if there are any questions.' There was no sound but the drumming of Prendergast's fingers on the lectern.

For a moment he thought he would get away without any objection. His decision to hit them hard and fast seemed to have paid off. He was slipping his notes into his document case when an elderly man who was traditionally if drably dressed struggled to his feet. It was Professor Abbott.

'Mr Plenderleith, you've declared your intention to turn this beautiful and listed building of Fallowfields into premises for gardeners and pedlars of quack remedies. But it's well-known that you – the university – do not own Fallowfields. It's the property of the Attwood family, who, I'm glad to say, take a more exalted and less functional view of higher education than you do. I'm confident they'll refuse permission for it to be put to such use.'

Prendergast decided not to reveal that the Attwoods were on the point of selling.Instead he gave Abbott an ingratiating and very dental smile and said: 'I'm sure we'll find that the Attwoods will be on the side of progress.'

'I remain . . . ' There was a paroxysm of coughing. 'I remain . . .'

'Only just, George,' said a voice behind him.

'– confident that the Attwoods can distinguish between progress and a phil– a phil – '

'A fillet steak?' queried the voice.

'– a philistinism, Mr Gormenghast, that one has a right not to expect from the custodians of the academy.' Dabbing his pink forehead with a handkerchief, Abbott subsided into his seat to some scattered clapping.

To general surprise, the next person up was Eric Uggles, belying his nickname of Eric the Unready. 'Mr Prendergast, you take the language of management and the weasel words of our politicians and blend them in the fond but false belief that they'll generate admiring assent. In fact, they evoke disbelief and contempt.'

A roar of 'Hear, hear!' rang round the lecture room and the clapping was louder and more prolonged.

'You have the speciousness of those who know the price – or, as you would say, the market modified retail sales signifier – of everything and the value of nothing. Because they fail to meet some factitious benchmark devised by marketing men, bureaucrats and bean-counters, you dismiss subjects that have challenged and developed minds for generations. You wheel out words like "robust" and "fit for purpose" as if they were magical incantations that will save this university. They will not save it, they'll destroy it. You don't hold aloft the light of learning, you simply parrot the mantra of the utilitarian and the commercial. I will oppose with every nerve in my body these ridiculous and demeaning proposals, and I'd be grateful if you would place matters academic in the hands of those who have some understanding of them.'

The applause became a torrent. Many leapt to their feet, and stamped an accompaniment to the clapping. But this kind of fight was what Prendergast was bred for. Hiding his contempt for the throng behind a rictus of smiling concern, he waited for the din to die down. As it did, a tall, slim woman got to her feet. She was in her thirties and peered through round spectacles in a way that was at once donnish and appealing. Around her neck she wore an elegant foulard scarf, and when she spoke it was in tones that suggested a privileged background. Prendergast would have described her as 'posh'.

'I'm Kate Huckerby, and I work here in the Department of Media, Literature and Culture. I lecture in film theory to students of Media Studies, one of the degrees you intend to axe. With my students I discuss realism, auteur theory, conceptualisations of genre, ideology and class, psychoanalysis, gender and aesthetics, globalisation and documentary, audiences and reception theory. So I'd be obliged if you didn't pretend that the likes of *moxibustion*, which as I understand it is the burning of leaves near to a person's skin as a counter-irritant, would represent an exciting update of my skills. I hope that in future there'll be somewhere in this university where intellectual and cultural matters might continue to be taken seriously. But if they're going to be abandoned altogether – if, in the words of Macbeth, it were done when 'tis done – then 'twere well it were done quickly. Without holding out false hopes, Mr Prendergast, and without pointless delay. Finally, just to be clear, Macbeth is not currently a lecturer at this university.'

Prendergast was needled by this, but before he could reply she'd sat down and been replaced by Gary Dorn, who was looking heroically shabby in a scuffed leather jacket, T-shirt and jeans. Gary felt it was time for some eloquent words from the Left. But as he began to speak, Prendergast realised that however awkward the comments from the floor there was little need for him to say anything further. Most of the speakers were more interested in venting their complaints than in hearing his reactions to them. All he had to do was wear a look of attentive concern throughout the meeting, thank the audience for their observations, and then go off to the next one. And when the members of all the departments in the university had got their grievances off their chests, he and his two senior colleagues could simply drive their plans forward as if nothing had happened.

'Some of us do accept that change is inevitable,' Dorn was saying. He shot Uggles a quick and condescending look and the lecture theatre fell silent. 'We can't go on teaching an elitist literary canon. Promoting a bourgeois culture that leaves most people cold. We've got to accept that students no longer get their intellectual nourishment from books but from cinema, television and new media. YouTube, iPads, iPlayers, iPhones. We in Media Studies have always known this so we teach students to be critically reflective about these things. What the university should be doing is widening student access to courses like ours, not closing them down and replacing them with job training programmes that don't involve any reflection at all.

'These proposals are a bulldozing exercise on the part of the management. But what we need is a democratically-constituted course-reviewing body that'll balance serious academic content on the one hand with the need to attract students on the other.' (Gary felt it was now time to heighten the rhetoric.) 'We need to engage students, not alienate them, inspire not depress, imbue confidence not sap their will. Too many of our courses do the second rather than the first. We must be alert to the needs of the contemporary student. If your reference to new assessment modes, Ed, means we'll finally get rid of written exams, if it means we're going to assess the whole student not just limited aspects, that'll be a move in the right direction. These are things I've been arguing for since I came here. But they can't be done by a clique sitting round the vice-chancellor's table. We need a properly elected, fully representative, cross-curricular working party to analyse provision and set it against needs, and then come up with proposals that make sense of what young people want to do in a society from which they feel alienated.'

He paused, but Prendergast looked smilingly round the auditorium as if inviting other comments. So before yielding the floor Gary decided to tick a few other politically-correct boxes. 'And of course there has to be student representation, a proper balance of gender, sexual orientation and ethnicity, and a neutral chairperson.' He sat down to scattered cries of approval from fellow union activists and eye-rollings from his more conservative colleagues.

Fiona Maddingley, Lecturer in Media and Gender, got to her feet. She was a thin, nervous woman, wearing half-moon spectacles which were attached to her neck by a cord. 'Like Gary, I want to oppose any notion that Media Studies should be axed. We're a key contributor to the university's overall aspiration of freeing young working class people from the repressive elements of their conditioning, and enabling them to see society for what it is: selfish, corrupt and unequal. We're here, as universities always have been, to challenge the prevailing order, not meekly collude in the obscenity of a society where the gap between rich and poor is celebrated rather than condemned.'

Fiona sat down and rummaged in her handbag for anything that would assist the recovery of her composure. A female colleague sitting next to her whispered, 'Well said, Fiona. What an odious man this Prendergast is! Will you get away to your place in Tuscany for Christmas? And did you find a local builder to do the patio?'

Marjorie Steerforth, who taught the Romantic Poets, was now speaking. 'I hoped to stay on for another year or two, but my sister would like me to join her in Argyllshire. She's much less mobile now. Would there be any prospect of, well, favourable terms if these changes go ahead? I've still got the mortgage, you see, but if there could be what they call additional years . . . ' Prendergast arranged his face into an expression of intense, compassionate interest and let her roll on. This, he thought, shouldn't be too difficult.

It wasn't until he was driving home at the end of an exhilarating day that he had a chance to recall the student prank which, but for Brian's local knowledge, might have seriously delayed him. Was it just an innocent instance of performance art? Or was Tom Burley, with or without the support of his colleagues, using his student minions to enhance the national reputation of the Department of Art and Design? It had been rather well organised: someone had gone to some trouble to stage the whole thing. He stopped at a set of lights and re-ran the dog parade through his head, realising, with a start, that he'd seen the girl in the swimsuit once before: indeed, he'd seen even more of her. She was the girl in the lift.

Gary Dorn was also musing. Prendergast's proposals were as bad as he'd feared. The media degree, indeed the entire department, was to be forced to wither away. In less than three years it would disappear, and he'd be out on his ear. He was enough of a realist to know that the changes were inevitable. Prendergast embodied the spirit of the times. Before long, every third-rate university like Mixton would've been turned into a commercial and industrial training centre. On the other hand, Gary was still enough of a good old-fashioned Marxist and muck-stirrer to be determined to put up a fight. Prendergast and his allies might win the day, but at the end of it they'd have wounds to lick. He was determined to mobilise the opposition to the changes so that even if they couldn't be prevented they'd be delayed, and what Gary wished to delay most was his department's removal from Fallowfields, the only pleasant building in the university and one which gave him the rare luxury of an office to himself.

His long-term aim was, of course, to gain employment at another, less vulnerable and more reputable university, but he hadn't the faintest hope of doing so until he'd completed *Culture, Identity and the Postgendered Imaginary*. And he hadn't the faintest hope of completing that if he were transferred from the sole occupancy of a pleasant room in Fallowfields to a communal office in a mud-surrounded portakabin in the middle of Mixton. Most lecturers, of course, had the occasional option of working at home, but Gary's domestic circumstances made this impossible. His ex-wife, Cynthia, lived only a few hundred yards away with their two teenage sons, and visited him at all hours of the day and night to blame his neglect rather than her own maternal inadequacies for the fact that their two sons were effectively out of control. His younger son had twice been excluded from school, once for threatening the woodwork teacher with a chisel and the second time for putting his hand up the skirt of the French *assistante*. Moreover, Gary's live-in partner, Rebecca, who was in the final stages of her PhD in economics, was jealous and neurotic, and ascribed to his lack of support and frequent, unexplained absences the fact that she couldn't concentrate and her research was in disarray. The two women loathed each other, and their screaming matches had more than once brought a threat from the neighbours to call the police. In a crowded portakabin, a mere stone's throw from his wife in one direction and his partner in the other, Gary would be able to get little work done.

If he were honest, he'd have to admit that there was another reason he was loath to quit his single office, and one that often conflicted with his will to work. Gary was a tireless womaniser. There was scarcely a nubile female on the staff whom he hadn't propositioned, with results that were sometimes ignominious. But when the object of his pursuit was complaisant, where better to enjoy her complaisance than behind the quietly locked door of his Fallowfields office and on the broken-down sofa he had purloined from the SCR?

So Gary was determined to fight Prendergast's plans, but he was also aware that he needed to tread carefully. As the teacher of two third-year modules on the media degree, he had a better chance than many of his colleagues of being retained for the remainder of its life. But if a mean bastard like Prendergast saw him as ring-leader of the opposition, he would be likely to sack him immediately and replace him with part-timers. This was why, in the public meeting with Prendergast, Gary had struck a measured pose, accepting the need for change but arguing that it should be more democratically managed. So was there anyone among his colleagues whom he could encourage to lead the fight on his behalf?

Tom Burley in Art and Design? Not a hope. Its hugely popular degrees were not at risk and Burley himself was a star turn. His national reputation was beginning to rival Damien Hirst's, which explained, Gary thought bitterly, why the university allowed him to get away with murder. But more than this, Burley wasn't interested in Dorn's kind of politics, perhaps not in politics of any kind. Gary remembered getting him to a union meeting once, believing that Burley's artistic anarchism might take a political turn. After ten minutes, Burley left to go to the lavatory and never returned. A better hope probably lay with Kate Huckerby, the film theorist. Kate was tough, serious, articulate and post-feminist. If she could be persuaded to champion the cause, he'd support her with all the energy and time that he could, well, make available. But on second thoughts, she was a no-hoper. While they held similar political views, their personal relationship was now wary. This stemmed from an occasion when Gary thought that his combination of personal charm and incisive cultural analysis had made an irresistible impact, and delicately propositioned her. Even now, the curl of her lip and the contempt of her answer were painful to recall. Best leave Kate Huckerby out of it.

Students? There wasn't really anybody. When he was at university there were politically dedicated students who lapped up the thesis, the antithesis and the synthesis. Now all they lapped up were coke and pizza. What about Holly, that little chick who'd flashed her legs and boobs at him in the tutorial, and whom he was trying to teach how to write? Could he enthuse Holly about political issues when he'd failed with academic ones? Could this be a means of giving her an intellectual focus beyond what, he suspected, was an existence dominated by celebrity magazines? It was never hard for Gary to dress his motives in a lofty rationale. He'd be enriching her life, broadening her horizons. But she did not present as the natural voice of protest. He would have to walk her through the issues, focus on the shabby treatment of the students, instruct her in what she was to protest against and how she was to do it, and above all, make her understand that he could not be associated with any action that ensued. To achieve all this, he'd need to get closer to her, and quite quickly.

11. BRENDA'S LITTLE SECRET

Elated by what he regarded as a successful debut at Fallowfields, Prendergast had addressed the other university departments with similar gusto. Everywhere, the sequence of reactions was the same: shocked silence, denunciations as furious as they were impotent, then sententious observations along with one or two diffident inquiries about severance deals. When the process was concluded, he decided to phone Brenda Hodges. It would be useful to keep her up to date, make sure she knew he was delivering what she wanted: on time and on budget.

'We're cooking with gas, Brenda. I needed to push and shove to get Turpin and his posh pal to realise it's got to be all-change, but they're bowing to the inevitable.'

'Glad to hear it. But universities often promise a new future and quickly relapse into old habits.'

'With me on watch, Brenda, it's not going to happen at Mixton.'

'We've hardly started yet. Things are going to get a whole lot harder.'

'Good. That's what I'm here for. Bring it on.'

'Bring what on?'

After a puzzled pause, Brenda resumed. 'We've already done a lot to make sure that those who go to university are the ones who should be there, and we want to make sure they'll have useful jobs at the end of it. But we've been re-doing our sums on student finance – on how much we can expect back, and when, from the students who've graduated.'

'I thought it was the repayment of a fixed percentage of income above a certain level.'

'So it is. Except it's clear that many who are graduating will never complete the repayments. Some won't even start them.'

'Because they won't earn enough?'

'That, and because they go abroad, disappear, change their names or set up fake companies to disguise their real incomes.'

'Ah,' said Prendergast, a hint of improper pleasure in his voice, 'just like some members of the cabinet.'

'I'll pretend I didn't hear that. But the treasury people keep re-doing the sums and the difference between the cost of providing a university education and the money we claw back from the graduates is about the same as the GDP for Denmark. It can't go on.'

'So you reduce overall costs or lower the fees somehow or . . .'

'Not "or" – "and". By shortening the time spent at university from three years to two.'

With a grim smile, Prendergast realised that the meetings he'd just held at Mixton were a mere skirmish compared to the battle that would be fought when plans for two-year degrees were unveiled.

'When the time's right, we want you to trial these new degrees at Mixton, along with a few other universities of similar, er, status. Do you think you could do it – and in such a way as to win the battle for hearts and minds? Bring students, staff and the hard pressed tax-payers on board?'

Prendergast's mind started to race. He needed to show Brenda that he was equal to the challenge. 'Er, we'd need a catchy title for the campaign. How about "Two is the new three"?'

'Many of our young people already struggle with arithmetic, Ed. Let's not make it even harder for them.'

'Right. Um, we call it Two for Three, and then do that in numerals, "2-4-3: when shorter means faster, shorter means better, shorter means cheaper." We could easily cover the existing courses in two years. In fact we'd be doing the students a favour because over the present summer vacs they probably forget half of what they've learned. They could do two years of 36 weeks each, which would include work experience to accompany formal learning. Then they're job-ready twelve months ahead of the competition. How's that?'

'And the staff?' inquired Brenda.

'We'd be completely open with them. There are now two kinds of uni, the research-led ones and the rest. At Mixton we're part of the rest. We shift to a longer teaching year, but the staff would still get more holidays than most people. They should count their blessings.'

'It'll take longer than counting their research citations,' responded Brenda drily.

Prendergast grinned. 'Have you told Turpin?'

'I'm writing to him and the VCs of the other universities that'll be involved in the trial. I suspect that when Richard learns about it, his language may be vivid. But I must stress this is all in the strictest confidence. We're not ready to go public on it just yet. Despite what you say, the students' and lecturers' unions are strongly opposed to two-year degrees, and they'll fight them tooth and nail. So not a word out of any of you.'

Prendergast put down the phone, tilted his executive chair back, and pressing the tips of his fingers together, contemplated the ceiling. When the plan for two-year degrees was announced he'd look forward to the fight, to flattening his feeble opponents all over again. Meanwhile, however, he wanted Brenda to appreciate him a bit more, force her to see him as absolutely indispensable to the government's strategy. And slowly an idea formed in his mind. With the approval of the Vice and the Toff, which should be easy to obtain since they had no ideas of their own that were remotely practicable, he would stage an event to which various key figures, both national and local, would be invited. Its centre-piece would be the plans for the new Fallowfields campus, but these would be bigger and better than he'd at first envisaged. For hadn't Turpin advised them that if Fallowfields could be bought by the university, Compton Farm would be pounced on by the council? And if the two sites could be merged into one, all manner of synergies could be developed between the university and the community. It could be home not only to the planned degrees in environmental technology and complementary medicine but to a custom-built, state-of-the-art village. The village would act as a test-bed for new ecological developments and alternative health treatments, and at the same time provide work experience for the students. It would be the Connected Community of the government's dreams. The more he thought about it, the more he liked it.

Prendergast reached for his phone. Time to get some key people on board, and best to begin with the council. He arranged to have dinner in a few days' time with Geoffrey Edgerton, the Member for Housing. Then he punched in the number of the MP for Mixton, Harry Hunter, but found himself talking to an answerphone. 'Harry, when did we last see you at the university? I know you're busy, but come and have some lunch. I want to share some exciting news with you. Can you spare me an hour or two? It'll be good for the university, for the town . . . and for you.'

12. TROUSER TROUBLE

As they drove into the street of shabby terraced houses in the town's student ghetto, Gary was struck by a thought. 'Most first year students are in university halls and flats. How come you've got your own place?'

'My brother used to live here. He graduated last year and I've taken his place. I used to come and stay with him and his mates. It were wicked.'

'Danny Ainscough,' Gary made the connection. He remembered Ainscough for excelling in nothing so much as the art of dumb insolence. In seminars, he used to sit slumped and silent, legs wide apart and feet set firmly on the ground, staring at the lecturer with an expression of belligerent uninterest. 'Has he got a job?' Gary asked, hoping he hadn't.

'He makes promotional videos for the Sally Army.'

Gary managed to find a gap at the kerb between an overflowing skip and a camper van that was partly propped up on bricks. He jerked up the handbrake but kept the engine running.

'How many of you live here?'

'Eight. I'm on the ground floor. Come and have a coffee.'

And before he could reply she leaned across him, reached through the steering wheel and switched off the ignition. Then she opened the passenger door and got out. He followed her. To his mild surprise she reached out and took his hand, like a mother helping her wayward child to catch up. With both hands behind her back and clasping one of his, she led him up the short path to the house. In the front garden fragments of an old pram and several burst sacks of rubbish could be glimpsed among the weeds and slivers of snow. Instead of curtains a blanket had been clumsily pinned up inside the front window. She released him, walked into the porch and fiddled with the front door key.

He hesitated a yard or two behind her. While he'd been led here by another part of his anatomy, his brain was now, at last, flashing hazard warnings. Dorn was not the most scrupulous of men and his life was already strewn with wreckage – his ex-wife and their two unhappy sons, his neurotic girlfriend, Rebecca. Experience had taught him that with any woman adventures of this kind seldom end cleanly, and Holly was not just a student: she was his tutorial student. The real issue was whether a liaison with her would help his campaign against Prendergast. As his adoring lover, she might be prepared to do anything for him, including hiding his own role in the campaign. On the other hand, if, as he dimly foresaw, he were to grow bored with her and try to shake her off, she could wreak a horrible revenge. She could not only reveal that he'd masterminded the opposition to Prendergast but claim that their close relationship had ruined her studies.

Something put a prompt end to Gary's inner debate: it was the jut of Holly's rump inside her tight little skirt, and the crook of her leg as she reached towards the door lock. He took a deep breath and followed her inside. The hall was dark and he waited by the door while Holly groped along the wall for the switch. In the sallow light, she walked quickly back to him, and colliding with him rather than embracing him, kissed him moistly on the mouth. Then, like someone bringing home a trophy, she led him along the passageway. It smelt of cats and ancient dirt. Below the dado rail was dun-coloured paint, above it, torn anaglypta. Some of the decay had been masked with a huge poster of a glowering and half-naked David Beckham. From somewhere upstairs came the babble of a television set. Leaning against the staircase were a brace of mountain bikes, and along the floor lay the usual detritus of student living: untidy heaps of magazines, mostly *Heat* and *Hello!*, tabloid newspapers, empty beer cans and wine bottles, scattered pizza boxes, milk cartons, an old computer keyboard. Holly's room was near the end of the passage and as she fiddled with another key Gary glanced down at a splayed copy of *Heat* by her door. On one page were photos that revealed that a certain female movie star had a cellulite problem, and on the other was a feature claiming that an international male tennis champion had just treated himself to a 'back, sack and crack wax'.

Gary felt the condescension that comes with expertise. As a media scholar he was wise to this sort of stuff. In our post-religious age, Marx would probably agree that the obsession with celebrity was the new opium of the people, the classic effect of a polity that has been corrupted by the hegemony – yes, that *was* the word – of a few conglomerates with a stranglehold on the press. Still, it was academically important that Gary should monitor the phenomenon and, indeed, all current developments in popular culture. Perhaps when he left he might take the magazine with him.

Holly pushed open the door to her room and switched on a couple of heavily shaded lamps. He followed her in uncertainly. She crossed to the hearth and lit a gas-fire, then turned to face him with her usual winning smile. His eyes could roam the room for just long enough to take in a low double-bed with stuffed animals and dolls on the pillow, a vase of paper flowers, some family photos, a poster or two of showbiz celebs on the walls, and a very modest row of books, mostly set texts for the Media course. Then she stepped swiftly towards him, threw her arms round his neck and pushed him against the door so that it banged shut behind them. In an instant her lips were on his, her tongue pushing into his mouth. Lower down, he could feel the pressure of those breasts that had so discomposed him in the office, and lower down still her pelvis matched something of his own fierce rigidity. He clasped her buttocks and yielded fully to the kiss. Passion drowned his last feeble misgivings. For this moment alone, the world was well lost.

Down on to the bed they crashed. Off came Gary's jacket, up went Holly's jumper and skirt. She was wearing a lacy pale-blue bra which, when he reached behind to unhook it, proved typically refractory. He could feel her giggling slightly as he struggled. Finally she sat up, unloosed it and tossed it aside and he had full, glorious sight of what had started all this turmoil. Now they were perched side by side on the edge of the bed, engrossed in the inelegant, unromantic business of tearing off the rest of their clothing. For Holly, a skirt, tights and pants were relatively easy to shimmy out of, but Gary made an unwise attempt to shed trousers, pants, socks and shoes in a single downward movement that was hampered by a sturdy, horizontal erection and shoelaces that had never been so tightly tied. More mildly embarrassed giggles, but desire was not so easily quenched by absurdity, and within seconds they were back on the bed, naked and busy. Cupping her left breast, Gary nibbled the lobe of her right ear and then made steady downward progress with his tongue, pausing to savour the generous mouth before moving to the base of her throat.

'Gary,' she murmured. He raised himself a little and looked at her. From this perspective she now had a slight double chin. It did nothing to lessen her allure. 'You're a wicked bastard, Gary.'

'Mmm.' He wished to ponder only the flattering connotations of this remark, for nemesis would arrive soon enough. But with his manhood lying on her downy pelvis, a veritable tank on her lawn and poised to bring the house down with a burst of gunfire, he could feel only the goad of lust and once more fell to his work. As he moved over her contours an innocent pink nipple popped into his near view and he rolled his tongue round it. The pace was quickening. She rolled him on to his back, flattened herself on his chest and began to suck his left nipple, perhaps to teach him how to do it properly. The activity was local but the effect was pervasive. Gary opened his eyes and smiled beatifically at a crack in the ceiling. In the see-saw of self-indulgence and postponement that love-making involved, he was not sure he could hold out much longer.

He sat up and threw her roughly on her back, and as her head bounced against the pillows she looked up at him with apprehensive pleasure. Poised between her parted knees, he was motionless for a moment or two, just drinking in her wondrous, dishevelled prettiness. Then he kissed her smartly on the mouth and they began the old dance. Yet even as he erupted, there was already a worm in the apple of his bliss, the end of his pleasure in sight even as it was beginning. The strength ebbed out of him, and he subsided on to her bosom and buried his face in the pillow beside her head. For a moment, there was a silence as she stroked the back of his neck. Then with a sudden, possessive ferocity, she hugged and kissed him repeatedly, locking her arms and legs around him so tightly that he had to resist the impulse to fight free. At last she released him and he rolled off her, moved a stuffed giraffe aside and lay staring at the ceiling.

His sun had set, but hers was rising. 'Thanks, Gary, that were fantastic!' she said, and hugged and kissed him again. Then

67

wrapping herself in a coverlet she leapt to her feet, switched on an electric kettle at the hearth and spooned coffee into mugs. By now she was chattering incessantly. 'Strong, weak? How many sugars? You'll never believe, my friend Shannon at home, she's a hairdresser, she takes three and still has a figure to die for, whereas Lindsey, who's plumper, eats absolutely bugger-all . . . '

What the hell was he doing here? 'This is another fine mess you've got me into,' he said silently to his manhood, now shrivelling with shame. Returning to the bed with the mugs, she kissed him briskly and continued her monologue – about timetable clashes in the Media Department, her assignments, Matt Bentley who wasn't pulling his weight on their group project, and it wasn't fair 'cos they all got the same mark for it, her best mate Katie back home, her dad's devotion to his garden, her mother's Tupperware parties and how she got Holly to help organise and promote them, and how Stevo here in the house kept nicking her groceries from the kitchen. A process of free association seemed to be at work. She sat up beside him, partly draped in the coverlet, occasionally sipping coffee but apparently needing no response from him. She could have been a gossip at a knitting circle. When she became especially indignant at one of life's small injustices, a crease appeared for a moment by her mouth but then disappeared as her thoughts took another and lighter turn. In his girlfriend Rebecca that crease would be a permanent line, in his ex-wife a wrinkle. As she prattled and sipped, he thought about what they had done to each other and took in every detail of her beauty. And despite his plans for her, he had an uneasy feeling that he'd started something he'd be unable to control.

13. ED DINES A DINOSAUR

Prendergast watched the *rillettes de saumon* and melba toast disappear into the ravenous maw of his dinner companion, Geoffrey Edgerton, the council member for housing.

'I've just been re-reading the party manifesto you issued at the last local elections,' said Prendergast. 'It mentions your ambition of building local homes at the rate of two hundred a year.'

Edgerton eyed him warily, gulped his glass of wine as if it were orange squash and continued to chew busily. 'Yes, well, we have fallen a bit behind.'

By about a hundred and fifty, thought Prendergast. 'Did you see that article in the Chronicle last week?' he said. 'Under the headline "Looking for a new home in Mixton? Buy some binoculars!".'

Edgerton burped surreptitiously and dabbed his mouth with his napkin. 'D'you know the editor of the Chronic, Bill Castles? Friend of mine. He will have his little joke. But if you're buying Fallowfields and you'll give us access, there's no question we'd purchase the Compton Farm land.'

The waiter took away the empty plates and returned with two portions of *côtelettes d'agneau à la sauce d'Estragon*.

'But we wouldn't have a great deal of space, even there,' Edgerton shot his cuffs and studied his plate with relish. 'What we'd want to do is maximise our income from private developers who'd build high quality dwellings with large gardens and forecourts. But we can't get away with that now. We're under pressure from central government to build "affordable homes", so we'd have to turn it into a mixed development. We could throw up some properties on the cheap, squash 'em in and pile 'em high.'

'Good thinking,' Prendergast topped up his companion's glass. 'But we wouldn't just give you access. We'd want you to get into bed with us.'

'Eh?'

'The university would like to form a full partnership with the council so we could treat Fallowfields and Compton Farm as a single, large, integrated development. Picture it. A delightful eco village with its very own university – and all on a single rural site with shared amenities, including retail outlets. Then we could give your higher-end residences a bit more space and a delightful, open prospect.'

Edgerton's small eyes grew yet smaller and twinkled shrewdly. 'I like what I'm hearing, Ed.'

'But there'd have to be a trade-off.' The departure of the second set of used plates and the arrival of the *croustade de pommes et de pruneaux à la Gasconne* provided a happy interruption. 'We'd have to agree that all properties had solar panels and there'd be wind turbines on the higher ground.'

Edgerton's mouth, which had opened wide for his first spoonful of dessert, was now fixed in horror. 'You're kidding me, Ed. Mirrors and windmills? They're a bloody eyesore. We can't promote upmarket homes if the owners have got to look out at those.'

'Think about it, Geoffrey. A mixed housing development sharing a university campus in a beautiful setting. It's the Connected Community. And as eco-friendly as you can get. Between us we'd tick all the boxes.'

'This eco stuff is just piss and wind. Except there isn't enough wind.'

'Two firms have already expressed an interest: Wind Wynders and Solar Panel Beaters, both standing to benefit from government start-up cash.'

'Wind Wynders?'

'Good name, eh? Surprised no one thought of it before. They specialise in smaller turbines, find sites to make sure the energy sums add up, and position them so they don't offend.'

'And the solar firm? Can they get sunshine out of cucumbers?'

'Cucumbers – or perhaps sunflowers. To be frank, they're a bit glitzy. Trying hard, like their name. Big on PR. *But*, they've just developed a panel with an improved solar-energy-to-wattage ratio. Not massively better, but in that business every little helps.'

'It's fantasy, Ed. I like everything about your scheme, except this.'

Prendergast refilled his own glass with mineral water and summoned the waiter to fetch a brandy for his guest. There was a pause.

'Geoffrey, you could go down in history as a man who masterminded the dream of a genuinely connected community. Care for a cigar?'

'Ed, you won't win me over by bullshit and . . . . oh, El Rey del Mundo. Well, OK, but only to avoid offending you.'

They went out to the terrace, and as Edgerton struck a light and puffed intently on the cigar, Prendergast pressed home his attack.

'If you don't care about your legacy, you should at least consider your future. Aren't you due to retire in the next year or two?'

'Yes, I am. What are you driving at?'

'You're too young to stay at home and just smell the roses, Geoffrey. When I was talking to Wind Wynders and Solar Panel Beaters, I happened to mention that their access to the potentially lucrative domestic housing market would be significantly improved if they retained a consultant with experience in the workings of local government. But I pointed out that the services of such a person wouldn't come cheap . . .'

Either the fee which Prendergast then mentioned or the pungency of the cigar produced in Edgerton a spell of violent coughing.

'And I told them that I knew just the right person for the role.'

'Hello Mr. Pickles, it's Geoffrey Edgerton. You remember, the council member for housing. How are you? Yes, I'd heard that you and Mrs. Pickles had been unwell.Very sorry to hear it. Such a demanding job, farming. Calling to ask after you, obviously, but to say that things have moved on since we quite properly refused to countenance the compulsory purchase of some of your land a few years back. However, I wanted to be the first to tell you that the council itself is prepared to make a new offer, a better offer, you'll be pleased to hear. Only problem is that there's a rather small window of opportunity. Of course, I could pop over and see you. And I'll bring a small gift to cheer up your lady wife. Does she prefer flowers or chocolates?'

Mr Pickles told Mrs Pickles about the call, but with a cynical slant of his own.

'If it's a second chance to sell Compton, love, I think we should take it and retire to the seaside,' she replied. 'On balance, I'd prefer a memorial stone in the cemetery at Skegness to one in the cattle shed.'

14. BRIAN GOES TO WORK

Brian walked along the corridor amid a fading smell of disinfectant and floor polish, and stopped at a door on the right. It bore a metal plate on which was engraved: ELECTRICAL APPARATUS. HIGH VOLTAGE. DANGER. DO NOT ENTER.

Glancing up and down the empty corridor, Brian shifted two carrier bags to his left hand, took out a crowded key ring, and selecting the key for a five-lever Chubb let himself in and closed the door carefully behind him. Inside, the only immediately obvious pieces of electrical apparatus were a kettle and an old telephone, both on a desk close to the door and bespattered with ceiling emulsion. The room was windowless. There were three chairs, one on castors, the other two on their last legs, and a large table containing items that looked as if they'd been deposited by a tornado. These included newspapers, magazines, two grimy sugar bowls, several unwashed teaspoons and mugs, an assortment of tea bags, some used, some not, and a large jar of cheap coffee. Above an ancient laboratory sink with a central tap, pin-boards and shelving filled the walls, and on the lower shelves was an array of books about computer programming, all very new and each bearing the stamp of Mixton University Library. On the upper shelves stood Microsoft manuals dating back many years, two never-opened copies of *Mixton University: Standing Orders and Regulations Governing the Conduct of Senate*, university study guides for the last decade, a transistor radio and, partly concealed by a half-empty Weetabix packet and a carton of milk, a Netgear router, its green fluorescent icons winking complicitly at the new arrival. Beneath the router were electrical items of a more modern kind than the kettle and phone, including a trio of multi-screen monitors and a very high-spec personal computer.

The room had been Dr Cunliffe's office until his incessant complaints about the feeble lighting and excessive heating forced Estates Management to accommodate him elsewhere. At the same time, a D408 had been issued to de-commission the room and get all the equipment removed, and on several later occasions Brian had seen Terry, a new recruit to Estates Management, wandering up and down the corridor looking for Room CG545, whose name-plate lay on the desk at which Brian now sat. On Terry's last visit to the corridor, just before he left the university to join the army, Brian had heard him muttering that he had better effing things to do than go round looking for effing rooms that didn't effing exist.

Brian gave the plate a quick polish with his sleeve and put it to one side. Then he lifted one of the two carrier bags on to the desk and carefully removed the contents. They comprised a sandwich box, two cans of Coke, a copy of the *Sun* newspaper and a high-spec digital multi-meter. He opened the sandwich box. It contained a packet of cheese and onion crisps, a sandwich consisting of a slab of corned beef smeared with PanYan pickle and pressed between two heavily buttered slices of Mighty White bread, a banana and a giant bar of milk chocolate. He placed these on the left-hand side of the desk and reached inside the second bag. From this, he extracted the very latest Apple laptop with a Bart Simpson sticker on the lid.

Brian set the two bags down on the floor, produced a USB 8.0 memory stick from his pocket, and plugged it into the computer. For the next ten minutes he scrolled deftly through the items stored on the stick, deleting some and transferring others to one of three folders on the hard disc. The first was labelled 'Maintenance Manual', into which went the emails that Brian had intercepted from management to non-teaching staff. The second was labelled 'Equipment Updates' and contained the emails he had intercepted between academic staff; and the third, 'Furniture Requisitions', was completely empty except for a single file containing the words 'Check with Jones'.

Brian minimised the file and opened up an email address in the name of Hugh Jones. It was still an active email account but one that had got less busy over the years. When Brian had worked out how he could break into many of the university's high-security files and emails, he soon realised there was a small business opportunity to be exploited. The university's Teaching and Learning Committee had issued a diktat that all lecturers who set examinations for their courses must draft outline model answers to each question and deposit both questions and answers in the databases of the departments they worked in. Brian managed to hack into these, but then proceeded with caution. In his tours of duty throughout the university he came to know students from all departments, and it was not difficult to pinpoint those who were growing anxious about the forthcoming 'time-constrained unseen assessments' – what he used to call 'tests' in primary school and 'exams' in secondary. Only days before these were due to take place, some of the laziest students would visit the library, often for the very first time in the academic year. The volume and frequency of foul language declared their anxiety, and from his own unpleasant experiences as a schoolboy Brian could sympathise with them. But, of course, sympathy came at a price: Brian had a living to make. He chose the students to approach, and the moment to approach them, with great care.

'What's up, Darren? You look all stressed out, mate.'

'You'd be effing stressed out, Brian, if you had this bloody exam coming up. I just haven't had the time for revision. And I couldn't get to a lot of the lectures, either. If I fail, I'll have to repeat the year.'

'Yeah, I can see it's a real problem. What's your course? Oh, that. Well, one of last year's students told me he got a bit of help from a Mr. Jones.'

'Who's he ?'

'No idea but . . .' Brian would pause and start to pat his pockets, 'I think the student wrote down the email address. It might be here somewhere.' The student looked on sceptically as Brian pulled out used tissues, half-consumed tubes of sweets, a variety of shopping vouchers and bits of lined paper on which various reminders had been written, for when Brian looked at them he would say 'Blimey, must do that' or 'Whoops, should've done that yesterday'. Eventually he'd find a badly crumpled scrap containing an email address scrawled in pencil. 'Here we are. You could try that.'

'What sort of help does he provide?'

'No idea. But the student that gave it to me got a one-two – no, sorry, a two-one. Good luck.'

The next day Hugh Jones's inbox would contain an enquiry from the student Brian had been speaking to. It was often couched in words of muted desperation. The student then received a sympathetic reply affirming how hard exams could be. It was accompanied by a menu which set out in columns the number of exam questions that could be provided for any particular course, the charge that would be made, and whether, for an additional payment, the purchaser would require a copy of the model answer. Before he or she could sign up for the service the student would be obliged to agree a set of terms and conditions which were much briefer than those usually encountered on the internet. Effectively it made clear that if any information about the transaction was leaked, the relevant authorities would be informed, and the student failed and expelled for improper conduct. This warning had been sufficient to allow 'Mr Jones' to be philanthropic in a way that was very profitable, but as Brian now scanned the file it confirmed a suspicion he'd been harbouring for some time. The gradual abandonment of exams and their replacement by 'continuous assessment' was reducing the income stream. 'Country's going to the dogs,' he muttered. 'In my day, it was all tests and stuff, none of this write-when-you-feel-like-it nonsense. Good for a year or two more, I reckon, but then I'll have to think of something else. Sorry, Jonesie, but you're on your way out, pal.'

Brian shut the lid, then took out three more items from a jacket pocket. The first seemed to be a sellotaped packet of sweets, the second an asthma inhaler and the third a small oil-can.However, hidden inside the first was a tiny camera, inside the second a recording device, and inside the third a hand-held scanner. The scanner could be used to record and store information both from the printed page and the computer screen. This was Brian's most recent acquisition and he was keen to see whether it matched the performance claimed for it. Reaching to the side of the table at which he was sitting, he pressed a switch and typed a code into a keyboard. The names of several of the university's departments came up on the screen and he selected *Media, Literature and Culture*.

'Time for a spot of telly,' he said aloud.

The trio of multi-screen monitors quartered into separate frames, each containing its own image. Brian clicked on the top left-hand image which zoomed up to fill the whole screen of the first monitor. It was of the office shared by Eric Uggles and George Abbott. Uggles was typing in a ponderous, two-fingered fashion and staring glumly at a computer screen. At the desk opposite sprawled Abbott, gazing at nothing in particular and munching stolidly on an enormous slab of cake. For anyone called 'Professor', Brian felt the exaggerated respect of one who had himself undergone no more than a rudimentary schooling: yet whenever he switched the spycam on, the old boy never seemed to be doing anything but eating or dozing. Mind you, the cake looked very nice.

Brian zoomed out and brought up the top right-hand image: Kate Huckerby's office. Empty. He dismissed it, went to the bottom left-hand one and brought it up to full screen. Sitting at her desk and almost hidden by precarious piles of books and papers, Marjorie Steerforth was talking earnestly into her telephone and nervously winding its wire round her fingers. It looked like a slow day until Brian brought up the bottom right-hand image – of Gary Dorn's office. Gary was sitting at his desk but facing a student who was seated beside him. Brian bit into his sandwich and craned forward. He recognised the student as a pretty young fresher named Holly Ainscough, and had lately observed that she'd been visiting Dorn's office more often than his other students. Moreover, there was something about their inaudible conversation, and Dorn's physical posture, that suggested an unusual intimacy. Gary was leaning towards her and peering up into her lowered face. At the same time, he placed a gentle but deliberate hand on her thigh and pushed it under her skirt. 'Well, I'll be . . .' Brian's mouth hung open for a second, and a half-chewed plug of corned beef sandwich fell into his lap.

15. SHAKING THE TREE

The meeting had been arranged so that Prendergast could report on the reactions of the teaching staff to the university's rescue plan. Turpin hoped to hear that it had won a measure of assent, but Marian had barely poured coffee before Prendergast was speaking in the boastful tones that irritated Turpin and dismayed Unthank.

'There was some opposition, but nothing I couldn't handle. People are realising that the writing's on the wall, it's in large letters, it won't go away, and if they don't like it they'll have to lump it.'

'What issues did they raise?' inquired Turpin. 'Concerns about the new courses, loss of existing ones, what the future holds?'

'All of that,' responded Prendergast, leaning back in his chair and flipping a gold propelling pencil between his fingers. 'But if a decision's right it usually attracts opposition, so it looks as though we're getting it spot-on. They'll soon come to realise the only way forward is ours.'

'Are we going to get protests, demonstrations, round-robins, union action?'

'I'm sure that's exactly what they're exercising their tonsils and keyboards about. And they won't be saying nice things about us. But reality will soon kick in. If they start playing silly buggers, are they really going to make Mixton the first choice, or any choice, for prospective students? No. Is there a shortage of places at uni's like Mixton? No. Are applications in decline? Yes. Are customers being put off by the size of the fees? Not put off, scared witless. Does Mixton have something special that'll allow it to beat the competition? Not yet, but it soon will.'

He paused to take a sip of coffee. 'Having worked out the answers themselves, the   staff will either work with us or commit hara-kiri. And I'd be happy to provide the sword."

'It won't be easy,' said Turpin. 'Some of those you met have given their working lives to the university.'

'I'm sure that's right, Vice. But when you shake the tree, the oldest fruit drops off first.'

Unthank was about to deplore the callousness of the metaphor but Prendergast continued. 'One odd thing, though. On my way to the meeting at Fallowfields, I got held up by some silly business on the main road. At first, I thought it was a stunt by the RSPCA, but then someone said it was students. Our students. I found a way round them but next time I'll find a way over them.' Prendergast allowed himself a smirk and flipped his pencil through his fingers a final time before setting it carefully down on the table. He turned to Unthank. 'Any good news from you, Robert? Have your approaches to our local schools doubled our intake for next year?'

'Yes, Robert,' said Turpin. 'Have you managed to make any visits yet, and, if so, how did they go?'

Unthank's reply was cut short by the thumping music of Prendergast's iPhone. Prendergast waved his hand to indicate it was vital that he took the call. 'Yes. No, I didn't say that. You'd better get your facts right – and fast. Don't trouble me again.' He ended the call, giving a look which suggested that one of the many crosses he had to bear was being troubled by the ignorant and stupid.

Unthank's report was more measured than his colleague's, and briefer. He'd imagined that the schools he contacted would welcome him, but they made difficulties about their timetables, expressed doubts that the pupils would be interested, and asked whether he'd had clearance to work with young people. ('After the third call I began to feel like an importunate paedophile.') None of this impressed Prendergast. He was minded to compare his own ruthless efficacy with Unthank's hapless pussy-footing, but thought better of it. While Turpin murmured understanding words, he settled back into his chair with the air of one who would have achieved rather more.

As the meeting broke up Turpin handed his colleagues copies of *The Guardian* and *The Mixton Chronicle*. 'What you saw along the Mixton-Glabthorpe road, Ed, was not nonsense but performance art staged by our Art and Design department.' Prendergast's response was to snort and roll his eyes to heaven. He didn't get to read them until the evening, when he was sipping a glass of wine back at his flat.

The Guardian Editorial
In praise of . . . Mixton University
Gormley's Angel of the North casts a long but benign shadow – at least as far as Margate, where Tracey Emin and friends are attempting to add style to the candy floss and jellied eels. The celebration of what is happening outside London and the big cities may cause us to forget that provincial art is not recent. Overlooked for many years, the Midlands and North have made an impressive contribution to the nation's cultural heritage. Wright of Derby, Joseph Farington and Lowry have perhaps been eclipsed by Gormley and his contemporaries. In recent years, a new energy has surfaced in the provinces which is neither influenced by what has preceded it nor opposed to what is happening in the metropolis. It has a palpable

rawness, an immediacy that can both startle and delight. So in this context, but with surprise, we welcome the performance art, embryonic and exploratory though it may be, that is coming out of Mixton, not a name that is normally associated with experiment and the avant garde – or, indeed, with very much at all.

Yet the combination of the interactive and controversial, the iconoclastic and the inventive, has caught the imagination of many and aroused the ire of some. The latter springs not just from a preference for the Stag at Bay. It exists because the interactive art is causing delays on the roads and in the shops, and consternation in the parks. The Mixton councillors could doubtless invoke a plethora of by-laws and health and safety regulations to shut down overnight the whole outreach work of the University. They could – but they shouldn't. Art is challenging or it is nothing. We wish Mixton University well and hope that the activities of its students will revitalise a languishing town and win the admiration of its citizens.

The Mixton Chronicle Editorial

We have had a number of complaints from our readers about the activities of the university students. Some are perennial grumbles about late-night drinking, too much rowdiness and queue jumping at bus-stops and in supermarkets. But more recently the complaints have focused on the interactive artistic activities that have taken place across the town.

We will not defend those who seriously inconvenience their fellow citizens but we would hope that our readers' impatience can be tempered with understanding. We were all young once and, within reason, should allow the young to fulfil their ambitions and delight and amaze the rest of us. We can do no more than remind our readers of the immortal maxim, Ars Longa,Vita Brevis (Life is short but art outlives us all).

It was perhaps the mellowing effect of the wine that stopped Prendergast from uttering a single obscenity and, instead, to pour himself another and re-read the items. Personally, he thought performance art was bollocks, but if others who were influential thought otherwise, he should enlist them to his cause. The next day, he got his secretary to phone Bill Castles, editor of *The Mixton Chronicle*, with an offer to buy him lunch.

Dear Bill

It was good to see you and I hope you thought the food at the restaurant was worth the slightly longer journey.

It was most helpful to meet with you and I am pleased to confirm that the University will ensure that copies of The Mixton Chronicle will be distributed throughout the campus and that it will meet the cost price of a thousand copies a week. The Chronicle will be of great benefit to our students, keeping them in touch with local affairs and all the entertainment available within Mixton and beyond. You will therefore be able to inform your advertisers, both actual and prospective, that an extra and large group of consumers will be regularly perusing the Chronicle's contents. I am hopeful this will be of advantage to all parties.

I'm putting Josie Davenport, Deputy Head of Public Relations, in touch with you to discuss the possibility of a monthly student supplement, which I'm sure has great potential.

With kind regards
Ed
Ed Prendergast
Director of Academic Development
University of Mixton

16. BRIAN FIXES IT

At the knock on her door Marian gave a slight tut of annoyance. Grumble Guts was out of the office for the afternoon, and she was looking forward to a nice long gossip on the phone with her friend Cath, who worked round the corner in the council offices. She'd quite forgotten that that lumbering ESMO, Brian, had arranged this opportunity to repair the cleaning cradle that had jammed outside Turpin's window. She'd already punched in Cath's number when

Brian came puffing into the room, and she cupped her hand over the mouthpiece. 'I'm on the phone, Brian,' she said, stating the obvious in order to imply that the call was especially important. 'You know where it is. Go straight in.'

Carrying a large toolbox, Brian went through the connecting door and briefly surveyed the expanse of Turpin's office. He crossed to the window, which he opened with some difficulty, and examined the cradle. Though slightly askew, it was right alongside the sill, and he should be able to fix it merely by leaning out. He placed the toolbox on a nearby table, opened the lid and rummaged noisily among its contents. By this time Marian's conversation was in full flow: '. . . she's had no end of trouble with him, Cath. He blames his ex but I think he's scared of commitment . . . '

Whistling briskly, Brian moved back to the middle of the office, where, through the half-opened connecting door, he could see Marian seated sideways at her desk with her legs crossed, palavering intently into the mouthpiece, one finger twirling the phone cord. She was well away. Producing a USB from his pocket, he stepped round to the front of the computer on Turpin's desk, plugged it into a free port and switched on. Still whistling, he returned to the window and the cradle, busily clattering his tools. He plied an oil-can, a monkey wrench and some kind of implement that was worked with a ratchet, giving an occasional glance back at the computer as it warmed up and icons appeared on the screen. Marian was just getting into her stride. 'Have you tried Debenham's? They've got some beautiful fabrics in their sale.' Brian sauntered back to the computer and pressed some keys, talking silently to himself. 'Blimey, is this all the security he's got? The cleaners could get into this. Academics, eh? They're like babes in the wood. *Very* irresponsible . . . Let's see, what've we got here?' Brian found a folder marked TOP SECRET & CONFIDENTIAL. 'Hmm, this looks promising. We'll probably need the higher end megabytes for this.'

He became aware that all had gone quiet in the adjacent office. Still whistling, he peeped through the doorway but was at once reassured. Frowning with concentration, handset wedged between jaw and shoulder, Marian was now doing her nails, and evidently listening to a monologue from Cath. He returned to the open window and the cradle, completed the repair, winched the cradle down a foot or two ready for lowering later, closed the window, rattled his tools once more, and whistling a new and jaunty tune, returned to Turpin's computer.

' . . . so I thought I might have it ruched or gathered, but I wonder whether it would make me look too broad across the hips.'

With a tap or two on the keyboard, he had copied the entire contents of the confidential folder on to the USB. He unplugged it, dropped it into his pocket, switched off the computer, and in a noisy finale gathered up his tools and walked through the connecting door into Marian's office. 'Job done!' he announced, and Marian, head still clamped to the handset, gave rapid nods and smiles intended to be at once grateful and dismissive.

With a careful glance up and down the corridor, Brian let himself into his secret office, sat down at his computer, plugged in the USB and tore open a family-sized bag of cheese and onion crisps. He scrolled through the confidential folder, noting various documents of interest, but one in particular caught his eye, perhaps because its top secret nature was so stridently proclaimed in large capital letters. 'They never learn,' he said to himself, 'if they filed it under Boiler Maintenance they'd help themselves a bit.' He read it carefully and stroked his chin. If this were in the public domain, he thought, as he munched his way through the crisps, it could give the management a lot of grief – and serve them right after what they've done to the likes of George Abbott and Eric Uggles! Those poor old sods in Media, Literature and Culture wouldn't say boo to a goose, always let him have any spare cake that was going, and now they've got shafted for their trouble. Brian printed the document off before dropping the entire folder into his larger folder entitled 'Equipment updates'. All that was needed now was to get this document into the hands of an unscrupulous mischief maker. Who might that be? An hour or two later, Brian found himself in a deserted Fallowfields, and the door under which he slipped the document was Gary's.

17. LET'S RUN OVER LALIQUE

Tom Burley sat in what passed for his office. It was a large space in the annexe at Fallowfields and had been created by knocking together two of its rooms. Its size had been further increased by breaking through the ceiling to the space above. This was strictly contrary to the conditions under which the premises were leased to the university, but Tom had decided not to bother the authorities with such a minor matter and done the work over a single summer vacation.

The Head of Art and Design was Barry Powell and when, on his return for the new academic year, he saw what Burley had done he came close to a heart attack. That summer Powell had been the designated person for the oversight of property integrity and security, a humdrum role that was allocated on a rota basis and effectively sabotaged any prospect of a sensible break – in his view, one of six weeks or more. Powell therefore took counter-measures. He circulated an email which included his contact details and the announcement that he would be looking in at frequent intervals. This was to make his colleagues feel that he had his eye on them, but the contact details could, of course, be accessed from any part of the globe. He logged on weekly from his holiday cottage in the Algarve, and dealt with what were only the few minor matters which his colleagues, also looking for a sensible break, raised with him. Unhappily, however, they disregarded the warning that Powell would be looking in at frequent intervals because they'd learned from his secretary, who'd booked Powell's electronic airline tickets, that he wasn't due to return till September. On the day of his return, and gazing up in horror at the new ceiling of Burley's office some twenty feet above him, Powell felt it would be best not to report the matter. The Attwoods seldom ventured near the place and by the time it was discovered by anyone who mattered, he'd be long gone.

There was a desk in Tom Burley's cavernous office. It was circular and ten feet in diameter and would have lent itself to meetings of all kinds, but its actual use precluded such things. A model railway track ran round its perimeter, on which were situated stations labelled 'Renaissance', 'Impressionist', 'Cubist', 'Gilbert and George' and 'Conceptual'. In the middle were assembled figurines which the initiated might have recognised as Rembrandt, Van Gogh, Lalique, Turner, Rodin, Henry Moore, Rousseau, Lichtenstein, Warhol and Tracey Emin. Each had an additional feature. Van Gogh had a plaster over one ear, Turner a pot of paint on his head. Rousseau was pulling a tiger on a leash, and Warhol had an egg-timer in his right hand. Emin seemed to have an obsession with feminine hygiene. Across the diameter of the table ran a racing track for model cars. Burley had devised matters so that when the train passed a car parked at one end of the diameter, the car was released and travelled to the other end. When the train reached the further side of the table it released the car again to make its return journey. The figurines seemed to be watching the car as it shuttled to and fro.

The walls of the room were stuck with a variety of polystyrene shapes that had once protected televisions, lap-tops and a variety of domestic appliances from damage during transit. Out of their boxes they looked strangely naked, as if embarrassed to be there. Piled up against the walls at heights seemingly calculated to stub toes or bark shins were various artistic materials: pots of paint, brushes, palettes, tubes of cardboard, picture frames, an abandoned TV with some if its entrails poking out, and a set of four-foot-high plaster figures in faintly suggestive poses. There was a second, smaller table at which Burley sat. When Powell walked in, his lap-top was open in front of him and he was looking at YouTube.

'Ah, Tom, how are you, and how are all your friends?'

'We are all well, except Astrid Castles. She is upset, but she still can't draw, paint, sculpt or show she has the slightest trace of imagination. She has failed the module, and that is *absolutely fucking final*.' Burley swung round in his chair and smiled glacially at his visitor.

'I haven't come about Astrid, though my secretary tells me that last week she was outside my office. Weeping her way through boxes of Kleenex. No, it's the street demos, Tom.'

'You must mean conceptual art. How lucky are the Mixtonites to have art on their doorsteps, in their shops, and next week, maybe, in their council offices.'

'I've had the police on to me about the activities on the Mixton Road. Traffic held up, bystanders threatened, the peace breached.'

'Dear me. Very sad. Who could be causing such distress?'

'They wore T-shirts, a good number of which had slogans across them saying things like "ART FULL DODGER" and "ART MART".'

'They can be picked up anywhere. I've seen them on eBay. Probably students from another college.' Burley looked totally unfazed, a mannerism that Powell never failed to find irritating.

'Tom, you know I have clear views about all this conceptual rag, tag and bobtail. This contrivance over artefact, this self-preening, self-regarding collection of emperor's new clothes. This, this bloody nonsense that you – '

'It's such a shame you feel this way, Barry,' said Burley. 'But so fortunate that I enjoy the support of our higher management.'

'Don't be too sure. When I bumped into Dr Turpin a few weeks ago he complained to me very forcefully about one of your childish stunts.'

'I find that impossible to believe.'

'Claims he and Prendergast were showing a VIP round the uni when one of your life models got into the lift with them. Stark naked.'

'How wonderful for Dick Turpin and his guest that their ride in the lift should be changed from banality into an aesthetic experience! I know you're head of art, Barry, but you seem to have forgotten that the female form is a thing of beauty.'

Like a landed fish, Powell opened and closed his mouth soundlessly. Burley continued. 'I must find the life model and congratulate her on dreaming up something so brilliant.'

'Oh for God's sake, Burley!' Powell found his voice at the moment he lost his temper.

'Barry, let's talk about this with the air circulating.'

Burley reached across the desk and picked up a control box from which an aerial stuck out. He pointed it upwards. Powell looked up and saw what he'd previously missed, a model aeroplane suspended from the roof of the void above them. The plane was much more solid than the balsawood models that are usually sold in shops and had a black pod at the end of each wing. The plane started to circulate slowly, wafting the air.

'Who put that up there?' asked Powell.

'British Airways. And it carries a message from its sponsor.' Burley pressed another button and the pods revealed themselves to be loudspeakers. 'This is your captain speaking,' came a tinny, cackling voice. 'All engines have failed. We are losing height and will strike the water imminently. Those of you who paid NO ATTENTION to Stewards Sandra and Sven when they went through the safety drill need not worry. No wide-bodied jet has ever survived a crash into open water. Please adopt the brace position. Place your hands behind your head, your head between your knees, and kiss your arse goodbye.' This was followed by the noise of a prolonged crash, a gurgling sound and then the gentle lapping of waves. The surrealness of this had been magnified by the sense of the message swooping round in the air above. It was like kinetic surround-sound.

'Isn't that nice, Barry? I asked for proposals from the Second Year Conceptuals to liven this place up a bit. The top three proposals get installed for a month, then there's a final vote for the winner. Do you want to be a judge?'

'No, I don't. All of this, but especially the street stuff, will have Health and Safety crawling all over it like flies on carrion. Something's going to go really wrong and it won't just be you in deep paint.'

'Did you know, Barry, that Health and Safety won't allow the Director of the Newcastle Art Gallery even to stand on a chair to put a picture straight. The kids want to be artists; they are living, sentient beings. They've got blood in their veins and all kinds of other bodily fluids elsewhere. They want to live, they want to dance the dance.'

'Well, they're going to die the bloody death if they're not careful. Any more of this street nonsense and I'll get you and all your works closed down. That's a promise.'

'Think about it carefully, Barry. We are the rock on which the department stands. You'd be left with a handful of engravers, potters, needle-workers and kids doing potato prints. Not,' Burley smiled disarmingly, 'that I've got anything against potato prints.'

'They're students who should be developing their skills to make something valuable. Not wasting their time prancing across zebra crossings. God, don't you ever wish you could do something like, like . . . .' In his search for inspiration, Barry's gaze fell on the figurines at the centre of the railway track, 'like Lalique? Beautiful objects perfectly produced? Things with craft, skill and taste?'

Burley picked up the figurine. 'Poor old Lalique. Producing gewgaws for bourgeois drawing rooms. This is what we think of Lalique.'

Burley laid the figurine across the railway track and set the train in motion. The figurine turned out to be much less solid than it appeared, the train much more so. As Powell watched, the train sliced through the prostrate form and continued on its way.

18. PILLOW TALK

'Oh, Gary, I can't do that.'

'Why not? You've done everything else.'

Holly giggled. 'I know. But this isn't, you know . . . .' She giggled some more and ran a finger across his chest.

'If the students don't do something they'll get the rough end of the pineapple shoved up their arses. Not only will Media be axed: they're moving it out of Fallowfields and into a load of prefabs. Then they'll say the premises aren't big enough to teach everyone, and the degree will have to close even earlier. And finally they'll claim this confirms their view that it was never viable in the first place. It's going to be a self-fulfilling prophecy.'

'What's that, Gary?'

'You predict something's going to happen, then take steps to make sure it does.'

'You mean if I said that we were going to, you know, and then . . . .' her hand slid down over his stomach and Gary grabbed her wrist and sat upright in bed.

'Well, yes, I suppose that might be one example, but this is rather different.'

'But we'll be alright, won't we? They couldn't stop the courses part-way through. I'd be able to keep seeing my favourite tutor and finish my degree.' Holly stretched her limbs and started to move a crimson toe-nail up Gary's left leg.

'They're certainly saying they'll allow all the current students to finish their degrees here, but – ' Gary pushed away the ascending toe, 'saying's one thing and delivering's another.'

'But they wouldn't make promises if they weren't going to keep them?'

'Think about it, Holly. They announce that various degrees are going to close. Which of the staff will hang around to deliver courses that are going to be shut down? They'll all push off somewhere else, retire, get jobs at other uni's.'

'But Gary,' Holly sat up sharply and looked at him, 'you're not going, are you?'

'If they shut the degree early I may have no choice.'

'But what'll happen to us – the students? Are they just going to hang us out to dry?'

'They'll probably get you transferred to other uni's. But . . . ' Gary was now improvising desperately, 'you probably won't be able to choose which ones. I, er, heard a rumour – only a rumour, mind – that the uni was planning a fallback deal. If the Media and English degrees had to end early, you students would all be moved to Bolton.'

'Bolton? Bloody hell's teeth! That's a bloody outrage! Who the hell wants to study there?'

'That's why I want you to mobilise the students. Organise a university-wide protest. Against closing the degrees, or at any rate closing them early. Against being shifted from Fallowfields and stuffed into crap accommodation. Why should the students get screwed around just because the high-ups have decided we need to fill the world with solar panel salesmen and massage-parlour receptionists?'

Holly pouted thoughtfully and ran a finger round the pattern on the duvet cover. 'But Gary, that's not gonna work. We'll never get the whole uni out. The only students who'd protest are those on courses that are facing the chop. The other students won't give a monkey's.'

Gary leant behind her and reaching down to his trousers on the floor beside the bed, pulled a piece of paper from the back pocket. He'd prepared for this. 'What you've got to get across to everybody is that your courses are only the thin end of the wedge. With that bastard Prendergast in charge, *every course in the uni is at risk*. Just run your eye over that.'

Holly unfolded the paper. It appeared to be a sheet of Prendergast's headed stationery.Marked IN STRICTEST CONFIDENCE, it was addressed to various heads of department. She read it slowly and with some difficulty.

Further to our recent review of all the degree programmes which are taught at the university, I must inform you that a need for further rationalisation has become apparent. I will shortly be inviting you to meet with me and other senior colleagues to give closer consideration to staffing and student numbers set against the trans-UK median for those universities comparable with Mixton. Please bring to the meeting all relevant information relating to student enrolment over the last five years, student drop-out rates and departmental outcomes. I already have all the necessary information on staffing costs and turnover, much of which, I need hardly remind you, makes less than comfortable reading. The university is entering a very difficult period and you will appreciate that none of its programmes is sacrosanct and that no remedy, however radical, can be ruled out . . .

'What's this all mean, Gary?'

'What it means is that no one is safe. The axe is about to be swung again and a good number of heads'll roll. You need to alert all the students that the tumbrils are on their way.'

'Tumblers? Sodding hell! Can I keep this letter, Gary, and show it around?'

'I'd like to say yes but I can't. They'd ask where you got it from, and you wouldn't have an answer. But you can assure them you've seen it.' He stuffed the paper into the pocket of his trousers and dropped them back on the floor. He felt quite proud of this letter, which he'd concocted the previous evening over a warming glass of whisky. 'The point you've got to get across, Holly, is that every student at this uni is under threat.'

'But what can we get them to do?'

'Picket the vice chancellor's office, hold meetings in the canteen, organise a march from Fallowfields to Mixton, write to *The Mixton Chronicle*, get on to the local MP. Do something eye-catching and dramatic.'

'What, like those eco warriors?'

'Exactly. I've got nothing against them, but there's no reason why the eco courses should come to Fallowfields. Do you know any students in Art and Design?'

'Loads. We all work in Tesco's at weekends.'

'They're always doing weird stuff – performance art, and all that. Get them to think up something dramatic. And make sure the local TV and radio stations know about it.'

'Gary, that'd be great. But what could we do? Everyone does marches and picketing and stuff. No one's going to turn out for that sort of bollocks.'

Gary had an idea. 'You could get the mountaineering club involved. They could abseil down the main block. Put big banners up. "Mixton sacrifices students", that sort of thing.'

This litany of revolutionary options began to kindle Holly's interest. Her eyes gleamed. 'Gary, Gary, if I kept a diary of it all, could I use it for the module on Interpersonal Media – "Affecting Me, Affecting You"?'

''Course you could. You'd score twice, be a revolutionary *and* record the revolution. Brilliant idea. You're a genius.' He took Holly's head in his hands and kissed her.

'Talking about scoring twice . . .' Holly slid down the bed and nestled her nose into Gary's navel. 'I do love you, Gary, my gorgeous Gary, shmy shuper coddly liddle jimjam, shmoody doo, shmy . . .'

Gary looked at his watch. His next lecture was in forty minutes. He really shouldn't. But as Holly was his only, if slender, hope of delaying the loss of Fallowfields, it would be unwise to disoblige her.

19. THE SECRET LIFE OF BRIAN

Brian was spending more of his lunch hours in his 'office'. He didn't mind mucking in with Tosh and the others in the staff mess, but there were times when he'd better things to do than debate the merits of the day's Page Three Girl. The secret room afforded him peace and quiet, and the mobile phone and pager, always set to vibrate, warned him if he was wanted elsewhere.

Today he was doing his accounts. These were in two separate files. The first was titled 'Mixton and Domestic' and tracked his salary payments from the university, basic, overtime, additional duties and deductions. The second was titled 'Special Services' and detailed payments into an account in the name of Hugh Jones, who'd previously occupied the small terrace house where Brian lived. Letters for Mr Jones continued to arrive long after he'd left and, lacking his forwarding address Brian had opened them. Some were from organisations who believed they were owed money, but there were also bank statements, credit and debit cards, and numerous invitations to Jones to raise his credit limit, increase his mortgage, take out a loan, buy a new car and avail himself of many offers of consumer durables which could be enjoyed for up to two years without money changing hands. Some of the subsequent letters were anxious to correct a possible misapprehension that, after the offer was taken up, nothing ever had to be paid. To these, Brian, who'd never met Jones and who during his purchase of the house had dealt only with the estate agent, replied that Jones had gone to visit an aunt in New Zealand and left no forwarding address. The follow-up inquiries gradually tailed off.

Brian then tried an experiment. He signed for the receipt of a new credit card which had been posted to Jones: it had an increased limit and would be valid for five years. He was familiar with Hugh Jones's signature from the conveyancing process, and if they'd been block capitals its clear upright letters could hardly have been easier to forge. At this point he learned that once organisations become convinced you're a certain person their conviction is hard to shake. Accordingly he moved to an online account set up with the usual security checks. He enjoyed fabricating Hugh's middle name, Owen, and his mother's maiden name, Thomas, and was happy to determine his favourite food, Welsh cakes, and his favourite flower, the daffodil. Hugh was very much a boy from the Valleys, but he'd stretched Brian's knowledge of Welsh culture to the limit.

Payments into the account attracted no attention, and neither, subsequently, did modest withdrawals. From that point Brian used the Jones account for all his covert transactions. He now pulled up the statement and went through the details. The cash flow had been lively, but was becoming rather less so. There were payments from those students who'd availed themselves of Mr Jones's assistance in helping them pass their exams, but these were falling victim to the growing craze for 'continuous assessment' and 'projects', two forms of assignment which, to Brian's disgust, afforded a paradise for plagiarists. He moved across to the eBay account, his preferred trading venue for the expensive books that disappeared at some point after they'd been delivered to the university, but before they'd been subjected to the library's identity stamp, a stigma which, Brian discovered, reduced their resale value as well as all too evidently signalling their provenance. The identity stamp was a disgraceful reflection of student dishonesty: in his day, nobody ever thought of nicking library books.

Back in the Hugh Jones account, many of the out-payments were in respect of a wide range of electronic products concerned with surveillance, security and mobile communication. They included the latest phones, memory sticks, some with encryption, some not, Blu-Ray devices, miniature recording equipment, a range of security cameras and associated wiring, and wi-fi items and memory cards. The sales pitch that accompanied many of these products stressed how easy they made it to record, listen to, view, and play back audio and visual material in a wide variety of settings, from home to office, to car, to wireless hot-spots. But Brian wanted them for other, more sophisticated purposes than monitoring sleeping babies or uninvited callers or the rare birds that might visit his back garden.

His musical tastes were limited and the play-list on his MP3 player featured only twenty songs and five artists. Similarly, his store of visual items comprised no films nor even YouTube clips, but it did include a portrait gallery of persons employed by the university. These were accompanied by a number of video clips, the product of tiny cameras which he'd installed in various rooms to spy on those who occupied or visited them. The clips showed him not only who knew whom within the university, but who in certain circumstances would place a comforting arm round a depressed shoulder or even lock her legs round the small of another's back.

The 'Mixton and Domestic' material was all on a standard Office spreadsheet, but the Special Services transactions had been loaded into an SQL programme with its own computing language of primary and foreign keys, constraints, drop, alter, select and join. Brian, who had not so much 'got on' with maths at school as declared the subject a sworn enemy, had been an accidental convert to programming. On one slow evening shift at the university, he was checking out a lecture room in which a few personal belongings had been left behind. They included a sheaf of lecture notes entitled 'Elementary Programming for Beginners' and some very tired cheese sandwiches. Brian had started reading and discovered that programming wasn't like school maths, it wasn't those hateful fractions or algebra. His experiences at school had been unhappy. Never the quickest of learners, he'd been a pupil in an era when teachers looked not for potential but to administer prompt punishment for failures. Failure and Brian, especially in maths, were intimates. He would curl his arm round the exercise book in an effort to stop anyone from reading what he'd written, but his primary school teacher, Miss Watts, was all-seeing.

'What secrets have we here, *Brian*?' she would say, stressing his name as if to convey a special warmth. 'Some secret method of solving all these sums in a flash? Let's have a look.' Brian's endeavours would be plucked away from him. On a good day they'd simply acquire a column of red crosses, like a check-list for the angel of death. On a bad day they'd be announced to the entire class. While some teachers were head-slappers, Miss Watts's speciality was flicking ears 'Not,' *flick*, 'good enough', *flick*. 'We must, *Brian*, try harder.' Flick, flick. Brian thought it could never get any worse. But then, at his secondary school, he encountered Mr. Davis, and algebra. And worse was what it got.

Life had not been kind to Mr. Davis. A deformity of his neck caused his head to be permanently cocked, so that he seemed to be approaching you sideways. That and his invariably bad temper caused him to be nicknamed Crabby. He came to school on a motor scooter, and countless generations of pupils noted that the wing mirrors had to be set at peculiar angles to accommodate the rider's sight-lines. With the compassion for which children are renowned, they often readjusted the mirrors, and then, at leaving time, watched delightedly as Crabby, realising that the only rear view he had was of the pavement on one side and the sky on the other, came to a swerving, skidding halt just before the school gates. On one occasion Brian was standing nearby, so Crabby jumped to the conclusion that he was the culprit. This led to the misery of extra maths homework, and when that proved unsatisfactory, to detention. For the rest of his schooling, Brian then became Crabby's *bête noire* and was detained rather a lot. In the end, Brian felt he'd done more time than a serial killer in Parkhurst.

While maths was his worst subject, there was none he shone at. He left school with a minor qualification in Woodwork, the sole official recognition of his eleven years of full-time education. But on that slow evening shift at the university the student had left not just the notes but the information needed to log on and access the programme on the university's server. Brian hesitantly followed the instructions just to see what it was about, and discovered it was a bit like entering an enchanted forest. Absently munching his way through the tired cheese sandwiches, he did the first few worked examples and with growing elation watched the answers fall out. It was the joyful moment of a hitherto joyless life. What he'd supposed was impossibly difficult was in fact not much more than common sense. The very word 'program' had always put him off. But he was learning that programmes weren't like Miss Watts's maths, they were recipes. And just as, if you followed the recipe you ended up with Yorkshire pudding or blancmange, so with programming the rewards were equally logical. Brian never looked back. He discovered there were quite a number of programmes, C++, XML, Java, UML, BASIC. They each had their own quirks and flourishes, but all came with simple and structured explanations.

And nobody appeared at your shoulder who shouted at you or flicked your ear.

This adventure into programming was what forced Brian to acquire certain textbooks from the library. Not a great reader, he'd mostly confined himself to the *Sun* and the *Daily Mirror*, with odd forays into magazines that the students had discarded round the university. But as his confidence and proficiency in computing grew, he was eager to attempt another kind of reading. Books about computing were a shocking price, so there was nothing for it but to borrow them from the library on a long term, indeed permanent, loan. This he did, not by checking the books out in the conventional way but by putting them into black sacks, which were then left in the refuse bay for collection the following day. The collector was Brian and the receptacle was the boot of his Cavalier.

His success with programming led him into technology. He could easily and legitimately study the lecture notes for individual technology modules by accessing them on the university website, but most of these were heavy going and often failed to provide the answers he was seeking. He turned instead to the collection of computing magazines that stood in racks around the 'Relax and Learn' areas of the library. These rapidly became shabby, torn and dog-eared, a reproach to an academic ambience that Brian and his colleagues struggled to keep tidy, so he improved matters by transferring them at regular intervals to his secret office. Here, at leisure, away from eyes prying or otherwise, and with a thermos and a packed lunch, he could discover what was new, what was rated and what was rubbish, which gizmos did what and how much they cost. The mismatch between his lowly wages and his new appetite for learning was a social injustice that he would remedy by providing a paid service to those who desperately needed it, the students with unseen exams to take. This was, alas, a declining market, but some departments had oddly persisted with them, even the arty ones. He would continue to make hay while the sun shone, even if the sun was slowly setting.

His experiments with surveillance had been sparked by a curiosity as to what could be done with all the new electronic products coming on the market. And they never troubled his conscience because by keeping an eye on things in a way which was highly effective, even if not quite within the terms of his job description, Brian was clearly doing the university an immense favour.

20. UTOPIA COMES TO MIXTON

Prendergast was right. The Vice and the Toff were only too pleased for him to stage his 'event', the unveiling of the development plan for the Fallowfields campus, and for themselves to assume roles that were merely ancillary. This would be a huge publicity coup for the university, and when Prendergast assured them that the unveiling would be 'impactful, persuasive and dynamic', they understood that he had in mind something more than a flip-chart presentation. He was practised in persuading the doubtful, the wary and the cynical that whatever project he was inviting them to invest in was a winner. Appealing to heart, head and wallet in equal measure he'd always made sure that the sums added up, the project showed logic, and that even as they counted their huge returns the most hard-boiled of his listeners could believe themselves to be philanthropists. He was also aware that today's audience, though different in composition from those he was used to, would have very similar values. The representatives of local and national government would be hazarding other people's money but their own reputations. He also knew that much would turn on his ability to deal crisply and clearly with the follow-up questions.

He phoned a wide range of individuals, including ex-colleagues and those who knew about planning law, brown belt redevelopment, construction times, local land values, supply chain issues, and design and tender timescales. He called up contacts in aerial photography, scale modelling and graphic presentation. That the event would take place very shortly was a problem he overcame simply by sparing the university no expense. He was also anxious to keep his preparations private, and while he assembled some elements of the presentation in his own office most of the work was undertaken in one of Tom Burley's storage spaces. Burley's discretion, as well as some of his creative flair, was bought with a twenty per cent increase in his materials budget.

Prendergast's presentation would have several aspects. He had to persuade his audience that the two new departments at Fallowfields would be the saving, indeed the making, of Mixton University, and that their degrees would have the blend of theory and work experience that would make their graduates fit for employment. By serving as a resource for it, the departments would also make a huge impact on the local community. Prendergast's own interest in alternative medicine was non-existent, and his commitment to ecological matters no greater than was attested by a 2.8 litre BMW, a collection of domestic appliances that included a 42-inch television, and a deployment of central heating and air conditioning which ensured that the optimum temperature prevailed at any time in any place he lived. He never worried greatly about double or secondary glazing, insulated lofts or other energy saving measures. However, he recognised that he was swimming against the current – the rhetorical current, at least. Conversations with Brenda had revealed that the government's mighty promises on these issues were matched only by the feebleness of its performance, and this was why he was calculating that it would claim the new developments at Fallowfields as proof it was in earnest.

The Big Society and the local community were two other things about which Ed never troubled himself. He perceived them as a matter of those who had large houses and vast incomes exhorting those who had neither to help each other out while the provisions of local government, the health service, the emergency services and the legal system all dwindled. Just as taxes were really for the little people, from whose incomes they could easily be deducted at source, so were the notions of inter-dependability, community care and 'love your neighbour'. Prendergast didn't even know who his neighbours were and wished to keep it that way.

For professional purposes – the task in hand and his long-term ambitions – all this had to be set aside. What Brenda wanted to see was how key government policies could be realised, and that was what she was going to get. Mixton, the university with uni-versatility. Fallowfields, the campus, the courses and the community, whose tripartite synergy would set a standard for the rest of the country to aim at. Prendergast didn't have to be an idealist to dream, but much more of this and Brenda, Turpin and Unthank would be dancing round a maypole set up on the high street roundabout. Today's event was a lunchtime buffet and Prendergast had outlined his presentation to his two colleagues and assigned to them their supporting roles: Turpin would welcome the guests and introduce Ed, who would be followed by Turpin again, with some closing remarks by Unthank. Prendergast continued to regard Unthank with a certain contempt. The 'academic development' which formed part of his own title, and which this project embodied, also embraced the 'outreach and enterprise' that were supposed to be Unthank's responsibilities. The Toff had brought little to the table but airy-fairy musings and a stock of smart-arse foreign phrases. Yet Prendergast was astute enough to know Unthank's value to this occasion: though he himself had little time for such qualities, seeing them as effete and irrelevant, Unthank's charm, and the cultural allusions with which he sprinkled his conversation, would give the project what their audience would perceive as 'class'.

Prendergast had made careful arrangements to transfer those guests arriving from both train station and university car-park to the conference room near Turpin's office. The lift was manned by Brian, who had been smartened up. In fact, he looked as unprepossessing as ever but in a way that attested to the importance of the occasion. His meagre hair was wetted and flattened, he wore a fresh white shirt beneath an unusually tight tie, his shoes, though unlaced, were shining, and he'd managed to button parts of his ESMO uniform over his belly. Marian took coats, distributed name-tags, and ushered the visitors into the conference room, where catering staff served drinks and coffee. After a short interval in which the guests had a chance to meet one another, they were invited to occupy chairs that were set out in three or four rows.

'Ladies and gentlemen,' began Turpin, clasping his hands in a gesture of greeting. 'We're honoured and delighted to welcome so many important people here today. The Minister of Education and his permanent secretary, Ms Brenda Hodges, have kindly found the time to come up to Mixton, along with their colleagues from the Departments of the Environment and of Business and Enterprise. From closer to home we have our local MP, Harry Hunter; Geoffrey Edgerton, head of housing on the local council with two of his colleagues; and Bill Castles, the editor of *The Mixton Chronicle*.

They can all offer an informed local perspective which I am sure our guests from London will find invaluable.

'Ladies and gentlemen, my colleagues and I have a plan – indeed, a vision – which we wish to share with you. It is nothing less than the transformation of the University of Mixton from just another university – albeit, *ahem*, a highly reputable one – into the leader of the field, an institution which will embody a new concept of the academy and show the way in which higher education must develop over the next decades: as the unifier of research and theory on the one hand with the world of practical affairs on the other, as the catalyst of business, enterprise and industry, and as the servant of the wider community. Let me now hand you over to my colleague who is Director of Academic Development at the university, Ed Prendergast.'

Prendergast leapt to his feet, pressed a button which caused a screen to descend behind him and gave his PowerPoint presentation. He was a man for whom PowerPoint might have been invented. It afforded him the opportunity to flash his smile, shoot his cuffs and press the button for another set of slogans to cartwheel across the screen. He used the laser pointer as deftly as a sharp-shooter, targeting a key word while stabbing the air with a forefinger. His presentation was a mesmerising blend of audio-visual gimmickry, commanding gestures and slightly overheated rhetoric. '. . . . so, in conclusion, we have an overall vision which will appeal to all parties. We boost the fortunes of Mixton by the swift and radical development of its university, and we offer a vision of the future through the new Ecological and Environmental Department and the Department of Complementary Therapy and Outreach Care, both of them power-houses of cutting-edge research. We'll engage young people in the cause of saving the planet and preserving the health of the community through practical means which are integral to their studies. And we'll create a significant residential matrix which hits government targets by turning endless promises into real homes. This is a green agenda in which education is allied with practical experience; housing needs are met, yet with reductions in carbon footprints; and young people can study and work both for themselves and for the wider society. I invite you to join the party – not a political party in the conventional sense but a party of the purposeful, the pragmatic and the realistic, underpinned by shared commitment, a strong local economy and a strategic vision – a vision which is made real in this room. Please gather round and enjoy it.'

He pressed more buttons. The screen ascended into the ceiling and behind it curtains opened to reveal, mounted on a table, a huge scale model of the proposed Fallowfields development. Among the approaching guests, even the most cynical could not fail to be impressed. In fact, it displayed more than the Fallowfields site, for it also embraced the adjacent land of Compton Farm and omitted the fence that divided them. This happy amalgamation was the anticipated result of the new offer made to the owners of Compton Farm, Colin and Edith Pickles, by Geoffrey Edgerton of the local council. When he made the offer Edgerton also mentioned that their neighbours, the Attwoods, had agreed to sell Fallowfields to the university. For Colin and Edith it seemed the ideal time to retire to Skegness.

The historic Fallowfields buildings – the main house, the former stables and outbuildings – were instantly recognisable and the focus of the model. The narrow road that had led up to them was replaced by two separate roads, one for access, the other for egress. To the rear of the buildings were some new structures, arranged and landscaped in such a way as to respect the Attwoods' aesthetic concerns and fears of overdevelopment. However, a new road ran along the side of the site to the old Compton Farm land, and here development was rather more intensive. An assortment of bungalows, semis and low-rise blocks of flats, interspersed with larger detached units of accommodation, was arranged not in conventional rows but in two sets of semi-circles. There were no boundary hedges or car-parks. At the centre of the semi-circles were community facilities – a nursery, a clinic, a meeting hall, a playground. But as Prendergast eagerly explained, these buildings also offered an array of 'fusion services', combining the roles of post office, pharmacy, wireless hotspot, food store and library. 'Our slogan will be "Most of what you want exactly where you want it",' he added smoothly. To disguise the density of the development, the modellers had been artfully liberal in their use of foam rubber trees. Tracks were provided for prams, scooters and communal bikes, but not for motor vehicles. Prendergast also drew attention to the wind

100

turbines, to the fact that many of the buildings enjoyed a southerly aspect, and that the tiny mirror-like squares on their roofs represented solar panels.

It was now that he invited questions, and the moment was well-chosen. These were pertinent – 'How are you going to enforce the restricted car policy?', 'What links will there be to the wider world?', 'What will stop Fallowfields from turning into a concrete wilderness littered with beer cans and broken promises?' – but they were not so much strident challenges as constructive queries from a group who were admiring a fait accompli. Prendergast was able to deal with them almost effortlessly, usually thanking the questioner for the shrewdness of her or his question and then answering with a specious combination of promises and overstatements. After a due number had been addressed, he handed back to his colleague, Dr Turpin.

Turpin's theme was that 'connected communities' were not an impossible dream but a realisable ambition. As the model showed, there was an absence of barriers of any kind. The new-build would benefit from high speed cable broadband, allowing all residents to subscribe to Fallowfields@community.com. This would be for a micro-community version of SKYPE to be called HYPE, Harness Your Personal Expertise, and would encourage each member of the community to act in a caring and helpful manner. Another version of this would enable them to have medical consultations in their own home – an initiative to be led and supported by the university's new Department of Complementary Therapy and Outreach Care, to be known as DoCTOC. A second new university department, of Ecology and the Environment, would cooperate with the community in matters of fuel and energy conservation, assisting its members with composting and recycling. Turpin concluded by hoping, in a strained little joke, that his audience would excuse the small piece of whimsy by which the Fallowfields community bikes would be known as UNI-cycles.

The presentation was concluded by Robert Unthank, the Director of Outreach and Enterprise. Unthank's way of addressing an audience was not Prendergast's, nor to Prendergast's taste. Where the latter used bombast, the former breathed charm; where the latter boasted, the former offered endearing self-deprecation. There were cleverly-apt references and some elegant ironies, but far from undermining the project their effect was to imply that it was so well-grounded that humour was an easily-affordable luxury. The contrasting personalities of the university's triumvirate proved to be a powerful asset, and at the ensuing buffet lunch there was much animated conversation and useful networking.

As the event came to an end, Marian gave each departing guest a 'goody bag' consisting of a pen-drive and a ball-point, both emblazoned with the university's logo, a glossy brochure outlining the Fallowfields development, and a DVD in which computer-generated imagery was accompanied by a stirring soundtrack of Edward Elgar. The event suffered only one final, trivial hitch. Brian stood respectfully at one side of the lift as the main body of guests surged into it. Not appreciating his official role, the last of the guests pressed the button that would return them to the ground floor, and it was only by wedging himself between the closing doors that Brian managed to hold the lift. The doors parted once more and he squeezed in and again pressed the button. This time, however, the doors failed to move, and an automated voice barked 'Weight limit exceeded! Lift unable to operate! Weight limit exceeded! Lift unable to operate!' There was a silence. Everybody looked at Brian, who, whistling soundlessly and gazing up at the ceiling, affected not to notice. The silence was about to become awkward when a voice spoke crisply from within the throng: 'Brian, pop back and make sure nobody's left anything behind while I see our guests out.' Brian turned to see Marian fixing him with a baleful smile and shuffled out. The doors closed at once and the lift sank gratefully to the ground floor.

Last to leave the conference room was Brenda Hodges, who shook hands with Turpin, Unthank and Prendergast in turn. When she reached the latter, she gave him a faint, sardonic smile. 'Goodness, you *have* been busy,' she said.

It was a trifle, but exactly what he'd been waiting for.

21. GARY MAKES AN OFFER

'Hello, Dr. Dorn: it's Gary, isn't it? I have a busy schedule and, as you know, there's a lot happening, but take a seat.'

Gary realised he had to steer a course between the obsequious and the contrarian, present himself as a supporter of change while being sensitive to colleagues who favoured an eternal status quo. 'I don't want to keep you long, er- Ed, but I thought you might like the staff/student perspective on the forthcoming changes at Fallowfields.'

'Keeping things as they are is not an option,' returned Prendergast crisply.

'Absolutely not,' responded Gary. 'The university has to adapt to changing times and changing imperatives. I recognise that.'

'Excellent, then we're on the same page. So how can I help you?'

'I wanted to make a couple of suggestions as to how the changes could be, er, managed. Some of the staff will jump at the chance to retire. The university won't mourn their departure. Maybe some of the students will transfer to other universities."

'What about you? What are you going to do?'

'Obviously, retirement's not an option. As the axed courses run down over the next couple of years, the teaching staff will run down too. But I'm confident that if I'm kept on for the full period I could do a valuable job. Make sure standards are kept up, student morale stays high and, most crucially, that nobody behaves in an, er, obstructive way.'

'And then you'll be on your bike,' Prendergast gave a sardonic smile.

Gary grated his teeth at this wanton bluntness. 'It'll give me the time to take a careful decision about where I go next, but as the overall teaching load reduces I'd also be available to handle other issues. And I'm sure I could be of real help in facilitating . . .' Gary sought the phrase that would best chime with Prendergast-speak, 'the forward trajectory of the university.'

'And how, exactly, would you do that?'

'As I made clear at the meeting, I see change as inevitable. But what I could do is provide you with an inside view of what's happening "on the ground", so to speak. Many of my colleagues are fairly passive, but there are a fair number who might want to make trouble.'

'If they made trouble, they'd be pissing into the wind. These changes are going to happen whether they like it or not, so they'll either have to accept them or go. My senior colleagues and I wouldn't be the slightest bit worried by any trouble they tried to make.'

Gary screwed up his eyes and gazed at some distant point beyond Prendergast's shoulder. 'I don't doubt for a moment that sooner or later the changes'll happen, but the university could suffer a bit of a mauling along the way.' Prendergast raised his eyebrows questioningly. 'Strikes, demos, disruption to classes, nationwide publicity that could be bad for both the uni and the government – especially if it prompted similar action in other uni's. I'm sure you'd agree it'd be much better if all that was avoided.'

Prendergast gave Gary a still sceptical but appraising look. 'Let me think about it,' and sensing that Gary was looking for something in return, added, 'There could be one or two aspects of the university's new – ,' he paused while searching for a glossy pamphlet on his desk, which he then held up, 'Prospectus for Progress in which we might be able to give you a part to play.'

Gary took a deep breath and decided to push his luck. 'That'd be easier if my department could remain at Fallowfields. As our student numbers fall to make way for the new courses and students that are coming in, it shouldn't be a problem. There'd be enough room.'

Prendergast smiled rather menacingly. 'You're not the only person to make this suggestion, but I suspect it's less to do with a concern for the university and more to do with not wanting their lunch arrangements disturbed. I can tell you that two-thirds of the staff at Fallowfields will very shortly be moved to premises in Mixton town centre. Only Art and Design will stay behind. For the incoming courses we need to refurbish the premises sooner rather than later. Now if you'll excuse me I've got to go and rattle a few teeth somewhere else. But I've enjoyed our little chat. Keep in touch.'

Back in his office Gary ran a probing tongue round his incisors. Prendergast's bluntness was in some ways a refreshing change from the circumlocutions, the hopping from one hesitant qualification to another, that characterised the speech of so many academics. Boiled down, his message was 'Tough shit. The removal vans – and the tumbrils – are on their way. Those who don't get in the first are destined for the second.' There'd been a hint that Gary's offer to help the management might be accepted, but he clearly couldn't depend on it. He had to delay their steam-roller, and the usual procrastinations of working parties and academic board meetings were no longer an option. He mused for a moment, then picked up his phone and thumbed an increasingly familiar number.

22. A SPLIFFING IDEA

Holly and her best mate Taylor were sitting on Holly's bed and reviewing their first efforts to radicalise the students. They'd not been successful. Fired up with love for Gary and his cause, Holly made the convert's error of supposing her zeal would be universally shared. She organised a protest meeting, but it foundered when the few who'd agreed to attend realised it clashed with a key premiership derby that was being screened live in several of the Mixton pubs. Seizing on Gary's bright idea, she approached the mountaineering club but soon discovered they were not interested in abseiling anywhere unless they were paid for it. One of their number, who looked like a bank clerk in boots, even wanted a risk assessment undertaken and an appropriate indemnity secured against, as he put it, 'the prospect of misadventure'. Holly told him to stick his pitons where the sun don't shine.

She refused to be discouraged. She arranged another meeting, on a date that would clash with nothing important, and assiduously drummed up support using the Student Union website, texts, tweets, emails and word of mouth. Her message was simple: every course in the uni was under threat, and all the students should band together and fight tooth and nail against closures and cuts. As a first step they should all come to the meeting on February 21st.

'But the thing is, Tayl, we can't just let it turn into a moaning session. We'll need to come up with a plan of action.'

'Those of us in Media and English have got a lot to moan about,' rejoined Taylor. She drew lengthily on the joint and passed it over. 'Not only are they closing the degrees, they're not even going to let us finish them at Fallowfields.'

'Which is the only bit of the uni that isn't a shit-hole.'

'Is it really true they're going to squeeze us into a bunch of portakabins in the town centre?'

'Yeah. They want to tart up Fallowfields for their sexy new degrees. All this ecological stuff and these courses for mini-medics.'

'Mini medics? Midgets? There aren't any midgets in Mixton, Holly. They all fell down the bloody big cracks in the pavement.' The girls rolled around on the duvet in helpless laughter,

'Oh, Gawd, Tayl. You know I didn't mean that. Gary ticked me off for saying that. Said I was size-ist.'

'Gary? Who's Gary?' said Taylor, her eyes re-focusing a bit.

'Gary Glitter. You know. The intense one who sits at the front in the Media and Gender lectures.' Holly swallowed hard and praised her own quick thinking. She'd have to lay off the happy stuff.

'Oh, *that* Gary,' replied Taylor. 'I don't know about Glitter but he's always trying to chat you up. He's probably got a day-glo line that runs all the way down from his Adam's apple to you know where.'

The girls shrieked again, marvelling at how witty they'd become. 'Any road,' said Holly at last, 'he says they're going to do a major conversion on Fallowfields. Strip it out and put in equipment and stuff for herbalists and puncture people. They're the ones he calls mini-medics. Plus the Green People.'

'You mean Robin Hood and his merry men?' said Taylor. More rolling and shrieking. Mascara dribbled down their cheeks, making them look like coal miners after a difficult shift.

'You know who I mean. The save-the-planet bunch. They're always going on about the environment and carbon, and cycling everywhere and re-cycling everything, and I know it's right but it don't half get on your tits after a while.'

'Which for you, Holly baby, must be a big pain?'

Holly guffawed and jutted her chest so as to indicate the size of any discomfiture. Much more of this, thought Taylor, and I'll have an accident. 'Anyway, apparently the whole uni's going to be overrun by these eco-people, who'll be like sort of hermits who live on nothing but wild berries and fresh air and use less water than my kid brother. They're going to be ecology managers and walk around with clipboards shouting about carbon footprints.'

'But won't they be rescuing the world, Holls? Shouldn't we be joining them?' Taylor stretched her legs and inhaled deeply from the spliff.

'Well, s'ppose, but . . . we didn't muck up the planet, we've only mucked up Mixton, and nobody'd notice that, so don't we deserve to have a good time? But as I said, we can't spend the whole meeting moaning.'

Holly stepped off the bed, switched on the electric kettle and found the instant coffee amid a mess of DVDs, knickers, phone bills, curlers and biscuits that had fallen out of a packet. 'We need to be ready with a plan of action. What are we going to do to fight the cuts? Organise a march, a rally, a sit-in, whatever?'

'Thing is, Holly, how many are going to shift their arses for something like this? Getting out of bed's a big challenge for a lot of students.'

'Then it has to be a sit-in. Little effort but big impact. That's what we'll suggest to the meeting. Where would be best? Library, lecture theatres, concourse, sports hall, canteen?'

'Somewhere comfortable and warm, good phone reception, good wi-fi for the lap-tops, and a nearby vending machine.'

Holly was growing rapidly in her role as protest organiser. It was much to her credit that the meeting went well. Some fifty people turned up, most, though not all, students of the degrees that were officially marked for closure. While not wholly articulate, Holly addressed them feelingly. She told them she'd seen a letter written by somebody high up in the university which was clear evidence that other degrees were being considered for closure. She was not at liberty to say how she'd come to see the letter or who had written it, but she'd swear to its existence on her mother's life. Her listeners were impressed by her air of truthfulness and conviction. However, she insisted that they hadn't gathered just to complain but devise a plan of action. The proposal of a sit-in was accepted, and there was much discussion about the venue. Someone suggested the canteen, but it was soon agreed that barring other students from the canteen was not going to bring the uni to its knees. Lecture theatres were swiftly ruled out when it was realised that the uni would simply move the lectures to another venue. At length, the sports hall was fixed on as a place that was pleasant and spacious enough for a sit-in, but a venue that would disrupt the university because it was much used by staff and students.

It was agreed to hold a second meeting four days later, at which the details of the sit-in would be planned, but at that meeting Holly was obliged to announce a change of venue. The university's martial arts club (Motto: 'Strength in Peace') had got wind of their plan, and threatened to beat to a pulp anyone who interfered with their training schedule. So it was decided that the sit-in would take place in the library.

23. STORMING THE BASTILLE

The library was the university's newest building and covered five floors. Designed for the twenty-first century, it therefore presented as something other than a place solely for silent reading, contemplation and study. In its amenities and general hubbub it was more like an airport lounge. It contained a snack bar, relaxation zones with easy chairs and low tables, seminar rooms, and a couple of tutorial rooms fitted with projection equipment as well as a lot of shelving, on some of which were books. All this swayed the students in their eventual choice of the library as the site of their occupation. They would be assured of reasonable levels of comfort and the chance to catch up on their film viewing, to which end a large number of DVDs had been stockpiled. These matters aside, it had been recognised that the library was still the most visited part of the university, even if what drew the students was less the books than the other amenities. Anyone who tried to visit the library would encounter the sit-in and learn about its causes and aims and why they should support it. The hope was that they, in turn, would be radicalised and swell the protest. Furthermore, the library's commanding height, its numerous windows and proximity to a main thoroughfare, meant that slogans could be displayed from it which would be seen all over the town.

The occupation was carefully planned. Shortly before closing time on a Sunday evening in early March, two female students began an argument just inside the exit turnstiles. Voices were raised and foul words uttered, violence was threatened, and the two ESMOs who were still left in the building felt obliged to intervene.

'Now then, girls, this isn't very nice,' said one of them. 'Why don't you kiss and make up and get yourselves off home.'

The girls interrupted their dispute to round on the common enemy.

'Kiss and make up? Don't patronise us, you sexist git.'

'Why don't *you* go home, rat-face, 'cos you're sod-all use here.'

'Yeah, I bet wifey's got a nice mug of cocoa ready for you. If I were her, I'd tip it over you.'

Then they resumed their own quarrel, which they continued out of the main doors and on to the library forecourt. The cause was apparently an expensive dress that one had lent and the other damaged.

The lender pulled it out of a carrier bag. 'Look at it. Totally ruined. I want a hundred quid for a new one.'

'Wasn't my fault. Your bloke chucked his drink all over me.'

''Cos you were giving him the come-on – wearing my fucking dress!'

Once they'd left the library, they were no longer a concern of the ESMOs. But such a furious row between two female students was so rare and the threat of violence so real that they stayed in the foyer to watch. Sure enough, actions followed words. One girl pushed the other, the other grabbed her throat. Hair was pulled, punches were thrown. Pushed backwards, one of the girls took off a shoe and smacked her opponent over the head with it. Amid screams and curses they grappled and fell, struggled up and grappled again. Lurching this way and that, they bumped into a male student who was crossing the forecourt to the main door and doing his demure best to ignore them. Staggering slightly, he recovered his balance and walked into the foyer.

'Don't you think you should be stopping them rather than just watching,' he remarked primly to the ESMOs.

'Yeah, come on,' said one of them sheepishly. 'We'd better go out and break it up.'

This was easier said than done. Ducking the flailing arms they moved to separate the women, but they were as ready to fight the ESMOs as each other. The mêlée moved further out on to the forecourt, with the ESMOs fully embroiled but still trying to calm the combatants down. Meanwhile, and noticed by no one, a file of students carrying rucksacks and other, less identifiable, equipment crept round the side of the library, went in, shut the doors and fixed a stout length of chain through the door handles, securing it with a padlock.

All at once, the scuffle stopped. The girls calmly disengaged themselves, straightened their clothes, laughed and embraced and ran away, leaving the two ESMOs staring bemusedly after them. Then, hearing banging on the library doors, they spun round to see a group of students inside who were mouthing and making faces at them. Assuming it was all a mere prank, the ESMOs tried the doors and asked to be let in, but the only intelligible response was a large piece of cardboard which was taped to the glass and declared: OFFICIAL SIT-IN. STUDENT PROTEST AGAINST COURSE CUTS. For a full half hour, the ESMOs stood on the forecourt and debated what to do. Nothing like this had ever happened before, and it was a right pain that it had happened on their watch. In the end, they felt there was nothing for it but to phone their boss. Already in bed and enjoying a late-night movie with his wife, the chief ESMO didn't wish to be disturbed, and said so in vivid terms. He decided that there was no point in turning out of bed at that hour, but he'd get into the university first thing tomorrow and try to reason with the students. With any luck he could persuade them to end their sit-in before the senior management got to learn of it. 'And you better pray that I'm successful,' he told the ESMOs in a fierce parting shot, 'or Prendergast will have your guts to keep his socks up.'

24. DARLINGS OF THE MEDIA

At 7.00 am the chief ESMO arrived at the library, and meeting the two who'd allowed the occupation to happen, administered an impromptu reprimand: 'You cloth-headed gits. How come you were both outside the library, and with your backs turned, while thirty odd students traipsed in behind you and locked you out? You sodding blind or did they slip you a bung?'

Kev, the taller of the two ESMOs, was stung. 'We was already dealing with an incident, boss. Couple of women students were fighting on the forecourt and we went to break it up.'

'Yeah,' added the other ESMO, known to his mates as Bomber. 'They was havin' a right go at each other.' And then with an ill-judged attempt at humour, 'Wish I'd filmed 'em on me iPhone!'

'Oh, do you now,' the chief ESMO pushed his face unpleasantly close to Bomber's. 'Well, if this bloody nonsense isn't ended PDQ, I shall look forward to filming you hanging by your bollocks from the nearest flagpole.'

He marched over to the main door of the library and hammered furiously on the glass. He then started shouting, first asking the students to be sensible, to be good boys and girls and come out and go home. When this had no effect, he told them that they were bang out of order and there'd be dire consequences. Silence. The ESMOs stepped back and looked up at the library building. There was nothing to be seen or heard: it was a tower of indifference. The chief swore again. 'Right you two, guard this door. I'm going to my office, but the minute anyone shows their face in there, call me on the walkie-talkie and I'll be straight back.'

It was nine o'clock before anyone appeared on the other side of the glass. This was a student in casual clothes that perhaps doubled as pyjamas: an oversized T shirt with SOUPED UP HERO written across it, some jogging bottoms and beach sandals. Looking much the worse for wear – unwashed, unshaven and unapologetic – he struggled to open a small window beside the main doors, stuck part of his head through it awkwardly, and then read, with many falterings, from a prepared statement:

'The students of Mixton University are making this protest because we totally oppose the university's plan to close several of its degree courses, which it has, er, implementated without any consultation whatsoever. In particular we oppose the plan to remove the Department of Media, Literature and Culture from Fallowfields before its degrees have even been closed. And we oppose all future attempts by the university to close its courses without first consulting the student body. We demand that the cuts are suspended immediately; that the university issues an apology for threatening the students' studies; and that the university undertakes not to impose sanctions against any demonstrating students who are only exercising their democratic right to . . . er, demonstrate against these totally arbitrary measures which, er, were done without proper consultation. Signed, the sit-in executive committee, on behalf of all sitting-in students.'

With a solemnity equal to that of Luther nailing his theses to the church door at Wittenburg, the student then blu-tacked the statement to the glass of the library's main entrance.

'Sod this for a lark,' muttered the chief ESMO, thumbing his phone. 'Time to call in the rottweiler . . . Hello, Mr. Prendergast, it's the head of estates management here, I've . . . no, I'm sure you're busy and I wouldn't normally trouble you, but I thought you should know that we've got a sit-in in the library. No, not by staff, most of them haven't come in yet. It's the students. Yes, I did say students . . .' He held the phone away from his ear so that his colleagues could hear the response. 'Right, see you in a few moments.'

'Fucking right you will,' snarled Prendergast, who was on his way to work in the BMW and had taken the call on his hands-free. Accompanied by the squeal of his own tyres and the irate horns of other motorists, he arrived at the university in moments. His first impulse was to smash the library doors open with a sledge-hammer, but the chief ESMO advised against it.

'We thought of doing that, and I got Kev to go and fetch one, but the students had worked it out.'

'What do you mean, worked it out? I'll work them out. Give me the bloody thing.'

Prendergast seized the sledge-hammer and advanced on the library doors. As he made to swing it, a line of students, all female, materialised on the other side, pressing themselves up against the glass.

'That's what I was trying to tell you,' said the chief ESMO, 'as soon as we – ' He broke off as one of the students held up a placard, something that had not happened before. It read: STUDENT IN PEACEFULL DEMO BLUGGEONED TO DEATH.

Prendergast paused, and as he did so a second, third and fourth placard appeared: FIRST FATALITY ON CAMPUS FOR FORTY YEARS and FAMILY GREIVE LOSS OF BRILLIANT DAUGHTER and POLICE LAUNCH MURDER ENQUIRY. A student in the middle of the line was not holding a placard. She was strikingly pretty, her bosom barely contained by a scoop-topped T-shirt. As Prendergast looked at her, she smiled sweetly, fluttered her eyelashes, puckered her lips and blew him a kiss.

'Shit!' He turned on his heel and strode to his office. The Vice and the Toff were nowhere to be seen. Too early for them, of course. But that was OK, Prendergast would deal with this nonsense single-handed, and take the credit for doing so. He arranged for a notice to be placed immediately outside the library informing the students that they were in breach of their obligations, and their failure to leave the premises forthwith would have very serious consequences. Flipping his gold propelling pencil between his fingers, he pondered what the hell to do next. His impulse was to issue writs against the students for trespass, then break into the library with a bunch of heavies, and using CS gas and rubber bullets, drag the occupants out by their hair. But this was a university, an institution full of wet, spineless liberals whimpering about human rights, freedom of speech, due legal process and health and safety issues. Some time later he was still pondering, when the phone jangled on his desk.

'Ed? Bill Castles here, from *The Mixton Chronicle*. What's going on up there at the uni?'

Bloody hell! Had Castles heard of it already? How much did he know? 'Nothing really, Bill,' he replied airily. 'Just a silly quarrel about moving the students to new premises. It'll be ended by lunchtime.'

'You'll be lucky. It's all over the media like a rash. And given that we're a local paper and you and I have a close, you know, relationship, I thought you might be able to give me the first bite of the cherry – how the dispute came about, the management's perspective, exclusive access to the student protestors, that kind of thing . . . '

This was getting out of control, and Prendergast reached for the verbal fire-extinguisher. 'Bill, if there was a real story here, you'd be the first to hear of it. The university will be issuing a statement very shortly, but believe me it's all just a storm in a tea-cup.'

Castles failed to get the favour he was looking for, and hung up with a frown. As a local paper in a dull provincial town, the Chronic needed the university as a continuing source of stories. But the university also needed the good will of the Chronic, and for this rebuff Castles was determined to exact a price. He also had to admit that it was a bit personal. His daughter, Astrid, was a student at the university and having issues with that mad art lecturer, Tom Burley. In Castles' private opinion, Astrid had no more artistic talent than the family cat, but given his own standing in the local community he felt that Burley, a university employee, should be encouraging what there was rather than condemning it out of hand. Her education was, after all, costing Castles nine grand a year.

As soon as he finished with Castles Prendergast called in his secretary and dictated an official statement on behalf of the university. It would be issued by its external relations office, to which all further inquiries from the media should be referred, and the office would be instructed to make no additional comment of any kind. It read as follows: *The present occupation of its library by the students of Mixton University is unhelpful, unnecessary and illegal. It will do nothing to halt the dynamic changes in course provision that the university is planning, and the university's directorate requires that the occupation be brought to an end at once. The university also emphasises that its priority is at all times to ensure the safety, security and well-being of its students.* By now, Turpin and Unthank had arrived at the university, the former agitated, the latter benignly puzzled, and Prendergast was summoned to a crisis meeting in Turpin's office.

Castles was right. Once their lie-in had ended, the students woke up rapidly to the opportunities for publicity that the modern media provide. At first, they did no more than shoot zany movies of one another and post them on YouTube. One clip also contained some shaky frames of the Director of Academic Development advancing towards the chained doors with a sledge-hammer, and of laughing young women making faces at him while pressing their breasts against the glass. From sheer force of habit almost all the demonstrators tweeted, blogged and texted ceaselessly. Very quickly realising that ponderous laments about the closure of their courses would generate as much interest as a documentary about sleeping dormice, they began to think of other ways of attracting the attention of the mainstream media. Fortunately it was what is known as a slow news day, and the newspapers, radio and television networks were drawn to some iPhone footage of a passionate female student declaring that if the university authorities tried to eject them, she would throw herself off the library roof. They were even more drawn to a clip of Holly in her low-necked T-shirt, leaning boldly out of a ground floor window and saying how unfairly she and the other students were being treated. Within minutes phones were ringing inside the library building: newspaper hacks were seeking interviews and photos, radio journalists wanted sound grabs, and the TV people demanded shots and comments from the student leaders, especially the one in the attractive T-shirt, so that they could run the story on the main national bulletins.

Thirty minutes later Holly was again leaning out of a ground floor window and explaining her views to a veritable gunnery of lenses and microphones, and it swiftly became clear that these things loved her as much as she loved them. Her arresting, dishevelled beauty, warm and ready smile and slightly hoarse northern accent, expressing views which, if artless, were direct, heartfelt and in the guise of ready-made soundbites, impressed the most hard-bitten journalists and most blasé of audiences. She was irresistible. And as the day wore on, there were other things to feed the cameras. Posters were stuck on the windows, banners hung from the roof:

STUFF THE CUTS! SAVE OUR COURSE'S!
STOP THE NO-DEGREE TREATMENT!
DELIVER WHAT WEVE PAYED FOR!

YOUVE TAKEN OUR DOSH BUT WE'RE UNDER THE COSH!

On every floor, students held up crudely lettered signs saying 'Support Tomorrows Workers', 'Death Before Defeat' and 'Top Marks to Marx: Revolution Now!' A few others said 'Coventry for the Cup', 'Man U 'till I Die' and 'I Love You, Mum', but all was grist to the media mill. The university's security staff tried to push back the scrimmage of reporters and cameramen but were pushed back in turn, eventually recognising that to quell the invasion would generate publicity that was even more adverse. From their offices in a neighbouring building, Turpin and Prendergast looked out and fumed impotently. By the end of the day, two huge television trucks had parked boldly in the service road behind the library building.

The sit-in, with Holly as its star, began to trend on YouTube. While the Sky and BBC lunch-time bulletins ran only brief clips, these had grown slightly longer by late afternoon and were being looped on all the major news channels. But not all of the demonstrators were happy with Holly's status. Some of the other female students criticised her, but Holly retorted that she couldn't help it if the media were focusing on her, and anyway she'd stay out of sight for the evening and let the others have a turn. This wasn't altogether altruistic. First, she suddenly remembered that she had to do a job for Gary, which he had impressed on her was crucial to the success of the sit-in: in the excitement, she'd almost forgotten it. She also reflected that she'd been in the same clothes for all of the day's interviews, and Taylor pointed out that if the media interest continued, she just had to get a new outfit.

'You never see Rihanna and Beyoncé and all them in the same stuff more than once. You've got to keep them interested. You'll have *OK* and *Hello* after you before long.'

'Oh, yeah,' said Holly. 'Do you mean the *OK Higher Education Supplement*? Ha-ha!'

But the exciting thought of further media attention would not go away, and when her phone went off yet again, her heart jumped. Recognising the number as Gary's she decided not to answer. She needed to be able to tell him she'd followed his instructions – which was exactly what he was phoning to find out. She got hold of Shaun and took him up to a quiet area on the third floor, where she had

116

access to a computer and printer. Gary had given her a pen-drive which he'd warned her to guard with her life, so she'd hung it from her neck as a pendant.

'What's it got in it?' she'd asked.

'A document, a list of email addresses and a press release,' replied Gary.

'What's the document?'

'Dynamite. Found it on the floor of my office. Someone must have slipped it under the door.'

'Who?'

'No idea. But I reckon they knew what they were doing' – and he told her what was in it. 'At the end of the first day of the sit-in, I want you to send it as an attachment to all the email addresses on that list. They belong to every students' union rep and every lecturers' union rep of every uni in the country. Then print off multiple copies of the press release. It's a summary of what's in the document, and tells who authored it and who it was addressed to. I've claimed the press release has been drafted by your sit-in committee. Then early on the second day of the sit-in, you need to get a megaphone and read out the press release from the balcony of the library. Finally you should distribute it to any media people who're there. Got me?'

'Got you, Gary.'

'You could get Shaun to help you with the emailing and printing, but you're not to breathe a word to him, or to anyone else, about where you got the document from. Are you clear?"

'Clear, Gary.'

No sooner had Shaun done the emailing and printing than her phone rang.

'How's it going?' asked Gary, after he'd checked that she'd done as he'd told her.

'T'rrific. There's over a hundred of us now. Everyone's brought in sleeping bags and rucksacks and food. We've put messages up at the windows. Everyone's taking photos with their iPhones, loading them on to the computers and sending them all over the place. I've had journos talking to me and taking pictures of me. You'll see me in tomorrow's papers.'

'Fantastic. I knew you could do it.'

117

'There are a few problems, Gary. Everyone's had a whopping time today, but some of them are already worrying about missing their hair appointments or the away match at the weekend.'

Jeez, thought Gary, they never had these problems storming the Winter Palace.

25. 'WHAT'S THIS MALARKEY ABOUT?'

That evening Brian paid one of his frequent visits to the Pearl of the Orient. After a hard day's work there was no restorative quite like a Chinese takeaway, and with a certain gusto he swung the springy white plastic bag off the counter and headed for the door. However, he could never resist giving himself a little *amuse-bouche* before he'd even left the shop, and he foraged in the bag for a fistful of prawn crackers. Cramming them into his mouth, he stepped into the street and almost bumped into Bill Castles, who was on his way in.

'Hello Brian, keeping the wolf from the door?'

They'd known each other since Brian's days as a window-cleaner. The firm he'd worked for was under contract to clean the windows of Tribune House, the home of *The Mixton Chronicle*, and they'd formed a cheery acquaintanceship which was cemented by an informal business arrangement. Brian agreed that outside the firm's time, he'd go round and clean the windows of Castles' private residence. Castles would pay less than the firm would normally charge, but all the money would go into Brian's back pocket. However, Brian felt that he worked for what he earned, for Castles' home was a veritable glasshouse. It was not quite what you'd expect of a provincial editor's home, but was a spacious, ranch-style dwelling with picture windows and sliding doors, an amply glazed conservatory, a large patio and, of all things, an open-air swimming pool which was in use for only a few weeks each year. There was a rumour that Castles had married into new money, and it was certain that while he maintained the shabby demeanour one might expect of a newsman, his wife had the smart, spruce air of one who enjoyed constant and costly refurbishment.

Although they were on good terms, Brian had to admit to himself that he didn't much care for Castles. He felt there was something unsavoury about the man. Perhaps he'd been contaminated by all that moral dirty linen that journos were obliged to sniff out. Castles was also endlessly sneery about the uni and its academics. Brian had heard that Castles' daughter was a student in the art department and not doing very well, and he wondered whether her father's sourness had something to do with that.

'So what's this demo malarkey all about, Brian?'

'Search me, Mr Castles.'

'I was hoping your bosses would give me an exclusive on it.' Castles was still vexed by his phone rebuff from Prendergast, and allowed himself to make a claim that, in a world of mobile media and tweets, he knew to be untrue. 'That way we could've spun the story to favour the university. As things are, it's all over everywhere. On the web and suchlike. When the dailies appear tomorrow, the uni's going to look pretty bloody silly.'

'You're right there, Mr Castles.'

Castles looked at him shrewdly. 'But you always keep your ear to the ground, Brian. Any new twist to the story, any little exclusive you can get me for the Chronic, and I'll make it worth your while. Here's my office number.'

'I'll see what I can do, Mr Castles.'

Brian dug into the bag for a last fistful of prawn crackers before he reached the Cavalier. It occurred to him that a window-cleaner-turned-janitor was hardly the career path of the successful entrepreneur, but if you kept your eyes and ears open and your mouth, for the most part, shut, there was some useful money to be made.

26. DEMOS FOR DUMMIES

Unthank reflected that he found his colleagues in a state of high dudgeon. Nobody was ever in a low or even moderate dudgeon. Why was dudgeon always high? He recalled that the word also meant the handle of a dagger. Didn't it feature in *Macbeth*: '... on thy blade and dudgeon gouts of blood'? Whose blood was going to be on whose dudgeon today?

'Robert, I sense that I don't have your full attention.' An unusually tetchy Turpin had been bewailing the negative publicity the university was getting, and how this was occurring at exactly the wrong time. It was the second day of the sit-in, and he'd called another meeting with his two senior colleagues to consider ways of bringing it to an end. 'I'm going to have the Department for Education on the phone asking what's going on. So I need everyone to pay attention and come up with some ideas about how we mitigate the bad publicity and, above all, get the bloody students out of the library.'

Wearing a primly ominous expression, Marian walked in bearing copies of the day's national newspapers and laid them carefully on the table in the centre of the office. The three men gathered round to view their front pages, on most of which the sit-in was the second main story. Each bore a photo of Holly Ainscough ranging from the demurely pretty to the boldly sexy. 'Revolting students storm their library,' harrumphed the *Daily Telegraph*, with a well-aimed pun; 'Feminist fresher fights the student cause,' preached the *Guardian*; 'Mixton not Ivy League – but There's Plenty of Holly' smirked the *Daily Mail*; and 'Holly Gets Prickly' panted the *Daily Mirror*, above a picture in which Holly's invitingly half-closed eyes and full, parted lips vied with her cleavage for the reader's attention.

The *Sun*, however, drew the simultaneous if reluctant attention of all three. Yesterday afternoon its reporter had passed up to Holly a pair of black leather high-heeled boots and asked her to don them for a photo-shoot. The result was a picture which occupied the entire page. Holly was reclining on her elbow along a window-ledge. One leg was stretched out, the other bent at the knee. Between the top of the boots and the hem of her skirt was a short but alluring expanse of thigh, and above everything the headline screamed, HOLLY KICKS AGAINST THE PRICKS.

'Coarse – and defamatory,' huffed Turpin.

'Quite funny, though,' mused Unthank.

'Glad you can see the joke,' growled Prendergast.

Each favoured a different way of ending the sit-in. Unthank proposed a meeting between themselves and the students which would be chaired by an independent third party. Turpin floated the idea of warning all the sitters-in that they were in breach of the conditions under which they'd registered as students, that they were imperilling themselves and others, and that the university was empowered to take disciplinary action which could include rustication. Prendergast pointed out that he'd already given this warning when he put up a notice outside the library, and that it had been ignored.

'I propose we give them an ultimatum: twenty four hours to clear out of the building. Then if they don't go, we remove them forcibly and bring charges against them of unauthorised entry, trespass and wanton damage.'

'Yes, yes, Ed,' rejoined Turpin, looking peevishly round the table. 'Wouldn't we all love to do just that! But having already been cast as villains by the media, we'd then be represented as little better than war criminals. No, I'm afraid we must find a subtler way of dealing with this. We have to find some form of conciliation.'

'I've been over there,' returned Prendergast. 'They're not interested in conciliation, they're interested in whipping up as much trouble and publicity as they can. All this' – he waved his hand at the newspapers – 'could just be the starters. We've got to get it sorted, and fast. I suggest we bring the police in and get them to scare the sh-, the pants off them. Their behaviour's irresponsible, unacceptable and downright unlawful, so there should be severe consequences.'

Turpin groaned. 'Look, Ed, I'm as exasperated by this as you are, but we've got to try and end it peacefully. We're not going to do ourselves any good if the media get pictures of students being dragged away by policemen wielding truncheons. We have to try Robert's conciliation route first.'

'I'm happy to act as an emissary,' said Unthank. "Ask them to let me in, sit down with them, and without any preconditions listen to what they have to say. I can then report to you both and I'm sure we could come up with something that would end the matter.'

'Total fantasy,' said Prendergast. 'You'll be talking not just till the cows come home, but till they've been fed, milked and turned into burgers. We've got to get in there and turf the sods out.'

'We can't take that risk,' insisted Turpin. 'In case either of you didn't know, the chief ESMO has told me that if we try to break in, a female student has threatened to throw herself off the roof. What is it now, Marian?' he added testily as she walked into the room.

'I thought you ought to know what's been going on. I can see it all out of my window. They've lowered a window-cleaning cradle halfway down the side of the building, and there are students on it. Just now it was three girls sort of dressed as ballet dancers, swaying to and fro.'

'Do we need to know this, Marian?'

'Just keeping you in touch, Dr Turpin. Oh, and the television people are back again with their cameras and those things like furry animals on the ends of poles.' She thought it prudent to exit before getting a further response.

Listening to the rumble of voices, Marian stayed glued to her window to see what was going to happen next. In all her years as Turpin's secretary never had she had such fun as this! And she had a grandstand view of the show. The cradle was being lowered again, but this time it contained three huge, crude dummies, in effect puppets, whose limbs were being operated with ropes by three students on the roof. As she gazed out of the window, she recalled pranks from her school days that had done little harm and created much merriment. This one seemed similar. And why shouldn't young people stick up for themselves?

Her thoughts were interrupted by a call from Turpin on the intercom, and she had to search hurriedly for some contact details he was demanding. 'Dr Turpin, I thought you ought to know that there are now giant dummies on the cradle,' she announced as she brought the list into his office.

'I don't give a damn if there are giant meringues on the cradle!' snapped Turpin.

She exchanged faint, complicit smiles with Unthank before hurrying back to her office. Now there was something new to watch, and the crowds of spectators seemed to be growing by the minute. The television crews were also back in place, and located in pods on the end of mobile cranes two cameras were being raised and lowered in front of the library building in order to get a close-up of the antics on the cradle. The dummies had been dressed in clownish suits, and, though unrecognizable as anyone, had been helpfully labelled NO-THANKS, TURPS and GHASTLY. The right hand of each dummy clasped a huge blood-stained butcher's cleaver, which the puppeteers on the roof moved stiffly up and down, and from the open windows of the library came chants of 'Turps OUT! No-Thanks OUT! Ghastly OUT-OUT-OUT!' The chant was immediately taken up by the spectators.

The cradle was then winched higher up the side of the building, and on a balcony below it, the young ringleader – Holly Somebody? – appeared with a megaphone in one hand and a piece of paper in the other, from which she began to read. From this distance it was impossible to make out what she was saying, but Marian felt she once more needed to brave the wrath of Turpin and alert the trio to the ridicule they were suffering.

'Dr Turpin, I'm really sorry to interrupt you again but all of you ought to come and see this.'

They looked at one another, filed into Marian's office and gathered at the window. As if on cue, the puppets on the cradle, now wearing Hitler moustaches, began to cavort ponderously to recorded oompah music, and thin squirts of water issued from their trousers on to the heads of the crowds below, who expressed their enjoyment in shrieks, laughter and applause. The symbolism had all the subtlety of a bulldozer.

'This is appalling,' murmured Turpin, his face waxen.

Prendergast's lips were shaping themselves into the usual fricative, when his phone began to jangle and thump. He took one look at the screen and immediately excused himself from the room.

'Will you tell me what in the name of Christ is going on up there?'

'It's a mess, Brenda, but it's a local mess, and I'm in the process of sorting it. Not helped, I should add, by the spinelessness of my colleagues. If it wasn't for them, it would be all over by now.'

'It certainly is all over – all over the media and all over the internet.'

'Look, Brenda, I know it's annoying, but it's a ten-minute wonder. As soon as I end the sit-in, the media'll bugger off and look for a new story.'

'No, Ed, they're going to stay with this one. Damage has been done. Serious damage. Somebody – somebody at Mixton – has leaked the government's plans for two-year degrees.' There was a pause. 'I'm watching Sky News on my computer, and there's our little Holly, on her megaphone, sharing our plans with the whole wide world. Even with her ghastly northern accent and problems with the big words, the meaning's unmistakable. And we're now getting reports that students, along with some staff, are organising similar sit-ins and demos at universities up and down the country. The minister's fit to be tied and our publicists are spinning so fast they look like dervishes. This is a total car-crash, Ed. Absolutely not what you were paid to achieve. I want that bloody demo ended. Now!' And the line went dead.

Prendergast swore softly and stared at his phone. He wouldn't waste time going back into that meeting with the Vice and the Toff. It was time for desperate remedies. He thumbed a number he'd never called before. Gary Dorn answered at once. 'When you came to see me a few days ago, you said you could be of use. Here's your chance. I want this sit-in nonsense ended within twenty four hours. Do that and you'll get a just reward. And the faster you do it, the juster – and bigger – the reward will be. Think you can sort it?'

'Leave it to me.'

'But listen very carefully. No violence, no messy business before the TV cameras, or on YouTube, or on anyone's phone. And if anything goes wrong, you're on your own.'

'And if it goes right?'

'You've got three more years at Mixton. Maybe more than that.'

Well, smiled Gary to himself, what the Lord taketh away, he can be forced to give back.

27. AFFECTING ME, AFFECTING YOU

Module Title: Human Interaction – Affecting Me, Affecting You
Level: One
Credits: 20
Student Name: Holly Rachel Ainscough

Student Number: 2329066
Student ID: HA445

For this section of the module the student must keep a personal record of a series of interactions with either a single person or a group of individuals with whom s/he shares a common purpose. These interactions should take place over a period of time of not less than one month. They should be of a significant nature and represent a composite psychological or emotional experience. The student's record comprises one element of the coursework and is worth 10 credits or 50 per cent of the module.

Holly started to look through what she'd written.

At Home for Reading Week

Monday 18th. Blazing row with mum about time I got back last night. Said I was old enough to keep whatever hours i liked. She said I was 'putting myself at risk'? Duh? Like, hello? I said exactly what that was suppose to mean. She went on for fifteen minutes about what she did do or mostly didnt do when she was my age. I told her I wasnt up the spout, wasnt going to get up the spout and stormed out.

Wednesday 20th. Mum brought me tea and bickies in bed. She'd got the stain out of my Hugo Boss top that I'd picked up from the charity shop. We had a chat, a hug and a cry.

Friday 22nd. Standup row this time with Dad just as I was going out. Usual stuff. Not working, not studying, not getting up, not going to bed, not this, not that, not, not not, not. I told him to 'get notted', and laughed all the way to Shannons place. Then we went out clubbing.

Saturday 23rd. Had to use Shannons mob to phone home. Lost mine along with purse, cigarette lighter, mascara and lippy. Dad went totally mental – but came out to get me – wherever that was.

I said I was really, really sorry. He put his arms round me and hugged me. It made me feel a whole lot worse. I cant wait to get back to Mixton.

She crossed all this out and started afresh.

Day Zero.

Our student action group met in the back of the coffee bar for an initial planning session. Everybody all agreed that our courses were at risk and something had to be done. Student J said that if we let them push us around now then they would Push us around for the whole of our three years. Student K said that for Cheryl whose repeated the first year twice already then it could be for much, much longer. Ho! Ho!

Shaun said he had some stunts up his sleeve to get some publicity which he said is to do with the dummies he brought in. Student K said are you talking about Cheryl again and we all cracked up and called it a day.

Day 1

Up a bit later than intended but slept OK but there are a couple of Snorers. I thought my Dad was bad ....

Theres about fifty of us. Everyones brought in sleeping bags and rucksacks and were stocked up on food. Theres a Microwave in the librarians common room. Weve put messages up at the windows. Everyones taking photos on their Phones, and sending them off to friends. Then we sent some to The Mixton Chronical. I should see me in tomorrows edition!

Day 1 – a bit later

Everyone was totally with my Sit-In Council idea and agreed that meetings should start no later than 9.00am and that anyone who wasnt awake by then would be counted abscent.

We have list of demands, and are getting hold of radio, tv and the papers. Student J said we must be having a laugh. Nobody was interested in Mixton. So I said we'll bloody see about that then.

Yes, yes, I was right. It's all kicking off! Have just done interview out of ground floor window. Loads of cameras and microphones. Could be on news later today!!! Must get different top and some more of Taylors blusher. Got to do the students cause justice. Whoopee.

Unbeleivable. We're all over the lunch time news. I'm all over the lunchtime news.

Taylor and I did great big hug and hooray session. Was leaning quite a long way out but as T says if youve got it flaunt it. Then that man from the sun got me out on the ledge and made me put on some boots for a photo shoot and kept telling me to pull my skirt up a bit. might as well not of been wearing one.

Day 1 – a bit more later

Shauns a sweetie – and told me about the window cleaning cradle. Not sure its for me but he said he'd hold my hand. Ive taken up tweeting. Got thousands of followers already. Its amazing. And theyre all over me on Facebook. Heres one message: Holly, babes, you are my hearts desire. Marry Me tomorrow. Rasta Putin. Ive had about fifty offers of marriage. Wicked.

Holly's phone rang and she put down her notepad and pen.

'How's it going?' Gary's voice was guarded. 'It looks pretty good from the outside. Have you got plenty of provisions?'

'Everyone brought summat in with them and there are two catering students who can work the coffee machine in the cafe.'

'You managed to get into the cafe?'

Holly giggled. "Well, a pane of glass fell out the door and we found you could open it from the inside."

'That was lucky.'

'Yeah. But some of them are worried about nicking the coffee. Will we get into trouble?'

''Course not. All you do is leave a big IOU on the counter and sign it with a few names – you know, M. Mouse Esq, D. Duck PhD, Mrs Turpin – that sort of thing. It's probably all past its "sell-by" date anyway. You're doing them a favour.'

'Great. What about the chocolate bars and fruit bars and stuff that we found when one of the storage cupboard doors, like, fell off?'

'Same thing – different names. Any other problems?'

'Not really. Someone was a genius and brought in a load of indoor sports kit. We're playing table tennis in the tutorial rooms and badminton along the passage. We've got teams and a league going. Shaun and me won the mixed doubles last night.'

Gary had an uneasy sense that the main objective of the sit-in was slipping away. 'Fantastic. But what are you doing about the demands? You've got to keep them at the forefront of the campaign.'

'We are, Gary. Promise you, babes. And we've added to them. We're demanding reduced library fines and reduced penalties on essays we hand in late.'

Gary composed himself. 'Great. But you've got to remember that the media can only really cope with one issue at a time. Journos aren't that bright. Make sure you lead on the "no-course-closures" issue, right? And pile on the agony. Students distraught. Parents heartbroken. Feel deeply let down. Mixton has betrayed its students.'

'I promise we will. We won't forget. I want you to stay.'

'And I want you to stay, too.'

'And this is really great for the diary I've got to write for the Human Interaction module. I'm getting lots of stuff down.'

'Cool, but make sure my name doesn't occur anywhere in it. Remember, this is a purely student demo, OK?'

'OK, Gary, promise. Oh, and just one more thing. There's masses of powdered milk for the coffee, but I prefer the full cream stuff. You couldn't smuggle some in through the window, could you? And some Tampax? I've run right out.'

Day 2

Its still totally mental here. Media everywere. TV crews perched on the end of cranes. Ive done more interviews today. Went on the window cleaning cradle with Shaun. Ooo-er !!

But was all OK. Did Silly Dance Routine with Taylor and Cheryl dressed in funny too-too's. At first most of them were dead scared but now they all want to have a go. Cheryl may be thick but she's a great mover – she's orditioning for the next show.

Day 2 – bit later

Shauns dummies are just bloody brilliant! He got them on to the cradle and he, Lee and Craig put name lables on them and worked them with the ropes like puppets so there choppers went up and down. Then he made them wee on the crowds below. I was laughing so much I thought I was going to do the same. But then I had to go on the balcony below and read the press release through the meggaphone. It werent easy but I did my best. They're going to make all degrees two years. Bloody hell! You'd be in and out before you knew it as the actress said to the bishop [last phrase scored through]. And what about Cheryl!!!! Anyway the media all seemed very excited and kept asking me to lean over the balcony saying they couldnt hear me. HA! HA! I had a meggaphone. I knew why – but gave them what they wanted. Taylor says I could be Page 3 Girl before long.

Day 2 – evening

The days are fantastic – lots of action – everyone loves me – I was in the Sun today – amazing - wearing Taylor's low-cut number.

Actually, not <u>everyone</u> is like delighted. I'm getting some real bitchy comments. Its all jealousy – not my fault. The media keeps asking for Holly – what can I do? But the evenings get a bit boring. We watch a lot of telly on our computers including ourselfs on the news and two of the blokes have rigged up a table tennis table. We also played football in the passageway 'til Mat bently booted the ball into one of the swingdoors and cracked the glass. Hes such a dick. Its been great, fantastic to get in to library and turn it in to a demo Centre and get all the publicity. But didn't bring enough clothes with me and none of us girls are that keen on doing our bras and knickers in the sinks in the loos. And I have to keep borrowing stuff. Can't keep appearing in the same outfit. Lots of offers to start off with – some you wouldnt be seen dead in and then they go like – Oh, not good enough for you Holly, now your a TV celebrity– but now all drying up.

Day 2 Bed Time – well, Sleeping Bag Time – forgot pillow, real bugger.

Went to discussion group that some Final Years set up to talk about Big Issues. We quickly knocked off student fees, plaguerism, the canteen prices and the unfairness of only being able to get low grades on resits because weve all bashed them around since day one. Then one of the Green People started up and I thought I was going to die of boredom. But I didnt it was really good. She didnt do all that whole planet, doomsday by the time were thirty stuff, but said what shed been doing with her mum and dad and brother at home to make the footprint smaller. The Greenie's are usually incredibly ernest and intence. They start of by getting you to feel like a criminal and then tell you it doesnt matter anyway, the whole place is going to go up in smoke, or carbon dioxide or methayne or something. But this one was like personal, and jokey and small scale. I thought she said her name was Sue but its Sioux she spels it like a red Indian. Told how her family dissed her at the start then started asking questions and gradually got keener on doing something. Think theres a grandchild somewhere which probley helped. The Boo People came in with how pathetic it all was, she couldnt save diddly squat and it was all there fault. But she didnt start knocking them she just talked about people together making changes, unions, suffergettes, the berlin Wall. I got a bit lost but were all going to meet again tomorrow evening and do 'personal carbon footprints'. We asked her what hers was and she said she wanted to be Darcy Bustle on tiptoe but at the moment she were just a fat lady in flatties. We all laughed.

NB. Whose Darcy Bustle?

28. LET'S CALL THE WHOLE THING OFF

When Gary came off the phone, he allowed himself to punch the air in celebration, for the memory of his interview with Prendergast was still raw. 'That'll teach you, you condescending shit!' he said aloud. What a coup! The sit-in was driving the suits mad and they needed him, Gary Dorn, to end it because nobody else could. Of course, now that his own position was secured, he was prepared to act for the good of the university. But let those bastards sweat for a while. He had lectures and meetings all afternoon, but since his partner Rebecca would be out at a seminar he'd have the flat to himself in the evening. So he'd finish work, go home, stick a pizza in the oven, pour himself a nice gin and tonic, and then phone Holly and tell her to call it off.

'Holly, babes, it's me.'

'Gary, Gary!'

'Shh, keep your voice down! How many times have I told you not to mention my name?'

'It's all right, there's no one around. Did you see the papers? I'm in nearly all of them. And I need to tell you about Twitter – gone totally manic. As for Facebook, Gary, they are *queuing up*. What's a girl to do?' She cackled and coughed into his ear. He'd have to calm her down.

'You've done brilliantly. Couldn't have done better. You've got the uni totally rattled. It's clear they're going to consider all your demands. Terrific stuff. So I think the time's come to bring it to a close.'

'Bring what to a close?'

'The sit-in – the demo. You've achieved your objectives. They're going to listen to what you have to say. You've all been a total knock-out. You need to finish on a really high note.'

'Gary, Gary. We're only just getting under way. I'm going to be sent contracts. Everyone's after me. I've been asked to go on the Graham Norton Show. I can't give it all up now.'

'But that's just the point,' Gary started to improvise, 'now's when you need to pull out, when things are at their highest. Quit while you're winning. It could all start to go pear-shaped. You know what journos are like. Love you one minute, start slagging you off the next.'

'I promise you, Gary, babes, it's not like that. It's like they're all wooing me. That's what one of them said: he's wooing me 'cos I'm wowing him. And we're practising some sharper dance routines for the demo tomorrow.'

'Look, Holly, I know this has got very exciting and all that but I reckon this is the tipping point. The others there are going to get bored, hungry, fed up. They'll want to be back home before the weekend. Now's the time to stop, and . . .' he groped for some further rationale, 'all that jumping around on the window cleaning cradle. One wrong step and you'll be a puddle of blood on the concrete. You don't want that, do you?'

'Bloody hell, Gary, you're starting to sound like that Health and Safety geek who gave us a talk at the start of the year. The one who told us to avoid slippery floors.'

'But this is riskier than slippery floors. I'm worried about you. The next time I see you might be in A and E.'

'You're so sweet, Gary, but don't worry, we're fine. We're going to call ourselves Dancers on Air or The Sit-In Sisters. What do you think?'

'What I think, Holly,' irritation seeped through him, 'is that you're missing your lectures, you're behind in your course work and you've got some serious deadlines to meet.'

'You didn't have these worries when you got me to start all this. Or when you had me reading out that two-year degree stuff.'

'Of course not. But you have to stay focused on what's best for the protest. It shouldn't just become an ego trip.'

131

'Ooh, Gary, I do believe you're jealous! Don't worry, love, you're still my top babes. I know I flash a bit for the cameras, but nobody gets to see as much as you do. And now we're here, we're going to see the job through. Look, I've got to go, love. We're all having a great debate about carbon footprints.' She made what he supposed were kissing noises and rang off.

Gary drained his gin and tonic and phoned back straightaway, but got the answer message, and then the same ten, fifteen and twenty minutes later. In a sudden fury, he kicked a chair over. Stupid little cow! This complete bubble-head, whom he'd done his best to help, and whom he'd given grades well above what she deserved, now imagined she was some kind of celeb who . . . He could smell smoke. He raced into the kitchen. The pizza was burnt to a frazzle.

Fucking fuck, fuck!

As he scraped the remains into the waste bin, he reflected that this whole business could backfire on him. He could persist in trying to get Holly to see sense, but time wasn't on his side. What the hell was he going to do? Prendergast had given him twenty four hours, effectively until the end of tomorrow morning. If he didn't deliver, that'd be the end of him – not only at Mixton but at any other university. In order to clear his head he decided to walk back to Fallowfields, but this produced nothing more than muddy shoes. As he walked into the main entrance he encountered a series of yellow cones warning of Work in Progress. This seemed to consist of nothing more than the replacement of a light bulb inside the lobby and was being sweatily and breathlessly undertaken by Brian on a stepladder.

'Evening, Dr Dorn – Gary. What brings you back at such a late hour?'

Brian, the dim-witted but obliging porter . . . They weren't exactly intimates but had always got on well enough. When Brian had caught him in the act of dragging the old sofa from the SCR to his office, Gary had expected to be told to take it back. But Brian had helped him carry it the rest of the way, observing tactfully that 'with all that reading you busy lecturers have to get through it's only fair you should be able to put your feet up from time to time'.

'It's this bloody student sit-in, Brian. It's becoming a real headache for all of us.'

'I know, I know,' said Brian. 'What a carry-on. Have you seen those young ladies dancing about? Could be auditioning for a night club.'

'Or heading for a long stay in hospital, if they fall off.' An idea struck Gary – or perhaps he'd merely thought of a straw he could clutch at. Brian would know the university premises better than anyone. But before Gary made his request, he felt the need to parade his liberal credentials, even to a lowly ESMO. 'I fully support what the students've been doing. Someone's got to make a stand against the attacks on the uni's, and they've done a better bloody job than the staff. So I'm all in favour. But they've made their point, there could be accidents, and their work's beginning to suffer. You're a man who knows his way around, Brian. Is there any means you can think of to, er, wind it up – peacefully but quickly?'

Brian puffed his way slowly down the ladder and rested an elbow thoughtfully on its top. 'When did you have in mind?'

'Soon as possible. Tonight.'

Brian rounded his lips and sucked in air in the time-honoured way of one who is being asked to do what is impossible at all but the highest price. And what, he wondered, was Dorn playing at? The reason for the demo was not just course closures but the government's plans for two-year degrees – and Brian knew better than anyone that the very person who'd leaked those plans was Gary himself. So why was he now in such a hurry to bring the demo to an end? Yet Brian had learned one valuable lesson, even if at neither of his lamentable schools: it's always better to seem more stupid and ignorant than you really are. Then others will worry less about revealing their hand. 'Daresay I might be able to do it, but I'd need a bit of assistance. So it would cost money.'

'Money? How much?'

Brian calculated for a moment. 'If you're looking for a ball-point figure, let's see . . . I'd need a bit of equipment and some helping hands, and the job would involve unsocial hours. I'd say five hundred quid should sort it. Cash. Half up-front. No questions asked.'

'Bloody hell!'

'But you wouldn't want to put your hand in your own pocket to solve the uni's problems, would you? So the whole thing's probably out of the question.'

'No indeed, but, er, some people in high places might want to. What time do you finish tonight? Can I make a few calls and then get back to you?'

'No problem. I'll be out at the gatekeeper's lodge. Don't come off duty till nine.'

Gary let himself into his office, sank into his swivel chair and gazed blankly at the poster of Karl Marx that adorned one of the walls. It was out of the question for him to ask Prendergast for cash. When Gary had been to see him, the implicit claim he made was that he had special influence with both his colleagues and the students. If Prendergast knew that ending the sit-in was a matter of mere money, he could do the job himself without needing Gary's help. And if Gary didn't do the business by tomorrow, his career prospects would be zero. He probably wouldn't even last for the remainder of the media degree, and even if he got his book published, would have only the faintest chance of getting a job at any other university. He decided to try Holly one last time, perhaps even play the emotional card by telling her he was crazy about her, and, without going into any explanations, beg her to end the demo for his sake. He pressed the buttons on his phone, but went straight to her voice-mail. Intoxicated with the whole damn circus, she wasn't picking up, and was unlikely to do so until the morning.

He swore loudly, tossed the phone on to his desk and himself on to the sofa. Where the hell was he going to lay his hands on five hundred quid? And in any event, the idea of doing university business with his own money was thoroughly repugnant. Yet the alternative was equally unthinkable: unemployment sooner rather than later and – at least until his book was published – unemployability. He swung himself back on to his feet and paced the room. The germ of an idea was occurring to him. One cause of the rows he had with his ex-wife, Cynthia, was her constant, and in his view excessive, demands for money for the upkeep of the kids. Why was she constantly pestering him for money when she had a part-time job at the Citizens' Advice Bureau? Eventually they'd managed to agree on a monthly payment, but what with all the other demands on his income Gary hadn't always been able to meet it. And then things turned from bad to worse when, instead of keeping the issue between them, she went snivelling to the Child Support Agency. The outcome of that unpleasant episode was that he'd been instructed to pay her £300 a month by standing order. It now occurred to him that if he could stop the payments for the next couple of months, he could purchase Brian's services without feeling the sting. It would, of course, mean that Cynthia would start moaning at him all over again, but he could point out that if he didn't spend this money on ending the sit-in, he'd lose his job: and if he lost his job, she wouldn't get another cent out of him. Put like that, it was a no-brainer.

Nevertheless sparing a thought for 'bloody Holly, who was costing him big-time', he pulled out his wallet, extracted his debit card and went down to the cash-point in the lobby. A few moments later, he put his head round the door of the gatekeeper's lodge. Brian was poring over the *Sun*, a large mug of tea at his elbow.

'I've been having a word with the powers-that-be,' said Gary conspiratorially, 'and they've, er, authorised payment.' He counted out twelve twenty-pound notes and a tenner and laid them on the table. 'Half now, the rest when the job's done. But, Brian: not a word to anyone, not even to the management. This is just between you and me, OK?'

'OK,' repeated Brian. 'No names, no pack-drill.'

'No names, no pack-drill. And no violence either – no nastiness, no screaming headlines. We want "Calm end to protest. University holds discussions with students." Are we clear?'

Brian was clear – very clear about the way in which he could gain even further reward for his efforts. When they parted, he got out his phone and thumbed Bill Castles' number at *The Mixton Chronicle*.

'Hello, Shaun, it's Brian. How're you doing in there?'

'Oh, yeah, great. We think we've got it sewn up. We're going to be broadcasting our demands all day tomorrow.'

'What for? Easier exams? Been busy revising, have you?'

'Knock it off. We can't study and demonstrate at the same time.'

'Thing is, Shaun, the uni ain't going to make any concessions over the exam timetable. All assignments have to be in on time, all exams as per schedule. I realise you're a bit busy at the moment, and wonder if I – if Mr Jones – could help out this year, same as last.'

'Actually, Brian, I was going to have a word with you when the demo ends. I could do with a bit of a leg-up when exam time comes.'

''Course you could. Perfectly understood. Give me the module numbers and I'll see what Mr Jones can do.'

'Brian, that's great. Same terms?'

'Well, I know how hard up you lot are, so I'll try and get a BOGOF deal for you.'

'Eh?'

'Buy one, get one free.'

'But I've only got one exam to sit – the Art History paper set by that bastard, Barry Powell. Bloody exams went out with the ark, but he's a total fascist and really believes in them. How can we be expected to remember a lot of facts, and write down essays and stuff with the bloody clock ticking away?'

'I can see your difficulty, old son.'

'Trouble is, Art History's a core module. If I fail, I'm in the shit.'

'Dear oh dear. Well, I'm sorry I can't get you a BOGOF, but I – Mr Jones – will do our best for you at the usual rate. But I need you to do a little something for me in return, Shaun. You're one of the people who's been operating the window-cleaning cradle, right?'

'Yeah, see, I got this mate and his uncle does that sort of work– '

'At 3.30 tomorrow morning, I want you to bring the cradle down to first floor level. No questions. And when you've taken the cradle back up to the roof, just make yourself scarce, and no one'll be any the wiser. Understood?'

'Brian, I couldn't drop my mates in the sh– '

'Exam deal's off then, Shaun. You'll be able to afford to repeat the year, will you?'

At 3.30 the following morning, two ESMOs, a man and a woman, placed light ladders against the window cleaning cradle which had been lowered to the first floor, climbed up and clambered in. With Shaun, they ascended to the roof of the building and then, without Shaun, made their way downstairs to the ground floor. They were dressed in T shirts and jeans and wore branded trainers and peaked caps. The woman had a rucksack over her shoulder, while her companion carried an open can of Coke from which he swigged as they made their way down the main stairs. On the ground floor, inert bodies huddled on chairs and benches were the only intimation of life. To one insomniac student gazing blearily at his laptop, they nodded and made a 'peace' sign. The library foyer was deserted: a general sense of security had reduced vigilance. The woman extracted a pair of bolt cutters from her rucksack and severed the chains that secured the main entrance.

Carrying flashlights, three large men in uniform came in and started to clear the floors one at a time. For the most part, the students were shepherded out of the building and on to the forecourt before they were fully awake. The few who attempted to resist were lifted off their feet and half-carried out of the building by way of a little-known and usually locked exit down in the boiler room. Blinking, sleepy and tottering, everybody else emerged on to the forecourt where, before them, was a van from which Brian and another ESMO dispensed hot tea and doughnuts. 'Well done, mate. Well done, love. Have some refreshments,' was Brian's greeting. And when faced by the distressed and the disgruntled, he added, 'No, you did great. But you've made your point. And you've got your studies to think of.' Holly, who had gone to sleep only about an hour beforehand, was thoroughly confused and dishevelled. Sleeping bag round her waist and her hair down in her eyes, she gratefully took a mug of tea even before she was fully aware of what was happening. ''Ere, put this on for a moment. Warm you up a bit.' Brian slipped an old donkey jacket round her shoulders, and as he did so she became aware of what, at this nocturnal hour, was an unnatural brightness. Somebody had alerted the TV crews in the trucks behind the library, and they were now setting up their lights, cameras and microphones.

'Looks as though the sit-in's over, Holly, what are your views?' asked a reporter.

Holly put the best face on it, and despite her fatigue, what an alluring face it was. 'We've made our point. We were, er, about to wrap it up anyway, 'cos we've forced the government and the university to listen to us. So I just want to say a big thank-you for the terrific solidarity we've had from the students at other uni's.

Also to the thousands of people who've sent us messages of support on the internet, and whatever. Love you all – and especially you, mum.' And Holly looked straight at the cameras with her big, glistening, panda eyes, blew kisses and wrinkled her nose in a happy if weary smile.

Beside her stood Brian. In the background, gazing longingly at her, lurked Shaun, burdened forever with a guilty secret. Later that day, on national television and on YouTube worldwide, she would charm the myriads of viewers all over again. There was a noisy deluge of follow-up questions, but with the proprietary air of someone who might have been her manager, Brian intervened. 'Ladies and gents, you'll appreciate Miss Ainscough's very tired and won't take any more questions. She needs to go home and have a long rest.' And with that, he resettled the donkey jacket over her shoulders and guided her off to his nearby Cavalier.

Much as she normally loved dealing with the media, Holly felt a surge of gratitude. The jacket, the hot drink and the lift back to her flat were the mark of a gentle and thoughtful man. And God, was she bushed! When she got home, she intended to sleep for a week. 'Thanks Brian, you're a love. I really appreciate the lift home.'

'That's all right, ducks. But I promised Bill Castles we'd drop into the Chronicle and give him just a few words and a photo for tomorrow's paper.'

'Oh, must we?'

'Won't take long. And, you know, the Chronic's a local paper, very pro the students. He's coming in to his office specially to talk to you. Be a good idea to keep him onside, eh?'

Holly closed her eyes and rested her head against Brian's uniformed shoulder. When they were shown into his office, Castles was sitting at his computer. 'Thanks, Brian, you can go now. I'll run Holly home.' But she insisted that Brian wait for her. The interview was friendly, brisk and quite brief. As if on auto-pilot, Holly repeated the principles behind the sit-in, and expressed her belief that despite its abrupt end it had been a success. 'Otherwise we'll do it all over again.'

'Right,' said Castles, rising from his chair. 'All we need now is to go along to the studio and get a nice photo of you for tomorrow's front page. Brian, you wait here.'

Brian settled into his chair, and finding a packet of Starbursts in his pocket unwrapped one. Chewing contentedly and with his hands clasped over his belly, he stretched out his legs and gazed admiringly round Castles' office. About ten minutes later, Castles and Holly returned. 'Thank you, my dear,' said Castles with a vulpine smile, and as he showed them out slipped a roll of banknotes into Brian's hand. Holly said little on the drive home.

'How did you like Bill Castles, then?' Brian asked.

'Creepy blighter. No wonder him and his weird daughter's got issues.'

The following day the university issued the placatory statement that it wished to support and work with, and for, all its students at all times. Prendergast, however, was in a different mood. 'I want the names of everyone who was in there,' he muttered, 'and if we get another peep out of any of them, they'll be part of the new road into Fallowfields.'

29. THE BOMBSHELL

At the morning's meeting of the senior management, the sense of relief could almost be tasted. The news that the sit-in was over had been swiftly relayed from Brian to Gary, who despite the time of night had been waiting with his phone switched on, and, first thing in the morning, from Gary to Prendergast. The latter had phoned Turpin and Unthank before they'd even come in to work.

Turpin opened the meeting by inviting Prendergast to explain how it had been achieved. Prendergast was quick to claim full credit for it, but added, with coy self-importance, that his colleagues must forgive him if he didn't go into detail. It had been a matter of activating his informal contacts among the staff and students. The sit-in had been ended without violence or further bad publicity, and, indeed, the university had emerged from the whole affair as a humane and forgiving institution.

'Amen to that!' concurred Turpin, looking round for the biscuits, 'and the institution – and indeed, we your colleagues – owe you our great gratitude.' Suffused with a sense of his own might, Prendergast nodded unsmilingly. 'Now, gentlemen,' Turpin continued, 'I've just come off the phone to Brenda Hodges. Can't pretend that she's best pleased with us, but she's at least expressed her gratitude that the sit-in has been ended, and says there are early signs that the demos at the other universities are petering out. And, of course, again thanks largely to Ed, we still have a great deal of credit with the government for our plans for the Fallowfields campus. Speaking of which, I know that Robert went to see Cyril and Betty Attwood yesterday, and . . . ' Turpin rubbed his hands together happily before selecting a biscuit from the plate, 'I'm hoping he has some more good news for us.'

Unthank felt the eyes of his colleagues on him. He glanced from one to the other, looked down at the notes he'd made, took a deep breath and began his account.

He'd decided to walk from his office to the Attwoods' house. A prior attempt on the phone to renew their acquaintance had not gone well: 'No, no, I really don't want to sell you anything, Mrs Attwood, it's a voice from the past. Do you remember Charles and Laetitia Unthank who lived in Cheshire? I'm Robert Unthank, their youngest.'

'Robert Unthank. Robert? There was Miranda and Annabelle. They were both very sweet.'

'Mirabel and Amanda, Mrs Attwood. My sisters. Always very good to me.'

'If they were then you probably didn't deserve it. Brothers can be horrid. They're the world's great destroyers. My brother was Genghis Khan in short trousers. But Charles was such a dear man. Are you nearby? Come to tea tomorrow.'

Like many English towns which have been haphazardly rebuilt over decades, Mixton is a broadly unattractive hotch-potch of brutalist shopping precincts and office blocks, grey multi-storey car-parks, streets of mean houses and delapidated factories. Yet it contains hidden jewels. Beside the parish church is a secluded, leafy close of town houses, at the end of which was the Attwood residence.

140

As he walked up the drive to the front door Unthank took in the handsome, ivy-clad building and its grounds. From its elegant proportions, the transom over the wide front door, the array of twelve-paned windows on the ground and first floors, and the dormers in the roof, he judged it to be late Georgian. Yet there were faint signs of neglect: some loose slates, a slightly sagging roof gutter, peeled paint, patches of brickwork in need of re-pointing. Tall chimneys stood at each end of the roof, and Unthank wondered if they still functioned or if their flues were occupied by the ghosts of wiry, blackened urchins who had climbed them in an earlier age.

'Rupert, come in. It's nice to see you after all these years. I'm afraid people like me say things like "You have grown!", but indeed you have.'

'It's Robert, Betty. And it *has* been twenty years or more. But it's very good to see you after all this time. Is Cyril at home?'

'Oh, didn't I tell you on the phone? Cyril died three weeks ago. Heart, you know. He took all those tablets with great punctiliousness. He was very particular about that, laid them out in rows on the breakfast table. They required two large cups of tea. But the condition got him in the end. Come into the living room and sit down and I'll organise some tea.'

Like the house's exterior, the living room was imposing, yet with hints of decay and makeshift repairs. A wooden chair by the wall had lost part of a leg and was supported by several ancient bound volumes of *Punch*. Unthank noticed that to prevent it from falling further, the slipped frame of one of the sash windows had been wedged with two silver tea-spoons. After years of occupancy, the fine armchairs and sofas had become faded and misshapen. Yet the room was comfortable: there were books and magazines everywhere, flower-filled vases a-plenty, and on the inlaid coffee table, a half-filled dog bowl. Betty Attwood served the tea in chipped yet exquisite bone china. At her insistence, Unthank updated her on the lives of his sisters, and then, tactfully but resolutely, explained how he came to be in Mixton.

'My colleagues were keen that I should come and thank you personally, Betty – and, alas, poor Cyril – for the long and happy association the university has enjoyed with you. Above all, for your kindness in agreeing to sell Fallowfields to us. We know you've had other and more tempting offers. Your decision couldn't be better timed. We mean to keep the property in all its present splendour but establish new courses there and attract more students. It'll be very much the showpiece of the university.'

'Ah, Roland, now there's something I must tell you,' Mrs Attwood lowered her cup to her saucer and placed both very deliberately on the coffee table. 'It'll be a great wrench, you know, allowing the premises to be used for non-educational purposes.'

Unthank was perplexed. 'But I can assure you, Betty, that they will continue to be . . .'

'Cyril's family were always keen on this. At the end of the war, Fallowfields was used by the government as a place for emergency teacher training. Cyril's father was happy to make a contribution to the post-war effort, but insisted that the college provide *Christian* training. The Attwoods have always felt that religion was very important, you know. It worked well for a good many years. The place expanded. Some tasteful additions were made. The Church smiled on the enterprise and . . . '

'God was in his heaven and all was well with the world,' murmured Unthank.

Whatever point Betty was making seemed to have become mired in nostalgia. 'It was all very civilised, you know. Cyril used to say that it served the best cream tea in the county. But then something happened in the seventies. I don't know exactly what. Student numbers declined. Those ghastly inspectors kept prowling round the place. And there was that unhappy incident with the bursar and the sacristan's daughter. Anyway, it had served its time as a teacher training place, so we had to let it out to the polytechnic. We tried to impose a condition that they teach theology there, but the place was run at the time by a frightfully vulgar little man and he wouldn't have any of it.'

Mrs Attwood sighed and refilled their cups, and Unthank saw his chance. 'With great respect, Betty, that was a long time ago. And if religious education's no longer in great demand, the next best thing is the secular education the university's been providing for many years now. Wouldn't you agree?'

Mrs Attwood looked resigned. 'Yes, you're right. Times change. And it's rather sad, in a way, that Fallowfields will no longer be doing even that. Under-gardener's orders, I'm afraid.'

Unthank stared at her, struggling to catch her drift, yet fearful of succeeding. He was about to speak, when a white pug suddenly trotted round the corner of the settee and leapt into Mrs Attwood's lap, slavering breathlessly. 'You naughty boy, Baggins,' she said in loving tones, and picking up the dog bowl from the table, tried to interest it in the contents. 'You rascal, turning your nose up at this food.' Unchastened, the dog craned and sniffed towards the tea-tray, indicating a preference for the plate of biscuits it held. 'Do you have a dog, Roger?'

'I'm afraid not,' but Unthank was determined not to be deflected by polite small talk. 'My dear Betty, I'm thoroughly confused. Do you mean you've decided *not* to sell to the university? And why are you taking orders in this matter from your under-gardener?'

Mrs Attwood became impatient. 'Haven't you been paying attention, Raymond? This is what I've just been explaining to you. Gardeners are our lawyers. We called Gardener Senior the head gardener, but he's retired so we call his son the under-gardener. And the under-gardener has advised me to sell to the highest bidder, the Arabian gentleman. I'm afraid the under-gardener's a rather brash young man. He's put a big NO WIN, NO FEE sign over the door of his office. Is that progress?'

'I really couldn't say. But why won't you sell to us? You're not obliged to take Mr Gardener's advice.'

'Indeed not. But since Cyril's death, I've discovered that our finances are in a worse state than I feared. There are debts to pay off, and I hadn't realised what a burden death duties can be – on the living, not the dead.' By now, Mrs Attwood was absently feeding shortbread biscuits to Baggins. 'Cyril had been meaning to put in place all sorts of wheezes, as he called them, to make sure I could manage comfortably when he'd gone, but he died before he could. I've discovered the poor dear was really rather hopeless about money. You see, Ronald, I do want to hang on to this house, but he didn't keep up the insurance cover on it, and now the Listed Building people are saying the structure may have to be underpinned. It's not so much *listed* as *listing*, they said. I imagine that's their favourite joke. Anyway, I've no choice but to accept the very generous offer from the Mohammedan gentleman. I think he'll take good care of Fallowfields – and I must say he has perfect manners.'

Unthank made efforts to get her to re-consider, but was inhibited by the knowledge that she needed to make as much money from the sale as she possibly could, and that the university would never be able to match its rival's bid. He walked back to the university with a heavy tread, not relishing the prospect of telling Turpin and Prendergast that their bold new master plan might have to be re-thought.

'Sell it to the Arab?' spluttered Turpin. "Renege on her promises to me and on five hundred years of history? Hand over our finest asset to some plutocrat from the Middle East? It's outrageous.' He stopped, becoming aware that he was displaying a prejudice which he had all his life striven to avoid.

Prendergast had no such inhibitions. 'So we're going to have to make room for the sultan and his harem. What does that make us? Eunuchs! Why didn't you tell her she was betraying the university?'

'This has happened very quickly,' said Turpin. 'The last time I spoke to her Cyril was unwell. Now, just a few weeks later, she's selling his inheritance not for a mess of pottage but a mass of money.'

'Mrs Attwood finds herself in a terrible predicament,' rejoined Unthank. 'She's lost her husband, and because Cyril never made the arrangements he said he would, she suddenly finds herself knee-deep in death duties. Now she's had an offer her solicitor has told her she can't refuse. And despite their religious differences, the buyer's found favour with her because he's mainly interested in the buildings, not the land. Unlike us, he doesn't want to alter or add to them.'

Prendergast listened to this in an anger tinged with panic. Instead of playing the gallant and defending this stupid old biddy, Unthank should've reminded her of her promise, and used fair means or foul to make her stick to it. Turpin's toff could be relied on for nothing. For all his mimsy philosophisings and cultured posturings he was utterly ineffectual. But more to the point, where did this latest disaster leave him, Ed Prendergast? In the deepest of shit. He'd

144

boasted to Brenda that he'd flattened the opposition to the changes she wanted, but then the students had staged a sit-in that had gone viral, leaked her precious plans, and caused demos at uni's across the country. If Brenda heard that after the ballyhoo of a few weeks ago they'd now lost Fallowfields, and with it the early chance of launching the new degrees, that'd be the end of him. As Turpin fretted on about the need to persuade Betty Attwood to change her mind and, failing that, to consider 'alternative scenarios', Prendergast focused on just one thought. To have any chance of retaining his role as Brenda's enforcer, he'd need to act quickly, drastically – and entirely on his own.

30. A CHANCE ENCOUNTER

Prendergast was about to climb the stairs when he was obliged to make way for Brian, who was puffing down with a computer screen under one arm and a power unit under the other.

'Evening, Brian. Off to write some emails somewhere?'

With a grunt Brian set the apparatus down on a table at the foot of the stairs.

'Blimey, no. Mr Burley's asked me to move this for him. Personally I don't have nothing to do with computers. I'm too old for that sort of thing. I've got Sky TV at home and it's encripped, but that's about as far as I go. What brings you to Fallowfields, Mr Prendergast?'

'Happened to be passing, and it's such a lovely old building I thought I'd look round. On the late shift?'

'Just about to knock off, Mr P. Can't wait to get home tonight. It's a good night on the telly and my mum's doing B and M.'

'What's that?'

'Bangers and mash – what those TV cooks call a signature dish. So I'm just going to make a final check. These lecturers may be clever people but they still leave stuff switched on, gear for others to trip over, don't shut the windows, don't put the milk back, and what not.'

'You always based up here?'

'Oh, no. I'm here, there and everywhere. That's 'cos our chief likes to rotate us.'

'Must make you feel giddy.' Prendergast so seldom attempted a joke that Brian seemed not to notice it.

'Makes no difference 'cos I know all the uni premises like the back of my hand.'

Prendergast remembered his very first meeting with Brian, when the latter forgot the way to the coffee bar. But he was now warming to his theme.

'Not only do us ESMOs know all the buildings, but in our line of business you have to do a bit of everything. Makes it easier to cover for sickness and holidays and gives us – ha ha, listen to this – a wide range of opportunities and broad working experience. The lads call it the JABT option.'

'What on earth is that?'

'Jack of All Bloody Trades, or, Mr P, because we get that equality training, Jack or *Jill* of All Bloody Trades.'

'Don't suppose there are many Jills.'

'There's Doris in supplies. Nobody gets on the wrong side of Doris.'

'Still, working out here must be better than other parts of the uni. Quiet. Pleasant.'

'Except when the art students are coming up to the last bit of the year, they want to stay here till all hours. Funny, innit? They sleep, smoke and drink for seven months and then work their boll– er, socks off for what's left. But we still help them.'

'How do you do that?'

'Let them work as late as possible.'

'Isn't there a security issue?'

'Not really – although the alarm system only covers the ground floor.'

'Why just the ground floor?'

'Anything worth nicking would have to come out the front door and that'd trigger the alarm. They keep meaning to extend the system, but last time the money got spent on re-laying the croquet lawn.'

'Perhaps I should have a word with Dr Turpin.'

Brian jingled his keys thoughtfully. 'You could do. But the place is pretty well covered. We ESMOs are here twenty-four seven 'cos it's so isolated. At night and weekends there's someone in the gatekeeper's lodge. Patrol every hour. And any alarm'd go off in there.'

'Glad to hear it.'

Brian made a wry face. 'Mind you, it depends who's in the lodge. This week it's Tosh and Mitch. Word has it they've got a mini-bar installed behind the fire screen and have the odd snifter while they watch educational videos.'

'Educational videos?'

'*Lustful Lezzies on the Job. Fifteen, Free and Frisky.* You know the sort of thing. But it's probably all gossip – someone having a laugh and indulging in a spot of bandage.'

'OK, Brian, I'll let you finish your shift and get home. I'll look round another time. Enjoy your night with the telly.'

Prendergast walked swiftly out to his car with a firm sense of what now needed to be done. The Vice's efforts had been as unavailing as he'd expected. Immediately after the meeting at which Unthank had dropped his bombshell Turpin had paid Betty Attwood another visit. She'd mistaken him for the dish-washer repair man. If only, he thought grimly, the Vice was that useful. At least Gary Dorn had proved dependable.

Brian watched Prendergast's BMW swish out of the car-park. He got into the Cavalier, took a gadget from his inside pocket, and switched on the stereo. Checking the Bluetooth connection was working, he pressed a button. '. . . round another time. Enjoy your night with the telly.'

'Ah, Mr P,' said Brian, addressing his dashboard, 'I don't just do the telly. You know what I mean, not just the *TV* telly. All these questions . . .Are you just the new boy learning the ropes? Or is there a bit more to it?' Despite the imminence of his mother's B and M, he took a Twix bar out of the side pocket of the Cavalier and chewed on it pensively.

Some time later, Prendergast drew up outside his flat. He took a phone out of the front glove compartment and punched in a number. 'Entry via the first floor. Ground floor's alarmed but nothing above.'

'Can I use an accelerant?'

'Absolutely not. Make it electrical. That shouldn't be too much of a problem. Do it away from the outhouses where the art studios are. And come in from the north-west of the building where you can more easily avoid the cameras.'

'Don't worry, I've got someone who'll do a recce for me. And the best time?'

'Go in at 1.30 am.'

'What about the on-site security staff?'

'Will be relieving the boredom by watching a movie.'

'How long before the engines arrive?'

'Depends on how soon it's spotted, but if the security staff are watching movies instead of the house, it should be at least half an hour.'

'Easy as kiss my arse. Usual arrangements?'

'Yes. Half before, half afterwards. No change to the account?'

'None at all. You've got the details. I think this is going to remind me of the poem.'

'Poem?'

'Red sky in the morning, shepherd's warning. Red sky at night, Fallowfields alight.'

'Cut the poetry. It must be on the date I've specified – the 20th. If anything causes that to change, you'll get a text saying "Guy Fawkes cancelled". In which case, do nothing till you hear from me again. Understood?'

'Understood.'

The connection was terminated. Prendergast opened the phone that he'd purchased on the way home in the name of Patrick Kinsella and took out its SIM card. Then he opened the car door and dropped the card into the drain beside the kerb.

31. OBSTACLES – CLEARED AND CREATED

Mark Middlemiss was aware that he'd probably drunk more than he should have at the Crown and Anchor, but he hadn't seen many of the lads for over a year, they'd had a lot to catch up on, and their rivalry always extended to seeing who could neck the most vodka in the shortest time. Back in the car-park he had a problem. His SatNav had been stolen the week before, there were no maps in the car and he didn't feel up to navigating by the stars. The journey out to the pub had been simple, as he'd just followed Les from Accounts. But Les had bailed out early, and as the other cars revved up around him he didn't want to look stupid by asking someone how to get home. So he polished the windscreen vigorously while shouting out cheerful obscenities to his departing mates.

Once they'd gone he looked around and tried to picture the return journey. He recalled a number of landmarks, and knew that once he hit the B6042 he'd be able to find his way home. But he was a long way from both. The right turn he now took into Badgers Lane, which he was sure he'd recognised as the short cut on the outward journey, ended up at a locked gate to some kind of college. Whatever it was, it appeared to be some distance away and suffused in a rosy glow. The lane was too narrow to turn the car round. He got out and stepped into a large puddle. He could see that back down the lane was an entrance to a field. He reversed with what he imagined to be great panache and swung the rear wheels round into the field, taking the unseen gate completely off its hinges. Half falling out of his car, he surveyed the damage with impotent fury. Lost, thick-headed and cursing without cease, he drove unsteadily away. Plodding languidly in his wake, a large herd of Friesians spilled out of the field and gathered in the lane.

A mile or two away, Tosh and Mitch had come to the end of *Blondes Like Bondage*, and Tosh, deciding that he needed some fresh air, pushed the door open, stepped out and looked up. 'Fucking hell. It's on fire.'

Mitch joined him to see flames leaping from the back of the main building. There was already a strong smell of smoke and a busy crackle of flames. 'Shit,' said Mitch. 'What the hell's happened? Get the extinguishers.'

'I'm not going anywhere near it,' said Tosh. 'We'll get barbecued.'

'Nobody's going anywhere near it. I'll just empty the extinguishers to show we did our best to fight it. Phone the emergency services. Tell 'em there's a fire at Fallowfields and we've been fighting it with everything we've got. Tell 'em it's just too big for us and they'd better get here quick.'

Along with all the other local public services, the county fire and rescue service had suffered its share of cuts. So what a few years ago might have been a ten-minute journey was now closer to fifteen. Even so, the tenders made good time, rousing the residents of half a dozen villages as they sped towards the fire. What delayed them was a huge herd of cows sauntering up Badgers Lane. The sound of the sirens and the shouts of the firemen unsettled rather than dispersed them and they began to mill about, lowing piteously. In their helmets and day-glow jackets the firemen waved and shouted in an effort to herd them off the road, but with only slow success. On the move once more, the tenders came up against the secured gate that had so annoyed Mark Middlemiss. The crew carried no keys but this failed to blunt the zeal of the driver of the first truck, who hadn't enjoyed the fun of a real fire for well over two months. He backed up and with a shout of triumph drove straight through the gate. Twenty-five minutes after Tosh's call, water jets at last began to play on the burning rafters of Fallowfields.

At seven that morning Prendergast heard the news on MIX FM, the local radio station. Already dressed and breakfasted, he picked up his car keys and camera from the kitchen table and drove straight to the scene. He spoke with Inspector Derek Foreman, the policeman in charge of the case, the chief Fire and Rescue officer, and two senior members of the ambulance service. After he'd established that nobody was hurt, and that the fire had been confined to the main building, he was told of the brave but unavailing efforts of the two ESMOs who had at first fought the blaze alone. Unfortunately, even the best efforts of the fire service had been unavailing. Reduced to broken and blackened walls and a tangle of rubble and fallen rafters, the once graceful edifice was now a pitiful sight. The single consolation, which, he was assured, was due only to the quick response of the fire service, was that all the outbuildings had been saved. While Prendergast was taking photos and shaking hands with the heroes of the hour, he took care to inquire how long they thought it would take to clear the site.

Back at the university he instructed Marian to phone Turpin and Unthank, both of whom he knew to be at a conference down in Oxford. She should reassure them that he was doing everything possible to allow courses to continue and would brief them on their return next morning. She was then to phone Mrs Attwood and break the news to her, but add that a senior member of the university's directorate would shortly be with her to give a very full account of what had happened. Over the next few hours, Prendergast briefed various senior members of academic staff on how they were to deal with the emergency, and drafted a statement which would be issued by the external relations office. Then he downloaded his photos on to a computer and got his secretary to print them off on A3 paper and in full colour. With these, he felt he could almost persuade Mrs Attwood that Fallowfields had suffered a belated visit from the Luftwaffe. He slid them into a portmanteau and left the university on foot. His first stop was the florists on the High Street, where he picked up the large and consoling bouquet that he'd taken the trouble to order some three days before. Then he strode up the close, flowers in his left hand and portmanteau under his right arm, to Mrs Attwood's house. She opened the front door, impeccably smart in pearls and a dark dress, her distress apparent only in the pallor of her complexion and the frailty of her stance.

'Mrs. Attwood, I'm Ed Prendergast, Director of Academic Development at the university. On behalf of Dr Turpin, Dr Unthank and myself, I've come to say how dreadfully sorry we are about Fallowfields. We don't know yet how the fire started. The evidence points to an electrical fault. But we know how distressing this is for you and the family. Dr Turpin and Dr Unthank are away at the moment, but they've asked me to visit you straightaway and express our deepest sympathies.'

'You're very kind, Mr . . . What did you say your name was? Please come in.' Betty Attwood accepted the bouquet with unsteady, mottled hands, and admiring their beauty showed him into the sitting room. 'You can imagine, Mr . . . that after Cyril's death this news has come as another great blow to the heart. I don't think I could survive a third.'

As he sat down Prendergast nodded silently and clasped his hands between his knees. They felt clammy. In a strange way her composure was harder to deal with than a display of anguish, yet he'd have to press on. As soon as Mrs Attwood's housekeeper brought tea, Prendergast moved across to the settee beside her, opened his portmanteau and took out the photographs. She picked up her spectacles, which hung from a cord round her neck, and looked carefully at each in turn. Only a slight tightening of the mouth and a flaring of the nostrils betrayed the grief within. But Prendergast passed them relentlessly, one image after another of charred timbers, scorched, tumbled walls, pools of water criss-crossed by the fire hoses. No word was spoken, no movement made. At last, she dropped them into her lap, took off her spectacles and stared thoughtfully at the fireplace. Baggins waddled slowly into the room, glanced lugubriously up at his mistress and sank down at her feet.

'I fear this is God's judgment on me for agreeing to sell to a Mohammedan, though I must say that he was such a pleasant gentleman. He loved the house very much and didn't intend to change a thing.' She swallowed hard. 'But of course, he won't be interested now, and I can see that I was meant to sell the property to the university.

'I can at least offer you some crumbs of comfort, Mrs Attwood,' murmured Prendergast. 'My colleague, Robert Unthank, told us you were facing all kinds of difficulties – death duties, the upkeep of this beautiful house.'

'Oh, yes. Randolph. Such a nice young man. He had tea with me only the other day.'

'If you were able to make the Fallowfields property over to the university fairly swiftly, we could help you with some of these. The sum you'd make on the sale would still be considerable, and we've got our own team of expert lawyers who could reduce your liabilities to a minimum.'

'That's most helpful of you. When I try to digest this awful calamity, I shall bear your offer in mind.'

'Another thing. Your husband was a great benefactor to the university for many years, and we'd like to mark this by calling the new premises the Cyril Attwood Building. Its centrepiece would be his portrait, and we'd be honoured if you'd come and formally unveil it. But I know that over the past weeks you've been through a lot, and now I'll trouble you no further.'

He drained his tea-cup and stood up. Mrs Attwood led him to the front door and stood beside him, looking out over her garden. She looked smaller and frailer than ever, but when she spoke, it was in a firm, clear voice. 'I'm so glad Cyril didn't live to see this happen. It would have broken his heart.' She turned to Prendergast and laid a trembling, bony hand on his sleeve. 'Thank you for calling, Mr, er . . . and for the beautiful flowers. Your kindness means so much.' She smiled and closed the door gently behind him.

As he walked down the drive, Prendergast felt, for the first and last time in his life, a stab of pure self-loathing, but he soon came to his senses. After all, he'd meant the old girl no harm. Betty Attwood was merely collateral damage in a political fight he had to win. And now, he thought, quickening his pace, it was onward and upward.

PART TWO

... in with the new

32. INQUEST, DIGEST, PROGRESS

'What happened? Was it a go-slow day for the fire service?' asked an exasperated Turpin.

'They got held up by cows and locked gates, couldn't locate the hydrants, and had to radio for more appliances,' said Prendergast. 'The real heroes were our security staff. They fought the fire unaided. It was only when they were getting beaten back that the fire service arrived. But now to the latest developments . . . '

Turpin and Unthank had hurried back from their conference the previous evening and been out to view what was left of Fallowfields. Now gathered round Turpin's conference table early in the morning, they were anxious to be updated. Prendergast gave them a sheet of paper outlining the actions he'd taken. They covered immediate health and safety issues, dealings with the various emergency services, clear directions to the relevant heads of department and proposals for the re-scheduling of lectures and related matters.

'There's some good news,' he said. 'Art and Design has come through virtually intact. There's a bit of water damage, but the workshops and other areas are usable once we get the all-clear from the fire service. What we've lost is the main building, which housed Media, Literature and Culture – the lecture and seminar rooms, social areas, SCR and a small library. Luckily Easter's late this year and we've had an unusually long term. This means the teaching on most courses has nearly finished, so for the rest of the academic year there'll be reduced demand for lecture and seminar rooms. Still, we need to keep both staff and students happy. I propose we reimburse staff against any personal losses resulting from the fire, provided they're reasonable. Books, laptops, odd items of clothing, probably some plastic lunch boxes.

'For the students, we run a "we feel your pain" agenda. We offer counselling and give them travel passes till the end of term. We also set up a Degree Classification Fire Review Sub-Committee. This would give sympathetic consideration to anyone who's been affected by the fire. To take account of their distress we'll postpone some of the exams and extend deadlines for the submission of coursework.

This'll show we're a caring university that always looks after its . . . '
Prendergast groped for the buzzword, '*stakeholders*.'

Turpin and Unthank looked dubious, and as the latter was about to venture that the balance in higher education may have tipped a little too far from the academic to the philanthropic, Turpin expressed their concerns more bluntly. 'Why not just *give* them their degrees on production of a Tesco Clubcard and have done with it?'

Prendergast was undeterred. 'I realise the students'll try to take advantage. Some'll be waving letters from their GPs claiming they've had a nervous breakdown. We'll commiserate, offer counselling, and, after the committee's looked at each case maybe shift most of them up a classification.'

'Perhaps the students decided to burn the place down in order to get better degrees,' murmured Unthank.

'The evidence points to an electrical fault,' said Prendergast, ignoring the joke.

'So where do we go from here?' asked Turpin. 'We've just lost our only attractive building. We'll have students running round like headless chickens and staff running round like headless students. While we've been shuffling deckchairs on the Titanic someone has set fire to the lifeboats. *Marian!*' he barked into the intercom, 'where the devil is the coffee?'

'There's one thing we haven't touched on,' said Unthank, 'we've quite neglected a major . . . *stakeholder*,' he uttered the word as if suddenly finding something unfamiliar in his mouth. 'What are we going to say to Betty Attwood?'

Prendergast jumped in smoothly. 'Ah, that's something I've not had a chance to mention. I managed to find a moment to drop in on Mrs Attwood and take her some flowers.' Turpin and Unthank looked at him with interest, and he pressed on swiftly, recounting how he'd comforted her with an account of the university's willingness to deal with the aftermath of the fire, and, by purchasing the Fallowfields estate, to relieve her of the worries about insurance, compensation, negligence, death duties and the like. There was an astonished silence, broken at last by the arrival of Marian with the coffee.

'I must commend your opportunism,' breathed Turpin.

'But she must've been in a state of shock,' said Unthank. 'We can't expect her to agree to sell the place off in half an hour. She needs time to reflect, take advice, decide.'

'Or,' rejoined Prendergast, 'to dither, delay and get screwed by her so-called advisers.'

Sipping his coffee, Turpin saw the matter with a sudden, exhilarating clarity. Ever since he'd learned that Betty had decided not to sell to the university he'd been unable to bring himself to break the news to two interested parties. The first was Geoffrey Edgerton and his colleagues at the council. Having committed themselves to buy many acres of low-grade farmland which would be worthless without access through Fallowfields, they'd be livid. The plans for a town-and-gown synergy lay in ruins, and the university's happy relationship with the council would be finished. Even worse, someone else who'd be livid was Brenda Hodges down at Whitehall. The loss of Fallowfields and the plan for a connected community would very likely mean the end of the government's backing for the new degrees, a stop on its funding of new construction, and perhaps sound the death knell of the university itself. Above all, it would mean the end of Turpin's own dream of gaining a knighthood. Yet now, amazingly, the wheel had turned again. It was a moment he could not let slip.

'I share your concerns, Robert. But you'll recall that Betty Attwood was in a similar quandary when you paid her a visit. Anxious to do the right thing, but worried about whether she could afford it. Toying with some dubious Middle Eastern gentleman one moment, then getting all tearful over Cyril's memory the next. This could play out endlessly.' He paused, and seeing that Prendergast was eager to add his voice, raised a hand to silence him. 'We can ensure that she'll be assisted financially. We purchase Fallowfields, she ceases to have insurance worries, she can settle with the Revenue. We can turn Fallowfields into a shining example of a university of which she – and Cyril, had he lived – can be extremely proud.'

'We could call part of it the Cyril Attwood Building,' suggested Prendergast, as if the title had just occurred to him.

'Excellent,' agreed Turpin, pushing the plate of biscuits at his colleagues. 'So, to sum it all up, we've recovered Fallowfields! And

157

in the knowledge that they'll have access through its land, the council can develop Compton Farm.'

'Thus turning milk cows into cash cows,' remarked Unthank, to nobody in particular.

'We can realise our plan to forge links with the local community,' continued Turpin.

'And now that the old Fallowfields building is no more,' added Prendergast, 'we can provide purpose-built accommodation for our two new departments. Perhaps, Vice, we should also have a word with Harry Hunter. We can tell him and the council it's a genuine fire sale.'

Turpin sipped and munched, and felt more in command of matters than he'd done in a long time. 'I'll contact Hunter straight away and explain that the, ah, glorious phoenix of Mixton University is about to rise from the sad ashes of Fallowfields.'

Watching with growing unease his colleagues' haste to profit from Betty Attwood's calamity, Unthank remarked, 'You could also tell him that God moves in mysterious ways His wonders to perform.'

The next morning, Marian laid the newspapers on Turpin's desk. 'THE GREAT FIRE OF FALLOWFIELDS' shrieked the front page of *The Mixton Chronicle* above a picture of the ruins. As he pondered it Turpin realised that in human terms the university had got off very lightly. There had been no deaths, indeed no casualties of any kind, just two 'heroes of the hour', with the suitably gung-ho names of Tosh and Mitch, who had fought the fire with everything they had. Yet he was astonished by the *deus ex machina* that the destruction of Fallowfields represented. As an averagely cynical man, he couldn't help but wonder whether it was the act not of God but an arsonist, yet all the evidence pointed to an electrical fault and not even the Chronicle had deviated from that line. And even if the fire had been set deliberately, what could have been the motive? He, Richard Turpin, remained in perfect ignorance of any possible guilty party, and it was going to stay that way. Moreover he was comforted that since only a handful of people were aware of Betty Attwood's intention to sell to the Arab, the rest of the world would have no reason to be suspicious. Come what may, his own hands were clean, no guilt could be imputed to him. Above all, he'd played the power-game long enough to know that you claimed full credit not only for your own achievements but for any stroke of luck that befell you – and exploited both those things with equal vigour. He tossed *The Mixton Chronicle* into the bin, turned to his computer and tapped the keys with renewed purpose.

33. WINNERS OF THE ASHES

Some two weeks later, Brenda invited Mixton's management trio down to London for an afternoon meeting in her office. She'd been evasive about its purpose, but reassuring too. 'Just an update and a friendly chat,' she told Turpin. However, unknown to both Turpin and Unthank, she was first having lunch with Ed Prendergast at a smart little restaurant round the corner.

'Well,' she began, with a nod to the waiter. 'It sounds as though Mixton University has been fired up literally, even if not intellectually.'

Prendergast was eager to explain how the fire had occurred but she was much more interested in what would happen next. He produced an iPad and scrolled quickly down. 'We've made a plan to turn the fire to our advantage. We're going to raise Felix from the ashes. Instead of being lumbered with a useless old monument we'll be able to provide gleaming purpose-built accommodation for our two new departments.'

'Excellent. I suppose you're looking for help from us.'

He'd hoped this matter would arise later in the conversation. 'Some additional capital would certainly help us create the leading-edge, totally fit-for-purpose departments that'll pull in the punters going forward. Say about thirty million?'

'Say about twenty. You've struck lucky. Some money reserved for the University of Cleethorpes is on hold. They've discovered a large number of bodies in the early part of excavation.'

'I saw it on the news. They think it's a lost Roman legion.'

'Or a bunch of academics who've expired from lethargy.'

She broke off while the waiter filled their glasses and took their order, then rested her elbows on the table, clasped her hands under her chin and looked levelly at Prendergast. 'There'll be a *quid pro quo*.'

'Delighted to hear it. Twenty million, you just said.'

Brenda realised that the only word he'd recognised was 'quid'.

'I'm talking about what the government will want in return. We want to revive the two-year degree initiative, but since you leaked it up in Mixton and caused a national outcry, we're having to tread carefully. So you can atone for your sins by trialling two-year degrees across the whole university.'

'Wow, serious stuff. But we'll handle it.' Ed was already picturing himself crushing any academic staff who dared to oppose him.

'It's actually an opportunity for you. Given the financial savings involved, we believe that in the long run two-year degrees will prove popular. And in piloting them, Mixton can represent itself as being in the van of academic progress.'

'Great. What else?'

'Learn and Earn. We want your trendy new courses to incorporate paid work experience. And you could also introduce Learn and Earn into some of your older and not-so-trendy courses. But in the short term we'll leave that to your judgement.'

'Brilliant.'

'Finally, and related to Learn and Earn, we want to push the idea of the Connected Community. As embodied in that fancy model you dragged so many of us up to see. But it has to be real and attract good publicity. We want more than the local Women's Institute selling cup-cakes in the foyer. If you're going to get some new build, it must be community-friendly. "The university with the community at its heart", that kind of thing. We need something that shows action. Then the Minister can pop up there, put on a yellow hat, and get himself photo'd with a cement mixer. Smiling family on one side of him and some fast-track students on the other.'

'Anything else?'

'Get Harry Hunter on board,' said Brenda, dabbing her rouged lips with a napkin, 'but keep an eye on him. Same with the local council. We can't be promoting connected communities while local politicians are kicking the stuffing out of each other.'

She scribbled carelessly across the bill the waiter had presented and looked at her watch. 'You've got an hour or so to do some shopping and join up with your colleagues before our meeting. As always, mum's the word. Leaving the talking to me.'

At the meeting Brenda set out matters with her customary crispness. For its twenty million pound windfall, the new, community-friendly Mixton University would introduce two-year degrees and integrated Learn and Earn programmes. Her words produced a thoughtful silence from the triumvirate.

Somewhat surprisingly the first to be heard was Unthank.

'We're all agreed, Ms Hodges, that we need to offer a university education to those who've so far been too poor to afford it. But in extending the opportunity in this way don't we run the risk of debasing it?'

Brenda looked at him through narrowed eyes. 'How so, Dr Unthank?'

'University has always been about more than studying a particular discipline. It gives students a chance to enrich themselves in a wider sense – culturally and intellectually. Universities aren't just forcing houses for youthful trainees. They give students opportunities for independent thought and larger reflection – opportunities they may never get again. We're now proposing to reduce these opportunities by a third – more, if we include the time they'll spend in the workplace. This'd make our universities little better than industrial training centres.'

Brenda drew a deep, patient breath. 'Like several before it, this government's committed to putting as many youngsters as we can through higher education. But how do you think this'll be paid for? For many, the cost is unaffordable – hence the loan scheme. On the other hand, the state can't assume the whole burden of it, and shouldn't be expected to.'

'Quite so, Brenda,' interposed Turpin, who sensed that the discussion might be getting out of hand, but Unthank was not to be deflected: 'Even if we give our universities the purely utilitarian role you've proposed, there are dangers. What happens if we train

161

legions of hotel managers and the demand for their services then dries up? Or we churn out scores of estate agents only for the housing market to collapse? Since our relationship with our students will be essentially commercial rather than academic – they won't so much be students as customers – will they be able to ask for their money back? After all, we no longer propose to equip them for life but for a trade. And if there's no trade to employ them, where are they to turn? I'm playing the devil's advocate here. I repeat that we all want to provide what's the best for the greatest number, but it's surely our duty to consider very carefully what "the best" might actually be.'

Turpin began some hasty equivocation. Dear Robert, such a nice and clever boy but, politically speaking, a bit of a loose cannon. 'In-in- in- a two-year degree programme,' he spluttered, 'it'll be the *especial* task of academic staff to ensure that training is enriched with, ah, the, er, more speculative activities that Robert has in mind, and so ensure that the student experience remains as rich as ever. And as far as the relevance of our degrees is concerned, sensitivity to market trends and a flexibility in responding to them must surely be our guiding principles.'

Brenda nodded solemnly. Unthank said nothing more. And since Prendergast had his own agenda, one that, even though he'd never reflected on it, happened to coincide exactly with Brenda's, he too remained silent. As the three men took their leave, Brenda called Turpin back.

'Richard, a word. I like your handsome and clever young colleague, Dr Unthank, but he's a bit too idealistic for this game, and certainly for Mixton. You'd better keep an eye on him.'

Shortly afterwards, she went to brief the minister, who was cleaning his fingernails with a paper knife.

'What do you mean, Brenda, good news from Mixton? April the First was last Thursday.'

'It *is* rather astonishing, Minister. But the bones dug up in Cleethorpes and the ashes raked over at Fallowfields have conspired to help us.'

'How, exactly?'

'As you know, Mixton's not so much one of our top spots as flop spots. Unemployment, housing concerns, food banks . . . we've got a chance to address some of this and, rather surprisingly, a chance to ensure the Connected Community doesn't go the same way as the Big Society.'

'What do you mean?' said the minister furrowing his brows.

'I'm sorry to tell you that the joke round Whitehall is that the Big Society went into a Blumenthal restaurant for lunch, and couldn't squeeze its way out again.'

'Very droll, Brenda. But the Connected Community was part of a three-pronged approach for Mixton, wasn't it? Where are we now with the 2-4-3, as you call it?'

Brenda recounted her meeting with the university's senior figures.

'Who's the local MP?'

'Harry Hunter. We met him when we went up for Mixton's "look at me" day.'

'What's his majority?'

'Three thousand. Second division marginal, but as you know the electorate seems to be rather fickle at the moment.'

'He's supportive?'

'He will be, because he knows what's good for him. He'll quickly get to love the Learn and Earn initiative and the Connected Community. They'll promote fusion between the workers by brain and those by hand.' She noted that the minister seemed to be shaping his thumbs and forefingers into some kind of magic quadrilateral which might conjure good fortune.

'You mean putting dons into donkey jackets?'

'Exactly so.'

The minister took Brenda's smile to be in response to his joke, but it was in anticipation of her own: 'Perhaps even putting cement into mortar boards.'

Their laughter, at least, was in unison.

34. DISS-APPOINTMENT

For Ed Prendergast the business of conducting job interviews was mostly boring. You had to feign interest in the candidate's answers, make careful notes, clarify what was ambiguous, probe for weakness.

He enjoyed the last two but not the first two. Swift encounters, crisp statements – mostly from himself – and sharp decisions minuted by a secretary made up his favourite style of communication. Moreover, he hadn't had much of a vac. Because Easter fell late this year, the ski season in Europe was almost over. So while most of his colleagues had pushed off to warmer climes for a couple of weeks, he and his partner had only managed a four-day break doing some power cycling in Britanny. For him, the vac had largely consisted of long days at the university followed by long evenings at his computer. He hadn't been able to set foot in the gym for nearly a week. Now, with the summer term beginning and his colleagues returning, he desperately needed to pump some iron, pound a treadmill, rev the cycling machine and rattle the cross-trainer. He sat flipping his gold propelling pencil through the fingers of one hand and drumming the fingers of the other on the table. The arrival of a poised and sharply dressed candidate for the post of Head of the new Department of Environmental and Ecological Studies suddenly commanded his attention.

'Dr Loren Lafayette,' announced Marian.

Dr Lafayette was tall, slender, finely proportioned. Her heels were high but not vertiginous. She wore light make-up but no adornments. On her right hand was a single ring which bore a stone carrying a complicated engraving. She was wearing a finely embroidered white blouse and a dark suit with a pencil skirt. Her face was animated, not exactly beautiful but one which would nevertheless draw the keener observer. Fidgeting in his seat, Prendergast imagined that the stone was to ward off global warming. The interview panel comprised himself as chair, Unthank, the bespectacled film theorist Kate Huckerby as representative of the teaching staff, and Professor Ansbach, a specialist in the field from another university.

'Dr Lafayette,' Prendergast began, 'we've all read your impressive CV but it would help us if you could identify the key aspects of it which you feel qualify you for the post.'

Answering the same question, the two previous candidates had wandered backwards and forwards along their life-history as if they'd dropped something useful and were searching for it. Lafayette was different. She outlined an employment history which embraced both private and public sectors. She summarised her experience across continents and her detailed contacts with socio-economic groups that ranged from the well-heeled of Kansas to the destitute of Namibia. She spoke in a deep and confident voice but with an accent he couldn't identify.

'You've had an unusual career,' Unthank smiled at her encouragingly, 'one with some sharp changes of direction. What brought these about?'

'I majored in chemistry and earth sciences at Cornell. The main career paths were into mining and oil firms, and I chose the latter. I developed a broader perspective very quickly. My key tasks were proclaiming oil's contribution to successful economies around the globe, and how hard we were working to minimise damage to the environment. But I was also expected to encourage scepticism about whether there was such a thing as climate change, and even if there was, whether there was any connection between that and fossil fuels. In the end my doubts got the better of me so I resigned and joined the Global Environment Corporation, which was then small and is now large. It took me all over the world and I started seeing the effects of climate change for myself. Then I moved into the embryonic Environment Regulatory Agency to find out what the rules were, how they were applied and what effect they had.'

'And what did you discover?'

'That the rules were rubber, their application piecemeal and their impact reduced by the power of the opposition lobbies.'

'And what brings you here today?'

'We need to establish academic centres that deliver clear messages about climate change and its impact. We need to persuade everyone – politicians, CEOs, opinion formers, perhaps most importantly the people in the street – of the nature and urgency of the problem. We can do that by teaching, by warning, by taking the message out of universities and into communities, by prising open the alliance between the oil lobby and their friends in government. Your university's attempt to link up with environmentally concerned firms to help create a low carbon micro-economy is what attracts me to this job.'

'So you're going to save the planet from the evil politicians,' observed Prendergast. 'Isn't there a danger of biting the hands that feed you? These people give us most of our cash.'

'Some would say we're biting the hands of those who are strangling us. People think the environment and climate are problems for the future. They think they'll only affect people in faraway places. That's a fallacy. And I and many others want our children to grow up in a world that's sustainable.'

'Children?' said Prendergast, 'you wouldn't experience any clash of interest by virtue of – ' he stopped abruptly with a stifled grunt. Kate Huckerby had kicked him hard in the left calf.

'What my colleague means,' she broke in, 'is that at Mixton we positively welcome those staff who have families. It keeps us all in the real world – the one we want to preserve.' She smiled winningly at Prendergast, who could only grimace his assent.

Professor Ansbach then asked Dr Lafayette a series of technical, research-driven questions which required statistical answers. She seemed equal to them all, and furtively rubbing his calf beneath the table, Prendergast closed the interview.

He knew why Huckerby had kicked him. To so much as hint to a female applicant who later turned out to be unsuccessful that child-care might have debarred her from the job was to give her clear grounds for appeal. Prendergast was annoyed with himself for having even gone near the issue. At the same time he was surprised that a subordinate, and a female one at that, should have presumed to correct him so forcibly. And finally he was roused by this sudden display of female violence. He decided the best reaction was feigned innocence. 'What was all that about? I was only going to – '

'No you weren't. You were in danger of saying something gross and sexist that would've embarrassed us all.'

'Of the applicants, who do we think will best head up the department?'

Ansbach thought Lafayette the best of the interviewees by some distance. Putting the applicants in descending order of choice, he then announced that he had to leave for another appointment and hastened to confirm his fee and the means of payment. Unthank also favoured Lafayette. As well as admiring her personal qualities he was attracted by her combination of expertise and idealism. Since

Prendergast agreed, they seemed to be reaching a swift decision until Kate Huckerby spoke again. 'She's good on paper – good qualifications, lots of research publications, wide and varied experience in business, the public sector and academia. But there's something slightly unsettling about her.'

'Is this female intuition at work?' asked Prendergast.

'Careful, Ed, we wouldn't want to see you limping for the rest of the week. Look at her references. They're very cautiously composed. These are written by people who seem to respect rather than like her.'

They looked at them again and Prendergast spoke: 'I don't see it that way. They don't gush but they're very sound. And they credit her with the qualities she claims. What more do you want?'

'I want a touch of the personal, and it's not there. I want some sense that the referees esteem her as a human. These are well crafted, but a bit detached.'

'I take Kate's point,' said Unthank. 'You don't learn much about Loren *qua* Loren.'

Prendergast felt he was going to be sick *qua* sick. Now the Toff was fence-sitting and pointlessly prolonging what was an open-and-shut case. Would he ever manage to get to the gym? He made an effort to conceal his impatience. 'Look, we all know how cautious about references everyone's become. Worried in case they get challenged on legal grounds. But I don't think we should let this cloud our impression of her positive qualities.' They continued to debate until it was determined that Lafayette should be offered the job.

'Don't say I didn't warn you,' was Kate's parting shot.

35. MINDING THE GAP

Later that day Ed Prendergast was briefing the two recently appointed administrators of the Learn and Earn initiative in order to ensure that they understood what was expected of them. Unthank should have been doing this: he, after all, was Director of Outreach and Enterprise. But his intellectual maunderings in Brenda's office showed that he was quite unsuited to the role. Prendergast felt that Brenda had entrusted L and E to him and he fully intended to take credit for its success. He flicked his propelling pencil deftly between his fingers and eyed them narrowly.

'We're in the business of establishing a cross-disciplinary, cross-modular matrix of training and learning arrangements that will serve the interests of the university, the employers we work with, and the students. We're one of the few recipients of funding that the government's putting into its Learn and Earn programme. So we're the pioneers of, er, cross-fertilisation between university and business, study and work.'

It was rousing stuff. His two apprentices, well-dressed and in their late twenties, nodded vigorously.

'We're talking fusion learning, fusion curriculum, fusion opportunities. We're bringing together those components of the students' development that have so often been separate. The Mixton student will be a product that is able to do something useful quickly, benefit employers and ensure their thinking skills combine with their practical skills and interlock with their life skills. Are we clear?'

Further nods showed that it couldn't be clearer.

'But what you'll be doing won't be without its challenges. You'll need to approach local firms and sell the concept. You'll need to stress quality experience, eager students, government subsidies, commercial benefits and very probably bigger profits. Understand?'

'Absolutely,' chorused Gemma Giddings and Ben Frampton, sparing further strain on their neck muscles.

What it all boiled down to was that the new appointees were to drive the Learn and Earn plan and persuade local businesses to provide work experience for the students.

'If there are problems, you talk to Dr Dorn here, who'll be overseeing the campaign.' And Gary nodded sagely at them, all the while thinking that the desire to save his bacon had forced him down a strange road indeed, and wishing he was somewhere else.

Ben and Gemma went to their office. Gary stayed with them only to tell them that he was a very busy man, to remind them it was Mixton not Silicon Valley, and that they might have to use their initiative if they were going to gain their Performance-Related Bonuses. They looked round the modest room with its one window, one desk, one phone, one chair, one table, one kettle and one rug, and quickly realised that this was the accommodation they'd be sharing.

'Any chance of getting this upgraded a bit?' asked Ben as Gary was on his way out.

'I'll have a word with Brian, one of the ESMOs. I'm sure he'll be able to sort something.'

'I think it's called hot-desking,' said Ben, looking helplessly round after Gary's departure.

'Hot-phoning, hot seating and hot-kettling as well. Perhaps it's a ploy to bring colleagues closer together. What do you make of it? We have to be innovative, flexible, imaginative, proactive, shrewd when need be and manipulative as the situation demands but . . . '

'We have to produce results.'

'Or else we won't get our PRB.'

'Which I have to do. Because I've got a mortgage and my wife's pregnant. What about you?'

'No mortgage, and no wife but a nice flat and some expensive habits, and I'd like to keep both.'

'Well, let's put our heads together and see if we can come up with a plan. Take a similar approach to students and employers. Probably best not to involve Dr Dorn too much.'

'Agreed. You nip across to Pic-n-Mixton and get some coffee and milk and I'll go and fill the kettle and hijack two mugs from somewhere.'

'Excellent. We'll drink to success with Nescafe and skimmed. What shall we toast to?'

'To each having a chair of our own,' announced Gemma with a wink.

They cemented this professional concordat with smiles and a high five.

36. PROFESSOR ABBOTT GOES ON-LINE – AND OFF-DESK

Professor George Frederick Abbott stared uncomprehendingly at the screen in front of him, his eyes watering even more than usual. Using his computer was something he'dtried hard to avoid ever since attending the induction programme for new staff, but now he'd arrived to find a notice on his desk printed in aggressive red capitals. It told him that he hadn't replied to a number of urgent emails. With some effort he'd logged on and managed to access the university's intranet. After a little help from a colleague he then found the messages that needed his attention. The first three were dealt with quickly. This was because Abbott accidentally deleted them and decided that since they'd gone he could say they'd never come. The fourth he managed to keep but as he stared at it uncomprehendingly, the colleague, now about to go to a lecture but noticing Abbott's difficulty, leant over his shoulder and said, 'You have to download the attachment, George', and did it for him.

He was now staring at a twelve-page questionnaire seeking details of his carbon consumption at home and at work, which consisted of intrusive queries about the 'eco-morality' of his lifestyle. Abbott was aware of global warming, carbon in the atmosphere and the demise of the rain forests, but like many intellectuals he approached them in an abstract way without giving much thought to their relevance to his own life-style. Yet he felt a duty to try and fill the questionnaire in. After a good two hours of introspection and sometimes painful honesty he was the only person left in the room. But when he tried to send it off he succeeded only in causing it to disappear – and despite his frantic pressing of keys he was unable to retrieve it. For the first time at Mixton, Abbott wondered whether it was all getting too much for him.

It was not the University of Mixton which had given him a professorship. He'd been elevated some years ago to the chair of philosophy at a well-known if middle-ranking redbrick university some forty miles away, where he presided quietly over a small group of staff who were as unworldly as he. He was a mild, pear-shaped man of irredeemable dowdiness, with pale blue eyes and exiguous, sandy hair: even in the form of a resolute comb-over it could not mask the large freckles on his pate. His shapeless jacket and dun-coloured tie bore the stains of a thousand carelessly devoured meals, and in his habitual grey-green trousers his lower body resembled the hindquarters of a small elephant. In his post at the university he'd been winding down to his retirement, heedless of the numbers of philosophy students who were winding down rather faster. But within the university as a whole a panic was spreading about spiralling costs and unsustainable staff-student ratios, and a firm of management consultants was called in to 'rationalise' – merge or close – those departments that were the worst culprits. For probably the first time in its history the philosophy department emerged, blinking and diffident, into the glare of managerial scrutiny. The consultants – three or four slick individuals in fat cars, sharp suits and designer spectacles – were at a loss to understand how a subject as useless as philosophy had come to be taught at a university. In an institution that should be focusing on income generation and closer links with industry it would have to go, and the vice chancellor and his acolytes enthusiastically agreed. But the consultants' bafflement increased when the life-line they graciously threw to the philosophy staff – an offer to relocate them within the School of Marketing and Business Enterprise – was unanimously rejected. The next offer Abbott received was a redundancy package, and this he eagerly took. He looked forward to a comfortable retirement in which he could revisit the moral theorists of the eighteenth century.

But he'd reckoned without his wife, Enid – a thin, strident woman who resented his constant presence around the house. Their only child, Daniel, though well into his thirties, still lived there too. A meek, ineffectual soul, he'd only recently found employment as a municipal gardener, but to him she was kindness itself. George, on the other hand, was permitted not a moment's repose. If he sat down with a book, she claimed he was 'under her feet' and sent him to the shops. Even when he locked himself in the lavatory with Bishop Berkeley's principles of knowledge, she banged on the door and reminded him that the dog needed walking. In despair he took himself off to the shed at the bottom of the garden with David Hume tucked under his arm, but within minutes she'd follow and order him to cut the hedges.

Things reached a nadir one winter's day when having dutifully done the week's shopping, George felt he was entitled to an hour or two of his own company down in the shed. When Enid unpacked the groceries, however, she discovered that he'd bought courgettes instead of cucumbers, and was so angry that after going down to berate him she decided without telling him that she'd lock him in the shed for an hour or two. Some time later, and very content with his own company, though barely warmed by the feeble heat of a paraffin stove, George was in no hurry to leave. But he discovered that he'd lost some of his notes on attenuated theism in Hume's *Dialogues Concerning Natural Religion*, and while hunting for them in the log basket that housed most of his papers he put the pile he was already holding on top of the stove. By the time he noticed the blaze his only option was to vacate the shed, but finding the door locked he could make his escape only by smashing the window and pitching himself through it. Miraculously, he suffered no more than a bruised elbow, but there was no further escape from Enid's stern surveillance.

Within a few months, however, relief came from an unexpected quarter – the University of Mixton, an institution George had never even heard of. Mixton seemed an unlikely place for a university. He'd assumed it might have some kind of technical college but nothing more. He received a phone call from one of his old postgraduate students, who was now working at the university and in charge of a newish degree in 'media studies'. George wasn't sure that he knew what media studies was: they hadn't taught it when he was a student, nor at the universities he'd worked at. However, the ex-student was aware that to meet even the inexacting demands of the university's course approvals committee, the degree needed some theoretical underpinning, a cloak, however skimpy, of intellectual respectability. If George were to join the teaching team, then with his background and professorial title he would confer on it a cachet it desperately needed. Would he care to sign up for a couple of days a week and take classes in social and political theory. George hesitated, but not for long: it would get him away from the imperious Enid. Within a few months he was installed at a desk on the Fallowfields campus in a spacious room, the catering in the SCR was

172

excellent, and his new-found colleagues were agreeable and helpful. But now, alas, the party was coming to an end. He was again facing redundancy, and after the tragic fire at Fallowfields he and his colleagues had been transferred to temporary accommodation, a cramped and squalid portakabin on a waterlogged car-park near the town centre. It was about as comfortable as an Anderson shelter. For a short time he pondered whether he should jump ship and return to the life domestic, but the prospect of Enid, full time and full on, was not enticing. Others had adapted to worse things, and so would he.

But now, after five o' clock, there was no one to help him find his email. He couldn't bear the prospect of having to fill the whole thing in again. The frustration that had welled up inside him as he'd plodded through the endless multiple-choice questions broke its banks. Feeling anything but philosophical, Abbott banged the desk in front of him and yelled at the computer screen as if it were a wicked child, 'You bloody sodding bastard. Where is it? You bloody heap of junk! I'm going to smash you up. Where is it? Where the hell is it?' He suddenly hit out with his right fist at the screen in front of him. The unit flew off the rear of the desk and crashed to the floor. Professor Abbott sank his head into his cupped left hand and tucked his bruised right fist under his left armpit.

'Not sure that'll help you find it, prof,' came a voice from behind him.

He looked round, startled. It was Brian. Abbott heaved himself up from the chair and leaning forward, peered over the edge of his desk at the wreckage on the floor.

'Not to worry. You're not the first to be angry with all this new technology. That's why I won't have nothing to do with it. I think I might be able to rustle up a spare for you from the stores. I suppose the screen just went blank on you?'

'No, Brian, I must confess I lost my temper and punched it . . .'

'Yeah, just went blank on you,' repeated Brian with a wink. 'Look, prof, you pop off home and let me sort this. I'll just need to know your university email address and password. What was it you lost?'

The next day Abbott discovered that Brian had been as good as his word – indeed, better. A new VDU sat on his desk, and stuck to it was a note which read QUESTIONAIR GONE OFF OK – B .

37. A DOUBLE WORK-OUT

Kate Huckerby set the cycle to Hill Climb, raised herself from the saddle and put all her strength into the pedals. The only way to dull this agony was to ponder the book she was working on, *A Handbook of Feminist Film Studies*, to be published under the distinguished academic imprint of Albright and Pifford. Had she, she wondered, included a full enough entry on 'auteur' theory – given it a sufficiently historical dimension or adequately inflected it through gender issues? Above her, a gantry of muted TV screens flickered endlessly, lending a nightmarish hue to the muted lighting of the gym. Many of them showed news and sports channels, and a few carried makeover shows and vintage detective series. Kate returned to the thoughts on her book. What about her discussion of sapphic motifs in the later films of Juliana Kretzmer? Was she right to critique them as politically timorous? Or was this too facile a dismissal of a creatively subtle, more nuanced approach?

She was beginning to find these self-questionings as arduous as the Hill Climb so she discarded them for the banal comfort of gazing round the gym. At this time of day, when everyone was on their way home from work, the place was full, and it was only a long board of studies that had kept her from her habit of exercising at off-peak times. Every one of the cycling machines in front of her was whirring, powered by frantic pumping legs, whether plump and smooth or scrawny and hirsute. Her eye ran idly along the row before it fell on the man riding diagonally to her right. He was wearing a sweat-band and a chunky athlete's watch, was dressed in tight black lycra and had a good physique. His frame was not large but it was strong and well proportioned, with full shoulders and a narrow waist. His back and buttocks were tightly muscled, his thighs powerful, and his well turned calves, one of which seemed to bear a large bruise, moved like well-oiled pistons.

Readjusting her spectacles, Kate made two simultaneous and contrasting discoveries. This individual was both highly desirable and Ed Prendergast, the macho man whom the university had hired to get rid of most of its staff and courses and launch vocational programmes – the man she'd saved from making an utter fool of himself during last week's interviews. But preoccupied with the figures on the console of his machine, Prendergast was oblivious to her and everyone else. He was, he thought, pretty fit but could be fitter, and the monastic life he was about to lead would provide him with the opportunity to become so. Soon after coming to Mixton he'd taken a small flat in the town, but his main residence, to which he repaired at weekends when work permitted, was still in London – a chic house in Hackney that he shared with his partner, Sally. She was the chief accountant for a highly successful retail chain and about to fly off on a ten-day trip to the States. For two consecutive weekends, then, Prendergast would find himself without company in London so had decided to spend them in Mixton. It was almost the end of the academic year and he had a fair bit of paperwork to catch up on, but that would still leave him with time on his hands in one of the dullest towns in the country. What better a way to spend it than to really get in shape? He moved the difficulty level up two grades and bent to his task.

'Surprised you can pedal at all after the damage I did to your leg the other day.'

He looked up to see a smiling Kate Huckerby standing beside him. She was wearing a sports top and below her flat, bare midriff, short trunks. Slim legs and shapely ankles ended in a pair of chunky Nike trainers. She was pink and perspiring freely, and inside the sports top her breasts rose and fell rhythmically. Prendergast thought she looked more attractive like this than in her everyday wear. 'I've just done ten kilometres in seventeen minutes,' he said. 'If you can beat that I'll buy you a drink in the bar.'

'You're on.'

The bike next to his had fallen vacant and with a brief, coquettish look at him she eased her bottom on to the saddle, swung her legs on to the pedals and pressed buttons on the console. If this is the monastic life, thought Prendergast, it could have its charms.

Glowing, fragrant, hair clean yet charmingly awry, Kate claimed her reward in the bar. 'Fifteen minutes. What was the difficulty level? It was more like freewheeling downhill!'

'OK, well done. I'll set you a harder task next time. What's it going to be?'

He ordered two large gin and tonics and they sat back in their easy chairs and gazed out at the grounds of Mixton Court Country Club. Over the years the premises had enjoyed several incarnations – as a convalescent home for tubercular miners, a private hotel, and latterly a boys' prep school which had closed only after half its staff had been jailed for paedophilia. It had been built in Victorian times as a mental asylum, for there never had been a Mixton Court in the town other than as a seat for the local magistrates. But during all its uses the grounds had been well tended, and the mature trees, lawns, shrubs and flowerbeds were like an oasis in the wider urban desert.

'I guess I should thank you for kicking me the other day.' He smiled ruefully into his glass and gave it a swill.

'Yes, you should. I'd rather we'd appointed someone else, but didn't want to see her claiming a fortune in compensation. To recoup the money you might've had to sack even more people . . . including me.' She twinkled at him over the top of her glass and took a sip.

'I take it you don't approve of the changes we're introducing.'

'No. I have this sweet old-fashioned view that universities are for the pursuit of knowledge, learning and research. Not boot camps to meet the government's employment targets. But the Philistines have won the day, at least here at Mixton. So if I can't beat you I have to join you – and then I at least get to kick you.'

Prendergast felt agreeably unsettled. He didn't exactly know what 'Philistines' meant but he had a pretty good idea. Most women he met liked his male vigour, his can-do attitude, his impatience with those who theorised, dithered, and did nothing. It was clear that Huckerby despised what he did, and in truth she was rather more of an intellectual than most of the women he mixed with. Sally, for instance, was a sharp girl with a head for figures, but you'd no more think of her as reflective than you'd think of the cat. Yet it also seemed to him that Huckerby didn't find him unattractive. It was almost as if she were baiting him. He shifted in his chair and stared out at a magpie bobbing along the lawn.

'You're rather quiet this evening,' resumed Kate. 'Has all that cycling tired you out? You're normally a veritable lexicon of management-speak. When I'm in meetings with you and you start to talk about learning outcomes, self-managed study, strategic reviews, recruitment targets, staff-student ratios and prior vocational accreditation, I'm so impressed. I feel as though I want to take notes.'

'Very funny. But the problem with you academics' – damn! she'd wrong-footed him again – 'with *us* academics is that we find it hard to live in the real world. We have to comply with the demands of a government desperate to put fifty per cent of young people through uni. Few of these will ever be able to enter by the traditional A-level route or take old-fashioned academic courses. And despite what some of our colleagues think, Mixton University will never be able to attract them. Too many of these courses are already on offer in the major league places.'

'When you say "some of our colleagues" you mean Robert Unthank, don't you?'

Almost every time Huckerby opened her mouth she disconcerted him. It wasn't just that she was shrewd and direct: she had no inhibition about the way she spoke to someone who was, after all, her professional superior. And not only was the effect disconcerting: it was exciting.

'Erm, you're wrong about Robert. Robert's a highly cultured man, and he's been brought in by the Vice as proof that we're not compromising our standards. But Robert's entirely on board and on-message. He understands the need for change. Look,' he added swiftly, glancing at his watch, 'this has all been hungry work. What about some dinner?'

'Round here? Where pie and chips reign supreme?'

'I was thinking of a mile or two further on. It won't be *duc à l'orange* but it shouldn't be toad in the hole either. I'll get us a taxi.'

Dinner with wine mellowed them both. Jagged conversational edges became smooth contours and smiles relaxed into laughter. Kate pointed out that if translated into French, toad in the hole became *crapaud dans le trou*, 'shifting it from the unappetising to

177

the downright disgusting'. It was she who did most of the talking, but she was witty and, notwithstanding the spectacles, unquestionably sexy. While he waved the empty wine bottle at the waiter she went on to amuse him with talk of *cordon bleu* restaurants whose food was so awful that they were more in need of a *cordon sanitaire*. Feeling a growing need to hold his own, he then sought to impress her with an account of his professional achievements, but though she listened politely he could detect no great sign of interest, and she soon cut him short with an invitation.

'How about a coffee or a brandy – at my place.'

Her flat was what might be expected of a scholarly woman who lived alone. Great cliffs of books filled the alcoves on either side of the sitting room fireplace, and while the room wasn't scrupulously clean, there were numerous and effective artistic touches – a large plant here, a notable painting there, a baby grand piano, some interesting bric-à-brac on the mantelpiece and shelves, and a variety of beautifully framed, if rather whimsical photographs. By now they'd drunk a fair amount and Prendergast sank into a long settee while Kate switched on various table lights and standard lamps and went out to the kitchen to make coffee. A long-haired cat sat on top of the piano and regarded him with disdain. He picked up a copy of *Screen* which was lying on the cushion beside him and flicked through it rather helplessly.

'I don't think that's your sort of thing,' said Kate smoothly, returning with a tray.

'Oh? And what *is* my sort of thing?' asked Prendergast, faintly nettled.

She sat down next to him and handed him a coffee and a brandy. 'You,' she said with a teasing, slurry emphasis, 'are Action Man. You don't think about things, you change them. And you like the sort of changes that involve moving people about like counters on a board. Putting new counters down, but better still, getting rid of the old ones. Hiring and firing . . .' She leaned closer to him. 'You're essentially a doer. Come on, why don't you show *me* what you can do?'

She kissed him full on the mouth and cupped a hand on his crotch, squeezing gently. Prendergast rose to the challenge in both senses. He pushed her down on to the settee and began to unbutton her blouse, but she disengaged herself almost immediately. 'Come on. This way,' she said, and led him into her bedroom. He followed meekly enough, but resolved to show her a thing or two when they were stripped for action. He shrugged off his jacket, kissed her face and neck and again tried to remove her blouse, but again she broke away almost immediately.

'Why don't we each take off our own clothes?' she suggested. 'So much less complicated.'

So sitting side by side and in silence they undressed methodically and dropped their clothes into separate piles. When they'd finished Prendergast was just beginning to think that the encounter was turning out to be a little too clinical when she pushed him back on to the bed, removed her spectacles and placed them on the bedside table. She smiled at him brightly and then took the initiative in so pleasurable a way that he was obliged to think of something completely irrelevant – his interminable meetings at the uni – in order to prevent any premature conclusion. Then unease seeped into him. It really was time that he, Ed Prendergast, should assume his rightful place: in the driving seat. He gently disengaged, kissed her briefly and laid her on her back. She smiled short-sightedly up at him but still with a hint of mockery on her lips. He knelt up and arranged her limbs, almost as if setting out knives and forks on a table, and then gave her the full benefit of his portfolio of skills as a lover. Kate panted with growing satisfaction. A rivulet of sweat trickled down between Prendergast's shoulder-blades. But while strength and stamina were important he was not oblivious to the need for delicacy and skill, and he combined his exertions with kisses and caresses. Yet something was not quite right. For all her apparent contentment, the kisses and caresses seemed not to add to it: they were somehow deflected. He felt that she'd not wholly succumbed to him – that whatever his prowess as a lover, she would always be more than equal to him, always hold something back. And quite suddenly she eased him off her and resumed the initiative until matters were concluded to the audible approval of both.

'That was wonderful,' he said.

'I'll call you a taxi,' she replied.

She climbed briskly off the bed. Handing him a box of tissues, she smiled at how much better it was to conduct these assignations at her place rather than somewhere else. But requests to stay were always refused. Better to let him, whoever 'him' might be, get up, get dressed and brave the night air. She had her own life to lead and these trysts did not extend to having her bathroom cluttered up with foreign bodies or the sharing of breakfast. For his part, Prendergast again felt unsure of himself. In spite – because? – of her elusiveness, he'd enjoyed himself immensely and wished to repeat the experience at some point. But there were professional complications which would only be made worse if she told him that she didn't, and he was now keen to get back to his own flat. As he pulled on his trousers, he decided to say something which would sound both appreciative and non-committal.

'Let's have another dinner at some point,' he suggested.

'Let's wait and see. I know what a very busy man you are.' The note of mockery had returned.

38. UNTHANK TAKES SOUNDINGS

It was September, the beginning of the new academic year, and Robert Unthank reflected that it had been a momentous summer. The government, in the form of Brenda Hodges, and the university, in the guise of Turpin, Prendergast and himself, had jointly announced that in a year's time Mixton would begin to offer two-year bachelor degrees, the first public university in the country to do so. It was a move which left only Unthank with an uneasy conscience, and which had not so far provoked the widespread opposition that had occurred when it was leaked back in March. What had changed?

Unthank had to admit that both the timing and the wording of the announcement had been astute. Unlike most other organisms, universities hibernate in the summer. Offices, lecture theatres, seminar rooms, libraries and laboratories are all deserted. So when the announcement was made both staff and students were away – at home, on the beach, scattered about the globe – and their respective trade unions were caught napping. Their public reactions lacked both coordination and conviction. The announcement was also very artfully worded. Much was made of the fact that the two-year degrees would save students a considerable sum of money, and that they would turn Mixton University into 'a dynamic, innovative institution' with a sufficiently powerful vision to set it apart from the rest. Even some of its own staff were perversely pleased that it had achieved a distinction of some kind.

The popular newspapers, in particular, took up the refrain which was begun in the official announcement. Here was a university, they said, which was at last going to tackle the problem of astronomical fees, make students work harder, teach them a useful trade, and force them on to the job market sooner. Perhaps it was also a sense of the public's approval that made the unions so muted in their opposition. It was true, furthermore, that the higher education sector did not display the sense of solidarity that might have been expected. When the news was leaked in March it seemed that the entire sector was being threatened with two-year degrees. Now, it was only Mixton that was being singled out for the trial, apparently with the willingness of its management, so staff and students at other universities kept fairly quiet. They'd have a few more years in which to orchestrate their own opposition. It looked to Unthank as though the government and Mixton were going to get away with it, though a part of him was sorry that they were.

He'd also been reflecting on the results of his visits to local schools back in May, June and July. Most recorded the reactions of their pupils and passed them on. Since he was advised by the covering letters of the careers teachers that some of the more offensive remarks had been removed, the reactions he read were doubly dispiriting. 'If thats uni then give me the abbatoire' and 'Why get a debt bigger than my auntys bum' might have been withheld on the grounds of spelling, if not taste. The remedy, he felt, was to liven up the university's open days which, so he'd been told, had hitherto been limp affairs at which parties of restive schoolchildren had not been won for Mixton by the droning rhetoric of staff from engineering and business studies.

The man to help him was Tom Burley. Burley not only had a national, indeed an international, reputation as an artist, but was a livewire – both outgoing and eccentric. He was exactly the sort of figure who'd appeal to sixth formers on the lookout for an exciting

181

place to study at. Unthank got into his car and drove up to Fallowfields. The surviving outbuildings, in which Burley's office was located, were handsome and well-kept but, for those who remembered the edifice to which they were annexed, wore an air of melancholy. Yet Unthank was heartened by the thought of the exciting developments that would enhance them. As he made his way to Burley's office, he saw two familiar faces.

'Hello, Holly, what are you doing here? I thought your lot were over at Mixton now?'

'We are,' affirmed Holly, 'but Shaun here's going to take me out for a ride in his souped-up Ferrari.'

'Not a souped-up Ferrari but a clapped-out Fiat,' sniggered Shaun, looking at his feet.

'Have a good time. And, Holly, my daughter Dora would like to join you on Facebook. She was very impressed by your exploits. Since you're a media star, I think she'd be really thrilled if I got your autograph.' Holly laughed, found a notebook in her bag, and tore out a page on which she scribbled her signature, underlined with several kisses, hash tag, phone number and email.

'Finally, Holly, I wonder if you'd do a favour for me? I need help with certain university matters.'

Holly nodded vigorously. She thought Unthank was a doll and would willingly help him with anything. He thanked her and promised to be in touch again shortly.

Burley liked to judge people by their initial reaction to his office. Barry Powell loathed it. Prendergast was bemused by it. Unthank rose effortlessly to the challenge it implied: 'Tracey Emin, Grayson Perry, David Hirst . . .' he said, identifying each of the figurines on the large oval desk.

'Not bad,' said Burley. 'It's Damian Hirst, actually, but we might enrol you on our introductory course in finger painting. You also mixed up Matisse and Rousseau, but how did you know it was Grayson Perry?'

'The frock and the five-o-clock shadow were a clue, but my knowledge of contemporary art is pretty limited. Still, I wonder if you'd be willing to help me with what cynics might describe as Mission Impossible – to persuade young people in the schools hereabouts that Mixton University should be their next step.'

'Are all these fired-up wannabes going to apply to Art and Design?'

'Not necessarily, but as a well-known icon of the university, you could persuade them that it's a vibrant – er, funky? – place to study. I've visited a few local schools and didn't arouse much interest. You're much better attuned to the way youngsters think."

'What do you have in mind ?'

'I believe we can do more by bringing them to us than going out to them, so I think we need to liven up our open days. And we should be more responsive to their concerns.'

'Those being?'

'They're not convinced that a books-only, heads-down degree will get them a better job. They think that mixing it with work experience would help. Then they're worried about racking up debts they can't pay off. So two-year courses will be attractive: they'll qualify quicker and do it cheaper.'

'Ah, yes, the two-year degrees. I thought we'd put an end to that idea back in March. But what you management people can't bring in through the front door, you'll smuggle in through a side window. What makes you think I'm willing to go along with it?'

'I'm a reluctant convert to two-year degrees, Tom, but you and I studied for free. And the youngsters realise that studying locally's cheaper than doing it far away. Most of them seem resigned to living with their mum and dad until they're forty. Perhaps we could make that thirty-five.'

'We can have a go. Is funding available?'

'Of course. And another thing. With all due respect to yourself, the uni's recently acquired another icon. Holly Ainscough. Do you think you might be able to find a role for her?'

Though Holly's celebrity rivalled his own, even surpassed it in some spheres, Burley was disposed to be generous. He would use her because he rather liked Unthank, despite the man's patrician air. Turpin was remote and indifferent, Prendergast a mere bully, but Unthank had taken the trouble to come and talk to him, try and charm him, show an interest in what he did. He promised his help and made Unthank a gift of the Grayson Perry statuette, along with some eye shadow.

'Look after him or her. He or she is part of the future.'

183

39. DAY TRIPPERS AND PHOTO BOMBERS

At different times Turpin, Prendergast and Unthank had all visited the Fallowfields site, but had never done so together. They therefore planned to hold one of their meetings at the new campus in order to inspect progress and provide a local 'media opportunity'. The external relations office was instructed to make the arrangements and did so with great zeal, if little judgement. A schedule was fixed, and invitations were sent out to VIPs. Cameras captured the arrival at the site of the three senior managers who had driven there in Unthank's new electric car. They parked at the top of Badgers Lane, and then mounted the UNI-cycles to complete the journey. But first they handed their documents and laptops to Marian, who placed them in a small trailer attached to the back of a fourth bicycle. On its handlebars had been mounted a calorie counter bearing the words 'Faster, Fitter – it's Fallowfields'. Eff words, noted Marian, as she mounted the bike and pedalled gamely after the trio. Soon feeling the strain on her lungs and calves, she resolved that she wouldn't be available for any further media opportunities.

Progress on the site was impressive. The first phase of the university development was beginning to take shape, and on the land that was once part of Compton Farm, about a dozen two- and three-bedroomed properties were rising up within nests of scaffolding. Two Wind Wynders turbines were visible in the distance and much of the ground once used for farming had been smoothed and contoured. Parking their bikes at the university development, Turpin and Prendergast strode into the area where the main atrium was taking shape, while Unthank helped a grateful Marian to dismount and unpack the documents and laptops. The atrium would be a notable feature of the Connected Community initiative, with retail outlets available to staff, students and local residents. At present these were little more than concrete shells, but with the help of the university's catering department the external relations people had improvised a light-hearted foretaste of the future. Inside one of the outlets the caterers had set up tables and chairs and a makeshift counter with a buffet whose dishes were identified with large, zany labels. Greeted by two waiters in silly hats and short capes that were a parody of academic garb, the trio sat down and ordered 'Fresher Fayre'. On the menu were Mortarboard Mash and Don's Delight, as well as a 'sandwich course' and Campus Coffee. It struck Unthank that this was a far cry from the academic life he'd known at Cambridge.

'Ladies and gentlemen,' preened Turpin, 'this could be our *annus mirabilis*. Now, let's get the guided tour under way. Where's Holly? Oh, when you've finished, of course, Marian.'

Still hot and breathless, Marian had only just begun the Diet Coke and 'glad-u-ate' sandwich that Unthank had hastily ordered for her when a smiling Holly arrived to lead them all away

AFFECTING ME, AFFECTING YOU - continued
The private dairy of HOLLY RACHEL AINSCOUGH!!

When I handed in my Journal last term I got a really rubbish mark for it. A bare pass. Dr Chandler said while she wasnt too fussed about grammer and spelling it was hard to make sence of sometimes and the ideas were nave and banale. Well sod her because I really enjoyed writing it so now Im going to turn it into a private dairy.

Taylor keeps saying what a turn-up for the books. I made them all really antsy over the library sit-in but theyve now forgotten and forgiven and Im Top Girl again. Dr U has asked me to be a Campus Scout for the VIPs who visit the Fallowfields site. I get free outfit of my choosing – cool or what! And theres always lots of people taking film and photos.

Dr U also wants me to do publicity for Tom Burlys 2-4-3 campagne but Im not so keen on that. Not only is Burly raving mad, but part of the sit-in was to campaine against 2-4-3. So what kind of a berk will i look like changing sides. Gary seems keen for me to do it though. Sometimes i cant work him out.

Turned up for the Big Three today. Love Dr U but not so keen on Turps and Ghastly but obvious mustnt show it. Picked up the other Premium Punters – Mr. H MP and the Housing Councellor, Ejerton or some name. Dr U calls him A. E. House Man and gives me big

smile. Doh!!!??? – ???? Castles, ed. of local paper plus some of their bobbers and nodders, and Barry Powell, Shaun's HoD – a GATE CRASHER!!!

We take the usual route – over to where the Green With Envy houses are going up. Mr House man gives his usual spiel but this time theyve got the people whove already bought some of the homes. Theyre all lined up outside the houses - arms linked, smiles and lovey-dovey, and kitted out like Robin Hood or Maid Marian all holding up a notice saying Green All Over. I joined them and I'm like Beyoncie at Mumsnet and the Big Three and the others but just as the pics are about to be taken someone in green top, shorts and tights with an orange safety helmet does a photo-bomb, squeezing in next to Hunter. Its none other than that cow who did those stunts last year, got in the lift in the buff with the Big three. Within two shakes of her ass she and Hunter are Best of Friends. Oh yeah!!

We finished of with a look round the work thats still going on and surrounded by hordings. A lot of the hordings now have these Luv Uni – Luv Mixton bits of art on like comic strips. Couple of kids going into Bog Standard Uni – then asleep in lectures – then holding up placards which show a Debt Thermeter with the red up to the £15 thou mark, then looking ten years older – then at degree ceremony with notice saying Sponsored by Friendly Fertiliser Ltd – then with speech bubbles saying I ow 5 Billion Quid then selling Big Issue outside Mixton Poundland. The second set was about getting rich quick via Mixton: I told Shaun Im still waiting. People got very excited by the new wind turbines but seen one seen them all.

RESULT! Next day Im in the papers again, Marian said come up and see her and have a look as I had come out well in the ones shed taken. I had, even when that cow pushed in. All the papers did the same picture

The Mixton Chronicle called it 'Holly Gets Even Greener'.

The Builders Times 'New Construction Delivers on Carbon Targets'.

And the Uni Mag 'Its Green For Go at Fallowfields'.

So whose the photo bomber then? Must be one of Burlys life models – pops up pops off. She was all over Hunter like a rash. But if she tries something like that again I'll axe her legs. Bloody good legs though – the B*tch!

40. TWO CLOSE ENCOUNTERS

'Everybody says you were brilliant as the campus scout. Did you have a good time?' Gary was lying on his back, and Holly was sprawled on his chest, munching languidly. He opened his mouth and she popped a chocolate into it.

''Course I did. It were like making a comeback after the sit-in.'

The sit-in was still a sore point between them. This might be a time to apply further balm. 'I know you feel it ended badly. But I thought you'd all made your point very effectively. And, Holly babes, it couldn't have lasted for ever.'

'Even so, I'd like to know how security got in and turfed us all out. Some bastard must have shopped us.'

Gary shifted underneath her. She suddenly felt rather heavy and the chocolate was sticking in his throat. 'It gave you star status. And there's no reason why fame and fortune can't return. Have another of those chocs I bought you.'

'You've never brought along chocs before. You trying to get round me?'

'Certain parts of you,' smirked Gary. 'I know we fought hard against the idea of two-year degrees, but they're becoming a reality – at least at Mixton – and we're just going to have to accept it. Even better, we've got to turn it to our, er your, advantage. If Unthank wants Burley to use you in some of his stunts, er, promotional activities, why not go along with them?'

'But why me ?' Holly planted a sticky, chocolate-coloured kiss on his chest.

'You're a big name, a recognisable face. You're the Mixton brand. The youngsters love you. You'll pull them into the uni by the hundred. Unthank reckons that 'cos of the publicity you got during the sit-in, you've bumped up even this year's recruitment figures.'

'But I'd be working for Burley, and he's a nutter.'

'So what? Didn't he tell you that Unthank'd pay your expenses?'

'What does that mean – bloody bus fares?'

'Probably a clothing allowance, like you got for being a campus scout. And you'd need some make-up. Which is expensive. And new shoes.'

Gary drew a pound sign in the air. There's no aphrodisiac like money, he thought, as Holly began to express her appreciation in an immediate and dramatic manner.

Kate opened her eyes and looked around at the unfamiliar bedroom. The abundance of mirrors gave it an uncomfortably al fresco feeling. Some reflected the sky outside the windows, others threw light around the room and from the door of one wardrobe to another. Another mirror with a highly decorated frame stood on the bedside table beside her, and yet another with the etched motifs of orchids graced the dressing table. Between the two windows were pictures of African origin, majestic women in brightly coloured clothes that were tied round waists or thrown over shoulders. There were no photographs that she could see, but on the floor was a tangle of her own clothes. Her eyes went up to the ceiling on whose whiteness a handful of luminescent stars had been irregularly stuck, presumably to replicate one of the constellations. This could not have been a man's bedroom.

'Tea or coffee?' Loren's voice was mellifluous, deep. She was fully dressed, ready to start her day. 'Of course, I only have green tea,' she added with a half smile. Was this self-directed humour or the truth? She remembered why she was where she was and why she should really be somewhere else.

Yesterday evening she'd gone to a cinema in Leicester, the only one relatively near to Mixton that might deserve the name 'art house'. Directed by Ousmane Sembène, the film was one she'd normally have ordered for her university film club. But sometimes she needed to get away from both the uni and her flat and savour the atmosphere of a real cinema. The big screen, the shared experience and the anticipation of losing herself in a drama always sent a childish tingle up her spine. So when she saw that Sembène's last creation was showing within travelling distance, she determined to make the effort. But she was disappointed. The film addressed the big African issue of polygamy, a favourite with directors wanting to draw attention to what was seldom discussed in other media. But she thought the film tried too hard to find a fresh perspective, the irony was too delicate, the observation too cool for the subject. In the end it seemed that polygamy caused the wives no worse problems than could be offset by knowing smiles and barbed witticisms.

Emerging from the cinema and feeling she'd slightly wasted her evening, she bumped into a woman and began to apologise when she recognised her as Loren Lafayette. This was faintly embarrassing. Greetings were nervous, suffused with an affected warmth, and followed by an uneasy pause.

'Hey, I gotta go get the bus back to Mixton,' said Loren, glancing at her man's watch. 'Automobile's broke and won't get fixed till tomorrow.'

She was reluctant to accept the offer of a lift, finally doing so on condition that when they got back Kate would come in for a drink. As they drove, Kate found that prospect more and more tempting. She reminded herself once or twice that she'd been cool about Loren Lafayette's appointment as head of the new department. But she found they were of one mind on the weaknesses of the Sembène film. And Loren's conversation, mainly about the challenges she encountered as an American who was settling in to Mixton, was intriguing enough. Struggling to preserve some detachment, Kate was disturbed by another sensation. Loren was physically attractive. She was both spiky and sinuous, and, despite the seat belt, sat as if almost directly facing Kate. Her observations about life and her own situation were impersonal and reasoned, yet physically she seemed to be offering herself. Her expression and her light touches on Kate's sleeve hinted at a desire she herself was beginning to feel.

Kate sat down on Loren's sofa and barely had time to look round at the sitting room before her host brought two enormous glasses of wine and settled herself beside her. 'Now,' said Loren, clinking their glasses and curling one leg underneath her, 'tell me about you.' Kate had barely begun to gather her thoughts when Loren leaned forward, took the glass from her hand, and kissed her almost questioningly on the lips. Despite the suddenness of the gesture, Kate was ready with her answer. Their mutual exploration extended further, and taking their glasses and a bottle with them they eventually made their way to the bedroom in which she found herself next morning.

'Bloody hell!' Kate now said to herself. 'Coffee please, strong, black, no sugar,' she said to Loren.

'Fine. It's in the kitchen. Can you just stay tucked up here while I get Forest off to school? And look, I'm ever so late. Can I take your automobile?'

'Well, I suppose . . . What was that about Forest and school?'

'Forest. My daughter. Thanks, I've got the keys. Back in twenty.'

Kate got out of bed and went to the window. Loren and a girl were getting into her car. What sort of household had she stumbled into? Her one-night stand had been impetuous enough but, while Loren was unlikely ever to know, she'd also enjoyed it with someone whose appointment to the uni she'd questioned. However, Kate was a rational woman whose intellect was only occasionally ruled by her appetites, and she was determined to justify, to herself if not to Prendergast and Unthank, her suspicion that Loren was carrying some kind of dark secret.

She recalled the occasional encounters they'd had since her arrival. Loren was already well known around the university and beyond, not surprising since black women professors were hardly commonplace in Mixton. Especially, she thought, black women lesbian professors with children. They'd once chatted briefly in the canteen over coffee, but the difference of their disciplines meant they'd struggled to find common ground. Clearly, however, they shared two interests, African cinema and . . .

Kate washed and dressed hurriedly. What clues might the house reveal? She went downstairs and walked quickly from room to room. There were few signs that a child lived there – one or two games, three or four books, a small hooded jacket. There was a piano with scores on the stand that would be suitable for beginners, a pair of trainers on the floor, and on a chair something that looked like a handbag but could be a satchel. She'd been in no state to notice these things last night. She went back upstairs to discover what else she'd missed. A bright, girlish room with a single bed, a computer, books, an ark filled with soft animals, and some art work which Kate thought might have been produced by a child in the early stage of secondary school. On the walls two posters, one of a well known model, the other of a male pop star. She crossed the landing to the remaining room, whose door was shut. The handle turned to reveal Loren's study. A lap-top lay open on the desk in front of her. Kate touched the pad and an electronic diary for the day appeared on the screen. Kate looked at it and realised why Loren was up early and eager to get moving. She was due at the university at nine, with back-to-back meetings throughout the day. Kate moved the cursor to open up the next day, and then the day after that. All were predictable, meetings with the VC and other senior colleagues, then with one or two key members of the local community, an appointment with the estates management people. A busy lady, but nothing out of the ordinary. She moved on to the following month and opened a day at random. What she saw gave her a shock.

She ran down the stairs and into the kitchen. She spooned instant coffee into a mug and slopped in some tepid water from the electric kettle. She got out a bowl, shook in some muesli, splashed on some low fat milk, stuck a spoon in and put the bowl on the table next to the coffee. Then she took a piece of kitchen roll and made a deliberately clumsy attempt to clear up the spillage. She went back upstairs, looked out of the window to check that her car was still absent and returned to the lap-top. What she saw were future appointments, meetings that were not physical but via video links. She glanced round the desk and saw the camera at the back and the loudspeakers on each side. All unexceptionable for an international academic whose specialism took the world as its work-space. But the names of Loren's contacts were well-known. They were all members of 4DK, an American organisation which was thought to have links with some of the more extreme eco-jihadist groups. The name stood for 'Four Degrees Kills', itself shorthand for the proposition that if average temperatures on earth rose by a mere four degrees Celsius, most of its life forms would be imperilled. Kate sympathised with those who demanded conservation of the planet and strong action to offset climate change. But the activities of 4DK were a step too far. Had the university, Kate wondered, taken a viper to its bosom? Had those academic references, which she now struggled to bring back to mind, been hinting at something she'd not fully understood? Despite her protestations at the time, it was largely intuition that had caused her to be doubtful about Loren Lafayette. What was the wording that one of her former professors had used?

She took the department forward into challenging territory that might well have been eschewed by someone of a less determined and radical intellect. Did that translate as 'dangerous trouble-maker who could have destroyed the entire institution'? Did it come from the same lexicon in which 'extraordinary rendition' was a euphemism for kidnap and torture?

She minimised the web page, clicked on the email icon and opened the inbox. Among the senders were some of the names she'd recognised. She clicked and scrolled. Some remarks were edgy but hardly eco-jihad stuff. Some began warily but grew less reserved as she read on, prudence soon yielding to passion. This was hot material. She looked round for a means of copying some of it. Oh, for a memory stick. Could she forward the emails to herself and then delete the sent items? Oh, God. Too long and too risky. What to do? She pulled up one of the most outspoken emails and pressed PRINT. Nothing. Then, on a low table to the side of the desk, a wireless-connected printer suddenly clattered into life, giving her a start. 'Print, damn you, print!' she muttered, racing back to the window to look for Loren's return.

Kate heard the front door open, and as Loren appeared in the kitchen took another spoonful of muesli and a swig of coffee. 'Helped myself. Sorry, I've made a bit of a mess but I've got to rush, too.'

'Don't worry. Really grateful for the automobile. You're not going into the uni, are you?' Kate decided very swiftly that she wasn't. 'No problem, I'll get a taxi.'

While waiting for her taxi, Loren cleared Kate's dish and mug, and was surprised at how cold she drank her coffee.

A few days later, Kate skyped her former colleague in the States, telling her what she knew of Loren but not revealing the source of her information. 'It's a bit of a surprise to see her over here, Cassie, especially at a minor league uni like Mixton. I'd have thought she'd attract wider interest over there.'

'I know the name,' said Cassie. 'We were both at the University of Wyoming, but at different times. She left a while before I joined. I'll make inquiries. When am I going to see you?'

'You're seeing me now,' replied Kate.

'Don't, that makes it worse. You know what I mean.'

'Well, find me a job over there. Shout as soon as you see something.' In one of their little rituals, Kate puckered her lips close to the camera and Cassie did the same.

41. SOME OF THE EARTH HAD MOVED

Brian felt it was time he paid a visit to Fallowfields. Construction had been going on for the best part of four months, and he should by now be able to get a sense of what the whole development would look like and what challenges surveillance would pose. It was vast. At the Fallowfields end, the shells of some interesting new structures were rising round the old annexe, still home to the Department of Art and Design. Further away, towards the Compton Farm end, the outlines of a micro-village of mixed housing were already apparent. Two-storey portakabins were stacked along the perimeter, and cranes presided over several of the buildings. The entire site was ringed by a hoarding with port-holes cut into it to allow outsiders to watch progress. Brian mused that you'd need to be pretty sad to come all the way out here just to look at fat blokes with hard hats and a rear cleavage. But outside the hoarding and next to the annexe was another and more curious structure, a large tent with BIG TOP emblazoned across its roof. Brian peeped inside. It was equipped with tiered seating to serve as a lecture theatre, and setting out a chair and table on the podium was Mitch, the ESMO on duty at Fallowfields that day.

'Whose is this tent, Mitch?'

'Tom Burley's.'

'He don't need a tent. Art and Design wasn't damaged in the fire.'

Mitch straightened up, and gave him a shrewd look. 'You know Burley, he'll turn any situation to his advantage. Feed his ego. Claims he needed it 'cos he lost the shared lecture rooms in Fallowfields. Bollocks, if you ask me.'

Brian stepped back from the entrance and saw that to one side of it was a notice board bearing the message:

Here is art under canvas, not on it!
Please leave the following outside:
Muddy shoes
Copies of the Daily Mail
Artistic prejudices
On the other side was another notice:
The following are refused admission under all circumstances:
Breughel
Buffet
Constable
Durer
van Dyck
Powell
Prendergast
Turpin
If you see any of the above, call Security immediately!

Brian made his way over to the open gates in the hoardings which provided the main access to the site. Lorries rumbled in and out through a sea of churned mud. To complete his survey of the site he'd need to get closer to the buildings, and indeed get inside them – preferably when few other people were around. Time for him to pursue his subterfuge . . . The site manager's office was right beside the gates. Brian tapped on the open door with an air of timorous respect. 'You Brian?' The manager was sitting at his desk and eyed Brian's ESMO uniform. To enhance his authenticity, Brian had also pinned to his uniform an ID tag with a mugshot which he'd concocted in the privacy of his den. 'As I said on the phone, we already have our own security staff here twenty-four seven. But so much stuff gets nicked off of these sites that the more the merrier. If you're local and work here, you might even recognise some of the toe-rags what are doing it. Still, you'd better make yourself known to the lads. Security's second cabin on the right after the portaloos. And if they're happy to have your help, I'm happy.'

Brian did make himself known to the lads and won their happiness with a show of cheerful friendliness and a generous distribution of Twix bars. Within ten minutes he'd amused them with a colourful account of what he would do to any toe-rag he managed to catch, distributed his phone number so that they could always find him, and gained their ready assent to the fact that for the next six months he'd need to get into Fallowfields not only during the week but over the weekends.

As he left the site with an all-hours security pass in his pocket, he was reflecting on what a wonderful social catalyst the Twix bar is when he noticed a Prius drive up Badgers Lane and slowly circle the site. It stopped immediately behind a large lorry, and an elderly man struggled out of the vehicle and looked about him in bewilderment. Then he went round to the other side of the car, opened the door and kneeling on the passenger seat, put his head down and began to rummage in the glove box. He was oblivious to the rhythmic beeps of the lorry as it started to reverse. The warning shouts of the onlookers were in vain. The car was pushed inexorably backwards and rammed into the side of a half-demolished wall.

A few moments later, Professor George Abbott climbed out of the mass of compacted metal, confused but unscathed. He looked round for a face he might recognise. 'Ah, Brian, is that you? You see, I came up to Fallowfields because I normally take the bus to the new place, but on this occasion Enid let me have the car, so I just sort of took it on its usual route. Because I'd forgotten, you see. And then realising my mistake I was looking for my map in the glove compartment.'

Brian gave him a lift back to Mixton and nodded understandingly as Abbott sought to share his preoccupation with a Scottish empress called David Hume. Why an empress should exist in Scotland and be called David was beyond Brian, but he'd long ago stopped expecting to hear anything intelligible from academics. 'Thank you so much,' said Abbott as he got out. 'I fear Enid will be displeased. Do you think I'll be able to claim on the insurance?'

42. ECO-WARRIORS UNITE!

When Professor Lafayette emailed every student in the university to propose the formation of an eco society, there was widespread curiosity. The email was rather charmingly phrased. It wasn't for her, she said, to presume to tell the students what to do, but she'd welcome the opportunity of meeting with anyone who was interested in forming one and exploring with them what might be possible. Lafayette was seen by most students as a rather exotic addition to Mixton's academic staff. There were few black lecturers at the university, and she was the first to have been appointed professor. The area of her appointment added further spice. Her department was already staffed in readiness for the launch of its degree in the next academic year. To invite all students to get involved in green issues in advance of having any students of her own seemed generous and inclusive.

About seventy people gathered in the lecture theatre for the inaugural meeting. Holly noticed several who had helped to organise the sit-in. Shaun, Taylor and Donny were there, along with Aisha Khan, another Media Studies student, whom Holly sat next to. Aisha had used the library sit-in as material for a project for one of her modules.

'We all thought you did wicked, Holly. I know they got you out but you did great while you were in. It was so much better than just groaning and moaning.Sioux said you took her side against the deadbeats and the macho brigade.'

'Seems a long time ago now, Aisha. Gary said– ' Holly swore under her breath. 'Once we were inside one of my, er, mates gave me some idea what we should be doing 'cos he thought we weren't serious, just having a lark.'

She really needed to stop dropping Gary's name. He'd been a great mentor, but her feelings about him had become slightly mixed. He'd egged her on, then told her to pull out. Now he'd made her change sides, and do stuff for the top brass, and was telling her she was brilliant and buying her chocolates. If she didn't love him, she'd have dumped the bastard by now. There were plenty of other fish in the sea, she thought, glancing at Shaun. Shaun smiled back devoutly.

'Speak of the devil, here's Sioux now.'

Sioux was a smiling, dainty girl who from the waist downwards nevertheless resembled a storm trooper. She wore baggy green camouflage trousers tucked into huge army boots. Above the waist, she was slight. She was wearing a sleeveless khaki vest that revealed an array of tattoos on her upper arms. She had piercings in her mouth and nose and her hair was drawn tightly into multi-coloured braids. She looked like Medusa after a visit to a paint shop.

When La Lafayette, as they'd already started to call her, made her entrance she silenced the lecture theatre. Academics are not generally known for their dress sense. At Mixton the men fell into two categories, those who wore a tired jacket and baggy cords and those who adopted a shabby T-shirt and dirty jeans. The women were scarcely less dowdy, favouring shapeless smocks and leggings or dull blouses and dun coloured skirts and trousers. Lafayette was astonishingly different. She wore a long flowing dress in bright blue and orange. Her long ear rings turned and sparkled in the lecture room lights, and embedded in her hair, which was dramatically tied up, was what looked like a sapphire. She walked elegantly to the podium, placed her notes on the lectern, looked up and bestowed a warm and winning smile on her audience.

'As you know, I've been appointed by the university to head up the new Department of Environmental and Ecological Studies. Our first students will be arriving next year, but I don't want to wait until then before we start to put green ideas into practice. I think we should be the green conscience of Mixton. We should draw up a list of issues that we want to progress over the next year. That way, others'll see things happening and want to join us. I'll be working hard with my colleagues here to make us greener and better. And I'll make sure you know what we're doing because I'm going to persuade the uni to set year-on-year targets to show we're about actions, not just words. This is an issue that unites us all, staff, students of all disciplines, the local community. So I'm here to get the ball rolling, and, along with my colleagues in our new department, to offer advice and information. But this is intended to be a forum where you students can trade ideas. You need to do it because you want to do it, not because anyone tells you to. Now I'm going to ask my good friend Sioux to speak.'

Sioux left her place in the auditorium next to Holly and Aisha, and strode to the podium. Slight though she was, Sioux had presence. She proposed a Mixton Manifesto on how the university could colour itself green and an eco monitoring unit to ensure that it was happening. The unit, she believed, should name and shame the

197

back-sliders and praise the trail-blazers. She wanted help in determining the current carbon benchmark and how best to ensure that Mixton would join the top ten per cent of the greenest universities in the UK. She then asked the audience to shout out their proposals. These ranged from the piously impractical – everyone should forswear motor transport of any kind for the next five years – to the solidly achievable, everyone should establish their own carbon footprint; and from the blatantly delinquent – frackers should be sent death threats – to the vaguely aspirational.

'We've got to grab people's attention and force them to go green.'
'Blockade the staff car-park and make them walk.'
'Boycott the student buses till they go electric.'
'Burn Jeremy Clarkson's books.'
'Burn effigies of Jeremy Clarkson.'
'Burn Jeremy Clarkson.'

This was greeted with a loud cheer.

Professor Lafayette rose to her feet and said she'd leave them to continue their discussion, but before she left she wanted to show them a short film entitled 'De-Nial Is Not Just a River in Egypt'. At first it seemed to be no more than a montage of disparate clips – of icebergs, deserts and the mean dwellings of the wretched of the earth. But these were soon succeeded by what must have been computer-generated imagery. Continents of ice melted, fell apart, merged with the waters surrounding them. Deserts swiftly encroached on the fertile areas that bordered them. Slums in the Philippines and Bangladesh were lapped by rising waters, then collapsed in the flood and were swept away. All this was intercut with clips of politicians making statements at press conferences. Some were declaring their commitment to carbon reduction, a decreased dependency on fossil fuels, a desire for sustainable energy and a secure and happy planet. Others were stating emphatically 'The climate's always changing, nothing new there', 'Global warming is nonsense', and one American even averred that he was 'Happy to burn coal – and put a few eco-nuts on top of the fire'. The closing sequence showed water lapping at the Houses of Parliament, and a well-known climate-change denier apparently drowning as the Thames burst its banks. A speech bubble was superimposed above the individual with the words 'Well, maybe a *bit* of warming', and the film closed to loud laughter and clapping.

In another and distant part of the building, a separate screen flickered into life and automatically sequenced through the cameras providing the feeds to it. Most of the images were of empty rooms but a few showed staff who were staying on, and one revealed George Abbott, who was going through his usual pre-leaving ritual of patting his pockets and rummaging in his briefcase. The meeting in the lecture theatre was coming to a noisy end and Sioux was holding her arms aloft amid shouts of approval. Brian checked the balance and focus and then zoomed in on a smiling individual in the audience. 'So our young activists are planning to change the world,' he reflected, dipping his hand into a packet of marmite flavoured Quavers. 'But, Holly love, what you see in a plonker like Gary Dorn will always be a mystery to me.'

The plonker remained as influential as ever. That evening in Holly's bed he elicited a full account of the inaugural meeting, then poured cold water on her involvement. 'Stick with the 2-4-3 campaign. That's where the perks are.'

'Why shouldn't I do both? I already do green stuff as a campus scout. Dr Unthank thinks I'm great.'

'Yeah, but if this eco lot start doing demos and sit-ins, the management will just see you as a trouble-maker. Then you'll lose your job as campus scout – and everything that goes with it.'

Holly frowned and ran her finger round Gary's left nipple. He was probably right. She'd better keep the eco society at arm's length. But not to worry. Shaun, Taylor and Sioux would keep her informed of developments.

43. CARDS ON THE TABLE

Gemma Giddings and Ben Frampton, the Learn and Earn administrators, were both out, and Gary and Kate were conferring in the office that had been assigned to them. It gave them more privacy than the open-plan spaces in the portakabins, and Brian had furnished it with comfort, if not taste. As well as two desks and chairs, there were blinds for the window, a microwave and an electric kettle. The walls had been repainted and the floor carpeted. Brian had added a final touch of which he was proud. He'd rescued a large framed painting of Princess Diana which a mate of his, who ran a bric-à-brac stall in Mixton market, was just about to throw into a skip – an act which for Brian bordered on sacrilege. Dusting it down, he bore it reverently to the main university building and nailed it high up on the wall of their office.

Gary had sought this meeting with Kate, not altogether willingly in the light of their personal history. But it became necessary when Prendergast had casually mentioned that after the Media Studies degree came to an end in eighteen months' time, he was minded to retain Kate Huckerby as Gary's collaborator.

She nevertheless opened the discussion. 'What's Prendergast keeping you on for?'

'I'm supervising the, er, Learn and Earn duo,' muttered Gary sheepishly. 'And now he wants me to help push the 2-4-3 agenda. Said you might help.'

'What's the payback? Has he said you can stay on after our degree's closed?' Her manner was that of a schoolmistress extracting admissions from a naughty child.

'Yes – but nothing in writing, and I don't know for how long. Is he promising you anything?'

'Nothing I want. I didn't come into this profession to be a bureaucrat, I want to write books and teach. I'm looking round for other jobs, and there's not much about. But I want to avoid a car crash – unlike the lady up there.' She nodded at the portrait.

'Same here,' agreed Gary.

'I've tried not to get too involved in uni matters, and I certainly don't want to take the lead on this 2-4-3 nonsense,' continued Kate, who was rather more interested in describing her situation than in hearing about his. 'But I said that despite my reservations I'd be willing to give you some support.' She made no mention of the circumstances in which she'd expressed her willingness and the condition she'd imposed that her contract be extended for another three years. 'So how you going to peddle this stuff?'

Gary explained that he'd arranged meetings with groups of staff in parallel with the university's advertising and recruitment campaigns for the two-year courses. 'I don't like it any more than you do. But I can't see an alternative – except more and more course closures.'

Kate adjusted her glasses and squared her shoulders. 'The university has to promote itself as a front runner, ahead of the curve and at the cutting edge. We've seen the future and we know it works.'

'You sound like Prend – '

'It's intentional. If we don't act like organ grinders we'll be taken for monkeys.'

'Right, let's go and deal with the first group.'

As expected its reactions were hostile. Two years was not a sufficient amount of time for students to graduate, whether in terms of knowledge and expertise or character development. Nor did an extended teaching year allow time for staff to prepare lectures, research and publish the material that was integral to their work. But then the remarks and questions became personal.

'Dr Dorn, er Gary, can you assure us that these proposals have the full support of the Socialist Workers Party ?'

'Gary, can you tell us how these proposals express that Marxist doctrine that is so dear to you?'

He was nevertheless prepared. 'I can. We'll be producing not workers by hand or brain but by brain *and* hand. We want them to learn practical skills alongside theoretical ones and we don't want them to leave uni with enough debt to last a lifetime. Perhaps anyone here can advise me if they graduated owing anyone a sum in excess of thirty thousand pounds? . . . I thought not. So be careful about wishing on others what you were lucky enough to avoid.'

Kate thought this a deft stroke. Dorn might be an odious, randy sod but when cornered he could put up a fight. And she had some weapons of her own.

'But all we'll be doing is generating fodder for McJobs," complained another member of the group. 'Burger flippers in a drive-thru, goods packers at Amazon.'

'And these proposals are a unilateral change in our conditions of employment,' said another. 'None of us came here to work a fifty-week year.'

Gary was about to reply that some never came to work a twenty-week year but thought better of it. The exchanges went back and forth until the meeting ground to a disgruntled end. They went for coffee before the next group arrived and agreed it hadn't gone too badly. Thirty minutes later the third group of staff had started to file in when Gary's phone rang. 'Sorry,' he grimaced, 'Gemma and Ben need to talk to me' – and leaning over to murmur 'this lot shouldn't be too bad', departed hastily.

Another group, more rows of clenched faces. Kate met the familiar objections by playing up the increased numbers of furloughs which would be available, along with enhanced salaries and remission from teaching for part of the year. Few were appeased, and, growing tired, she decided to resort to an easier option: threats. 'This is the way it has to go at places like Mixton. We're just too expensive because most of our students will never repay the cost of their tuition. We either adopt two-year degrees or become part of LetzLern, one of the private providers now pitching to the government.'

'Scare-mongering nonsense!' someone shouted. 'We're not going to get those third-rate charlatans here.'

'Aren't we, though?' Kate was suddenly enjoying the fight. 'I've taught in the States. They're shifting from the Harvard/Caltech model to one much more like Wal-Mart, where the student-customers fill their trolleys more quickly, attend less, pay less and don't always end up with what they wanted to buy. But that's the trend. As in so much else – extreme wealth, extreme poverty, extreme obesity, extreme religion and extreme politics – where the US leads, we follow. The only question is how quickly. You need to understand that many of this country's secondary schools are now run by private enterprise. The universities are next in line.'

The group's blood was up, too. What about travel in vacations, someone asked – students broadening their minds, seeing new places, meeting new people? Her response was blunt. 'You're reminiscing about your own time at uni. Hitch-hiking to India during the long vac. Sleeping on the beach in Kerala. What the youngsters do now is buy a brief package deal in the Med, get hammered, arrested and fined, and come back with a hangover and a sexually transmitted disease.' This provoked an outcry, and she was inwardly ashamed of resorting to such a stereotype but needs must. If peddling dodgy degrees would buy her the time to get a post she wanted, and this is what she had to say to justify them, so be it.

Now the attack became legalistic. Nothing in their conditions of service, said a lecturer in leisure and hospitality studies, obliged them to teach two-year degrees. And nothing forbade it, returned Kate. Then, with a faintly long-suffering air, she reached down to a document case beside her left foot. She opened it and waved a piece of paper at the audience. 'This is a copy of a recent advert for a temporary lectureship at Mixton . . . and these,' she reached down into a briefcase beside her right foot and produced a bunch of files, 'are the fifty applications for the post.'

'So what?' came voices from the audience. 'Fifty applications are what you'd expect.'

Kate waited for the hubbub to abate. 'I agree,' she said quietly, 'but these represent the *short* list – from eight hundred applications. And no disrespect, but may I add that a lot of the applicants seem better qualified than some current staff –which is not, of course, to say that they'd display the same level of dedication and commitment.' That's settled their hash, she thought in the sudden silence that followed. And no thanks to that skiving weasel, Gary Dorn.

44. SHOCK, HORROR AND CAKE

Brian was in his secret office when his phone started to vibrate. He had a quick check on the video screen to see if there was anyone in the corridor outside before he took the call.

'Is that Brian? It's Professor Abbott – George. I've got water coming in through the roof, Brian. What should I do?'

Brian resisted the temptation to tell Abbott he could take a shower. 'Is it coming just, you know, drip, drip, drip?'

'No, Brian, it's splish, splosh, splash. Ha, ha, onomatopoeia.'

'I thought you said it was water.'

'It's turning into a deluge. Do you think you could help?'

'I'll come and have a look, prof. Where are you now?'

'I'm in the big office in Portakabin D.'

As he made the short drive in his Cavalier it struck Brian as odd that very clever people like Abbott were almost babyish in their dependence on others to get them over the simple hurdles of life. And in his worship of ideas the poor old boy seemed to be at war with the physical world. He recalled Abbott's fight with his computer, and then the encounter with the reversing lorry at Fallowfields. He shook his head and chuckled.

When he opened the door to the portakabin he couldn't see anybody. He looked at his watch and recognised that at seven fifteen in the evening it would hardly be buzzing. But Abbott hadn't exaggerated, a curtain of water was running down the far wall. Something rather serious had gone wrong in the roof, but where was Abbott? As he walked towards the prof's desk, Brian was suddenly halted by a horrifying sight. Lying motionless on the floor behind a filing cabinet was a pair of betrousered legs and shoes.

'Holy shit, what on earth has he done now?' exclaimed Brian.

On his back and with mouth half-open, Abbott was clutching an electric plug which he'd attempted to remove from the wall socket without first turning off the power. Brian now faced an unsavoury dilemma. In the health and safety course that all ESMOs had to take, he'd learned about mouth-to-mouth resuscitation. But that had been with a dummy on which their instructor had drawn the face of a well-known film star with inviting lips. Still, there was nothing else for it. Trying to make his mind a blank and focus on the task before him, Brian closed his eyes and bent his mouth slowly towards Abbott's. But as he did so Abbott murmured, 'Oh, Enid, really my dear, I didn't think you still . . . Enid?' To his great relief, the old boy was coming round.

The following morning, to save Abbott from further catastrophe, Brian moved his stuff into a corridor in the main building. Because the corridor was no longer a thoroughfare it had become a storage space for broken furniture, and was quite near to Brian's office, so Brian could keep an eye on him. Amid the clutter he found an old desk with three good legs, and made good the fourth one by propping it with a pile of study guides and books of regulations that had filled one of the shelves in his secret office. Then he cleared enough space round the desk to accommodate George's filing cabinet. 'You'll be alright here till the repairs can be sorted. The cleaners'll look after you.' And the cleaners did, especially Janice Hancock, who took him to her heart, for Abbott showed an engaging mixture of courtesy and absent-mindedness. She thought it a disgrace that a professor should be parked on his own in a corridor as if he were a disruptive pupil. Abbott, of course, scarcely noticed the isolation, but what he did notice was Janice's kindness. As her shape attested, Janice was an enthusiastic baker, and each day brought George a very generous sample of her produce – slabs of fruit cake, Victoria sponge, Battenberg, coffee and walnut cake, parkin, Swiss roll, gingerbread, lemon drizzle cake, blueberry muffins, doughnuts, chocolate brownies. And clutching a mug of tea in his pink fist to help him wash it all down, Abbott rose magnificently to every challenge she set before him.

'Do you good, professor, build you up,' Janice would say, leaning over him maternally. 'You need a spot of nourishment stuck out here in this draughty corridor.'

'You're too kind, Janice, my dear,' George replied, as his pale blue eyes eagerly followed the descending plate.

45. THE GREEN GORILLAS

Six students sat round a table in one of the little-used rooms at the further end of the old Fallowfields outhouses, which were still home to the Department of Art and Design. Fired by the inaugural meeting of the Mixton Eco Society, they'd decided to form a more militant and secret caucus of their own, and had called themselves the Green Guerillas. One of them, Donny, was tearing open the large parcel of T-shirts they'd ordered so as to identify themselves and promote the cause.

'This meeting is strictly confidential. It is not taking place. You have not come to it. Understood? Right. We all know that if people like us don't do something then nobody will. Loren's right. Endless talk, debates, hot air – it all goes nowhere. People only take notice when something happens. Something that affects their lives. Otherwise, as we know, they shrug their shoulders and tell you to piss off. Right?'

The others murmured their agreement, then all turned to admire the T-shirt that Donny triumphantly yanked out of the parcel and held in front of him. The green lettering leapt boldly off the white vest. But admiration was swiftly succeeded by a silent, more doubtful feeling.

At length, someone said: 'That's not how you spell "guerilla", is it? Who ordered these?'

'I did,' said Donny blankly.

'This means apes you see in the zoo.'

'I thought it was the same word. 'Cos guerilla fighters are sort of fierce, like apes.'

'You fucking idiot. It's different. It's spelt g, e, er- u . . . anyway, it's different. What a pack of prize arseholes we're going to look. Send'em back.'

'We can't send them back. That's the name we wrote on the order form.'

In the heated debate that followed, Steve, who was their chair by virtue of the fact that he had the loudest voice, found a statesmanlike solution.

'We can't afford to get them re-done, so we'll have to live with them. But it's no big deal, 'cos gorillas live in the rain-forest, right? And that's endangered by logging and pollution and such-like. And also they're nearly extinct because hunters kill them and eat their bollocks as an aphrodisiac.'

Nobody felt able to refute these remarks, authoritatively expressed as they were, and the meeting continued in a more orderly fashion.

'Right, we're the Green Gorillas – like Mao's Red Guards, just a different colour. We operate in stages. We've got three categories of action, light, moderate and heavy. We start light next week. There are separate campaigns to be operated by different cadres.'

'Carders?' came a quizzical voice.

'Groups – *teams*, you shithead. Team One hands out the questionnaires. The traffic for Fallowfields comes to the top of

Badgers Lane where the cars have to be left. Then you get on a UNI-cycle. Everyone will be asked to complete a questionnaire to help rate the Green-ness of the uni. While that's being done a photo's taken of car, driver and number plate. Then we can work out who owns what motor. After Fallowfields we do Mixton. Team Two does the next level, which is Naming and Shaming. Some lecturers drive into university in their mini cars, all low mpg or electric or mixed propulsion, looking as smug as an MP on a bike. But back home, they've got bloody great four-by-fours that do five miles to the gallon. So over the next couple of weeks, we'll track them to their homes and take pictures of any other motors they've got.'

'No sweat, we're on it, Steve.'

'Do a cruise round some of the streets with the upmarket motors in. Get number plates and addresses. Can everyone do that?'

Everyone could.

'But don't let them see you hanging about or loitering. And no in-your-face garb. The people who own these type of cars are the sort that if they see anyone in a hoodie or baseball cap, they'll get the coppers out. Everyone understand?'

Everyone did.

'Team Three's the heavy mob for the Five Levels. And we hit everybody with these, uni people, fat cats, the lot. We don't muck about any longer. We do things. By agreed stages. Number One, Footprints. Number Two, Cucumbers. Number Three, Green Warning. Number Four, Dead Dummy. Then Number Five . . . ' There was a pause before they all said 'Boom! Boom!' – and somebody added, 'Loren would be proud of us.'

The meeting ended with raised fists and high fives. In his red heaven, Mao would have turned green with envy.

46. HOMES FIT FOR HEROES

It was a fine Saturday morning in February, and Brian had just finished installing his surveillance equipment in the new buildings at Fallowfields. His all-hours security pass had enabled him to do most of the work at weekends, a time when few other ESMOs volunteered for duty and few people were about. The new premises had made the job much easier for him. The coving that housed some of the wiring was easily removed, and the purpose-built conduits that carried other parts of it were easily accessed. He scrupulously maintained his habit of hiding his equipment and tools at the bottom of a carrier bag. At the top, and clearly visible, were one or two innocuous contents – a newspaper, pot noodles, a can of Coke, a packet of sweets or a chocolate bar. Never cut corners, was Brian's guiding precept. Pleased with his work, he had only to check on reception quality when he got back to his den at Mixton. Pausing outside the new university buildings, he noted that the houses at the far end of the site, the so-called 'green houses' of the Compton Farm Estate, were nearly finished. He walked over to them and seeing that one of the doors was open decided to take a look inside. As he stepped in he almost bumped into someone who was leaving.

'Well, love a duck, it's Brian! Big Brian, Burger Brian – and looking even bigger.'

To Brian's dismay, it was Doug Schmeltzer, his old colleague at Central Energy, the company he used to read meters for. Doug's brand of brash, insulting bonhomie had never been to Brian's taste.

'What you doing, then?' Brian asked.

'Installing the FIT meters – you know, Feed-In Tariff. Mind you, you could do with a FIT arrangement, you haven't got any slimmer since your "Big Brian breaks it" days, have you?'

Between them was a half-secret knowledge that delighted Doug and embarrassed Brian: how Brian had given up window cleaning because the ladders wouldn't hold him and he got vertigo half way up; how he'd quit his meter-reading job when a chair he was standing on in an old lady's cottage collapsed beneath him. It turned out to be a rare Jacobean chair and cost the company a fortune in insurance money.

'What's this FIT about, then?' asked Brian defensively.

'Don't you know anything? It's changed since your day, Brian – though how that could happen without your keen brain amazes me. All this solar and wind energy comes in to these houses and the uni as well. It's all part of the government's "Let's go green" gimmick. When it shines and blows, the properties produce more energy than

208

they consume and what's left over gets fed back to us. Which we pay for. Everyone's a winner.' He paused and looked at Brian keenly. 'Well, nearly everyone. But what are you doing here?' Then Schmeltzer raised both hands with a terrified look on his face. 'For Christ's sake don't lean against the wall – we don't want to bring the house down.' He slapped his thigh and pretended to double up in silent mirth, then went off to check the next property.

But Brian had a stroke of luck. Walking further into the house, he noticed that Schmeltzer had left his coat behind, draped over a portable stepladder. Brian went through the pockets. He took Schmeltzer's official ID card out of his wallet, ignored the folding money and loose change in the pockets, and then found a large bunch of keys, which he removed. As he made his way out of the site he put the ID card in his back pocket and dropped the keys down a drain. Hearing a distant plop, he murmured 'Sod you, Schmeltzer. You'll need a Fish-Out Tariff to get that back.'

47. CARBON FOOTPRINTS

When Kate returned to her car after her last lecture of the day she was mulling over whether the French philosopher, Levinas, provided an ethical context in which one could examine feminist films from the Middle East. She was edging towards the conclusion that he did, but her rationale would be too complex even for a third year module. Still, it was a sufficiently interesting question for her to consider writing a paper about it. It'd be a welcome antidote to the endless, grinding encounters with her colleagues over 2-4-3 and her tricky balancing act between Loren and Ed.

Thus preoccupied, she got into the car, put her handbag on the front passenger seat and fished around in the glove compartment for a CD. Only after she'd fed it into the stereo did she notice the painted footprints which had been stencilled across the windscreen. Irritated and puzzled, she got out of the car to get the plastic ice-scraper from the boot. On the rear screen was another footprint, this one about twelve inches long, with some writing across the instep:

'Reduce carbon footprint now. Go green before it's too late.' As she scraped at the markings, she felt aggrieved. Her car was an elderly Volvo which her father had given her when she got back from the States. Parking between the four-by-fours that seemed to dominate every car-park, she felt like a tramp steamer hemmed in by cruise liners. Why didn't these stupid sods pick a more deserving target? She got back into the car, switched on the ignition, and realised as she did so where she'd seen the footprints before.

She drove straight home, ran up the stairs to her study and yanked open her filing cabinet. Where the devil was that file? She sat down at her desk with it and laid out its contents, looking through the e-mails she'd hurriedly printed off at Loren's house. Finding the one she wanted, she flattened it out on her desk. At the foot of the page was a series of black markings decreasing to a size that made them look like the result of a slight printing malfunction. Kate reached for a magnifying glass and examined them. They were miniature replicas of what she had struggled to remove from her windscreen. They reminded her of the cryptic fish symbol which had been used by the early Christians.

She re-read the email she'd previously only skimmed before more pressing matters had obliged her to lock it away. It was a fierce diatribe issued by 4DK that made 'J'accuse' read like something out of *The Reader's Digest*. Minatory bullet-points banged out the evils that were destroying our planet, and the action that would be needed to combat the indolence, stupidity and mendacity of the politicians and the greed of the coal and oil giants. The key section, 'On the Escalator', was printed in bold and set out increasingly radical actions by which individuals and organisations could be goaded into action.

- All owners of private vehicles with a CO_2 output in excess of 200g/km to be given a series of warnings, and then their vehicles to be INCINERATED!
- Prominent climate-change deniers to be selected for trolling and hacking, and then their homes to be DAMAGED!
- All energy companies which did not agree to take severe measures to combat climate change to be . . .

Feeling fatigued and alarmed by the fusillade of bullet points, block capitals and exclamation marks, Kate realised she needed to know more. Had Loren signed up to this? And was her sympathy merely notional or was she an active eco-jihadist? Had she set out to mobilise certain students or had they become green activists on their own initiative? And, indeed, was the graffiti the handiwork of students – or of others? The next afternoon she skyped Cassie in the States.

'Hi-ya, sweetie – and in a new top as well!'

'We like to surprise rather than disappoint. Now please tell me you've found me a job and what you've learned about La Lafayette, the Verdant Pimpernel.'

'Jobs are tight, sweetie. But for your sake and mine, I'm watching like a hawk. And I've learned a thing or two about La Laf. I told you we were both at Wyoming, but she was there a while before me. So I contacted a few of the old colleagues we shared. She was the mother of a couple kids and well liked, but she's been on the move a lot. Never stays anywhere long. And some of the eco activities certainly seem to go with her. Some folks say she was an agitator . . .'

'An *agent provocateur*?'

'Your German's better than mine, sweetie, but that could be the word. And some say she was the victim of jealousy and racism. But I'm still on it.'

'And get me a job. This place goes from bad to worse.'

'I'm on that too, sweetie. I wanna see you so badly.'

'You're seeing me now.' Kate undid another button of her blouse.

'Don't, that makes it worse.'

'I'll send you a copy of my CV, what you Americans call a *ray-zoom-ay*, and you can give me some hot coaching tips.'

She moved close to the camera and Cassie did the same. As their lips met, four thousand miles apart, Kate felt that skype should be renamed Tantalus. Only later, while sipping a coffee at her computer and pondering how she might write about Levinas, did she recall that Cassie had mentioned Loren's *two* kids. Yet Loren only ever talked about one, a girl whom Kate had briefly seen for herself. She even recalled the child's ecological forename, Forest. Where, she wondered, was the other? Perhaps in the care of a former partner . . .

48. GORILLA WARFARE

Bill Castles was already perched at the bar of the Carpenters Arms and had ordered two pints of its best bitter. The second was for his pal and police contact, Inspector Derek Foreman. 'Hello, Derek. How are things? Have you come across this footprints-on-cars business?'

'It's cats, Bill. They walk across vehicles and leave their footprints. Very inconsiderate. But not an arrestable offence.'

'Then they must be police cats 'cos they've got bloody big feet. It's more serious than you're making out. A number of people have contacted us to say they've had footprints spray-painted on the windscreens and rear windows of their motors. Along with a message saying "Carbon Kills – Go Green". Carbon mostly gets spelt with a C but sometimes a K.'

'Perhaps it's homework for primary school children.'

'Come on, Derek, I know this won't be your top priority but . . .'

''Course it is, Bill. Murder, theft, fraud, domestics, all way down the list after painted footprints on car windows.' Over years of interviewing evasive crooks, Foreman had developed a line in ponderous sarcasm.

'OK, OK. But I'm going to do a piece warning readers about it. Tell them to keep their eyes skinned. I'd like to say that if they're concerned they should contact the police.'

'No problem. We do have a lot to do, but if it means nipping something in the bud, Bill, then in the bud we will nip it.'

As they each took a sip of their beer, Castles pondered the paradox of going green and nipping things in the bud.

A few days later Castles was at Mixton Golf Club with his regular playing partners, Harry Hunter and Geoffrey Edgerton. They were teeing off at the fifth hole, and conversation was relaxed and desultory.

'Odd thing happened to me last week,' mused Edgerton as he watched his ball soar above the fairway. 'Couldn't get my car to start. It's usually very reliable. An Audi A4. When I called the AA, the patrolman told me someone had stuffed a giant cucumber up the exhaust. When he got it out, a message fell out with it. It said, "If you stuff the environment, we'll stuff you". And then it said, "Signed, the Cucumber Company – cool and green".'

'I'll be buggered,' exclaimed Harry Hunter, dropping his club into the trolley bag. 'Similar thing happened to the missus. She drives an old Toyota, a four-by-four. Parked it at Sainsbury's while she did a shop. When she came back she found a life-size doll sitting in the front seat, with a notice round its neck saying, "You killed me. Stop global warming now". Is there much of this going on, Bill?'

'Have either of you had footprints stencilled onto your windscreens?'

At different times they had. 'I just thought it was the local yobs,' said Hunter. 'Do you think it's a bit more organised?'

'Dunno. I had a word with one of my sources in the plod, and they don't seem to be taking it very seriously.' But when he got home that evening, Castles told his wife Iris to make sure their Range-Rover was always parked in the garage.

'You say you were kidnapped, sir?' said the police sergeant at the counter. 'That's a very unusual crime.' The young man across the counter was smiling and relaxed despite what should have been a traumatic experience. 'Just tell me what happened. Do you think you might need counselling, sir?'

The man, who had identified himself as Sam Usher, replied with a smile that he didn't think that would be necessary. 'I'd just left my home in Creighton Drive at about nine o'clock. It was a nice spring evening so I decided to stroll down to the pub. I'd only gone about fifteen yards when this old banger of a car screeched up alongside me. Out jumped three young blokes wearing hoodies and scarves over their faces and bundled me into the back.'

'Any reason they should've picked on you, sir?'

'None whatsoever. And that's why I wasn't too worried. I only left university last year, so I just assumed it was a rag stunt, and they were going to auction me for a local charity. "What's the game, lads?" I asked them. But then I got a bit alarmed because they were really aggressive. Told me to shut my fucking face. And they were driving the old banger like they were doing a bank job.'

'Where did they take you?'

'We tore down to the motorway and headed south. Then one of them turned to me and said "Right, Kyle. Here's the deal. You're worth a fucking fortune to United, so you're our little gold-mine. Keep your fucking gob shut and you'll be OK." I then got an inkling of what'd happened and said, "Look lads, you've got the wrong bloke. I think you've mistaken me for Kyle Yardley".'

The desk sergeant's jaw dropped. 'Kyle Yardley, the Mixton United striker they signed last year for several million quid?'

'The very same. But then the bloke said, "You don't fucking fool us. We know bloody well where you live: 46, Creighton Park." "No I don't," I said, "I live at 46, Creighton Drive, and that's where you grabbed me from".'

'Then what happened?'

'We were doing about ninety, and the driver suddenly brakes hard and yanks the car on to the hard shoulder. Then they all started arguing among themselves about who'd got the address wrong. They were calling each other a lot of foul names.'

'And?'

'After a bit they came over all polite. Apologised to me. Said they'd wanted to kidnap Kyle Yardley because Mixton United are sponsored by a company who cause a lot of pollution. They reckoned they could get a packet of ransom money.'

'And what did these individuals look like?'

'Couldn't really tell you. Their faces were muffled up, and apart from when they got angry and started swearing at each other, it wasn't always easy to make out what they were saying.'

'So then what happened?'

'It was all rather sweet, really. They kept saying "Sorry, sorry" every other minute, turned the car round at the next intersection, and drove me home. And then when they dropped me off, one of them forgot I wasn't Kyle Yardley and asked me for my autograph.'

'Nothing else you can tell us, sir?'

'No. Sorry, sergeant . . . Oh, I do remember one thing. One of the blokes opened up his hoodie to scratch himself, and I noticed he was wearing a T-shirt with a picture of a gorilla on it. A green gorilla, oddly enough.'

'Mr. Foreman – sir? Sorry to trouble you so early, sir, but we've had reports overnight of five vehicles having spontaneously combusted, including a serious incident at Mixton Court Country Club. May be a coincidence but they were all 3Gs.'

'Three what?'

'Apparently that's what the eco activists call them: GGG. Stands for Great Gas Guzzlers. Two of the owners said they suspected foul play 'cos they'd had graffiti painted on their motors telling them to buy an electric one. Or get a bike. And there was something about cucumbers and dead dolls.'

'What was the incident at the country club?'

'Mum with little girl, approaching her Jaguar in the car-park, when the bloody thing exploded. Fortunately they were twenty yards away and badly shocked, but not hurt.'

'Right,' said Foreman, cradling his phone with one hand and struggling to put his trousers on with the other. 'I want names and addresses. Makes and models. Statements from the owners. Questions asked of neighbours. Anyone who saw anything suspicious. And forensic reports on the vehicles. Usual drill. And make it sharp. These don't sound like old dears worrying about their bins not being emptied.'

'There is one other thing, sir.'

'You're not going to tell me someone's just ram-raided a bank, tied up the staff and taken the customers prisoner?'

'Not as bad as that, sir. But we had a young bloke come in about eleven last night, claiming he'd been the victim of an attempted kidnapping. Do we know anything about green gorillas?'

On his way into the station, Foreman used his Bluetooth connection to make a couple of calls on his phone. The first was to his lady-friend, Marian Bussell. Hearing only her voice-mail, he left a message. He'd have to cry off this evening's date. His wife Jenny was becoming sceptical about the number of evenings he'd told her he was doing overtime – and, ironically, he probably *would* have to do overtime tonight because things were kicking off down the nick.

His second call was picked up. 'Bill, it's Derek. All right, all right, you were on the ball about the footprints on car windows. May've been a bit of a prank to start with but now it's getting out of hand.'

'You don't have to tell me. Who's behind it, then? What are you lot doing?'

'We think it may be a bunch of eco-activists. But we can work together on this. I'd appreciate it if you could do another of those Watch Out articles in the Chronic. Say the police are on the case and if anyone's seen anything suspicious they can report it on a hot-line.'

'And what can you do for me, Derek?'

'I'll deliver updates to you personally, and when we make arrests and detain for questioning, you'll be the first to know about it.'

'OK. Anything else?'

'We might stake out a number of vehicles that are likely targets. If we do I'll take one of your photographers along to snap all the action.'

'Deal!' replied Castles, replacing the phone and turning back to something intriguing on his computer.

Foreman had now arrived at the police station. As he approached, he saw his reflection in the plate glass doors, and was not displeased by it. He winked at himself, squared his shoulders and murmured, 'Cometh the hour, cometh the man: the FORE man!'

49. HOLLY'S LITTLE HELPER

It was late September, the start of the new academic year, and Mixton University was bustling with optimism. Though not without its teething troubles, the new Fallowfields campus was largely completed and had extended a dazzling steel and glass welcome to the first students of the exciting new two-year degrees in Environmental and Ecological Studies and Complementary Therapy and Outreach Care. In contrast, the old degrees in English and Media were beginning their final year, their students contemptuously crammed into portakabins in the town centre. Yet even here the mood was upbeat. Entry into the exciting world of employment was, supposedly, only a few more months away. And to cheer everyone further, the weather was wonderful. If autumn was in the wings, summer, still radiantly centre-stage, was heedless of it.

Holly and her friend Taylor were not yet certain of their passage into the final year because they'd both failed an exam in May and were obliged to re-sit it. Yet they shared in the general jollity, and for reasons that were partly chemical. At the beginning of September, the therapy and care department, or DoCTOC as it quickly became known, had made an early impact throughout the university by offering all staff and students something called 'free health profiling'. It would be carried out by the new departmental staff under their head, Dr Wilkinson, although part of the exercise was to teach diagnostic skills to their own students. Holly and Taylor decided to go along for a laugh, and discovered, to their mingled delight and apprehension, that their own profiling would be conducted by Dr Wilkinson himself. Clive, as they were promptly invited to call him, was youngish, pleasant-looking if rather bedraggled, and with a manner at once languid and efficient.

As they entered the diagnostic suite, Holly and Taylor began to titter uncontrollably, for the same unspoken reasons. Was he going to get them to strip? Would he perform some kind of intimate examination? And if so, would they submit or resist? But the profiling turned out to be disappointingly mundane. He dealt with them separately, Holly first. The only thing they were obliged to remove was their footwear while he measured their weight. He also took their height and blood-pressure, and then conducted an oral questionnaire about their health history, dietary habits and life-style. When Taylor came out of the suite, Holly was waiting for her. Even more disappointing was the fact that Clive had given them both the all-clear. There wasn't a thing wrong with either of them.

'I feel bloody cheated,' announced Taylor, plumping herself down on a chair.

'Me too,' said Holly. 'Especially with our re-sits coming up. I was hoping if we did badly we could've had a medical excuse.'

'Let's have another word with him. Tell him we might *look* well, but these re-sits are doing our heads in. Making us *really bloody* stressed. He seems a cool guy. Let's get him to write each of us a note we can hand in before the exam. Just in case we screw up.'

Neither Holly nor Taylor, alas, knew anything about the discreet and selective exam-assisting service provided by Brian's friend, Hugh Jones. The only one in their circle who did was Shaun. But Shaun was no longer at the university. He'd graduated in the summer, and although he was still hanging around Mixton and likely to remain as long as Holly was there, he had his own reasons, notably the inglorious way he'd helped to end the sit-in, for keeping his knowledge to himself. Giggling and nudging each other, Holly and Taylor went back to see Clive, who by this time had returned to his office. Once shown in, they gave a very credible impression of two young women on the tearful brink of a breakdown. Wilkinson listened and smiled benignly, but it was impossible to tell whether he believed them. Having heard at length how oppressed each felt by the medieval barbarity of having to sit exams, he leaned forward and clasped his hands on his desk.

'I do understand what an ordeal exams can be. But I'm not able to write the sort of note you want. My field's *complementary* therapy. It's by definition something additional to mainstream medicine, but not part of it. So if you're both very badly stressed you'd need to go to a proper, er-, a conventional doctor, a GP. And get a sick-note.'

The girls were downcast.

'However . . . '

The girls looked up again.

'In DoCTOC we're about to trial . . .' and here he reached into a drawer of his desk, 'this alternative medication.' He held up a small glass bottle. The girls looked at it, mesmerised. 'It's herbal and it's entirely legal. It doesn't mimic traditional illegal drugs like cannabis and ecstasy. But the preliminary signs are that it's a very effective euphoric when used under stressful conditions.' He shook some out into his hand and gave them each three small blue pills. 'Keep them safe. Then each of you should take one tablet, and one only, about an hour before the exam starts. You may find they do the trick.' And he gave them a shy smile, though his raised eyebrows seemed to hint at an ulterior meaning.

The venue for the re-sits was a hall in one of the new Fallowfield buildings. The girls took their pills as advised, and by the time the exam began they were suffused with a breezy self-confidence and unusual clarity of mind. The questions seemed easy, the exam passed agreeably quickly, and at the end of it they almost skipped out of the hall.

'How did you get on?' cackled Taylor.

'Bloody brilliant! I was absolutely *motoring!*' hooted Holly.

'And I was *flying!* D'you think we've passed?'

''Course we have. And even if we haven't, who gives a sod?'

They doubled up with laughter and then, arms round each other's necks, reeled down the corridor, bouncing off its walls. Rounding a corner, they ran rather heavily into Brian, and although he was forgiving he didn't share the general mood. In an effort to cheer him up they steered him into the snack bar and got him a cup of tea.

'It's mad at the moment,' he grumbled, stirring in a third spoonful of sugar. 'Hundreds of students milling about, rooms double-booked, fixtures and fittings not yet completed, new furniture not arrived, and some of the audio-visual kit in the lecture theatres don't work properly.'

He took a slurp of tea and managed a half-smile as Holly felt in her shoulder bag and put a large packet of chocolate-coated biscuits in front of him. 'Don't worry, love, it'll soon shake down.'

'Yeah,' he munched ruefully. 'But now the Cavalier's started to play up. There's a funny noise coming from the gear-box.'

Holly and Taylor got him another tea and split open the rest of the packet.

'And then look at this.' Brian leaned back and showed them that the lower two of the four buttons on his ESMO jacket were missing. Holly and Taylor expressed sympathy while warily noting the size of Brian's girth and the task expected of the buttons.

'We can cheer you up, Brian.' Holly rummaged in her shoulder bag and produced a small twist of paper, which she opened. Inside were the remaining two pills. 'Have one of these. We got them from DoCTOC. They're stress-busters we took for our exam. They're brilliant. Go on, have one.'

Brian eyed the tablets nervously. 'No thanks, love. I don't do drugs. Got enough vices as it is' – and he gave a nervous chuckle.

'*Go on!*' urged Holly. 'They're not, like, druggy-drugs. They're perfectly legal. Just ease the stress and make you feel better.'

'I really won't . . . '

219

'Brian!' she looked hurt. 'You've been a pal to me in the past, now let me do you a favour.'

'Oh, OK, love,' he had no wish to offend her and took one. 'I'll try it later.' He dropped the tablet into his pocket, intending to throw it away at the first opportunity. But then his phone rang. He was being summoned to the third floor, where the toilets were blocked, and in the excitement he forgot all about it.

50. BRIAN'S LIST

At about the same time, Gemma and Ben were sitting in their office and taking stock of Learn and Earn while awaiting their monthly meeting with Gary. It was not something they were looking forward to. They'd now been in post for more than a year, and Gary's evident lack of interest in what they were doing was discouraging. Yet it was somewhat offset by the attentions of Brian, the fat and shabby ESMO. Filching desks and furnishings from here and there, he'd made their office as comfortable as he could. The portrait of Princess Diana was a bit overpowering. In its own crude way it was a good enough likeness, but the eyes were rather poorly executed. The left one suffered from what seemed to be something between a glint and a squint. Neither Gemma nor Ben was an ardent royalist, but they were able to live with it.

Thus far they'd been successful in their efforts to find work placements for the students – or *internships*, as they were sometimes more grandly called. The local employers, including Bill Castles at *The Mixton Chronicle*, had responded enthusiastically to Learn and Earn, and there was in any case no demand from those degrees that were being phased out, such as English and Media Studies. For the exciting and well publicised new degrees in ecology and complementary therapy, there were many offers of placements. The construction company in charge of the Fallowfields site, as well as Wind Wynders and Solar Panel Beaters, had told Ben they'd provide work placements to students on the environmental and ecological degree, or EnvirEco, as it was already becoming known. And whether because of the shortcomings of the NHS or because there was a local epidemic of hypochondria, there were scores of complementary therapists, naturopaths, alternative medical practitioners and wellness consultants who could also offer internships.

Yet there were problems ahead. When a degree signed up to the scheme the aim was to extend it to every one of its students, and during the coming academic year a number of the older university departments wished to join. The total number of students needing placements would shortly exceed the number of placements that Ben and Gemma could find. They'd already extended their search for suitable employers to within a fifty-mile radius of the town, but with little success.

'What the hell are we going to do?'

'There's only one option,' said Ben.

'I hope you're not thinking what I think you're thinking.'

Ben nodded. 'Brian's list!'

They both laughed, and as he walked over to the filing cabinet Gemma's phone rang. It was Gary. Something important had come up and he couldn't join them: he'd catch up with them next month.

'Break my bloody heart,' she breathed, as he rang off.

The list was another little favour that Brian had done them, one which at the time seemed as clumsy as it was well-meant. A week or two before, and somehow divining that they were beginning to struggle in their quest for placements, he'd walked into their office brandishing a piece of paper.

'I've worked round here, man and boy, for a good few years,' he said expansively. 'I've cleaned windows and I've read meters, and I'm on first-name terms with a lot of people who run businesses and services, and suchlike. I've had a word with one or two of them, and I know what they're looking for.'

He dropped the paper on to Ben's desk. 'There's forty seven names on there, plus phone numbers. Mention my name. Say Brian says 'ello. I'm not smart young things like you but, you see, I do speak Mixton.'

And he left with as near to a swagger as his shape would allow.

The list contained not only the names of employers but the likely internships they could offer, and it was the absurd meniality of these that had triggered their mirth. They'd dropped it into the filing cabinet – under J for 'Joke'.

'We can't use this,' said Gemma at last, tossing it aside. 'These aren't internships, they're just jobs for skivvies. They don't bear any relevance to the students' courses.'

'Sod that. Think of our performance-related bonuses. Let's get the placements, then dream up fancy names that'll make them *seem* relevant.' And very quickly they improvised a kind of parlour game which in its way was deadly serious. One of them read out the placement while the other supplied the fancy name.

'Home delivery staff for a supermarket's "shop and drop" scheme.'

'Retail strategy and distribution. That's one for students on the BA in Business and Marketing.'

'Flogging electric bikes in Mixton market.'

'You mean ecological sales promotion. That's another one for Business and Marketing – or possibly students on the environmental degree.'

'Speaking of whom, here's a further opening. Selling and installing double glazing and thermal insulation.'

'Ah, energy conservation specialists.'

'Yep, also grave digging and dustbin emptying.'

'The terminology you were groping for is "environmental management".'

'Here's more of a challenge. A takeaway in the town centre could use someone to deliver pizzas.'

'Ideal for students on the BA in Leisure and Hospitality Studies – once we've rebranded it as "community catering logistics".'

'Safe-with-Us, a personal confidence and security service, want a telephone adviser, working nights.'

'You mean, as a "safer neighbourhood" consultant: that'll be popular with the BA Social Work students.'

'Finally, I've got a vacancy for someone who'll cold-call people on the phone to drum up business for a firm of solicitors.'

'"Local justice facilitator" – ideal for the BA in Legal Studies. I think we might get our PRBs after all!'

They sat back in their chairs. 'What do we tell Gary?' asked Gemma.

'Not a lot. He takes no interest. Got his own agenda. If anything goes wrong he'll lay the blame on us.'

'And if anything goes right?'

'Then glory be to Gary.'

'What about Prendergast?'

'He's put Dorn between us and him, so that if the shit hits the fan it won't soil his suit. But you can be sure he's desperate for this scheme to work. That's why he's put us on bonuses.'

'That leaves us with selling these placements to the students.'

'On that front we need to be very clear. Tell them these are just the first steps on the working ladder. If they do OK, they'll be moved up.'

'And if they cause trouble?'

'They'll be thrown off the scheme and lose their weekly payments. Then they'll be cut into small bits and made into beefburgers.'

'And we keep calm and tell certain fast-food outlets that if they need it we can provide them with a substitute for horse meat.'

51. CAUGHT GREEN-HANDED

Like everyone else who was teaching on the degrees that were being wound down, Eric Uggles was pretty demoralised. It was now late September, the beginning of the last year in which English Literature would be taught at Mixton University, and only a small band of students was left. Eric and the other academic staff in English and Media who couldn't yet find new jobs were crammed into portakabins in the town centre. Surrounded by a vast and puddled car-park of broken tarmac and compacted cinders, the portakabins had the air of a holding camp for deportees. Like most of his colleagues Uggles had been desperately applying for posts at other universities, but had not been shortlisted for so much as one. In despair he'd applied for redeployment within the university, which would probably mean a job teaching grammar and report-writing to science students, but Human Resources had so far come up with nothing.

Today, however, he had a small reason to be cheerful. The improbably named Mixton Literary Appreciation Society, a small group of elderly widows and home-bound graduate mums, had asked him to give a talk on 'Love, politics and wealth in the Victorian novel'. It was fixed for tomorrow evening, but he hadn't yet managed to prepare it. He couldn't make up his mind which novels to choose or which critics to cite. Standing before his bookcase in the portakabin, he ran his eyes back and forth along a whole shelf of books but still couldn't make up his mind. He now had only a short time left in which to write the talk. Not for nothing had his colleagues dubbed him Eric the Unready. In the end, he dumped the contents of the entire shelf into a cardboard carton. He'd take the whole lot home and prepare the talk this evening. Struggling out of the double doors, a briefcase in his right hand and the bulging carton under his left arm, he encountered an ESMO, a wiry, youngish man whose face was vaguely familiar.

'Want a hand with that, Dr Uggles?'

'Most kind of you. My car's just over there. I've seen you around a lot and I really ought to know your name.'

'Call me Bomber. Everyone does.'

'Bomber – a military man! Oh no, that would be Bombardier, wouldn't it? Although . . . good God! There's a pair of legs sticking out from underneath my car.'

'Fucking right there is,' said Bomber, dropping the carton of books in a puddle and sprinting over to Uggles's car. Bending down, he seized the ankles and yanked out a young man whose hooded top rode entirely over his head and shoulders, exposing a white midriff. Bomber hauled him to his feet and snatching down the hoodie, exposed the face of a terrified youth with ginger hair. 'What you up to, sonny? This isn't your motor.'

'No, but I've got one like it and was just checking . . .'

'Don't give me that bullshit,' Bomber, who was certainly trimmer than most of the ESMOs, held the young man by the neck of his hoodie and rammed him against the side of Uggles's car. 'Dr Uggles, do me a favour and have a look underneath.'

With some difficulty Uggles crouched down and peered under the car. 'There seem to be various bits and pieces under here,' he grunted, and pulled out a rucksack and what looked like a flower-pot full of powdered metal.

Bomber took the flower-pot and waved it in front of the terrified face. 'What's this? If you've been buggering about with motors in this car-park, you'll be feeling this in an unusual place.' He released the youth, opened the rucksack and foraged inside. 'Well, well. Green paint, cucumbers, and . . .' He pulled a reel of metal out of the rucksack. 'What's this? You're not a gardener. What's your name?'

'Danny. I do a bit of gardening, that's why I've got these old clothes on.'

'You're going to have to think up a better story than that,' rejoined Bomber, and foraged some more. He pulled out a squashy mass of multi-coloured rubber, then pulled, stretched and peered at it. Meanwhile Uggles was unfolding one of the notes that had been wrapped round the cucumbers. He read it aloud. 'NEXT TIME – BOOM! BOOM! What does that mean?'

'As I thought,' said Bomber, who had now found a nozzle amid the mass of rubber. 'This is a blow-up doll. He's one of those eco-terrorists what's been damaging people's cars and making threats. Call themselves Green Gorillas.'

Uggles's liberal decency now came to the fore. Wanton vandalism was one thing, but action which was ideologically motivated, however misguidedly, deserved respectful consideration. And mercifully, no damage had been done to his car. Perhaps he should invite Danny back to his office, where they could have a serious dialogue about the ethics of direct action to save the planet. But when he made the suggestion, Bomber would have none of it. 'Dr Uggles! What you on about? There's been several very serious incidences of cars being damaged and lives being threatened. No way is our Danny going anywhere except down the nick.'

'Please don't hand me in to the police,' whimpered Danny. 'It won't happen again, honest.'

'Too right it won't, you little bastard!' Bomber once again banged him against the side of the car, and for good measure added, 'That's the last incidence you'll be involved in.'

Uggles felt a pang of pity for the youth, who seemed much punier than one imagined an eco terrorist to be. But Bomber's point was unarguable. The Gorillas had caused so much mayhem that the matter would have to be dealt with by the police. They marched a still whimpering Danny down the few streets to Mixton Central police station, and there he and his equipment were placed in the hands of Inspector Derek Foreman. Uggles and Bomber each gave a signed statement about the citizens' arrest they'd made, and then went their ways.

To anyone who heard the official recording, Foreman's interview with Danny seemed to be conducted according to the letter of the Police and Criminal Evidence Act. Yet to a person of Danny's timid disposition and lively imagination it was the ordeal of a lifetime. He'd never been in trouble with the police before. His activities with the Gorillas seemed like a lot of fun that was dignified by the worthiness of their cause. He'd hardly given a thought to their unlawful nature, or the inconvenience and harm they produced, or to the possibility that he'd one day be caught and charged with criminal offences. And now here he was, in the nick, being processed by the desk sergeant and in horrible proximity to roaring drunks and swearing brawlers. Grim reality had irrupted into his world. Worse still, there was something about Inspector Foreman that was absolutely blood-freezing. It was a kind of menacing cheeriness, the way in which he called Danny 'Sunny Jim', even though he'd been told his name, a sense that despite all the rights and safeguards extended to suspects, Foreman might at any moment kick off and beat him to within an inch of his life.

As Foreman conducted him into the interview room, Danny was so frightened that he could barely put one foot before the other. So when Foreman offered him an informal piece of advice before formal proceedings began, Danny embraced it as the kindness it seemed. Foreman suggested that while he was entitled to free legal representation, they could get through matters much more quickly without it and then work out how they might get Danny police bail. There was even a hint that if Danny answered as fully and frankly as he could, he might get off more lightly than his accomplices. Danny was grateful beyond words. Hence, when the tape-recorder was running and Foreman read out his entitlements, he was able to add that Danny had waived his right to have a solicitor present.

226

'Right, Danny,' began Foreman, 'tell me how you got involved in these activities.'

'It all started with MIXES.'

'Mixes? What were you mixing?'

'MIXES, Mixton Ecological Society – at the uni.'

Once he started Danny couldn't stop. He was part of a secret breakaway group. He and a few others had agreed that lots of people were gobby about eco issues, but never did anything. And if nothing was done lots of people would die. Poor people, kids, babies, the ill, the sick. And those causing it couldn't care less. Coal, oil, if it makes money, must be good. He explained how the Green Gorillas had acquired their name.

'Right, Danny. Tell me what you were doing under Dr Uggles's car. What was in the flower-pot and what was the metal ribbon for?'

The flower-pot contained thermite, and the metal ribbon was like a long fuse which you could light. It gave you time to get away before the contents of the flower-pot exploded. 'We all thought it was a good idea. The flower-pot. Nobody suspects someone with a flower pot.'

The interview developed a kind of cyclical rhythm. Danny would talk very freely, and feeling that this pleased Foreman, grew more relaxed and confident. But with this came the realisation that he was shopping his mates, and he would then try to put a brake on his disclosures. At that point Foreman would stare at him stonily while methodically cracking his huge, hairy knuckles, a gesture frightening enough to give new momentum to Danny's candour.

'Now Danny. I want names. First of all, who's the ringleader of this outfit?'

'No one. We're democratic, like a collective, all equal . . .'

Back came the stony gaze. 'I'm not sure you're being fair and square with me, Danny.' *Crack, snap, crack.* 'Surely someone has to decide who does what . . .'

'Yeah, no, well, that is . . . I suppose you could say that would be Steve.'

Foreman clasped his hands and leaned slowly forward. The hawk was about to pounce. 'Steve who?'

'Er, oh God. Must I?'

'I need a surname for the ringleader, Danny. And while I haven't got Steve's, I've always got yours . . . .'

Within forty-eight hours everyone had been rounded up and charged. In the rain-forests of Mixton the green gorillas were as good as extinct.

That evening Foreman was in bed with Marian and seeking to impress her with the tale of how skilfully he'd made Danny confess. Marian smiled and listened, but in fact there was only one thing about Derek that impressed her and it wasn't his skill as a detective. 'Calm down, dear,' she advised. 'You've done very well. Performed beyond the call of duty. Now what about a reward?'

52. EROS AND THANATOS

Some weeks later Holly was in a state of agitation. 'Gary, you've got to help me. This bloody assignment's impossible, everybody says so. Two thousand bloody words. I've got five so far and that's the title. You said you'd help, but you haven't.'

Gary sighed quietly. When they first got together she'd been deferential, apologised for troubling him, told him how hard she'd been working on the assignments, and requested just a bit of help so that she could get them in on time. This deference in academic matters had been matched by an enthusiasm for physical ones, and a tolerance of the fact that he couldn't always be with her for as long as she wished. But then she got cross because she caught him checking the time at a moment when his attention should have been elsewhere, and she now insisted that he stopped wearing his wrist-watch in bed. She'd also become much more peremptory in her demands that he help her with her studies. For his part, Gary was discovering that a vigorous sex life was not enough to sustain his relationship with a woman whom he otherwise had little in common with. He'd made this discovery with almost every woman he'd known, yet it never failed to take him by surprise. The problem was that, even if he wanted to, he couldn't just enjoy the sex and ignore the rest. The rest made the sex itself become a bit workaday. With Holly, he needed to spice things up, and the only way he could presently do so was by imagining he was making love to somebody else. He often found himself thinking about that striking black lady who was the new head of ecology and the environment. Then again, there was the work placement woman, Gemma Giddings. She wasn't especially attractive, but the fact that she was accountable to him was a faint turn-on. There was also the moment when it was hot in her office, and as she took off her jacket he noticed the way her blouse tautened over her breasts. So he'd started to court her in a low-key way, despite what he sensed was her initial hostility. Once or twice, he complimented her on her hair, but made sure not to overdo it. And one day, when Ben was out, he perched on the edge of her desk and feigned interest while she told him about her previous job as a sales rep. Gary Dorn, he felt sure she would think, was not such a bad bloke after all.

'Look, Holly, I'm sorry, but I've been very busy these last few weeks.'

'I know, Gary. You're always bloody busy. It's as if I've got nothing to do but sit around and wait for you to remember who I am.'

'Holls, honey, it was probably not best to have got so caught up with all that 2-4-3 stuff. I mean, I know you've been doing the uni some real favours – '

'I've been doing you some real favours, Gary. So what about some payback? Now!'

'The assignment doesn't look that hard. What reading have you done for it?'

Holly's pretty face grew sulky. 'Not a lot. I hate bloody reading.'

Gary sighed again – a sigh of infinite patience. 'Holly, if you're a student you have to read books. All right, let's meet this evening. But I've got to go at nine. I've promised to see Cynthia about the kids.'

'I'll come to the portakabin.'

'No, we'll meet in the library, look out some books, and then I'll talk you through a plan for the assignment.'

Their session in the library was both constructive and pleasant. With Holly in reluctant attendance, Gary looked through the shelves and found a handful of relevant books. They took these to a table

229

and sat together with a notepad before them, so that Gary could talk her through an essay plan. As they worked, Holly realised that it was in these situations that she liked Gary most. He was knowledgeable, casually authoritative – in control – and she felt she could rely on him utterly. She pressed a little closer to him, and under the table gripped the inside of his thigh and began to caress him. Growing slightly pink around his ears, Gary gamely ignored the distraction and finished the impromptu tutorial.

'Look, babes, I've got to go,' he said, glancing at his watch.

'You're a doll, babes,' said Holly. 'Can you drop me off at my place?'

Their way to the car-park lay through the main building, and as they walked down the dark, deserted corridors, Holly slipped her arm round Gary's waist, pushed her hand inside his belt and stroked his buttock. Desire crackled through him. With a quick look up and down the corridor, he pulled her round to face him and kissed her deeply, cupping her breast. This was risky, but it added to the thrill. Gary thought again about spicing things up. When lovers are obliged to have sex in doorways, they dream of having sex in bed: when sex in bed is routine, they once again dream of the doorways. Gary broke off and looked up and down the corridor once more. Deserted. To one side was a dimly lit passageway which had been blocked off at the far end and was little more than an extended alcove. Along one side of it tables and chairs had been stacked and on the other was a large old-fashioned filing cabinet. Gary steered Holly into the passage, stood with his back against the cabinet and pulled her to him. They kissed again hungrily. But from this position he could watch over her shoulder for anyone approaching.

How clothing can be adjusted to make coition possible, yet kept sufficiently in place to provide a veil of decorum, can be ascribed only to the ingenuity of lust. At all events, Gary and Holly managed a very enjoyable knee-trembler. The only problem was that their activity caused a rhythmic thumping against the steel cabinet, as if they were being accompanied by a bass drum, and the noise made them giggle. But aroused by the thought that they might at any moment be discovered, they soon brought their encounter to a happy conclusion.

As they straightened their clothing and Gary was murmuring, 'Thanks, babes, that was wonderful', Holly's face froze. Glimpsing something behind him, she clamped her hand over his mouth. She put her finger to her lips and peered cautiously round the filing cabinet. She could see the rear end of someone sitting in a chair. Together they edged along the cabinet to get a better view. Behind it George Abbott was slumped over his desk, evidently fast asleep. On one side of him was a plate containing a half-eaten slab of cake, on the other a half-empty mug of tea. They retreated silently, and tittering and shushing one another, tip-toed away down the corridor, until they at last burst through the double doors and gave vent to their mirth in the car-park.

'Ooh, we're bloody lucky he didn't hear us!' gasped Holly, clutching her sides.

'I think the old sod's a bit deaf,' said Gary, as he opened the car door. 'All the same, he must have been well under.'

George Abbott was, indeed, well under. He was dead. At the post-mortem some days later he achieved a final distinction to add to those, such as they were, of his scholarly career. His blood contained the highest level of cholesterol that the hospital had ever recorded.

53. THE POSTHUMOUS TECHNOPHILE

Brian flattered himself that very few things happened at the university that he didn't know about. All the more ironic, then, that he was among the last to learn of Abbott's death, even though it had a special significance for him. On the evening Abbott died Brian had already gone home, and the following morning, when the body was discovered, coincided with one of Brian's days off. So immersed was he in the life of the university that even on his days off he often wandered into its premises to take a look round or slip into his secret office. But on this occasion it wouldn't be possible until the evening. Brian's mother wished to make her monthly visit to Mixton Retail Park and he was required to drive her there.

He helped her into the rear seat of the Cavalier, rescued the oil-stained travelling rug from beneath the car-jack, wheel-spanner and old copies of *What Car?* and arranged it carefully over her knees. Her lifelong dislike of cars meant that she never travelled in the front passenger seat, believing that it was only slightly less dangerous than crossing a motorway while wearing a blindfold. For many years Brian had been allowed to stay in the car while she made her purchases, but now he was required to push the trolley round, offer verdicts on prices and check the change. On this visit special offers abounded, they ate a lunch of Welsh rarebit and knickerbocker glories in the supermarket cafeteria, and it wasn't until mid-afternoon that they returned home. Brian's mother was exhausted so he was obliged to make the tea.

Having ensured that she was comfy in front of the telly and intent on an early night, he drove to the university and let himself into his office. One or two students in the Department of Engineering and Technology had already declared themselves in need of Hugh Jones's assistance in the forthcoming mid-sessional exams. But ever the canny operator, Brian was now taking extra care to cover his tracks. His kindness in giving George Abbott a replacement for the computer he'd smashed had not been wholly disinterested. Knowing the prof was ill at ease with technology and used it as little as possible, Brian warned him always to leave his computer switched on, ''cos that makes it safer. If you turn it off it won't come on again. Just leave it on and it'll go to sleep till you come in next day.' Then, having ascertained that George had followed his instruction, he carefully encrypted the Hugh Jones folders relating to exams and transferred them to Abbott's computer, where he could access and work on them from his own computer in the secret office. Such remote operation meant that in the unlikely event that the files were discovered, they would appear to belong to Abbott.

All this had now been thrown into jeopardy by Abbott's sudden death. Not long after the body was discovered, on the morning that Brian was pushing a trolley round Mixton MightiMart, Hamid and Mervyn, the university's IT management officers, laid claim to Abbott's computer and took it back to their workshop on the third floor. There was a chronic shortage of good machines in the university, and for months Fiona Maddingley, still hanging on as a lecturer in media and gender, had been pestering them to replace hers. She complained that it took ten minutes to boot up and suffered more crashes than a dodgem in a fun-fair. Hamid's and Mervyn's plan was to purge the computer of Abbott's material later that day ('Not so much a purge as a gentle wipe with a damp cloth,' grinned Hamid) and then hand it over to Fiona the following morning.

They were at work rather later than usual because that evening they were playing in an important five-a-side football match at the university's sports centre. In the staff league, Technical Support were up against Business Studies, and among those who would be cheering them on was Mervyn's girlfriend, Astrid, daughter of Bill Castles and failing student of Tom Burley. The two teams were first and second in the league, and their previous encounter had generated some needle in the guise of what are delicately termed 'off-the-ball incidents'. Kick-off was at 8 o'clock. So after a busy day, and before they were due at the sports centre, Mervyn could turn his attention to Abbott's old computer. Both he and Hamid were sitting at their desks in the classic posture of the modern office worker. Slightly slumped in his chair, each was staring glassily at a screen, and just occasionally waggling or clicking the mouse under his right hand. The long silence was broken by Mervyn.

'What age was poor old Abbott?'

'Not sure. In computer terms about four and a half months.'

'A brief tribute email's already gone round. Says he's a sad loss, and does anyone know where his library books are.'

'Not everyone's been gracious. When I was in the canteen this afternoon, Gary Dorn was moaning about how inconsiderate the old boy was. His death means Dorn has to teach some extra classes. Still, to his credit, George died on the job.'

'You mean he was still at his desk when they found him this morning. The cleaners thought he'd dozed off.'

'And so he had – but for eternity,' said Hamid.

'Did you know that he left a last message for posterity on his memo pad?'

'Was it philosophical?'

'Not exactly. It said "Get potatoes for Enid".' They both laughed.

233

'Actually, a bit sad,' said Hamid. 'He was a decent bloke. Just clean up his disk and then we can let Maddening Fiona have it tomorrow. Get some peace at last.'

'Bloody hell! What the fuck is going on here?' exclaimed Mervyn. 'Abbott's ghost has come back to haunt us.'

Hamid looked across and pulled his chair alongside. The screen was filled with a large number of folders which appeared to be associated with the name of Hugh Jones, and a cursor was moving adroitly between them. They watched, spellbound.

'Seems fair to say,' breathed Mervyn at last, 'that Abbott's become much more comfortable with IT since he died.'

'Those files can't be Abbott's,' said Hamid. 'Get into them and see what this Hugh Jones is up to.'

Mervyn wiggled the mouse and tapped frenetically on the keyboard. 'Can't open them. They're encrypted.'

'Can you work out where the controller is?'

More frenetic tappings. 'I'd need more time and – *shit!* We're going to be late for the match.'

'Right,' said Hamid, 'stick a pen-drive in and copy them, and we'll crack the buggers tomorrow.' Mervyn grabbed the nearest USB he could find, rammed it into a port on the computer and rattled the keyboard once more. Then without so much as a backward look, they grabbed their sports bags and raced for the door.

It was not until the following morning, when Brian returned to work and bumped into Mitch, that he learned about Abbott's death. During the next hour or so Brian would be put to the exhausting effort of dissimulation followed by strenuous remedial action. The news was indeed a shock, and Brian was fond of the old boy, but he knew that as soon as possible he needed to retrieve the Hugh Jones files that were still on Abbott's computer. On the other hand it might be suspicious, even to a man as unobservant as Mitch if, on hearing such news, Brian were to excuse himself too abruptly. To make matters worse, Mitch was inclined to be long-winded, and expounded a number of theories about the cause of Abbott's death. The cleaners had poisoned him. His wife Enid had thrown him out and he'd died of a broken heart. All that philosophy had addled his brain and caused a fatal stroke. Having patiently listened to this,

Brian took a casual leave of Mitch, but once out of his sight made a puffing, waddling bee-line for Abbott's old desk in the alcove. His fear was confirmed: the computer had already gone. No doubt the technicians had re-possessed it, and he needed to get into his office as quickly as he could and reclaim Hugh Jones's files before they were discovered or wiped.

Upstairs, Mervyn and Hamid were letting themselves back into the workshop and were in high spirits. They'd won last night's match and also had the better of the off-the-ball incidents. At the end they'd rejoiced in the sight of two members of the Management team hobbling off the pitch. Sharing their impressions of the match, they took some time to get down to work.

'Get that USB over here and we'll see what we have to crack,' said Hamid.

Mervyn did as requested. 'Sod,' he said. 'I stuck in a full one. It hasn't copied. We'll have to have another go.' He woke up Abbott's computer and the icons of all the Hugh Jones folders again appeared on the screen. He pulled a new pen-drive out of a packet, and plugged it in. But just as he was about to copy them, the files began to disappear before his eyes. He stared in disbelief. 'Hamid, Hamid! Come here. Look at this! Someone's wiping the whole lot.' So transfixed were they that before they could react, every file had vanished.

'Damn and blast and bugger it!' Hamid sprang to his feet, knocking his chair over, and began to pace the room.

'What do we do now?' said Mervyn.

'We do two things. We've got the IP address of the computer that's controlling this one, so we try and locate its exact whereabouts.'

'That'll take time.'

'Right. So the second thing we do is get into the staff database and find out who this Hugh Jones is.'

'I'm on it,' said Mervyn, and made a swift discovery. 'Hamid, there's no question these files are dodgy. I've checked the names of all staff the uni currently employs, and all those it's employed in the past. I've also checked the names of all past and present students.'

'And?'

'Nobody by the name of Hugh Jones has ever worked or studied here.'

54. KEEPING AN EYE ON YOU

The private dairy of HOLLY RACHEL AINSCOUGH!!
Hadnt heard from or even seen G since I thanked him in the way he likes most. Sent him snotty text asking was he still alive. Then he phones. Says hes v. Sorry but his boy was sick, serious earache and hed had to take him to the doctors who said he had to stay of school and Gary had canscelled his lectures to look after him.

Made me feel awful and had to give him a Good Time when he came round. Just to spice things up we had a couple of Clives tablets theyre bloody brilliant. Tried to get some more off of Clive yesterday but when I went to the department couldnt find him even though his secetrary Leanne said he was in his office. But last night Tayl bought a whole bubblepack of them from a DoCTOC student in the nightclub and like a true pal she gives me four of them. Theyre getting dead popular with the in crowd cos when you dance you fly and theyve knicknamed them 3Hs, or hip hop highs for short. Gary and I were like mental, i think they call it tantrum sex, then Garys MOB goes off - OMG!! He gets his knickers in a twist – or would of done if hed been wearing any. I nip off to the toilet and he shouts gotta go babes love you and when I get back hes gone - I don't even get a kiss goodbye?

Ive looked for the other 3Hs everywhere – and all Ive found are some ear drops. I'll have to search the bed again.

Gary's call had come from Gemma Giddings, to remind him that in half an hour they were due to have their monthly meeting. He felt a stab of alarm. He'd missed the last two meetings with her and Ben, and realised he couldn't let a third one go by. He'd also had a text message from Prendergast, who wished to be updated tomorrow. Shouting excuses and goodbyes to Holly through her bathroom door, he was turning to go when his eye fell on the bubblepack of 3Hs on the bedside table. They'd certainly livened things up with Holly. Perhaps they'd come in handy in any encounters he had with anyone else. He picked them up and dropped them in his pocket. By the time he arrived at their office, Gemma was alone. Ben was sorry he couldn't wait any longer, she said. One of his kids had flu and his wife needed him at home.

'*Really* sorry I'm late,' said Gary. 'Since Prof Abbott died I haven't had a moment. Can I get you a cup of coffee from the vending machine?'

Going through his pockets to find coins for the machine, Gary rediscovered the 3H tablets. As the coffee gurgled into the plastic cups he was seized by a mischievous impulse. Should he or shouldn't he? Breaking out one of the tablets, he dropped it into the coffee he intended for Gemma and gave it a vigorous stir with his ball-pen. Back in the office, they drew their chairs closer and studied the spreadsheet that Gemma and Ben had compiled. As she pointed her pen at the different columns, Gary seemed to be studying the figures as attentively as she could hope. But he also noticed her elegantly painted nails and the bangle on her wrist. At last, and in a small gesture of despair, she threw down her pen. Finding placements was really hard going, she said. She and Ben were doing their best, but it was like trying to sell fridges to eskimos. Gary, however, was reassuringly supportive – enthusiastic, even. She and Ben were doing really well in a trail-blazing job, and he'd leave Ed Prendergast in no doubt of the challenges they faced and what they'd achieved so far. Gemma was struck by how sensitive he seemed: she and Ben had perhaps underrated him. She felt that she wanted to share a bit more of herself with him.

'Speaking for myself, I think I might be doing better if I hadn't split up with my boyfriend last month.'

'Oh, did you? I'm sorry to hear that. Had you been together long?'

'About two years, and living together for much of that time.'

'I can sympathise. I've had similar experiences,' and he lightly touched the back of her hand. 'Can I get you another coffee?'

'No thanks. That stuff's pretty revolting. God knows what they put in it.'

She suddenly decided that she found Gary positively attractive. And rising through this discovery, like a porpoise leaping out of blue water, was a strange, carefree elation. She felt all-powerful, accountable to no one. Reaching out to his chin, she turned his head towards her and kissed him full on the mouth. Gary was taken aback. Though never inclined to underrate his appeal to the opposite sex, he had to hand it to these 3H tablets. He'd got lucky quicker than he'd dared to hope! Sliding his hand inside Gemma's blouse, he almost sniggered at his sheer good fortune. Then he sprang to his feet, locked the door and rearranged the chairs in what felt like a single, stylish manoeuvre. Gemma, meanwhile, was unbuttoning her blouse and shimmying out of her skirt. Matters took their inevitable course and reached a pleasurable enough finale. But as was often the case with Gary, the fall from bliss was rapid. Having slaked his lust, he felt no further interest in the lady and just wanted to be somewhere else as quickly as possible. Gone were the sympathetic murmurings that sprinkled his pre-coital conversation. Struggling into his trousers for the second time that afternoon, he could think of only one thing to say: 'Would you like a quick bite at Pizza Express?'

Gemma felt similarly. The effects of the tablet evaporated as quickly as her now-satisfied desire, and as she watched Gary trying to hop into a trouser-leg he struck her as deeply ordinary. What on earth had possessed her to do *that* – with *him*? So her response was equally sheepish. 'Very kind, but no thanks. I'm sure you've got things to do . . . and so have I before I go home.'

He couldn't get through the door too quickly, but closed it after him with exaggerated care. She stared at it for a moment, then rearranged herself, cleared her throat and opened a folder on her desk. She couldn't concentrate on its contents. Every now and then she seemed to drift away from her surroundings. What the devil was the matter with her? She dropped her pen and gazed at the wall. Princess Diana looked down at her in perfect composure, diamond drops at her ears, a serene smile on her lips, something amiss only with one eye.

In a sudden access of fury, Gemma snatched the coffee cup from her desk and hurled its dregs at the portrait, shouting: 'And you can take that, you squinting bitch!'

As the coffee dripped off her chin, Diana's smile now seemed to radiate forgiveness. Feeling even worse, Gemma sank her head into her hands.

55. HAPPY BIRTHDAY, ASTRID

'Do you think she's old enough to be left?' Iris asked again.

Bill Castles followed his wife into the back of the taxi. 'Trust her,' he said. 'She's a sensible girl. She's promised to take care of the place.'

Nevertheless, before agreeing that Astrid could hold her twenty-first in the family home they'd taken a few precautions. He liked the thought that Astrid's friends would be impressed by her parents' magnificent home, even if the money that bought it had come from Iris's family. But there had to be restrictions and conditions. There'd be no-go areas. The upstairs bedrooms and Castles' study were locked. The more precious ornaments in the downstairs rooms were stowed away, and the party would be restricted to eighty guests, whose names and contact details Astrid had written out for them. Finally, when Bill and Iris returned at 1 a.m., the guests would have to leave. So as they drove away in the taxi Castles felt reasonably happy, especially as their own agreeable evening was just beginning. They were joining some old friends for dinner at the country club, and would then retire to the friends' house for a nightcap or two. However, he rather wished he'd remembered to drain the swimming pool. Were it not for this endless Indian summer he'd have done it weeks ago. But it was at least covered, and a slight nip in the October air would surely deter any venturesome guests.

'Music's a bit loud,' said Iris, as they turned out of the drive. Hardly any of Astrid's guests had arrived, but the sound system was already banging out her favourite dance tracks. Looking forward to his dinner, Bill Castles tapped his knee in time to the beat.

If they felt a fine thread of apprehension about what was going on at home, Bill and Iris didn't allow it to spoil an excellent evening. Astrid, they told their old friends over the brandy, was a grown-up, sensible girl who'd make sure the jollity was kept within limits. Nevertheless, when the taxi arrived to take them back, they sprang readily to their feet.

Nearing home they could see the blaze of light from their house and hear the thump of the music well before they could see the house itself. With growing anxiety they paid off the taxi at their front gate. As they walked up the drive, their garden offered chilling omens of what lay in wait. An elderly Ford Focus had been parked at a violent angle to the driveway. Its front wheel rested on the grass at one side, having gouged a trench through the neat verge, and gravel had been sprayed on to the grass at the other side. Bottles and food debris were strewn across the lawns and flowerbeds. Saplings had been snapped. Two males stood side by side in animated conversation while relieving themselves against the magnolia. As the Castles approached the house in a horrified trance, a separate sound asserted itself against the background of thumping drum-and-bass. It was the plaintive twanging of a single, loudly amplified guitar. They rounded the rear corner of their house and halted at what was before them. The cover of their swimming pool had been removed, and bobbing gently in it, indeed dwarfing it like some idiotic, nodding leviathan, was Castles' shiny black Range-Rover. Water rippled along its bonnet and lapped at its windows. And reclining on its roof against a cushion that had been taken from the lounge was a youth with flowing blond hair. He was completely naked, his modesty preserved only by the cradled guitar. He strummed it lovingly and his eyes were shut in devout attention to his own caterwauling:

Oh, give me a home
Where the buffalo roam
And the deer and the antelope play-eeee!

Roused from his trance, and with the headline "CORPSE IN POOL SHOCK" flashing through his mind, Castles raced into the garage and switched off the power to the amplifier. Unfazed by this action, the youth continued to sing and strum almost soundlessly. Castles slammed the garage door shut, and he and Iris advanced grimly towards the house. Light streamed out of the lounge and across the patio like an open wound. But they once more faltered before the sight they beheld. Astrid, at least, seemed fine. Through the sliding patio doors, one of which was cracked and partly off its track, they could see her dancing vigorously. Her mascara was badly smudged, the flower in her hair was hanging limply and her red dress bore the marks of many spilt drinks, but she was clearly having the time of her life. The youth who was dancing with her wore a pair of men's Y fronts on his head, his thick brown hair emerging through one of the leg-holes. It took a moment for Castles to recognise him as her boyfriend Mervyn. In varying degrees of emptiness, bottles, cans, glasses and paper plates cluttered every surface. Food and cigarette-ends had been ground into the carpets. There were splashes on the walls, pictures were askew, and one of the settees had lost most of its seating and cushions. Paper streamers dangled from the pictures and light-fittings. Some of the guests were talking, some dancing, some necking, some sprawled on the floor in various degrees of animation. Beer had been spilt over the television set and party poppers had been fired at it, streamers clustered on its sticky screen.

Castles at last found his voice and approached his daughter just as she became woozily aware of him. But between them came an endless line of conga dancers, chanting their own musical accompaniment: *ta-ta, ta, ta, ta, DA-DA! ta-ta, ta, ta, ta, DA-DA!* They didn't improve Castles' temper. 'What the hell's going on here, Astrid?'

She flung her arms round him ecstatically and then embraced her mother. 'Isn't this the most brilliant bash? I'm *so* grateful to you both!'

'Evening, Mr Castles,' beamed Mervyn.

'I'd rather you didn't address me till you take those underpants off your head,' snapped Castles.

'Astrid, this really is – ' began Iris, but she was interrupted by a burly, bearded youth who seized her elbow. 'You must be Astrid's mum, or perhaps her sister,' he simpered, in a clumsy attempt at gallantry. 'Now this is what I call a *real* party. And I just want to say thank-you for having me.' He bent over and kissed her formally on each cheek before disappearing into the throng.

Castles tried again, shouting to make himself heard over the din. *'Have you seen what's happened to my car?'*

'Don't worry, daddy darling,' his daughter smiled a blurry sort of smile. 'Range-Rovers are *amphibulous.* You can drive them anywhere.'

'The hell you can. And this is not what we agreed, Astrid. There must be a couple of hundred people here. Get them out. This party is over!'

'It's not her fault, Mr Castles. It's the flash mobs,' Mervyn's effort to seem sensible wasn't helped by the underpants that were still perched on his head. 'It was all going great, and everything was in order like we promised it would be. But then Joey texts people on his phone and tells them all to come here.'

'Right, well, I want everybody out – now!'

'Oh come on, daddy darling, do lighten up,' Astrid lurched forward and kissed her father wetly on his left eye.

Castles yanked the wires of the sound system out of the wall sockets and clapped his hands loudly. The hubbub abated. 'Good night, everybody,' he shouted. 'This party has ended. I want everybody off these premises within fifteen minutes, otherwise I'll call the police.'

He'd no wish that the party should reach the ears of the police, still less the columns of his newspaper, but the threat worked. Several of the departing guests conferred unwanted affection on both Castles and his wife. They embraced them sloppily and clumsily, and told them they were great parents and that Astrid was a superstar. Aided by Mervyn, who had at last taken off the underpants, Castles herded people out and down the drive. Some went cheerfully, others grudgingly and with muttered threats. At Castles' polite request, one couple broke off their embrace, walked demurely to the front gate, and then, still holding hands, were violently ill over the dahlias. Two other guests posed a particular problem. One was sound asleep in the kitchen flowerbed. Another slumbered, fully dressed, in the downstairs loo, with his bottom on the pedestal and his head against the door. Since the door opened inwardly it took Castles some time to gain enough access to get him out. He and Mervyn ejected both by the same method. They slapped the victim's face sufficiently to be able to haul him into a kneeling position. Then each hooked an arm under the victim's armpit, and dragging him down the drive, propped him against the wall on the pavement outside.

As they deposited the second and turned back towards the house, another departing guest was walking down the drive in what looked like a fairly sober state. Castles stopped him and thrust a twenty-pound note into his hand. 'Here, son. Call a taxi on your phone and get yourself a ride home. But while you're at it, take those two stiffs who're outside the gate and drop 'em off where you like – as long as it's a least a mile away from here.' 'God bless you, chief. Will do,' said the youth, colliding only slightly with a bush before stumbling into the road.

Closing the electronic gates at last, Castles trudged back to the house surveying the scenes of desolation, the maimed garden and the gently bobbing Range-Rover. These would have to be left for now. But the evening was not quite over. Back in the sitting room, Iris had reassembled the missing parts of the settee and was sitting with her arm round Astrid, who was resting her head on her mother's bosom and sobbing stormily.

'What on earth is the matter?' asked her father.

'She's a bit overwrought,' said her mother, shooting him a significant glance. Mervyn looked on helplessly.

'I'm just so-*ho-ho* unbearably happy,' wept Astrid. 'it's been the best – *hoop!* – evening of my life.'

'So what's the problem?'

'*Hoop!*'

'Pardon?' Castles had seen his daughter tipsy on one or two occasions, but never quite like this. A sudden suspicion struck him. 'Have you been taking drugs?'

The question produced renewed wailing. Castles turned away in exasperation. At that moment Astrid's new best friend, Chloe Stark, crept in from the kitchen, where she'd been doing the washing up. Chloe was a student on the new EnvirEco degree. Much as he loved his daughter, Castles sometimes wondered how a sober and level-headed girl like Chloe had become her pal.

'Mervyn, Chloe, were drugs going round tonight?'

The youngsters hesitated, looking at each other warily. 'Someone gave Astrid a couple of painkillers because she said she had a bit of a headache,' offered Mervyn.

Astrid once again began sobbing noisily.

'Painkillers, my eye! Iris, take her upstairs and put her to bed. You two had better get yourselves home.'

'Don't worry about her, Mr Castles,' said Chloe, as she left. 'Everybody loves Astrid, but one or two people do take advantage of her. And sorry about all the mess.'

Feeling immensely tired Castles sank into an armchair, only to leap up again very quickly. Cursing softly, he found he'd sat on a plate of wine-soaked birthday cake.

56. SPOT THE GOOSEBERRY

Kate and Loren returned from the movie in high spirits. This was the third trip to the cinema they'd made together, and the date had been fixed in the knowledge that Forest would be having a sleep-over at a friend's house. They'd decided on a film that was less demanding than the others they'd seen, and it had been a good choice. They'd laughed a lot and held hands tightly whenever the boyish heroine seemed about to come to a sticky end.

Back at Kate's flat they made short work of the Chinese takeaway they'd picked up, and now their chat had turned from cinema to their experiences of living in the States. Kate was keeping the tone light but she was looking for answers to two sets of questions. The more immediate ones concerned the Green Gorillas. Their arrest had been given a great deal of coverage by *The Mixton Chronicle*, but no mention had been made of anyone but the activists themselves. Had Loren started the movement? And in any event, how much did she know about what the Gorillas were up to? From her own discoveries, Kate firmly believed that Loren was at the bottom of it.

The second set of questions related to Loren's background. Although Cassie had told her that Loren had been on the staff at the University of Wyoming, no mention of this had been made in her application for the post at Mixton. And then there was the curious matter of her children. Cassie had said 'kids' but Forest was the only child who was apparent. Had Cassie misremembered – or confused Loren with someone else – or … what ?

Kate decided to talk about her own career history in order to induce Loren to talk about hers. They cuddled together on the settee, and at length Loren began to open up.

'What I soon learned is that big businesses are hypocrites. They spend the greatest time and money posing as good guys. Community based, eco aware. But all the while they're lobbying to get the government to do their bidding. They give the public what it wants only when this puts money in their pockets – and even when it's doing the public no good.'

'What are you thinking of?'

'Food. The US food and farming industries have turned the States into the fattest nation on earth. And the unhealthiest. Now its people are held to ransom on the cost of health-care.'

Kate furtively stoked Loren's fire. 'Perhaps US government policy is "kill rather than cure". You haven't got anywhere on gun control either, have you?'

This had the desired effect. 'The gun lobby runs the show and presides day by day, year by year, over the killing of innocents. Some folks claim that those who shoot school kids are in the pay of the gun lobby.'

'How does that work?'

'After each slaying the sale of guns goes up, not down. Then all we get is the state governor and the president saying how sad they are.'

Kate tossed some more coal on the flames. 'The States also seems to be full of climate-change deniers. I suppose they want to protect their profits,' she observed, as if thinking aloud.

There was a silence, and then Loren spoke, so softly that Kate struggled to hear her.

'I have a story to tell about that. Some years ago, I held a non-tenured post at a college in the south. Near Baton Rouge. I was teaching classes in environmental science. A few of us on the faculty decided we had to campaign more effectively. The eco debate was being owned by the oil and coal people. One weekend we mounted a protest outside the offices of a big energy company. It was totally peaceful. The usual slogans, banners, bull horns, chants. We were getting good publicity and drowned out the spin-doctor who tried to make the company's case. I took my . . . two kids with me because if global warming became a reality they'd be the ones who'd take the hit.'

Loren paused and sipped her drink. Kate sensed a tightening.

'We suffered the consequences much sooner. An employee of the company drove through the police lines and into the protesters. He injured three people and killed . . . my child. My older daughter, Sky.' The words fell like a stone into the silence. Kate looked at Loren. Though quite expressionless, her face was streaked with two glistening lines. Kate took her in her arms and held her, and felt some facial movement against her shoulder. But no sound was made. At length Loren detached herself. Recovering her composure, she smiled at Kate, 'I think you promised me some cheese-cake.' Kate went to the kitchen, took the cheesecake out of the fridge and was brewing some coffee when the door-bell rang. Who on earth was this? She was expecting no one. 'Will you get that, Loren?' she called. Loren obliged, and was shocked to find Ed Prendergast on the step, clutching a bottle of wine. Each stared mutely at the other. 'Come in,' she said.

Perched in the living room on what felt like the tip of an equilateral triangle, Kate looked at her two companions. Each had a plate of cheesecake and a glass of wine, and each was labouring to think of something to say. At length Kate managed, 'I think this is the first time we've all been together since the interviews.'

'We were glad to appoint you, Loren,' Prendergast seized the cue, 'though there were a couple of applicants who ran you a close second.'

'Hope you feel you made the right call,' returned Loren. 'I know how hard it can be for those who know little about a field to reach an informed judgement.'

This wasn't a topic Kate wanted to get into. She sensed that Loren was looking at her for support, but Prendergast would remember her misgivings only too well. Not to mention the bruise on his leg. 'Let me pour some more wine,' she suggested brightly.

The next half an hour passed slowly. She alone knew the reason for this triangle, but she sensed that each of her companions was guessing at it. The only way she could think of diverting their attention was to patter on about university matters and the key challenges facing higher education, and then invite their opinions. It was Prendergast who brought the evening to an end. He mentioned casually that the bottle of wine was a little thank-you to Kate for her help with the 2-4-3 campaign, and then declared that he had a very early start the next day. Then Loren stood up and announced that she had, too.

'But what was she doing opening the front door to me at that hour?'

'She'd phoned me to ask if it'd be OK to drop round and have a word.'

'Does this often happen – colleagues turning up just before the ten o clock news?'

'I should be so unlucky, but it could have been worse. Might have been Unctuous Unthank with a bundle of Truth Tracts.'

'Why did she want to see you? You're not close colleagues.'

Kate explained how they'd met. Loren had never actually confided in her, she said, but on the evening Prendergast turned up Kate suspected she was being probed as to what the staff and students made of her. If there was anything Loren ought to be aware of.

'What sort of thing?'

'To be fair, Ed, she's high profile. In a new post, running a new department in new premises. Understandable she'd want to find out if others thought she was doing OK.'

'And what did you tell her?'

'I said I thought she was running a course that was very attractive to young people.'

'And did she tell you anything you didn't know?'

'Not really. She does think you're a bit of an axe man so she's glad her department's for growing, not culling.'

The axe man wrapped his arms and legs around Kate and determined to keep a close eye on a number of matters.

'But what was he doing on the door-step at that hour with a bottle of wine?'

'I can only think, for the reason he gave. Good progress on 2-4-3, thanks for my help.'

'Does this often happen – colleagues turning up bringing liquor?'

'I should be so lucky.' Kate explained that she'd been keeping Prendergast sweet simply in order to stay employed at the university till she could find a job elsewhere. They'd met by chance at a local gym and had coffee every so often. Seeing her as a source of gossip,

247

he liked to ask questions about particular members of staff. She'd given evasive answers but won his confidence by doing her best to sell 2-4-3 to her academic colleagues.

'A sweetheart deal, huh?'

'Not especially. But he asked me if I'd heard any rumours about how things were going at Fallowfields.'

'What sort of rumours?' asked Loren, running a curious hand up Kate's leg.

'He'd heard something about legal highs being doled out in DoCTOC,' and then Kate used Prendergast's curiosity as a stalking horse for her own. 'He also asked if your students were being radicalised.'

'Radicalised?'

'Planning to kidnap climate-change deniers and drop them down a disused coal mine.'

Loren laughed. 'What did you tell him?'

'I told him the problem with megalomaniacs like himself is that they believe everyone below them's either a criminal or a revolutionary. But I said I'd listen out. Later I assured him everything was OK. I said you were a scholar, not a closet eco-terrorist.'

The closet eco-terrorist wrapped her arms and legs around Kate and determined to go on acting with the utmost prudence.

Lying in bed by herself, Kate realised this couldn't go on much longer. She'd placated both her lovers, but in their different ways each was shrewd. Each would be watching the other very closely, and she wouldn't be able to talk her way out of any future triangle. Not only was she deceiving each about the other, she was deceiving Cassie about both. She lay back on the pillow and stared at the ceiling. Cassie was her Number One, but Cassie was a long way away, and in the meantime Kate was only flesh and blood. So what of the two lovers she possessed in Mixton?

Prendergast meant nothing to her. He was just a sex-toy, and she was uninterested in anything else he had to offer. She was faintly excited by his primitive qualities of aggression and competitiveness, but she admired neither his intellect nor his values.

For Loren her feelings were more complicated. They'd swiftly fallen into an easy relationship in which passion, though not continuous, flared intermittently. She was impressed by Loren's intelligence, intrigued by her background, and curious about the extent of her involvement, if any, with the Green Gorillas. But she was not in love with her. Loren had now embedded herself in Mixton: Kate, on borrowed time, was already seeing Mixton as her past and positioning herself towards a future that would be somewhere far away.

Closing her eyes, she felt life was getting on top of her. She couldn't sleep. At length she got out of bed and switched on the computer. It was midnight here but only early evening in the Mid-West, and if Cassie wanted Kate to be true to her alone, she'd just have to redouble her efforts to assist. Kate clicked on the skype buttons, and almost to her surprise a jerky, fuzzy, but unmistakable Cassie leapt into view.

'Hey you, good timing. Just got in from college and was about to skype *you*! I've found you a job.'

'Cassie, you cup-cake! Where?'

'Here. Celestia State, Arkansas. Teaching feminist film theory. They want to appoint quickly. I'm sending you the internet link. I circulated your résumé and took soundings. They recall your time here and the faculty want you to apply ASAP. They can fix a skyped interview.'

When their excitement had subsided, Cassie added, 'I've also got more dirt on your new best friend.'

For a second, Kate didn't follow her.

'La Laf, the Verdant Pimpernel!' Cassie recounted the death of Loren's daughter, Sky, and Kate duly affected shock. But Cassie had learned more. 'Afterward, LL became much more radical. Joined up with 4DK and got arrested at several demos up and down the land. Charged a couple times, but the charges were dropped. Not enough evidence. Last one was a big anti-fracking rally in Wyoming. Got real ugly. An oil worker was killed. Lot of machinery damaged. But they still couldn't get her ass in stir. Some folks said she was directly involved. Others said she'd been framed. Some folks refused to say anything at all. I've got statements, press clippings.'

'Send them to me. Then what happened?'

'The university and La Laf struck a deal. They wanted to move her on, and she agreed – but only if she was allowed to go with a clean record. She then worked for a couple different consultancies before she showed up at your place.'

By the time they 'kissed' goodbye it was the small hours, but Kate's mind was racing. For a while sleep would be impossible. She went into the kitchen and made herself a coffee, sat down at the table and sipped thoughtfully. With luck she might get the job at Celestia, and well before the end of the academic year be able to say an unsorrowful goodbye to Mixton. And what of Loren Lafayette? She'd already found evidence of Loren's involvement with 4DK, and from Loren herself learned of Sky's death in the eco cause. What Cassie now told her was that this tragedy had made Loren more extreme – led her into trouble with the law and then to the falsification of her employment record, which Mixton hadn't exercised due diligence in checking. Kate was more than ever convinced that, though never arrested nor even associated with them, Loren was behind the activities of the Green Gorillas.

Draining her cup, she padded into the bedroom and switching off the light said aloud: 'Don't worry, honey. Your secret is safe with me.'

57. HOME DIAGNOSIS

The fine new Fallowfields campus was all but completed. The EnvirEco and DoCTOC staff were in post, and the first cohorts of students were hard at work. The autumn remained mellow and the academic year was still young. Stifled by the endless meetings with Turpin, Prendergast and others, and tired of reading and writing lengthy reports of dubious usefulness, Unthank was desperate to get out of his office and see how all the newcomers were getting on. He was especially keen to visit the training suite for 'mediskype' in DoCTOC. Its aim was to teach the students how to use skype to diagnose patients within their own homes. It was just one of the many innovations that were putting Mixton on the academic map and making it the cynosure of scholarly eyes.

He drove into the car-park at the top of Badgers Lane. All vehicles were to be left here and charged at the virtuously extortionate rate of five pounds per day. Awaiting those who had arrived as motorists was a rack of brightly painted UNI-cycles beneath the admonitory sign, 'Save Money – Go Green'. Unthank mounted one and pedalled admiringly into the campus, reflecting that this was the first time he'd meet the Head of DoCTOC, Clive Wilkinson, since the farcical events that had surrounded his appointment several months ago.

Before the interviews for the post took place, Unthank had struggled to quell a suspicion that the new degree in complementary therapy and outreach care lacked the intellectual value that had been ascribed to it. He read up on chiropractic, aromatherapy, the Alexander technique and pilates but faltered before the arcana of shiatsu, rolfing, reiki and moxibustion, for all of which he spent several hours combing the internet. Prendergast, it seemed, hadn't bothered. He skimmed through the applications, labelling each candidate by what he took to be their specialism. The candidate who specialised in Alexander technique became 'Alex', the specialist in herbalism 'Herbie', the chiropractor became 'Cairo', the acupuncturist 'A-Cup', and the osteopath 'Ozzie'. The expert who'd been co-opted on to the interview panel was a stout lady named Jennifer Sheldrake, and it was at the end of the second interview that there was a descent into chaos.

Ms Sheldrake gave a sudden cry: she'd been smitten by a nose-bleed. Her efforts to staunch it, along with those of a hastily summoned Marian, were unavailing. Marian led her into the waiting area outside the interview room, sat her down and went off in search of tissues. To contain the flow, Ms Sheldrake tilted her head back, at which point A-Cup, returning from the toilet, believed she was having a fainting fit, seized her by the hair and forced her head down between her knees. With a version of the Red Sea now opening up on the carpet, Ozzie leapt to his feet, yanked Ms Sheldrake's head back and pronounced that a key should be dropped down the back of her neck. He snatched a set from a nearby desk and forced them inside the patient's collar. But Ms Sheldrake continued to bleed copiously, so Herbie raced into Marian's office and said that the contents of a first aid box were required. Marian raced to the box in

251

her room, only to discover that the key to unlock it was, along with several others, halfway down the patient's back.

As Herbie and Ozzie sought to unbutton her blouse in order to retrieve them, Ms Sheldrake resisted violently, and was pacified only when Cairo returned with an ice pack and a reclining chair. Meanwhile, Alex stood by and wrung her hands helplessly. Standing at the doorway between interview room and waiting area, Unthank and Prendergast witnessed the entire episode. It served as a handy demonstration of all the candidates' curative skills – or lack of them. Mindful of how everyone behaved during the emergency, Prendergast declared, 'I think we should go with Egypt.' By this, he meant 'Cairo', who was of course the chiropractor, Clive Wilkinson. Unthank reflected that Wilkinson's proficiency in first aid by no means met all the elaborate criteria that had been set out in the job specification. But he could think of no good reason to oppose the only distinguishable candidate in an undistinguished list, and from within a field of knowledge about which he knew almost nothing. So Prendergast's proposal won everyone's assent, Ms Sheldrake grunting hers from behind a wad of tissues.

Unthank now parked his UNI-cycle in the stand outside DoCTOC, and a secretary who introduced herself as Leanne ushered him into Wilkinson's office. There, he received a mild shock. On the day of the interviews Wilkinson had been dressed much more smartly than his rivals, something which, however implicitly, would have counted in his favour. He'd been well-groomed, dressed in a three-piece suit and a tie that was matched by the handkerchief in his top pocket. Now he looked unrecognisably seedy. His hair was much longer, he was sprouting an unruly beard, and his dress consisted of a T-shirt, jogging bottoms and trainers. Perhaps, thought Unthank, this is a shrewd change of image to distance the work of his department from the ministrations of stuffy old medics in the NHS. Wilkinson led him into the Distance Diagnostic Suite, explaining that in future 'you won't have to go to your healer' – Unthank smiled at this quasi-spiritual term – 'your healer will come to you, via a secure video-link that my colleague, Ms. Chalmers, will demonstrate'.

Ms. Chalmers was young, sharp and busy. Unthank began to introduce himself, but she interrupted and gave him his own life-history in a few short sentences. 'All on the internet, but nice to meet you in person. Haven't read your books. Let me show you what we're doing.' She said it was now vital for the medical profession to make use of distance diagnosis, treatment and ongoing care. 'The NHS has too few doctors, and they're increasingly overworked. What we need are more trained medics who in many cases will be able to diagnose, reassure and prescribe. The Distance Care Suite, through here – ' she ushered Unthank into what looked like a TV studio, 'enables students to conduct mock diagnoses on people who pretend to be patients, while at the same time being watched by their teachers. Once the students are good enough, they'll be able to do real diagnoses on skype.'

Unthank asked if he could role-play as a patient, and was shown into a nearby room which enabled him and Ms Chalmers to view each other over a closed-circuit link. This room was in dramatic contrast to the studio. It had been furnished in a domestic, neo-fifties style, with the settees, table cloths, heavily patterned carpet, fire tongs, net curtains and knick-knacks that Unthank had last seen in the homes of elderly relatives. Noting his astonishment, Ms Chalmers explained that the furnishings had come from a charity shop in the town.

'Now what seems to be the trouble, Dr Unthank?' Over the CCTV link, she adopted the cold concern of the professional medic.

Unthank was beginning to enjoy himself. 'I get very nervous when I speak to medical practitioners.'

Ms Chalmers neither smiled nor hesitated: she was equal to the challenge. 'That's what's known as "white coat phobia", for which we have the perfect cure. No white coats, no sterile clinic, just a warm smile and a virtual helping hand.' On went a smile, though without the warmth. Unthank admitted to an occasional problem with eczema, and was offered a remedy which consisted not of ointment but wholesale changes to his lifestyle. He then had a try at the self-assessment equipment for blood pressure, pulse, height and weight, and learned about his BMI and how it stood well within the guidelines for his age and gender. Finally, he was handed a print-out of outcomes and recommendations on his alcohol, salt and calorie intake. At the foot of the print-out ran the legend, 'This assessment sponsored by the Hotter Dog Company – Eat healthily and keep well!' His rating had come out as 'triple A'.

He finished his tour of DoCTOC by taking a banana from the 'five-a-day' fruit-bowl and picking up leaflets on a variety of ailments. He was interested to read that these had been sponsored by HoriZen, a local store selling herbal remedies and holistic medicines under the slogan, 'The neighbourhood pharma that gives you good karma!' Climbing back on to the UNI-cycle he felt, with an unusual sense of self-satisfaction, that no fiddle could be fitter than he. But by the time he'd reached his car, the feeling had been dissipated by thoughts of what he must return to at his office. He was involved in a series of meetings with Uncle Richard and Prendergast in which they were drafting the university's business plan, and as part of it he was obliged to produce a report on the impact of outreach on student recruitment.

The university's *business* plan . . . Was he the last person in Britain to sense an incongruity between the terms 'business' and 'university'? Was running a university just a scaled-up version of running an ice-cream van? Surely it was, or used to be, a place for the disinterested pursuit of knowledge and truth, a pursuit that was not to be prostituted to commercial considerations. Universities, like any other institution, must be subject to financial discipline, but not at the expense of their intellectual integrity. He thought again of the sponsors' slogans he'd seen in DoCTOC, those tiny symptoms of ownership. The university was being bought, debauched, and as one of the architects of this so-called business plan he was conniving in the process.

But wasn't this a rather puritanical attitude, even for him? Wasn't it a specious justification of his own preference for scholarship over the endless bureaucracy that money-grubbing seemed to spawn? Yesterday, and with a heavy heart, he'd come into his office to work on the outreach report. But lying on his desk was a new book on Empedocles that he'd just received. He sat down at his desk and turned the pages, and in a short while the report was forgotten. He began to muse on what sort of synthesis might be possible between Empedoclean cosmogeny and modern scientific rationalism when there was a tap on the door and Prendergast walked in, inquiring if the report was ready. Unthank guiltily tossed the book aside and saw Prendergast glance at it.

'I've been asked to review it,' Unthank explained.

Prendergast looked bemused. 'For me,' he said, 'the great thing about being in management is that we don't have to read that kind of stuff any more.'

Now he'd got back to his office, Unthank reflected on what he'd just seen at DoCTOC. His own dream, for whose realisation he could endure all the paperwork, was to open the doors of academia to everyone, irrespective of class and background, who could benefit from it. But had this happened only by debasing academia? Thinking back to the encounter with Brenda Hodges in Whitehall, Unthank again asked himself if we were not in danger of providing mere training instead of a proper education. But like many idealists he had a sanguine streak and began to reproach himself. Unthank, you're nothing but an intellectual snob! In despising vocational training you're guilty of the worst kind of elitism, for it's always been the world of work that's created the wealth on which academia could float. And even if certain disciplines are largely vocational, do they not make intellectual demands that are just as challenging as those of the more traditional forms of scholarship – demands which therefore justify their inclusion in the academic pantheon? As someone with a religious urge to chastise himself, Unthank could readily see his own intellectual arguments, however powerful, as no more than disguised moral weaknesses. It really was time he came to terms with the brave new world of mass higher education – the world he was helping to create.

Resisting the siren song of Empedocles he sat down at his desk and began to write the report.

58. CASTLES DECLARES WAR

Bill Castles was in a vengeful mood, and the object of his vengeance was Mixton University. Over the years he'd given the uni a great deal of favourable publicity, but what had he got in return? A measly deal by which the uni bought a few copies of the Chronic to distribute round its premises, and an occasional invitation to its lunch parties – but only to ensure that he'd continue to give it good publicity. Prendergast was always insisting that their relationship was social as well as professional, but when he'd several times hinted to both Prendergast and Turpin that Astrid wasn't thriving on her art degree and the problem was that lunatic Tom Burley, they'd done nothing. Castles himself had no very high opinion of Astrid's artistic talents, but what the hell. She was fit for little else and this arty stuff was all bullshit anyway. So why wouldn't they lean on Burley? Because Burley was quite famous, giving the uni the only distinction it could claim, and so they were more in awe of him than they were of Castles.

The biggest cause of his resentment had always been Prendergast's refusal to give him an exclusive on the sit-in. It was only a day or two after Astrid's birthday party, when he went down to London to attend the National Journalism Awards, that Castles learned how dearly this had cost him. He'd been given a broad hint from those in the know that he was in the running for the title of Provincial News Editor of the Year, an honour he'd coveted for most of his professional life. But the award went to someone else, and in the bar afterwards the chair of the judges left him in no doubt that it was the Chronic's failure to get a scoop on the sit-in, a story of national significance breaking on its own doorstep, that had made the crucial difference. The narrowness of his defeat tormented rather than consoled him. He recalled grimly that by the time the Chronic could get a local angle on the story – the interview and photo of Holly Ainscough – it was effectively over. He cursed at Prendergast under his breath.

Insult followed upon injury. When he got back to Mixton he discovered that news of Astrid's party had spread. That evening he and Iris felt like a takeaway, so he ordered a couple of home-delivered meals from Pizza Pizzazz.

'Hi, Mr Castles. One calzone alla ricotta and one marinara.' The uniformed delivery boy seemed to Castles to have set his baseball cap at an insolent angle. 'You going to have pizza by the pool and watch the cars go by? Ha-ha! That'll be eighteen quid – service discretionary.'

'I'll use my discretion, then,' scowled Castles, giving him the exact money and slamming the door.

Next morning Halcyon Glaze sent two young fitters, a youth and a girl, to replace the damaged patio door. 'Hello, Mr Castles,' said the girl, jerking her head towards the pool. 'All clear of cars now? Great evening, eh? Was it a Land Rover or a Water Rover?'

The car had survived its immersion. At considerable cost his garage had winched it out of the pool and checked it over. He was advised to let it dry out and then get rid of the chlorine by giving it a good clean inside and out. That afternoon, finding that the car was now drivable, he took it round to Happy Valet.

'You sure, Mr Castles?' asked a lad with a sponge and bucket. 'I thought your motor got a good wash last week – know what I mean?' He gave a stage wink and started to strum an air guitar. Castles felt that if he heard one more joke of this kind he might hit someone, so while the car was being cleaned he decided to let off steam by going to his local gym.

The young woman in reception greeted him warmly. 'I know you don't normally swim here, Mr Castles, but why not try a dip in our pool. It's completely clear of traffic.'

Since all word of the party had been kept out of the Chronic and few knew about it in the town, all these smart-arse jokers must be students. That settled it. Castles had been slighted by the university's management, and now he was a laughing stock among its students. The revenge he'd contemplated would now be of a more calculating and systematic nature. He'd compile a dossier on the uni of material he could use to embarrass it. There was bound to be dirt to dig, it was just a question of finding it. But like many journalists he was adept at persuading himself that what he was doing wasn't something personal, something capricious or vindictive, but disinterested endeavour by a guardian of the public interest.

As he walked from the gym to his office, he realised that the students he'd just come across could provide him with his first target. Were they merely doing menial jobs in their spare time – trying to make a few quid, as so many students do? Or were they part of the university's much vaunted Learn and Earn scheme? Since he'd encountered most of them during office hours, the suspicion formed in Castles' mind that they could be part of Learn and Earn. But this was not what the scheme was supposed to be about. The students' work placements, or internships, were intended to be integral to their studies – an experience of employment, certainly, but also a crucial part of their educational experiences. Castles had enlisted *The Mixton Chronicle* in Learn and Earn, and took his responsibilities to his interns very seriously. But if the uni was using it to push students into menial jobs that bore no relation to their studies it was a bit like forcing the editor of a national newspaper to sell copies of *The Big Issue*. Here, perhaps, was his first ammunition.

His current intern at the Chronic was a smart lad named Leighton Rogers. Though a Business Studies student Rogers wanted to be a journalist, and having sent him out on a few stories Castles soon formed the view that he'd make a good one. In fact he'd prove a damn sight better than some of the Media Studies graduates Castles had employed in the past. Their heads had been stuffed with a lot of rubbish about Marx, ideology and feminism. He called Rogers into his office.

'Right, son, you've done well so far – covering car boot sales, burst water-mains and the like. But journalism's more than just reporting stuff that happens. Sometimes you have to investigate, use your own initiative, dig a bit deeper. Think you could do that, son?'

Rogers thought he could.

'Here's a list of local firms who seem to be employing Mixton Uni students – Pizza Pizzazz, Halcyon Glaze, Happy Valet and the Fab Abs Health and Fitness Centre. There may be others. What I want you to find out is, are these kids just casual labour or working in a more formal, regular way? Find out what the arrangements are, who gets what, who does what. Above all, if these kids are supposed to be furthering their studies by working for these fourth-rate outfits.'

'I'm on the case, Boss,' Rogers got to his feet.

'But Leighton: casual and discreet, not nosy. Don't arouse suspicions.' When Rogers was halfway through the door, Castles checked him. 'Oh, and one more thing. Find out what you can about the local drugs scene. I'm pretty sure stuff was being passed round at my daughter's party last week. Don't exactly know what, but the supplier will almost certainly be a student.'

59. THE LAUNCH OF MEDISKYPE

There was an air of excitement at DoCTOC. After a month of mock diagnoses in the lecture rooms and CCTV studios, the students' mediskype training was over. Clive Wilkinson and Ms Chalmers had put the students through their paces, and they were almost ready for the real thing. All that remained was for them to watch their two mentors conduct the diagnosis of an actual patient. Wilkinson and Chalmers would be located in a studio in Fallowfields and by means of a skype connection diagnose the patient, who would be situated in her own home. The students would be watching 'split-screen' images of the interaction from a viewing room next to the Fallowfields studio.

This particular interaction had been set up by Unthank. Having conquered, at least for the present, his own misgivings about the direction in which higher education was heading, he'd decided to work harder than ever to assist it, and the home diagnosis project was something that, as Director of Outreach and Enterprise, he believed he might be especially able to promote. It occurred to him that those who stood to benefit most from home diagnosis were the elderly. Not only did his friend Betty Attwood fall into this category but he'd noticed from the inner columns of *The Mixton Chronicle* that she was president of the local bowls club. It was possible that she and several of her fellow members could be induced to submit to home diagnoses and try the complementary remedies that might be available for whatever ailments were discerned. A week or two before, he'd paid Betty another visit, and to his delight she readily agreed both to launch the mediskype scheme herself and bring it to the attention of her friends in the club.

And now the day, and the moment, had arrived. Mrs Attwood had needed several phone calls to remind her of the time of the diagnosis, and in the end a student was sent to her house to help her switch on the computer and align the camera properly. To create a greater sense of intimacy, the student was then instructed to leave

Mrs Attwood and return to the university. The skype connection was a good one. Seeming slightly bewildered but able to see and hear Clive Wilkinson in the Fallowfields studio, Mrs Attwood was sitting in front of the camera, hands clasped demurely on her lap. In the studio but presently out of shot were Unthank and Ms Chalmers, and observing in the viewing room nearby were about 25 students.

'Good morning, Mrs Attwood,' called Wilkinson, 'we're very grateful to you for taking part in this project and telling your friends at the bowls club about us.'

'Who are you?' snapped Mrs Attwood. 'I'd get a shave if I were you. Can I have someone without a beard?'

'I'll attend to it. But this morning all we are going to ask you to do . . .'

'I'm not taking my clothes off.'

'Absolutely not. We just want you to talk about the shoulder problem that you mentioned to Dr Unthank. He's here in the studio with us.' The camera turned to bring Unthank and Chalmers into shot.

'Ah Rupert, dear boy, how are you? At least someone's had time to shave this morning. But who's that woman with you? She's wearing too much lipstick. Now, where were we?'

Once reminded, Mrs Attwood talked very readily about her right shoulder, which played up when she went for a longer shot on the bowling green. 'I'm president of the bowls club and it's imperative I maintain my high standard. May I show you the problem?'

She got uncertainly to her feet, set her chair to one side and stepped back from the camera, thus revealing a much wider view of the sitting room. 'Now, if I pitch the bowl by pulling my arm back – *so* . . . ' The object she seized to illustrate this was the dog bowl, which was, for once, empty. And she rolled it on its side along the carpet.

This seemed to trigger a dramatic sequence of events both in Mrs Attwood's sitting room and at Fallowfields, nearly all of which occurred off-camera. In the former, it galvanised Baggins, who leapt to his feet, barking enthusiastically, and pursued the bowl across the carpet, knocking over a chair, a vase of flowers and finally the table with the computer on which the diagnosis was being conducted. The computer landed on the carpet, its camera still working but staring fixedly at a point on the ceiling. Meanwhile things were also happening at Fallowfields. As if triggered by Mrs Attwood's bowling action, the fire alarms suddenly shrilled out, and three or four ESMOs burst into the studio and viewing room, shouting 'Out! Out! Everybody out! Everybody please leave in an orderly fashion.'

'We can't leave now, we're in the middle of important business,' protested Unthank, as an ESMO seized his arm and steered him towards the door.

'Sorry, sir, health and safety,' and then, to make it rather harder for him to resist, 'Need to set a good example to the students, eh?'

'Bad boy, Baggins!' admonished Betty Attwood, at the other end of the link. She straightened up and looked round. The computer and its camera seemed to have gone.

'Where are you?' she called.

The sound link was still intact. 'There's a fire emergency,' shouted Unthank, as he was marshalled out of the studio.

'Fire?' heard Mrs Attwood. 'I'll get the fire brigade.' And she picked up her phone and called the emergency services.

As it raced to Mixton, with headlamps blazing, blue lights flashing and sirens howling, the huge red fire tender made an awesome sight. But it was just as well that the alarms at Fallowfields signified only a fire-drill and not a genuine conflagration, for in the time it took the firemen to reach Mrs Attwood's house and discover it was a false alarm, Fallowfields would once again have been reduced to ashes. Huddling against the November chill, the staff and students stood about in groups outside the Fallowfields buildings until the ESMOs declared that it was safe for them to re-enter.

As they filed back in, one of the students murmured to his pal, 'Fuck me, did you catch an eyeful of all that stuff in the old girl's sitting room? Like Aladdin's bloody cave.'

60. 'SOW A BIT OF DISCONTENT'

'Spare a minute, boss?' Leighton Rogers' head appeared round the door of Bill Castles' office.

'Come in, son. What have you got for me?'

Rogers sat down and pulled out a notebook. 'I followed up that list of firms you gave me and your hunch was right. They're all employing students.'

'And are these kids just working in their spare time for a bit of pin money? Or are they part of Learn and Earn?'

'They're all Learn and Earn.'

Castles jolted exultantly in his chair. 'As I thought! The scheme's being misused. They're just a bunch of drudges. How do they make it look like Learn and Earn?'

'A lot of students are on Facebook, so it was quite easy to track them down. I got some of them to talk to me. When students join the scheme, the two university people who run it, name of Gemma Giddings and Ben Frampton, give them a document to sign. It's quite strict. Looks a bit like a contract. There's a lot of guff in it about duties and obligations, but the individual copies give a formal title to the work the student's doing – and that's the way they've always got to refer to it.'

'So what're you supposed to call the job of a pizza delivery boy – and how does that relate to his degree?'

Rogers flicked open his notebook. 'He's studying for a BA in Leisure and Hospitality Studies. So what he's doing is "community catering logistics".'

'Holy sh-'

'He seems quite happy,' continued Rogers. 'If you look at his Facebook page he's got several selfies. One of him wearing a pizza as a sun hat. One riding on his scooter with his hands outstretched and a pizza in each one. One looking through a giant pizza with a hole cut out of the middle.'

'Speaks volumes for the standard of food hygiene at Pizza Pizzazz. What about the other people you tracked down?'

'One was the girl from Halcyon Glaze who helped fit your new patio door.'

'And what was she supposed to be?'

'Energy conservation specialist. Dovetails with her studies on the new environment and ecology degree. She seems less happy, though.'

'I'm not surprised.'

262

'Says the work's boring and the money's terrible. Even worse, one lad's working for Happy Valet, scrubbing cars.'

'And what fancy label do they stick on his job?'

Rogers glanced again at his notebook. 'His degree's in Business and Marketing. He not only cleans the cars but takes the money and rings it through the till, so his job's called "customer interface management".'

Castles exhaled slowly through puffed-out cheeks. There was always some new dodge to amaze even a cynical old newsman like himself. 'Right, son. I've heard enough of this drivel. They can think up all the fancy names they like, but these kids are getting screwed. They're nothing more than skivvies.'

'Some of them moan in a low-key sort of way, but they don't kick up a major fuss because – well, at least they're getting paid for what they do.'

'Listen, son. A good journalist covers stories. But a *really* good journalist makes stories happen. Get on Facebook or whatever and tell these kids they're being shafted. Put yourself about and sow a bit of discontent.'

Rogers flicked his notebook shut and got to his feet with a grin. 'Will do, boss.'

That evening Castles was obliged to drive Astrid to yet another party. 'Don't want to be late home, dad, 'cos Merv wants to leave early. He's got a big five-a-side game tomorrow. Can you come and fetch me at midnight? Oh, and park round the corner from the house. It's a bit embarrassing for me to be seen getting picked up by my dad.'

Castles sighed. Was there any limit to the humiliations of parenthood? But he decided to try and glean something for his trouble. 'Do you fine art students happen to be involved in the Learn and Earn scheme?'

'Nope. Our head, Barry Powell, wanted us to be, but Bastard Burley wouldn't have anything to do with it. There was an almighty row and Burley got his way, as usual. He made a video ridiculing it and stuck it up on You Tube. If I didn't hate the sod, I'd find it quite funny. When you bring me home from the party I'll show it to you.'

As they watched it on her lap-top at the end of the evening, Castles couldn't help but smile. The video was crudely made but packed a certain comic punch. It began with a rather stupid-looking student talking straight to camera within what looked like part of the Sistine Chapel. He spoke in a solemn nasal tone, at the same time climbing a long ladder with a two litre can in one hand and a large paint-brush in the other. 'I'm a Learn and Earn student,' he announced, addressing the rising camera through the rungs of the ladder. 'And since I'm studying painting I've been given a job as a cleaner in this old church. Gives me insights into the true meaning of art. Place is filthy. Looks as though it hasn't had a scrub in years.' Reaching the top he began to slap white emulsion on to Michaelangelo's masterpiece, then looked back to the camera and tutted, 'You wouldn't believe the rubbish they've put up here.' As he continued to ply the brush, the camera pulled back to floor level and was confronted by a bling-laden rapper in a baseball cap and behind him a line of dancers cavorting to his song:

If you sign yourselves up to Learn and Earn
You'll screw your studies, serve the bosses' turn.
Slave for peanuts – this is true,
Earn jack shit and learn nothing new:
But study full time and you can aspire
To be top-class dudes for the world to hire.
If you're only an intern, doing work placement
You've trapped yourself in the bargain basement.
Learn and Earn! Learn and Earn!
Screws the students, serves the bosses' turn.

Tapping his foot to the beat, Castles felt that, for once, Burley had got hold of the right end of the paint-brush.

61. BEATING THE PANELS AND WINDING THE WIND

When Prendergast and Unthank arrived at Turpin's office for their weekly meeting, they found him sitting at the table and frowning at a newspaper spread out in front of him. 'Before we attend to our other business, gentlemen, you might want to read the editorial in today's

Mixton Chronicle.' He indicated two other copies on the table. 'Rather disappointing.'They sat down and read silently.

FIT for purpose . . . or fit for nothing?

In Mixton, hopes and hearts were raised when Central Energy got together with Mixton University and the residents of the Compton Farm Estate to launch a bold initiative in 'green' power. On the university's new Fallowfields campus wind turbines would catch the wind and solar panels would trap sunbeams. Together they would generate more than enough power for the University and the residents. And Central would pay them for the surplus they fed into the national grid – an arrangement known as the Feed-In Tariff (FIT). Alas, new figures released by Central show that the electricity produced has fallen well short of expectation. After our long warm summer, this may come as a surprise to some of our readers.

All of us want to save the planet and put a brake on climate change. And we expect our universities, as powerhouses of knowledge and research, to come up with better ways of doing it. To this end, Mixton even runs a brand new degree in Environmental and Ecological Studies. So can we hope that FIT will yield genuine results? Or, with its panels and turbines, has the University succumbed to the wacky visions of hippies, flower-people and New Age travellers? The jury is out. But perhaps not for long.

Turpin was vexed. This was a classic piece of journalism – mischief-making posing as a disinterested concern with the facts. But the facts were highly selective. The piece failed to mention that the long warm summer had been succeeded by a chilly, cloudy and windless autumn. And in any event, the FIT scheme had been in operation for less than six months, not nearly long enough to determine whether it was a success. Finally, no one would have associated the university's green initiative with hippies and eco-nutters if the Chronic hadn't put the idea into people's heads. Why had the editor suddenly decided to write this?

'I'd thought Bill Castles was a friend of the university,' said Turpin. 'We always invite him to our major events, and he's written well about us in the past.'

'Perhaps it was a slow news day and he'd nothing much else to write about,' said Unthank.

'I have a close working relationship with Bill,' said Prendergast, who was never slow to claim a superiority, real or imaginary, over his colleagues. 'Perhaps we need to keep him sweet. I'll give him a ring and take him out to lunch some time.'

'Meanwhile, Robert, would you give Dr Lafayette a call and see if she might send something to the Chronic that redresses the balance – a letter or even an article? Now, can we start on our agenda before I get another call from Brenda Hodges? I wouldn't be wholly surprised if Castles has sent her a copy.'

Down in the porters' office, the ESMOs were also discussing the editorial. 'Look at this, Brian,' said Tosh, putting the paper down amid the plastic cups, sandwich crusts and chocolate wrappers. 'I thought you said these windmills was going to give the uni free electricity. And you said it was also going to get rich by flogging power to half of Mixton. Dream on, mate!'

Bomber leant over and read the article. 'It says here we're no better than a bunch of hippies.'

'Yeah, well that's the Chronic for you,' said Brian. 'Just muck-stirring.'

His work-mates weren't going to let him off lightly. 'Hold on, Brian,' said Mitch, with a wink at the others, 'you was a meter reader, wasn't you? Before you get a job with the electricity people, do they make sure you can't add your sums up?'

'No wonder my electric bills was sky-high,' added Tosh, 'you was probably the bloke what was reading my meter, Brian. Can I have a rebate?'

Everyone had a laugh and went their ways. But the editorial made Brian even angrier than Turpin. It was classic Bill Castles: underhand and snide. In his window-cleaning days Brian had done a few jobs for Castles and was as ready to take his money as anybody else's. But he'd never liked the man and had his own reasons for finding him unwholesome. In any event, as the editor of the local paper Castles should, in Brian's view, be one hundred per cent behind the university and the new things it was attempting. Most of the national media seemed impressed by them. But oh no, not Bill Castles. He was a viper in their midst, a threat to the uni and the livelihood of everyone in it. Drawing on his expertise as a meter reader, Brian decided to do his bit to remedy the FIT figures. That would wipe the smirk off Castles' face.

The following Saturday, on a dreary December afternoon, Brian turned into a cul-de-sac in the Compton Farm Estate. He was wearing a dark raincoat and carrying a small roll of tools. Under his coat he wore on a lanyard the ID badge he'd stolen some ten months previously from Doug Schmeltzer. Its photograph was helpfully fuzzy, and Brian had fuzzed it up further by working it over with an abrasive. Now he and Doug looked fleetingly similar. But he knew from experience that if you simply flashed an ID card, most people accepted your authenticity without peering too closely at the photo – something which seemed a bit rude. So by this means, and by making a point of saying, 'Good afternoon, I'm Doug Schmeltzer from Central Energy,' he gained admittance to six of the houses and made certain complex adjustments to the electricity meters. These were to be found in a small store-room that was set into the external rear wall of the house.

Each visit took about twenty minutes and followed a similar pattern. Brian began by explaining that he'd come to make some checks on the meters to ensure that the householders were getting their proper due from the feed-in-tariff. This made him instantly welcome and he was plied with tea ('Splash of milk, three sugars, please') and biscuits, and left gratefully undisturbed to do whatever he had to do. There was a minor variation only on the last call he made. The door was answered by a woman, but she was reluctant to let him in because she'd been told by her husband, who was presently out buying a paper, that since he was hiding her Christmas gift there she was not to go into the meter room. However, when she heard that Brian was calling to make sure they were profiting from the FIT scheme, she began to soften. 'You obviously know what you're doing, Mr er- Smelter, so you'd better come in. Can you find your way out to the meters? I'll go and make you a cup of tea.'

When Brian opened the store-room door he got something of a fright. His view of the meter was obscured by a blow-up doll, standing with feet and arms apart and fixing him with a gaudy smile painted on her spherical head. 'Hello, love,' murmured Brian. 'Pleased to meet you.' At that moment he felt a tap on his shoulder and withdrew to face a terrified husband motioning him not to say a word. 'It's a surprise for a friend,' he whispered. 'Blew it up just to check it'd work. Look, here's a tenner. For God's sake don't say anything to the wife. I'll get it out of your way.' He squeezed past Brian and pulled a nozzle in the doll's navel.

'Always glad to help,' said Brian, finishing his work on the meters while she shrivelled to his feet in a hiss of stale air.

'Thanks, mate. What did you say your name was?'

'Schmeltzer. Doug Schmeltzer.'

As he walked round the corner and back to the Cavalier, Brian reflected that adjusting the meters had been a doddle – and he'd even been paid ten quid for his pains. Now he was ready to do the same, if on a grander scale, at Fallowfields.

62. HOLLY GETS A SHOCK

In his own quirky way Tom Burley opposed and ridiculed Learn and Earn, but continued to promote 2-4-3. This probably had less to do with conviction than the fact that he despised his head of department, Barry Powell, who was an enthusiastic supporter of the former, and quite liked Robert Unthank, who had asked for his help with the latter. And in accordance with Unthank's request, he always enlisted the services of Holly, among many other students. In an era of sophisticated and multiple media, the isolated street stunts that Burley organised were an extremely crude and limited method of promotion. It had been naïve of Unthank ever to think otherwise. But Unthank learned quickly and engaged the services of a top advertising agency. So even though the first of its exciting new two-year degree courses had already been running for four months, the university continued to promote 2-4-3 as vigorously as it could through all media, old and new, local, national and global. In an era when the number of university places all but exceeded the demand for them, the aim was to maximise recruitment by hammering home a simple message: Mixton's graduates boasted the same qualifications as graduates everywhere, but they gained them in two-thirds the time and at two-thirds the expense. To this end, the university bombarded the world with website clips, radio and TV commercials, billboard posters, cinema and newspaper adverts, and so on.

Why, then, did Tom Burley persist with his primitive street events? Simply because he loved organising performance art, a love which had long pre-dated 2-4-3 and even the arrival of Prendergast and Unthank. And in truth, they were not quite as ineffectual as they seemed. The local media always covered them, and they were therefore noticed by those prospective students who wished to study in or near the place they lived. Moreover, as an artist, their organiser boasted a national and even international reputation. Anything which bore Burley's stamp was certain to be taken as a serious aesthetic statement – even, he reflected ruefully, his unmade bed. So these street events were also covered by iPhones and the like, and rapidly uploaded to YouTube and countless websites and Facebook pages.

If the idea of using such events as a promotional tool was naïve, their content was even more so. They were all shot in Mixton and had an engaging, self-mocking naffness that made them loved and laughed at by all. Two events had been scheduled for January, and at the first of them Holly found herself with a dozen other students, all wearing sports vests, shorts and trainers, and shivering and limbering up in the bitter air. Above them a large banner spanned the road. JOIN THE UNI RACE, it said: GET A MOVE ON AT MIXTON. The vests she and Aisha were wearing proclaimed, '2-4-3 The Mixton Remix'. The vests the lads were wearing read 'This Mixton Dude Is Ahead of the Pack'. Street stunts, thought Holly, were so much more fun than studying! It hardly occurred to her that she was enrolled on what was still a three-year degree, or that, come summer, when she was due to finish, the degree would finish with her.

The local press and TV crews were again out in force. Fur cylinders were being waved on poles, long camera lenses bristled like guns on the western front. His hair loosely tied with a black ribbon and wearing a long scarf and full-length leather overcoat, Tom Burley was striding about and shouting instructions through a megaphone. There were two running teams. The sports vests of the Mixton team – Holly's – were royal blue. The other team were wearing inflatable 'fat suits' under badly stretched vests which declared them to be the graduates of Plodder Uni, Slo-Mo Uni, Here to Eternity Uni and Neverland Uni. On their backs were the legend, 'Too far! Too long! HOW MUCH?'

The starting gun was fired and both teams trotted off briskly towards the finishing line several hundred yards away. Those in the fat suits soon began to stagger and fall behind, and after fifty yards several people who were dressed in the dark blazers and white flannels of racing stewards stopped them altogether and strapped towering packs on to their backs, each bearing the word DEBT. The runners were then allowed to continue on their unsteady way. Meanwhile, a great cheer arose as the Mixton team, running abreast and with linked hands raised, crossed the finishing line. They were welcomed by placards bearing the words GOOD JOB OFFERS. Soon after, and amid laughter and catcalls, their rivals collapsed beneath their loads and were led away to a desk at the side of the road which bore the sign 'Unemployment Office – Abandon Hope All Ye Who Enter Here'.

The second event, which took place a week or two later, was another race, this time held on a circular path in Mixton's municipal park. It was a parody of a grand prix, in which the racing vehicles were mobility scooters and bicycles. It began as such races began in former times, with the drivers lined up on one side of the path and the vehicles ranged on the other. As the starting flag was lowered, the competitors sprinted across to their vehicles, clambered on and pulled away as fast as they could. A banner above proclaimed the event to be the Uni-Prix, and on the space beneath the crossbars of the bicycles were signs bearing the legend 'Mixton UNI-Cycles – Two Wheels – Two Years'. The mobility scooters bore rigid flags with such legends as 'Snailbridge University' and 'A Tortoise Taught Us', and were equipped with smoke capsules giving off dense exhaust fumes and loudspeakers emitting the sounds of racing cars. But they were scarcely able to move. They were lapped repeatedly by the fit-looking young men and women on their UNI-cycles, who passed them shouting taunts and making rude gestures. The scooters soon came to a chaotic halt, and the drivers, who were made up to look old and infirm, were helped out by young women in alluring nurses' uniforms. They were escorted to a booth describing itself as the Big Debt Repayment Office for the Elderly. Over at the finishing line, the UNI-cyclists held up placards declaring 'We Really Motor at Mixton', 'Graduate in 2 Years at Mixton', 'Get A Headache Elsewhere – Get A-Head at Mixton'.

After both events, the TV crews made a beeline for Holly, and before the mikes and cameras she worked her unwitting magic, answering questions with a wide smile and artless words spoken in a Lancashire accent. The university was the first in the country, she said, to take young people to its heart and offer degrees tailored to their special needs. It was lifting a great barrow-load of debt off their shoulders. Yes, Mixton was a brilliant place to study, a fun place. Far better than Cambridge, which was just a pile of old ruins and packed with geeks.

At the end of the interviews following the second event, Holly noticed a tall youth hovering uncertainly on the edge of the media scrum and trying, so she felt, to catch her eye. He was about fifteen or sixteen years of age, with a gaunt, rather handsome face, a shock of dark hair and of gangly, raw-boned build. Having outgrown the sleeves and legs of his garments, he seemed to be all wrists and ankles. There was something about the way in which eagerness and vulnerability vied in his manner that created in Holly a slight stirring of tenderness. She walked towards him and smiled. 'You all right, love? I'm happy to give you an autograph but I am in a bit of a hurry. Have you got a pen?'

'No, it's not that . . . er, thanks. I know you're a friend of dad's. Just wondered if you knew where he was.'

Holly looked at him with complete incomprehension. 'Who's . . .?'

'I'm Johnny, Johnny Dorn. Gary's son.'

'Bloody hell! You're better looking than your dad.'

'I'm in a bit of a mess. Had a row at school.'

'With a teacher?'

'Well, first with a teacher. I lost my temper and told her to –'

'I can guess,' said Holly.

'So I had to see the educational welfare officer, she's supposed to help me.'

'And does she?'

'She told me to go back and apologise. Apologise! I hadn't done anything wrong. Just left my homework at home. So I got into a bigger row with the EWO and she sent me home.'

'Have you been excluded?'

'That's what they call it. Third time this term, and I think there's going to be big trouble. But first off I can't get into my house. Mum's away at some conference so I need to get hold of my dad's keys. Do you know where he is? He's not picking up on his phone.'

'Perhaps he's teaching.'

'Yeah, might be.' Johnny glanced away into the distance. Something in his manner suggested that he disbelieved it.

'Go and have a cup of coffee in the Student Union and keep trying him on his phone. And if I see him, I'll tell him you're looking for him.' Johnny looked awkward and lost, and again she felt a tenderness for him. 'Don't worry, love, these things happen. Sounds like the EWO were right out of order and had no right to exclude you. I'm sure your dad'll be very understanding.'

'I doubt it,' muttered Johnny, wiping his nose on the back of his hand. 'He's part of the problem.'

'How d'you mean?'

'He's been shagging her senseless for the last month. Here, there and everywhere.'

Holly looked at him, her face frozen by the chill that descended on her heart. Was this mere teenage malice, a way of excusing his own misbehaviour? But no, he was genuine, he wasn't lying. She couldn't doubt him. He radiated a kind of truth, something that indicated he knew his father only too well. And yet neither could she believe him: in this case, he couldn't be right. He must've made an honest error, for he'd no inkling of how fond of each other she and Gary were. Yet she could think of no words to put him right. She recovered her composure as quickly as she could, wished Johnny luck in finding his dad, and, without quite knowing what she was doing, walked quickly into the town.

63. DESKTOP AVIATION

'Right hand down a bit, Tosh.'

Panting heavily, Brian and Tosh were manoeuvring a polished new 'hospitality cabinet' into Dr Turpin's office, from which the vice chancellor would be able to offer his distinguished visitors a drink. The thing was huge and abominably heavy, and Brian wondered bitterly if the visitors were going to be offered everything in tankards. They'd had to wriggle it out of the lift at the cost of scraped knuckles, heave it across the landing, and through Marian's outer office, where she and her boss were conferring. Turpin waved them through, and they had a final struggle to get it past the connecting door. At last and with an exhalation of relief, they lowered it into the designated space. Brian rested his elbows on the top and mopped his brow with the jay-cloth he'd been using to wipe the cabinet down.

'I didn't know we'd be lugging it up stuffed with booze,' he said.

'We haven't,' said Tosh. 'We've got to go back down and bring the booze up. It's in a couple of boxes in the porters' lodge.'

'No worries, you go off. I'll get them later,' said Brian, slowly straightening up. He felt in sore need of a restorative and began rummaging through his pockets, where he'd almost certainly find a sweet or two. Bloody hell, the stuff he kept in them . . . biros, bulldog clips, odd bits of paper, coins, string, batteries, a pocket screwdriver, a crumpled fiver, a penknife. He really should have a clear-out. Encountering the tablet that Holly gave him a few weeks ago, he absent-mindedly dropped it into a half drunk cup of coffee on Turpin's desk and continued the search until he at last found what he wanted – a squashy, ancient toffee that he popped into his mouth.

'Brian, Dr Turpin will have no need of the drinks today,' said Marian. 'You can bring them up tomorrow.' He made a grateful exit.

A few moments later, Turpin returned to his desk, sat down and perused some papers relating to the university's business plan. Then he drained his cup, clasped his hands across his midriff and tilted his chair back. For once, his windows were clean and in the clear winter sunshine he could see the rooftops and steeple of the parish church.

273

A strange mellowness stole over him. After all the months of anxiety, the hectoring calls from Brenda Hodges, the meetings, reports, directives, memos and working papers, the university – dare he think it? – was beginning to thrive. The Fallowfields campus was complete, an attractive embodiment of higher learning in the twenty-first century. Exciting new degrees were in place and of a mere two years' duration, and in the care of those two young people whom Prendergast had employed, the Learn and Earn scheme was working well. Studying these days was very different from the idyll he'd enjoyed as an undergraduate at Cambridge, but he could be quietly proud of his own ability to pilot Mixton University through some of the most sweeping changes that higher education had ever undergone. After being something of an obscure joke, the university was now receiving constant and admiring publicity from the media. It was being represented as ahead of the pack, a trendy, innovative institution, and Turpin was expecting it to have moved up the league tables when they were next published. He suddenly felt elated. Indeed, only one thing irritated him. Why, given the size of his achievements, did he allow himself to be so regularly browbeaten, by Brenda Hodges? He was suddenly riding on a seismic swell of self-assurance. He felt omnipotent, irresistible – and by God, he'd give Brenda Hodges a piece of his mind! He pressed the speed-dial button on his phone, and almost to his surprise she picked up at once.

'Brenda Hodges.'

'Hello, my dear! How are you, Brenda, to whom we must all surrender? Brenda with the not-so-hidden agenda.' He chuckled, confident she would enjoy the levity.

There was a pause.

'Hello. Who is this? Is that you, Richard?'

''Tis I, Dick Turpin, the famous highwayman. A bit long in the tooth, but I can still *stand and deliver*!' He tittered helplessly. He'd no idea he was so amusing.

There was another pause.

'Richard. Are you ill?'

'I have never felt better in my life. But Brenda, my cuddly gauleiter, you must stop bullying all us hapless vice chancellors. You seem to think that with a snap of the fingers you can have us all liquidated. Formidable Brenda will drop us in the blender.' He roared with laughter and dabbed at his eyes with a handkerchief.

'Richard, you're drunk!'

'Don't call me Richard, call me Dick. You strike me as just the sort of girl who appreciates a Dick.' He wept. He'd never heard anything so funny in all his life.

'Richard, pull yourself together. Have you got something you want to tell me? Because if not, I–'

'My dear Brenda, I refuse to be intimidated by you any more.'

'What on earth are you talking about?'

'I shall court you instead. Because, as Shakespeare put it, "That which we call Brenda by any other name would be as tender".'

'I'm going to end this call now, Richard.'

'And you are indeed tender. And fragrant.'

'We'll forget it ever happened.'

'A fragrant violation of my peace of mind.' He was crooning with mirth.

'I'll talk to you again when you're sober.' The line went dead. He felt that it was all too beautiful, too . . . *logical* for words. He was a plane flying high above it all, but now the airfield – or was it his desktop? – was coming up to meet him rather fast and–

His head hit the desk with a bump, and he was instantly asleep.

'Dr Turpin, are you all right?' Marian was gently shaking him awake. 'I've brought you a cup of tea.'

Turpin sat up and stared about him. How long had he been like this? What on earth had happened? He had a slight headache and his mouth was dry. 'Yes, I'm fine, thank you. Not sure why, but I seem to have dropped off.'

'I was a little bit concerned about you,' said Marian, fussing around him. 'I think you've been overdoing it. Your job's very stressful, and, if I may say so, none of us is getting any younger. Can I get you anything else – an aspirin, a biscuit?'

'Nothing, thank you. But you could be right, I have been overdoing it. I think I might take the rest of the afternoon off.'

'Quite right, and leave your car here. I'll call you a taxi.'

As he sipped his tea and waited for the taxi, he tried to make sense of what had happened to him. It was quite unlike him to have succumbed to tiredness in that way. He also recalled murkily that while asleep he'd experienced a strange dream in which he'd had a highly inappropriate conversation with Brenda Hodges. Thank God it was only a dream, he thought, as he got to his feet and picked up his overcoat and briefcase.

64. LEARN AND EARN – OR CRASH AND BURN?

Leighton Rogers was as good as his word. He got on Facebook and sowed some discontent, essentially by claiming that his own Learn and Earn experience could hardly be better:

Im sure everyone agrees Learn and Earn's a brilliant scheme. AND great idea – not stuck in lectures all the time listening to the blah. Im at the Mixton Chron – all the news thats fit to print – sort of. Getting about a bit; meeting some interesting people. How's everybody else doing?

The hornets' nest was duly stirred.

Cumfy office, eh! I'm bashing my feet out knocking on doors trying to get people signed up for thermal insulation. How green is your home? What the F... do I care. How flat are my feet?

Mixton Chron sounds like a cushy number. I'm doing the BA in Marketing. And in my second week of You Shop and We Drop deliveries I feel pretty bloody dropped myself by half past eleven – AT NIGHT !

Even the compliments were gratifyingly back-handed:

Too much whingeing. It's not all bad. I'm BA in Marketing as well and do Pizzas on a Scooter. Vroom, vroom. Meet up with some Real Lovelies who want a dessert after the Pizza!! So I tell them I'll pop back later, darling. But it does make my hourly rate come out at about 40p!

Almost all the comments were negative. None of the employers seemed remotely interested in the educational development of their internees, and almost all were operating scams. Three of them were particularly illuminating:

I'm an EnvirEco student, flogging electric bikes coz theyre good for the planet. Do demonstrations every weekend in the town centre. Bit of a stitch up. They fix a race between me and the likely buyer – but the route goes uphill. Customer gets on normal bike with no gears and I ride the electric. At the end Customer usually ready for A&E and I'm fitter than a twerking pop star. Sold seven last weekend – was promised commission on top of the rubbish rate. Still bloody waiting.

I'm BA Leisure and Hospitality and delivering take-aways from the Indian in the high street when my scooter gets a puncture. I had to push the bloody bike back three sodding miles – then they deduct the cost of the repair from my wages.

I'm doing phone calls on Personal Insurance Protection. I have to ask if they have it and if they say yes I tell them it's a scam and they can reclaim money. If they say no, I tell them there's a new deal and a rep will call round.

Throughout January, Rogers worked on fomenting the students' dissatisfaction. In smug tones he continued to say how good his own work placement was, figuring among other things that it would do him no harm if his comments got back to Castles. But he also implied that his placement was the norm for Learn and Earn, so those who were complaining were getting an exceptionally raw deal. He also quoted shrewdly from the university's Learn and Earn regulations, which contained a great deal of wistful prose about 'the educative experiences of employment', 'a symbiosis of scholarly and professional insights' and 'enrichment in the academy, emolument in the workplace'.

After being subjected for a week or two to Rogers' artful provocation, one or two Facebook correspondents decided to take matters into their own hands: they called a gathering in a local pub of all those who held grievances. The ringleader, Barney Travis, was a student of the BA in Sports and Events Management for whom Learn and Earn was indeed a raw deal. He cut the grass and painted the white lines at Mixton United's football ground. After the matches he also had to swab down the floors of both the home and visiting teams' changing rooms, and clean up the disgraceful mess which was left by players who were paid thousands of pounds a week. He soon protested to Ben and Gemma, saying that to require him to do such a job was a bit like insisting that a civil engineer couldn't design a sewerage system till he'd cleaned out a few lavatories. But they fobbed him off, saying that if he was unhappy with a job at a premiership club, there were many other students who'd be glad to replace him.

At the pub gathering, which Rogers attended, it was agreed that Travis and two others would go and see Frampton and Giddings and ask them to meet the students so their complaints could be addressed. The next morning Rogers called in to see Bill Castles and ask if he should now write up the story of the Learn and Earn scam. Still pleased with his mischievous editorial about the FIT scheme, Castles was in no hurry. 'Not yet, son. We've already got a good story, but we could get a better one. Let's see how the university people react to the complaints. If they deny all knowledge of the scam, we can show they're fibbing. If they agree to improve the scheme, it's an admission they've always known it was dodgy. And if they try to deny any wrong-doing, it'll show them in an even worse light. Get along to the meeting and see what happens.'

The same day Travis and his companions went to see Ben and Gemma. Agreeing a meeting for early in February, Ben and Gemma adopted a relaxed and sympathetic air, saying more than once that they were looking forward to the opportunity to address whatever difficulties the students might have encountered. The moment the students left they succumbed to an obscenity-sprinkled panic.

'If this reaches Prendergast's ears, he might side with the students,' grimaced Gemma.

'And that could mean we lose our performance-related bonuses – or even our bloody jobs,' added Ben. 'Get Dorn here straightaway. He's supposed to be our line-manager. Always says what a terrific job we're doing. Says he never misses an opportunity to tell Prendergast. Well, now he can help us deal with the students. And if need be, defend us against Prendergast.'

As usual, Gary proved hard to get hold of. They left voice messages on his phone and on his home and office lines, texted and finally emailed him. Several hours later, he phoned them to say he was on his way. The moment he arrived, Gemma put the matter bluntly. 'Gary, we are squarely fucked. The students are up in arms about Learn and Earn. They've demanded a meeting on February

7th. They haven't said much so far but it's clear they're very unhappy about their work placements.'

'February 7th,' said Gary coolly, pursing his lips and pretending to consult his diary. 'Nope, can't do it. Son's got himself into a spot of bother at school. I've a meeting with his welfare officer which I can't miss.'

Ben Frampton, who was not tall but fairly stocky, had long since grown hardened to Gary's indifference to Learn and Earn – his lack of interest in the placements they'd found, or their difficulties in finding them, his frequent failure to turn up to the monthly meetings. But on this occasion he walked over to Gary, stood before him and looked him straight in the eye. 'No, Gary,' he said. 'This meeting you *will* attend. Reschedule the other one.' There was something about the way he said this that extracted Gary's gruff acquiescence.

65. GENTLEMAN WITH VERY FINE UNIFORM

Hamid and Mervyn were busy at their keyboards when there came a timid knock at the door. 'Bugger off!' they shouted in unison and continued with their work, punctuated though it was by desultory conversation.

'So what time's the bash on Thursday night, Merv?'

'Six till eight. Just a few drinks.'

'Dress code?'

'Astrid says, just smart-casual. Old man Castles isn't a stickler for these things. But she says we've got to behave ourselves after what we did to his house at her party.'

'After what *you* did, you mean!' replied Hamid. 'Don't implicate a man who never touches alcohol.'

A few moments later the timid knock was repeated. Hamid tutted and went to the door with hostile intentions.

'*Assalamu alaikum.*' Smiling at him were two quietly spoken Yemeni students, Sameer and Hussein, whom he knew from meetings of the university's Islamic Society.

He instantly softened. *'Wa alaikum assalaam.'*

'Can we talk to you for just a little minute?' asked Sameer. 'You are our very good friend and we cannot ask another.'They were ushered in and seated, but eyed Mervyn and said nothing more.

'Don't worry, Mervyn's a close mate. You can talk to both of us. If you've got a problem, we'll be happy to try and solve it.'

Sameer and Hussein were both students of the BSc in Engineering and Technology, and had just done very badly in their mid-sessional assessments, the result of which would contribute to their final degree-classification.

'Really sorry to hear it,' said Hamid, 'but there's nothing we can do to help.'

Hussein's dark eyes flashed with indignation. 'But we have been betrayed! We pay for help with exam papers, ten pounds per question, and only get bad result. We need better result for money paid. Can you help? But not to tell anyone.'

'How do you mean you got help with the exams? What sort of help?'

'From Mr Huge Johns,' announced Sameer, 'he send to us the answers.'

Mervyn and Hamid leaned forward in their chairs. After a pause Hamid said, 'I think that's probably meant to be Hugh Jones. But who is he? Is he a lecturer, another student?'

The students looked at each other, then said they'd never met him. 'He only on internet. And says not tell to anyone.'

'Or you get found out.'

'And sent home with nothing. Not degree, no nothing.'

'So how did you learn about this person, Hugh Jones?'

'From Mr Byron.'

'Who?'

'Gentleman with very fine uniform and large stomach.' Mervyn and Hamid looked at each other blankly. 'They can't mean Brian, the ESMO.'

'Yes, yes, yes! Mr Brian. Is ESMO. Very kind gentleman. He say Mr Johns help students all over university.'

'So what do you want us to do?'

'You find marks on computer, help us get better results,' Sameer pulled out his wallet and began to extract a wad of banknotes.

'No, no, put that away!' said Hamid hastily. 'Look, we can't do that. But security's been breached and you seem to have been swindled. We'll try to find out what's happened and then tell the university authorities.'

'Please, my good friend, don't do that,' said Hussein. 'I beg you not to give our names to anyone, or we will lose all things. Three years study, go back Yemen, nothing! Mr Johns give us strong warning.'

Hamid promised the two Yemenis that he and Mervyn wouldn't reveal their names to anyone or do anything to worsen their position. The best they could do was try to find out what had gone wrong. 'But if what you're telling us is true,' warned Hamid, 'you need to know that you and this Mr Jones have been breaking the rules, and if you get found out you could end up not just with bad degrees but no degrees at all.'

After the unhappy students left, Mervyn went straight to the Department of Engineering and Technology. He was well-known there, and on the pretext of trying to locate an IT glitch used one of their computers to get into the marks database. What he found was that both students had scored a first for the exam and scraped a bare pass for the three accompanying assignments – the opposite of what usually happened. 'So overall they got a third, Hamid. And I reckon what's happened is that they thought they were buying the outcome for the entire mid-sessional assessment and not just one part of it.'

'So what do we do now?'

'We could tell the head of department, but that'd drop the lads right in it, and you promised you wouldn't do that.'

'True. But from what they told us, this Hugh Jones helps out students across the entire uni. So why don't we go and see the Director of Academic Development – Ed Prendergast?'

'And what, precisely, can we tell him?'

'There's some kind of exam-cheating service going on, and it's being operated by a Hugh Jones –'

'Whose encrypted files we've seen –'

'And who students can access via Brian the ESMO.'

'What the hell is a numpty like Brian doing, offering this kind of service on behalf of Hugh Jones?' asked Mervyn.

'You know Brian,' smiled Hamid, 'kindly old bloke. Likes helping the students out. Probably doesn't realise he's doing anything illegal.'

'But he can't be as innocent as all that, because remember that I ran a check on "Hugh Jones" a couple of months ago? And nobody of that name has ever been at the uni.'

'Hmm. So Brian has a connection with someone that he must know is operating under a false name.'

Mervyn got to his feet. 'I think it's time I had a word with him and found out a bit more about this Hugh Jones. He's often in the canteen at this time of day, I'll see if I can find him.' He was almost at the door when Hamid checked him.

'No. Wait. Don't talk to Brian.'

'Why not?'

'Because there may not be a Hugh Jones. Or rather, Hugh Jones may be Brian himself.'

'What the hell are you suggesting?'

'I grant this all sounds a bit far-fetched, but hear me out. Someone other than Brian may have hacked into the system. And under the false name of Hugh Jones, he could be using Brian to tout for him.'

'Right!'

'But a much simpler scam would be for Brian just to hack into the system himself, then flog the data to the students under the handle of "Hugh Jones". One scammer, not two – less risk of discovery, no division of spoils.'

'Hamid, mate, have you met Brian? He's as dim as a nun's night-light. He can hardly dress himself. How's he going to hack a computer?'

'I know, I know. I'm not claiming it as fact, I'm just saying it's a possibility. But until we've ruled it out, we shouldn't say a word to him.'

They sat for a while in silence. At length Mervyn picked up the phone. 'There is someone we should say a word to, and that's Prendergast. I'll call his secretary and get us the first appointment that's available.'

Two days later they were in Prendergast's office and telling their story. He heard them attentively, but the way he flipped his propelling pencil between his fingers conveyed impatience. When they finished, he tossed his pencil on the desk and paused for a moment.

'Let me get this right. You're reporting an exam-cheating scam on the basis of allegations made by two international students who refuse to be identified. You believe the evidence lies in some secret files you can't produce. You think they might be stored on a computer not far away but you don't know where, and though you've looked for it you haven't found it. And you think they might belong to a porter called Brian, who even from my limited knowledge of him clearly knows damn-all about computers.'

He leaned back. 'Sorry, boys, you're going to have to do better than this.' Mervyn and Hamid shot a frown at each other. Determined to press their case, they drew breath for fresh words but Prendergast spoke first.

'I've heard from Victor Margolis – do you know him, Director of Learning Applications? – that a scam's suspected, but he reckons he'll soon get to the bottom of it. But look, boys . . .' he assumed the air of a sophisticate struggling to explain the ways of the world to a pair of country bumpkins, 'British universities depend more and more on overseas students for the higher fees they bring. So they can't look too closely at the students' entry qualifications or at the, er, kinds of assistance they get in order to complete their degrees. That's a fact of life and Mixton has to go with it.'

Mervyn and Hamid were dumbstruck, but Prendergast hadn't quite finished. 'In any event, we can all get too fixated on exams. At Mixton we're working on more imaginative ways of assessment. Exams are a very blunt instrument for assessing the range of skills most students have. So once we've rolled out these new ways, the odd fiddled exam result will be neither here nor there. But look, I appreciate your concerns,' Prendergast got to his feet, 'and thanks for coming to see me.'

They departed in a daze and made their way silently back to the workshop. Each was overtaken by a sense of outrage. They'd been made to look like a couple of simpletons. That they'd been disbelieved was bad enough. Worse was that their concerns had been dismissed as trivial – concerns about a fraud whose effect was to debase the very standards the university existed to uphold. The

283

implication was that they were wasting the Great Man's time. They dropped into their chairs.

Mervyn was the first to speak. 'We did what we thought was right. Reported a serious scam to the head of academic affairs. I wonder if the outside world would take the same relaxed view as he does.' He stood up again and kicked back his chair. 'We can't let this go. We need to tell the right person about this, even if it's no names, no pack-drill. And I think we'll get our chance this evening.'

Castles was fond of throwing the occasional drinks party. In the setting of his spacious house it was an opportunity to bestow some rather showy hospitality on the important people in the town such as Harry Hunter and some key players in the Freemasons and Rotary Club. Parties also yielded gossip and potential news stories. This one was to mark his and Iris's wedding anniversary. He'd toyed with the idea of inviting some of the senior figures from the university, but decided against it. He was still nursing his grudges and even entertained the hope that if news of the party reached Prendergast he'd feel insecure at having been snubbed. But someone on whose attendance he insisted was his daughter, Astrid. He was fond of her, indeed proud of her, and if he'd indulged her to the extent of allowing her to hold her own party a few months ago, and to trash their home into the bargain, the least she could do was show up at this one and behave sensibly to his guests. He also liked her boyfriend, Mervyn, and his mate from the uni, Hamid, and urged her to bring them along, too. And she could also ask her curvy young friend, Chloe. Castles hadn't altogether forgotten the matter of Mervyn and the underpants, but if an old newspaperman like himself couldn't take a tolerant view of drunkenness, nobody could. Basically Mervyn was a nice, decent lad, and so was his mate.

In the event, Castles' largesse was rewarded beyond his dreams, for when the party was ending and Astrid was helping her mother to clear up, Mervyn and his pal asked to speak to him privately. He took them into his study, where they told him the whole story of the files, the exam scam, the rebuff they got from Prendergast and their wish to blow the whistle on the entire scandal. Castles couldn't believe his luck. Never slow to take a moralistic view, he warmly endorsed their intentions. There was no question this should be in the public realm. But while skulduggery was clearly afoot, they hadn't yet got enough to go on. And smart as these two lads were, the idea that shambly old Brian might be a computer whizz-kid – the window-cleaner whom he'd seen struggle with a ladder and bucket – was quite beyond belief. 'But keep on it, above all keep it to yourselves, and when you've got the hard evidence we'll splash it in the Chronic. And I can promise no one'll ever be able to trace it back to you. Believe me, in my business we know how to protect our sources. If we didn't, we'd never get any stories.'

Then Castles clapped his hands together, got to his feet and led the youngsters back into the lounge. 'Right lads, this calls for another drink. Mervyn, gin and tonic? Excellent. Hamid, gin and tonic? Oh, course not. Well, how about a nice glass of orange juice?'

66. GARY BLUFFS IT OUT

The students who turned up to the Learn and Earn meeting – some twenty or thirty of them – were in an ugly mood. Nor was it improved by the fact that Gary was ten minutes late and Ben and Gemma were unwilling to start until he arrived. Then the students didn't wait to be invited to speak but weighed in with their complaints. However, Gary, somewhat to his colleagues' surprise, faced them squarely. As someone whose life was littered with crises, most of which were of his own making, he would do all he could to avoid their consequences. But when at last there was nowhere to hide and he found himself at bay, he could turn and fight as stoutly as anyone, and was not always scrupulous in his observance of Queensberry Rules.

'These placements or internships – whatever you want to call them – are a total con,' shouted one student. 'They're supposed to enrich our learning, but they turn your brains to sawdust. They're completely balls-aching and the pay's lousy.'

'Do you expect even the high-status jobs to be continuously fascinating?' asked Gary. 'Being a lecturer's supposed to be one of them, but I can tell you that marking student assignments isn't the greatest fun in the world. And every successful tycoon, every top member of a profession, will tell you that you have to learn your trade from the bottom. If you're going to run a restaurant, you've got to know what it's like to work in the kitchen and serve the customers. Even the bosses of the multi-nationals spend time on the shop floor so as to find out what it's really all about.'

'Oh yeah?' returned one student. 'That'd be fine if I wanted to be head of a graveyard or chief litter-gatherer, but I don't. I'm on the EnvirEco degree and I want to be a geologist. On Learn and Earn all I do is dig graves and fork up rubbish with a spiked stick and a sack.' There were gales of sympathetic laughter.

'Anyway it doesn't take more than five minutes to learn what we're expected to do for weeks on end,' said another. 'Let me tell you, Dr Dorn, once you've delivered one pizza you've delivered them all.'

'And the same's true of delivering bags of groceries!'

Feeling himself backed up against the ropes, Gary decided to throw some different punches. 'Knowledge and wisdom don't just come through books – lots of great thinkers have also been great doers. So even if you're doing a humdrum job, the experience itself's an education. When you're delivering pizzas, you're encountering the real world. It's called "the university of life". You're getting a fuller understanding of what people want, what they're about.'

'The only thing people are about is slamming the door in your face if you've brought the wrong flavour of pizza.'

'This is bullshit,' declared Barney Travis. 'If I wanted to study at the university of life I could've done it without paying a fortune in fees. And I might have found better-paid and more interesting work.' There was a roar of agreement.

'Better still, we could've signed up for the army,' shouted someone. 'And speaking of the army, sod this for a game of soldiers. Let's go to the top – see the head of academic stuff. Prendergast, he's called. Tell him Learn and Earn's a fraud and we want proper work experience – now!' The roar became a tumult. There were cat-calls. Fists drummed on desks, feet stamped on the floor.

Gary glanced at Ben and Gemma. They were wide-eyed and wordless, two rabbits before an army of stoats. Faced with another

286

threat to his standing with Prendergast, Gary decided on drastic measures. 'You're wasting your time!' he shouted. The noise abated. 'Mr Prendergast is already fully aware of your concerns and has asked me to remind you of Paragraph 14 of your Conditions of Temporary Employment. These are what each of you signed up to when you started.'

'What's that?' they chorused.

Gary had the relevant document in front of him and read from it. 'Any student failing to comply with the university's Learn and Earn requirements for other than certified medical reasons will be deemed to have terminated their contract with the university, and be required to leave and to refund all monies paid to them under the scheme.'

Many claimed they couldn't remember the document. Voices were raised in protest: we knew nothing about this, we never agreed to that. Gary produced the signed documents. 'We never read it. It was just one of those bloody bits of paper with stuff on like you get from the . . . '

'But you should've read it,' said Gary, 'because you signed it.' The students hesitated, and he drove home his advantage. 'As I said, Mr Prendergast knows all about your concerns, and he's authorised me to warn you that if you cause trouble the conditions I've just read out will be enforced. Your Learn and Earn contract will be terminated, you'll have to return any money you've so far received, and you'll be required to withdraw from the uni. I have to tell you there's no shortage of youngsters who'd be happy to step into your shoes. Our new two-year degrees are extremely popular. We could fill the available places several times over.'

For the first time, the meeting was relatively quiet. Gary decided to offer some final emollience. 'Look, we all want you to do well, get good degrees, get good jobs. I know Learn and Earn isn't a bed of roses, but it was never meant to be.' He improvised a final fib. 'But I promise I'll have a word with the employers and see about improving the conditions of some of the internships, getting you more interesting work and full feedback. So stick at it, my friends, it *will* get better. And thank you for sharing your views with us.'

The students slowly and grumblingly dispersed. 'How does he do it?' murmured Ben in Gemma's ear, but Gemma's question to Gary was more direct. 'Is it true that Prendergast knew the students were on the war-path? And did he tell you that if they didn't play ball you could threaten them with fines and expulsion?'

Gary grinned wolfishly. 'Ask no questions, hear no lies,' he said. 'We've quietened them down. Let's make sure it stays that way.'

'Mr Prendergast didn't attend the meeting. He sent a spokesman along – name of Dr Dorn, Gary Dorn.' Leighton Rogers was reporting back to Bill Castles, and this was the light in which he viewed it. 'Prendergast said that if the students didn't accept the Learn and Earn deal, he'd throw them out of the uni. He said there were hundreds of others who were desperate to take their places.'

'Did he, by God?' whistled Castles. 'He behaves like Hitler. What an almighty rip-off.'

'Should I write up the story, Mr Castles?' asked Rogers, getting to his feet.

'All in good time, son. All in good time.'

Castles sat for several minutes contemplating the picture on the wall opposite his desk. Something strange was happening to him, something of which he was scarcely aware. The Learn and Earn scandal, such as it was, was ready to publish in the Chronic – had, indeed, been ready since Rogers had confirmed it some two months before. Why, then, was he keeping it back? His personal vendetta against the university, his desire to inflict real damage on it, was beginning to get the better of his instincts as a newsman. Now, to his incredible good fortune, the rumour of another university scandal had reached his ears. It was true that the evidence Mervyn and Hamid had so far gathered was fragmentary, but it certainly pointed to some kind of wrongdoing, and he was confident that two such capable lads would come up with more. When they did, this second scandal – the organised leaking and sale of exam papers and the university's apparent connivance in it – would be far bigger than the one he presently had.

The plan forming in his mind was that he would bundle the two stories together, and indeed any other scandals about the uni that his contacts might dig up, and then run a grand exposé in the Chronic – one that, if need be, could be spread over several days. And as a final sadistic twist he might even adopt that pose of fair-mindedness so beloved of journalists and, just before he ran the exposé, warn the university of his intentions – though not so far in advance that it could take defensive measures. The university would then learn that however big and trendy it was becoming, it must respect those local institutions like *The Mixton Chronicle* on whose goodwill it depended.

67. ONLY THE BOWL GOES BEGGING

'Sorry, Mr Foreman, but we've had another two burglaries. Same MO. The houses in the roads got a leaflet through the door. One road got Yum Choi Chinese Take-Away and the other got Delhi Delight – at Your Door.'

'Any other similarities?'

'Usual one. It's not that you take away from them it's that they take away from you. So it is a takeaway, but not as usually understood.'

Foreman gave the sergeant a hard stare in case he was trying to be funny. 'What did they get this time?'

'From the Yum Choi place they got two iPads, two iPhones, a telly, and, a bit odd, an original and very valuable Chinese lantern. So we thought perhaps someone from the restaurant was nicking the stuff.'

'And were they?'

'No, sir. Place doesn't exist.'

'So what are these leaflets for?'

'We think they're sort of a decoy. Someone goes down the road stuffing them in the letter boxes but then actually calls on the house they want to do over.'

'Why?'

'If someone comes to the door they say there's a new restaurant opening and give them a leaflet. And if nobody answers . . . '

'They break in and take what's around.'

'That's about the size of it.'

'So what did they get from the other two places?'

289

'From the second, complete stereo system, very smart camera, two hundred and fifty quid in cash and a coffee maker.'

'A coffee maker? Are they getting stuff for a food kitchen?'

'No, sir. This was something called an integrated bean grinder. Costs about a hundred and fifty quid. So the poor sods who were done'll probably have to survive on instant for a day or two.'

'And how are these villains getting in?'

'Varies, sir. Some places just need a plastic card to get through the door but at others they have to get over the side gate, get round the back and then force a door or window. Whichever way it is, they seem to have a motor nearby and wear overalls of some kind so it looks as if they're legit.'

Next day the burglaries were splashed across the front page of *The Mixton Chronicle* under the headline CHINESE TAKE-AWAY – OR CURRY TO GO. There were photos, reactions from the victims, descriptions of the missing items, and a plea to all readers to keep their eyes open. A special crime number was provided for anyone who had any knowledge of the burglaries or wished to report something suspicious. Readers were advised that Inspector Derek Foreman was leading the investigation and any call would be treated in the strictest confidence. The week passed without any arrests being made, and culminated in another burglary that was something of a tour de force.

'They did a really big one yesterday, sir. That smart lady up the close. Mrs Attwood. She got totally taken to the cleaners. Even though that was the day her cleaner wasn't there.'

Foreman gave the sergeant a frosty look. 'What's been taken?'

Having read out a list of missing items, the sergeant added, 'Oh, and apparently her dog's disappeared as well.'

'Well, she'll have to get on to the RSPCA about that. We've got enough on our plate.'

This time the Chronicle took a more partial view: THIEVES RUN RIOT WHILE POLICE PLOD – ARE OUR HOMES SAFE? Foreman tutted when he saw it. He understood that in order to sell newspapers his mate Bill Castles had to colour things up a bit. All the same, journos had no loyalties. He'd slipped Bill many a juicy titbit in the past, and now the old scoundrel was biting the hand that fed him.

As soon as Unthank read the article he went to Betty Attwood's house to offer what comfort he could.

'Come in, Raymond, how kind of you to call. The place is a mess. Well, actually it's not, there's nothing to make a mess with.'

Unthank walked into the sitting room and gazed around him, thunderstruck. Its shabbily exquisite furniture and furnishings had mostly vanished. The room was naked, with only carpet and curtains to cover its shame. White rectangles on the wall bore witness to the stolen pictures. The mantelpiece was bare: even the coal-scuttle and fire irons had been taken from the hearth. Feeling a gust of cold air, Unthank glanced at the window and noticed that the frame had now dropped entirely because the two silver teaspoons that had wedged it had also been taken. In the middle of the carpet, and still full of biscuits, was Baggins' bowl. Betty Attwood led Unthank into the kitchen, where her housekeeper had set a tray of coffee on the table.

The burglary had taken place during a visit she was making to the bowls club, which always occurred on her housekeeper's day off. When she got back, this was what she'd found. She immediately called on her neighbour, who told her that she'd noticed a white van parked in Betty's drive and merely supposed that something was being delivered.

Unthank's repeated and various offers of help were gratefully declined. Her housekeeper had agreed to live in for the next few weeks, during which Betty would arrange for the house to be fitted with a burglar alarm and proper locks. As he was leaving Unthank observed that she would at least have Baggins to console her. 'It seems not, Roger. They appear to have taken him too, you see. At least, I haven't seen him since I was burgled.' Despite the value of all that had been taken, this was in its way the keenest loss of all. Unthank groped for comforting words. He felt a flash of anger that God, or the gods, should rain so many blows upon this wiry, eccentric and brave little woman. Tears and self-pity seemed foreign to her yet the less she flinched, the more tenderly he felt for her. 'Perhaps the intruders frightened him away, and he'll find his way back very soon.'

'I must hope so. I've put a notice in the Lost and Found column in the Chronicle,' she allowed herself to be kissed as he took his

291

leave. 'But in the meantime life goes on. The bowls club AGM takes place shortly, and I shan't be deflected from writing my annual report. I won't give the burglars that satisfaction.'

68. BASTARD!

One evening in late February, Holly was sitting in the library busily avoiding work. She was reviewing video clips on her iPhone. The first showed her as a campus scout on the half-built Fallowfields site and posing for a photo-shoot with the first occupants of the new 'Green with Envy' houses. In the next ones she was performing in Tom Burley's 2-4-3 street stunts. In the uni running race, she was loping ahead of the field with the full, rounded grace of a woman in her prime. Another showed her in a more comical but equally attractive light. She was wearing a skimpy parody of a nurse's uniform. The tunic was too tight and, scarcely buttoned, revealed bits of a lacy, push-up bra. Suspenders and the welts of her fishnet stockings were clearly visible, and she teetered across the road in high heels to help a decrepit three-year graduate out of his mobility scooter and into the Big Debt Repayment Office for the Elderly. It wasn't the first time that evening that she'd played the clips. She then turned to Facebook to discover that another twenty five people wished to befriend her. For the moment she could quell her unease about how much of her time these antics took up, feeling secure enough to open the envelope she'd just collected from the student office.

The library building was due to close in ten minutes' time and floor by floor Brian was clearing the students out. There was always a hard core who wanted to stay put. It was like 'drinking up' time in the pub. The hard drinkers knew the evening's end was nigh but ignored all intimation of it. As students caught his eye, he nodded and tapped his watch, and most began to collect their papers and shut down their computers, but a few showed reluctance. These were usually huddling round a single screen. They were the football fans who wanted to see the end of a match clip, or the gamers, even noisier, who were either jubilant at getting to the fourth level or angry at being dumped.

The top floor seemed deserted. Brian glanced at his watch because he was ready for his supper and didn't want to keep his mum up. He normally walked along every aisle between the stacks, but this evening he'd just take a quick look down each before heading home. He was approaching the exit door when he thought he heard a muffled sound, rather like a sniff or sob. He stopped, but there was silence. He started again, but this time the sound was unmistakable. He retraced his steps towards the aisle it seemed to come from. Rounding a corner, he saw a girl at a desk, head resting on her arms and some half screwed-up papers and a torn-open envelope scattered about her. As he approached, she raised a tear-smudged face and he realised to his surprise that it was Holly. He hadn't seen her in the library since the time of the sit-in: she was usually to be found in less studious settings.

'You all right, love?'

He was at something of a loss. Weeping women hadn't featured much in his life. He'd only seen this kind of thing in films. There seemed to be a range of masculine responses. You could take the girl in your arms, or you could tell her to pull herself together. Or – though he could never understand this one – you could start talking softly about something totally irrelevant to both you and the girl. Or in some cases, you could give the girl a sharp slap. The girl then slapped you back, and even more bafflingly, you went into a fierce clinch with her. Feeling none of these were appropriate, he decided just to be kindly. 'What seems to be the trouble? Lost a book or something?' Holly sat up, sniffed and smiled, and shook her head. Even Brian realised there must be a graver reason for her distress. He tried again. 'Failed a module, ducks?'

'I've failed the Media Today module, Brian. It's where you've got to, like, give a sort of description of media stuff. Different things. How they, like, relate. Or not. It's all bloody rabbit-rabbit. We've got to do it 'cos we've got to – ' Holly quoted from the guide in front of her – '"have a comprehensive understanding of how the media interface with both producers and consumers". I mean, what's that all about? I just watch the stuff. But you have to *interface* with it, Brian.'

Brian nodded, his face luminous with incomprehension.

'Some of my mates on the course just did the cut-and-paste thing. You cruise round the sites and stick bits together. Then you mix them up and add odd words and some spelling mistakes to put the plague hunters off the scent.'

'Plague?'

'Plague-yer-ism. It's where you nick the stuff from somewhere and don't tell. But I thought I'd do it properly. Apart from a couple of 3H tablets some mates in DoCTOC gave me, I didn't get help from anyone. I sweated blood over the books. Honestly, Brian, you wouldn't think there was so much to say about telly and stuff. I mean some's good and some's crap. But the people that write this stuff, they need to get a life.' Holly sighed and folded her arms and Brian couldn't but agree. 'I tried, I really did. And this is the bloody mark I get.' She scrabbled among the pages and pushed them towards him. Brian took in the mark of 28 at the top of the cover sheet, followed by what seemed to be some very hurtful comments. 'Twenty eight per cent, Brian. After all that work, that's a fail. I've got to do it all again.'

'You'll do better next time.'

'Impossible,' she wound a damp handkerchief through her fingers. 'If you fail, then for your re-sit you can never get more than a bare pass, which really stuffs you.' She pressed the hankie to her nose and fresh tears appeared at her eyes, but Brian had an inspiration, one which had never occurred to the romantic heroes of the screen. He produced a Twix bar. Holly smiled through her tears and shook her head. But this act of tenderness, however inept, seemed to upset her even more. At length she continued. 'There's been something else on my mind. Brian, can you keep a secret?'

''Course I can, love.'

There were further sniffs and pullings at her handkerchief, then she began to weep again. 'I think my boyfriend might be two-timing me.'

'A lovely girl like you? He must be mental. What makes you think that? Who is he? I'll wring his neck for you.'

Again she giggled through her tears. 'One of the lecturers. Gary Dorn. You know Gary?'

'Yeah, I know him. I've helped him out once or twice.'

'I've helped him out a lot more than that. We've been together for two years – almost the whole time I've been a student at Mixton. I love him, and he keeps telling me he loves me.' (In fact, he told her only when pressed.) 'I bumped into his son the other day. Yeah, he's got kids, but him and their mother's divorced so he's not two-timing me with her.'

Not *two*-timing, thought Brian. Pick a higher number.

'But his son, Johnny's his name, told me without knowing about me and his dad that Gary was shagging someone at his school.'

Perhaps a much higher number, thought Brian.

'Anyways, I tried to have it out with Gary. Told him what Johnny had said, but he totally denied it. Said he had a difficult relationship with his son. It were just a nasty lie 'cos his son goes round making up stuff about his dad 'cos he blames him for the break-up with his mum. Gary said Johnny's in a heap of trouble himself, and no one should believe a word he says. What do you think, Brian?'

Brian pursed his lips and gazed at the spines of the *Encyclopaedia of British Film* ranged along the shelf in front of them. Holly had told him little he didn't already know – she would have been surprised to learn how little – and he had no wish to distress her further. But she was a sweet kid, and he felt he owed her a truth which, while adding to her pain in the short term, might liberate her in the long. He inwardly braced himself. 'If you'd asked me a few days ago I'd have told you not to worry. But as it 'appens . . .' Brian grunted and lurched and fishing in one of his pockets produced a pen-drive. 'I don't know what this thing is but Tosh gave it me. Says it's got film from one of the security cameras he monitors, and if you plug it into your computer you can view it. He was all nudge-giggle-wink, and said something like, "Cop an eyeful of this. That Dr Dorn's a bit of a lad." Don't know what he means, haven't had a chance to look at it myself.'

Holly plugged the pen-drive into her lap-top, and Brian squeezed into the chair beside her. So eager was she to see what it contained that she didn't notice how adroitly this well-known computer dunce advised her to 'skip to this' and 'click on that'. At length there appeared an elevated fly-on-the-wall image of an office, one that gave a relatively wide-angled view. Standing in front of a desk a

295

man and woman were kissing and groping each other hungrily. Holly vaguely recognised the woman as Gemma Giddings, the Learn and Earn administrator. The man was unmistakably Gary. He disengaged, walked over to lock the door, and returned with a chair which he set down in the middle of the room. The woman meanwhile had wriggled out of her lower clothing. He sat down on the chair and she straddled him eagerly.

'The bastard! The fucking BASTARD!' Holly's words rang out across the darkened spaces of the library. 'The leching, whoring, two-timing, dick-sticking BASTARD!' She'd seen enough and yanked out the pen-drive. Then she sat and wept silently, elbows on the desk, fists pressed to her eyes.

Brian was fleetingly sorry not to have been able to watch to the end of the clip, because the final shot was the best. There was boring footage of the couple putting their clothes back on and rearranging the furniture. Gary soon left and Gemma returned to her desk and sat quietly for a while. But then she looked up towards the camera and suddenly grabbed the cup beside her and hurled the contents at it. The image of her was instantly replaced by a brown curtain, and then failed altogether. Princess Diana's squint, which had so infuriated Gemma, had of course been Brian's fault, for when he'd hung the portrait he'd been obliged to drill a small hole in the lady's left eye in order to accommodate the lens of his spycam. He'd been ashamed by this disrespectful, if necessary, measure and felt that he'd now been duly chastised, except that he really liked the dramatic way the clip ended, and it'd been the princess who'd suffered the chastisement.

He now put this to the back of his mind as he extended a comforting arm round Holly's shoulders. 'Forget him, love. He's no good for you. Fine young girl like you don't have to dangle after a worthless old goat like Gary. You can snap your fingers and have any number of nice blokes. But look, you've only got another term to go before you finish. Just concentrate on your work and get your degree. Then you can put all this behind you.'

After a few moments something slightly surprising happened. With a final sniff and blow of her nose and wipe of her eyes, Holly got to her feet with some composure, and though deathly pale began to gather up her things. 'Yeah, Brian. You're right.' She declined any further comfort or a lift home, promised him she was OK and wouldn't do anything drastic either to herself or anyone else. Then she put an arm round Brian's neck, and kissed him firmly on the cheek. 'You're a nice man, Brian. Better than most.' And she turned on her heel and was gone.

69. HEADING FOR A CELESTIAL STATE

One day in March, Prendergast received an email which he read, re-read and then continued to stare at for several minutes. It was a request from the head of human resources at Celestia State University in the United States, informing him that, subject to satisfactory references, it had appointed Dr Kate Huckerby to a professorship in feminist film theory and that she had cited him as one of her referees.

This had come as a bolt from the blue, and yet, deep down, he was not surprised. Since that first encounter at the country club, nearly two years ago now, their relationship had settled into a curious routine. They dated about once every four or five weeks, when Prendergast would turn up at her flat with a bottle of good wine. They'd eat a home-delivered meal together and then retire to the bedroom, but she never allowed him to spend the night with her. At the end of the evening, never later than midnight, they would then determine his next visit by consulting their iPhone diaries. They might have been two strangers arranging a dental appointment or a business meeting.

The encounters themselves were almost as impersonal. They were the slaking of a cold, bloodless lust. Conversation was mundane. From time to time they discussed things like the cost of property or the freakish weather, current stories in the media, or educational and university politics, though not usually as these impinged on either of them. Broadly speaking, this suited Prendergast. He was not a man whose emotions were highly developed and not keen to discuss his private life. He liked the absence of attached strings, and Kate provided an occasional midweek alternative to the weekend sex he enjoyed with his partner,

Sally, down in London. But sometimes, just sometimes, he had the desire to make a full conquest of her, to gain her heart as well as her body. To this end he'd attempt an occasional compliment or begin to say how clever he found her, but with her sardonic smile she deflected all expressions of affection, parried all inquiries about her personal life. She had no interest in yielding her own heart, nor in capturing his. She'd never stayed at his Mixton flat, never even visited it. She showed no curiosity about his life and no wish to discuss her own.

Yet perhaps for these very reasons he trusted her entirely, above all never to discuss with others the liaison they enjoyed. After the initial price she demanded for it, she'd never sought to vary the deal or exert influence over him in university matters. She never asked him for favours. The price had been that she should be allowed to remain at the university for up to three years while she looked for a new job that suited her. And when the job or the termination point arrived, that would be the end of her life at Mixton – and, implicitly, of their affair. But as the months went by and she mentioned nothing of any jobs in prospect, her departure became harder to imagine. He realised that he would be more than happy to keep her on permanently, not just because of their relationship but because she was tough-minded and efficient. She'd crushed the opposition to 2-4-3 much more efficiently than that apathetic and slippery eel, Dorn, the back of whom Prendergast would not be sorry to see. Yet now, suddenly, here it was. She was going. Even macho Ed was only flesh and blood. He would try and tempt her to stay. Their next date was not for several weeks, and in any case he sensed that a date would not be the occasion to discuss the matter. So he got his secretary to ask her to come and see him in his office, and this she did early the following day.

He handed her a printed copy of the reference request. 'I see you're leaving us.'

'Yes,' she agreed. 'I should've told you I was quoting you as a referee, but the interview came up quicker than I expected and I didn't get the time. Apologies.'

Prendergast sighed.   'I remember when you discussed your ambitions with me a couple of years ago. I know we're not Oxbridge and we're not the Russell Group. But since then, a hell of a lot's changed here, and in selling 2-4-3 you can take much of the credit. You gave your colleagues a wake-up call. Made them understand we can adapt without sacrificing standards. So in the end, we might just put all those older universities in the shade. Mixton's going places, and we can do it better with your contribution.'

Kate crossed her legs, leaned back in the chair and fixed him with her mocking smile. 'Ed, don't waste your PR-speak on me.'

'I mean it. I should've said this before, but I'd like you to consider staying on with us. What we need is a Teaching and Learning Ambassador to carry the Mixton message to other universities.'

The mocking smile grew broader. 'What would that involve?'

'We've led the way in both 2-4-3 and Learn and Earn. New courses need new teaching methods. Students have to be taught more intensively. Education and work have to be integrated through student-centred learning. We need someone from Mixton to tell the other uni's where their future lies. We need to show them how our students get a better deal than theirs.' The more amused she seemed, the more strenuously he sought to persuade her. 'You'd be the ideal person to pros- pros, er, spread the word more widely.'

'Why would I wish to proselytise for Mixton? Why would I want to pick up the Mixton baton and run round the country with it? Would the university provide me with shorts and a sports top, like that girl Holly selling 2-4-3?'

'Kate, be serious. The fact that you're an academic, and an increasingly senior one, makes you the ideal person for this job. I know you'll want to pursue the academic stuff you enjoy doing, and I'm sure we can give you a bit of research time for that. What do you say?'

It was about as far as he could go. She might guess that behind this professional offer lay a personal motive, but his pride would not allow him to declare it. He waited. She took a deep breath and the sardonic smile receded. 'I'm flattered by your offer. But how would I end up if I stayed here at Mixton? It seems I could be an administrator, a spin-doctor, an entrepreneur, even a media star. But the only kind of person you haven't got room for in this academy is an academic. Sorry, Ed, my mind's made up. I'll be leaving at the end of next month, but look . . .' she consulted her iPhone, 'we've got one more date in a couple of weeks' time. A modest celebration's called for and I'll stand us a bottle of bubbly.' She got to her feet and her smile had returned, though without its usual mockery.

Prendergast spent a long time staring at the door she closed softly behind her.

70. FIT-ED UP

Gemma and Ben always knew that the cream of the Learn and Earn internships would have to go to students of the university's new flagship degrees in environmental studies and complementary therapy. Learn and Earn had to be seen to be a success on these if on no others. Such was the demand for internships that they struggled even here, and it took all their skills in euphemism and jesuitry to pretend that cemetery and parks maintenance was suitable work experience for students of environment and ecology. Nor, as the recent rebellion showed, had they been wholly successful. However, the favourable publicity that had surrounded the launch of the new degrees made them attractive to those organisations that wished to offer work experience, and most of the students were lucky enough to get good placements.

One of them was Astrid's new friend, Chloe Stark, who was a student on the EnvirEco degree and had been allocated to Central Energy, the local power company. She was a quiet, buxom, homespun girl, and her unlikely friendship with the scatty and self-dramatising Astrid could only be seen as an attraction of opposites. Sensible, placid Chloe kept Astrid relatively grounded: self-confident, vivacious Astrid lent glamour and excitement to Chloe's otherwise humdrum lifestyle. But Chloe didn't greatly like Astrid's father, Bill, the editor of the Chronic. Though fond of his daughter, he clearly preferred male company and got on well with Astrid's boyfriend, Mervyn, who worked in IT management at the uni. Castles was civil enough to Chloe, and though she sometimes noticed him giving her an appraising look that made her uncomfortable, he otherwise paid her little attention.

Central Energy took good care of her. On her very first day, she'd been provided with a mentor and a daily schedule which set out what she'd be doing and with whom. Over the next days she learned about energy supply and distribution, about kilowatt-hour usage, about the pros and cons of different forms of power generation and the ways of accessing it: coal, gas, oil; drilling, mining, excavation, fracking; solar power, wind power and wave power. Her hosts were impressed by her intelligence and curiosity. In her second week, as they sat down together at a computer, she asked her mentor about the FIT scheme. Could the company identify how well the scheme was working in so particular a locality as Mixton? Of course, he assured her. Was it even possible to measure the impact of FIT over a mere neighbourhood, such as the Fallowfields campus and the neighbouring Compton Farm Estate? Nothing easier, replied her mentor. And for even greater illumination he'd show her the figures for the current quarter, and compare its energy profile with that of another part of the town that consumed a similar amount of energy but hadn't joined the FIT scheme. Looking at energy consumed and energy generated, they should then discover that for the FIT subscribers the costs were lower because they were buying less power from Central, and, with luck, feeding a modest surplus back into the national grid.

But as he accessed the relevant pages on the computer screen, his suave and knowing facade began to slip. 'So if we just bring up these figures here, we'll see . . . no, I must've gone wrong. Ah yes, so if we go here and look along here, we can see that . . . Hang on a sec, have I got that right . . . ? No, it must be under . . .' There was a long silence as he brought different pages on to the screen and his cursor raced along rows and down columns like a bluebottle fretting at a window pane. At last, he pushed the mouse aside, gripped the edge of the desk and leant forward to peer closely at the screen, his mouth wide open.

'Frack me gently,' he breathed. 'If these figures are to be believed, we're not looking at Fallowfields but Barbados. Seems the area has a micro-climate that never falls below thirty and blows a non-stop hurricane. Something's gone badly wrong here. Smells distinctly fishy. I'd better get on to my boss.'

71. MORE THAN JUST DESSERTS

Gary didn't know what had got into Holly, but whatever it was it couldn't have come at a worse time. Both his ex-wife Cynthia and his partner Rebecca were giving him hell because Johnny had ratted to them about his dalliance with the welfare officer. And instead of focusing on Johnny, the welfare officer was focusing on Gary, to an extent that was becoming embarrassing. He'd somehow have to cool that relationship and spend a bit more time with Holly. But now Holly was also acting strangely. Of course, Johnny had ratted to her, too, but Gary thought he'd managed to convince her that Johnny was just a lying little sod.

For a week or two things seemed to be OK, but then her manner changed somewhat. She became wheedling, demanded frequent tokens of affection from him in ways that suggested her suspicions hadn't been wholly assuaged. One of her complaints was that he'd never delivered on a long-standing promise to take her out for a posh dinner. He reassured her that as soon as he could find the time, he would. She replied that he could always find time for a date that involved taking his clothes off. At length, and admitting to himself that even his liaison with Holly needed occasional nurturing, he adopted an air of munificence and told her to go ahead and book somewhere nice for Friday evening. He could ill afford it, of course, but to an artless northern lass like Holly, 'somewhere nice' would be a local pizzeria or *The Star of India*.

The next day she bumped into him in a corridor and gave him some cheerful news that made his blood run cold. 'Found somewhere nice. I've booked *La Jonquille* in Glabthorpe.' *La Jonquille* was one of the smartest restaurants in the area, and had just been awarded several stars by a top food writer. He couldn't object. To have given her a free hand and then complain about the cost of her choice was something even Gary couldn't sink to. So he tried to transpose his initial response, 'Holy fuck!', from one of incredulous horror to incredulous enthusiasm. 'Make sure you look smart,' she called back to him as she walked down the corridor.

As their date approached, Gary struggled, with some success, to see it in a positive light. If the evening was going to set him back a fortune, he'd be twice a fool to sit through it wretchedly counting the cost. He'd try to enjoy it as best he could. Holly would be a very glamorous companion, even, thanks to her media exposure, something of a celebrity, he could steer her towards the cheapest dishes, and afterwards he'd be in her good books for the foreseeable future. Since Rebecca was spending a long weekend with her parents, he didn't even have to worry about spinning her a yarn. Waiting for the taxi to arrive, he patted on some aftershave, and stood before the mirror to check his appearance. In a beige suit and his best white shirt, he was a guy any girl would want to be seen with.

When he picked her up, Holly was wearing a short blue silk dress. She looked delectable. Not for the first time Gary marvelled sadly at how a simple, unremarkable creature could assume such awesome beauty. Before a girl like this the most gifted and successful men in the world – generals, scientists, poets, politicians – might prostrate themselves and offer all they possessed. And yet, Gary told himself, you're the bloke she's preferred. You barely lifted a finger for her – *and* you've got a couple of other chicks on the go. He smirked at his reflection in the taxi window, but their arrival at the restaurant soon brought him to his senses. Glabthorpe High Street was a pretty parade of Georgian and Victorian houses and shops, with only a sporadically ugly in-fill of more modern buildings. *La Jonquille* was in what had once been a shop, but he was well aware that expensive restaurants often present an unassuming exterior. As he paid off the driver he was mildly vexed that Holly had gone straight in and not waited for him to escort her. But then given the places she usually ate at, this was forgivably gauche. A girl doesn't wait to be escorted into Burger King.

Behind the front bar the restaurant was situated in a large, tastefully appointed room that gave on to a floodlit garden. Pen and ink drawings of buildings and landscapes were hung round the walls, and on the tables was crisp white linen, a vase containing a fresh flower or two, gleaming glassware and opulently weighty cutlery. There were about a dozen tables, at all but one of which diners were already seated. With a professional smile, the maître d'hôtel conducted them to the single unoccupied table in the very centre of the room. Waiters shunted them gently into their seats and placed napkins across their laps, and as they studied the menu Gary did his best to focus on the description of the dishes and not on their prices. Conscious of the many glances directed at his companion, he at last began to feel like a man about town.

Almost at once, things began to slip out of his control.

'Would you care for a drink while you're studying the menu?' asked the waiter.

'No, I don't think – ' began Gary.

'Yes, I'd love one!' said Holly, and promptly ordered the most expensive cocktail on the list. Gary looked warily at her over the top of his menu, but the last thing one can do when taking a lady out to dinner is admonish her for her extravagance.

When the cocktail arrived Holly took a sip and grimaced. 'It's crap,' she announced. 'Crap on ice. Bring me a buck's fizz instead.' Unperturbed, the waiter removed the drink and went to fetch the buck's fizz. Now staring openly at her, Gary was met with a sticky, innocent smile.

'You OK?' he asked.

'Fine,' she said. She made a swift, almost indifferent choice of dishes, then leant forward with her hands clasped between her knees, and rocking back and forth glanced in turn at the pictures on the wall. She was beginning to act like a bored child who'd been instructed to be on her best behaviour. When the starters arrived, Holly, who had ordered spinach gnocchi, took a dislike to it at the first mouthful. 'Not really my thing, Gary, would you like a taste?' Before he could reply she scooped up two or three gnocchi with her fork and passed them across the table. As she tipped them towards him, they fell like bombs into his own starter, spattering his suit and shirt front with beetroot soup.

'Oh, sorry, love. Here, let me. If you mop it quick it won't stain.' She seized her napkin, plunged it into the jug of iced water, half rose from her chair and began to sponge him down.

'It's OK, it's OK,' protested Gary, pushing her away.

They were beginning to attract interest from the other diners. Sitting in a shirt and jacket covered in red smudges and spooning the balls of gnocchi out of his soup, Gary wondered what was going on. Was she an awkward, working class girl who didn't know quite how to behave in a posh restaurant? Or had she been popping the 3Hs again? He'd heard they took people in different ways. They had little effect on some, while others were said to go totally ape-shit. They usually just made Holly a little bit hyper, but if she'd been upping the dosage it would explain a lot. He thought it prudent not to ask till later, and they finished the course in near silence. Once again he resolved to make the best of the occasion, but he noticed that Holly was gulping down the expensive wine and not waiting for him to empty his glass before re-filling her own. The wine waiter was never quick enough to serve her.

Their main course was loin of venison with celeriac remoulade, pomme Maxine and juniper jus. Holly recognised none of the food and few of the descriptions but relished every mouthful, and at first they were too busy eating to talk. Then with fork halfway to his mouth, Gary paused in dismay as she once again attempted to re-fill their glasses. She served herself first and then poured so much into Gary's that it overflowed and made a red puddle on the white tablecloth.

'Holly, what the hell are you . . . ?' but she silenced him with a finger to her lips, and then, to his horror, lifted the bottle to her mouth and drained the rest. With a hand over her lips she burped demurely, tittered at him and extended the bottle to a passing waiter. 'Can we have another bottle of the same, please?'

'The Premier Cru Clos Saint Jacques, madam?'

'Holly, I really don't think we – '

'That's right, love,' she said to the waiter. 'Premier Crew Closet Saint Jack. Great.'

Gary was no longer willing to hide his annoyance. 'Holly,' he snapped, looking round at the other diners, 'for Christ's sake pull yourself together.'

The waiter had returned with a fresh bottle. There was a painful pause while he uncorked it and offered it to Gary to sample.

'No, love,' said Holly loudly, 'it'll be all right. Just glug it straight into the glasses.'

With pursed lips and raised eyebrows, the waiter did as he was told. No sooner had he departed than another waiter arrived with the dessert menu.

'I don't think I can manage a dessert . . . .' began Gary weakly, but Holly said that a meal out was nothing if you didn't have pud. So she chose spring fruit pavlova, a flamboyant confection of meringue, whipped cream, freshly imported strawberries and red berries. And as an afterthought she ordered herself a glass of vintage port.

Gary was steeling himself to make a grand if *sotto voce* protest when she leant forward, and with her chin on her hand smiled winningly at him. 'It's been lovely being with you, Gary, but what's going to happen to us when I leave the uni?'

This was unexpected. 'Er, well, we'll keep on seeing each other, of course. It may not be quite so easy, but unless you – '

'Unless I what? Unless I refuse to be like all the other women and be your plaything whenever you fancy it?'

'Come on, Holly, let's not go through all that again. I told you before, you're the only one I'm seeing – '

Holly chuckled. 'I do love it when you make me laugh!' Then she picked up the bread roll from her side plate and threw it at him, hitting him on the forehead.

'What the fuck are you doing?' hissed Gary, as he bent down to retrieve it from the floor.

'What do you mean, what the fuck am I doing?' she was still smiling but had raised her voice. 'The question is, sweetheart, who the fuck are you fucking? How many and how often?'

The room had fallen silent. All the other diners seemed to be engrossed in their meals, but each now strained with every fibre of their being to follow the events at the centre table.

'Holly, I don't know what's got into you. Calm down, here are the desserts. Let's have a quiet chat, sort out any problems.'

'There wouldn't be any problems,' she continued, in a loud voice, 'if you could just bring yourself to tell the truth. But you talk all this rubbish about me being the only one.'

'You *are* the only one,' he muttered, eyes flitting to left and right.

'Oh really? Who's this, then?'

She suddenly thrust her iPhone into his face, so closely that he couldn't make out the moving image on the screen. He pulled his head back to see Gemma Giddings and himself, coupling briskly. Panic flooded through him. 'Oh, God. Where did this come from? Look, it's not what it seems, we were, we were . . . it was just a one off.'

The other people had now lost their inhibitions and were gazing frankly at the drama in the middle of the restaurant. Opened mouths awaited food that was suspended in transit. Wide eyes stared over the rims of tilted glasses. Frozen waiters held out bottles as yet unpoured.

Holly got to her feet. 'I'm leaving.'

Gary rose too, and went round the table to restrain her.

'Don't touch me,' she said.

He tried a sterner approach. 'Sit down, Holly. Stop making an exhibition of yourself in front of all these people.'

'All these people? Oh yes, I'd forgotten about them,' and she at once assumed the air of a public entertainer. 'Good evening, ladies and gents, sorry to have spoiled your nice quiet meal. But think of it instead as dinner with a cabaret. Now, ladies and gents, my boyfriend is such a randy old skunk that his privates get overheated – and they need cooling off.'

She turned back to him, seizing the jug of iced water.

'He's a *lying* . . .'

She yanked out his waistband and tipped the water into his trousers.

'*cheating* . . .'

As he bent forward from the shock, she emptied the red wine over his head.

'*double-crossing. . .*'

Blinded, he couldn't stop her from pouring the port into his top pocket.

'*BASTARD!*'

And with all her force she rammed the pavlova into his face. Then she turned on her heel, smiled sweetly at the maître d'hôtel and walked out.

72. BEATEN TO THE PUNCH

Before her departure from the university became public knowledge Kate needed to break the news to Loren, and for a week or two she couldn't decide how. The obvious way was when they were in bed together, but such was the companionate, fairly low-key nature of their relationship that the intervals between their trysts were quite lengthy. Recently, pleading pressure of work in running her new department, Loren had even been obliged to cancel two of them.

In the end, Kate surprised herself by resolving to tell Loren not in bed but over a prearranged meeting in a coffee shop. It would be hard to tell her anywhere, but Kate felt something else she couldn't admit to herself – a glee at the sadness it would cause. This was not peculiar to Kate, for in the words of the poet, William Blake, a lover often 'joys in another's loss of ease'. On the other hand, she was fastidious enough not to want too much emotional mess, and in a public setting the matter could be more cleanly managed, brought to a speedier conclusion. The sadness that must be half-suppressed in a coffee shop would be every bit as gratifying to her as the tears that would flow freely in a bedroom – and rather less embarrassing.

Without hinting at the reason Kate therefore arranged to meet Loren one Thursday morning in the Coffee Mill on Mixton High Street. Loren arrived only a few moments late, breathless and strikingly smart. As soon as they'd ordered, Kate came straight to the point: she'd been offered, and had accepted, a post at Celestia State and had handed in her notice. 'So now, at last, I'm on my way,' she concluded, and as an attempt at mitigation reached for Loren's hand across the table and added, 'You've always known, haven't you? – ever since you arrived and we became close – that I was on borrowed time here.'

For a few moments Loren's eyes remained lowered. When she looked up, however, there was no clear sign of sadness. Her mouth was set in a rueful line, but her eyes were clear and smiling, as if she knew that regret was expected of her yet wasn't fully able to feel it. She squeezed Kate's hand and exclaimed, 'I'm so thrilled for you. I really am.'

Kate felt a certain disappointment. Perhaps Loren hadn't quite taken the news in. She'd spell it out. 'Now it's happening, I'm almost sorry to be leaving. I'm going to miss you badly. I shan't just be leaving Mixton but the UK. Off to your homeland – all the way to the States.'

Loren nodded pensively. Then suddenly she became airily cosmopolitan. 'Hey, think of it as time, not distance. We'll only be a few hours apart. I can go over there to visit pretty often and you can come back here.'

Kate pushed harder, feigning more than she felt in order to elicit a stronger sign of regret from her companion. 'That isn't much comfort, when we've been . . . lovers,' she murmured.

Loren withdrew her hand, smiled warmly at her and sat up straighter. She picked up a teaspoon and stirred her coffee slowly. Then she placed her hands flat on the table, looked her in the eye and spoke very deliberately. 'Kate, I've gotta say this is kind of a blessing in disguise, because I need to tell you something. Something I should've told you before. You've been very special to me . . .'

Kate felt a sudden chill.

' . . . but I know there were limits to what we shared.' Loren took a deep breath, raised a spoonful of coffee and tipped it back into the cup. 'I've been wanting to tell you that as of a couple of weeks ago, there's now someone else in my life. Name of Sioux.'

'Sue?'

'She was a Fine Art student here. Just graduated, but always been very committed to the eco cause. It's hard to explain. But we've worked and planned together, and we've gotten . . . close.'

For a moment Kate stared at her. Then she laughed brittly and put on her gloves. 'Well, then, that makes it so much easier, doesn't it? For both of us. I'm pleased for you.'

She walked back to the university struggling to feel the serenity that the fixed smile on her face was meant to declare. She would try not to feel bitter that Loren had failed to appreciate how much Kate had protected her, try not to believe that her new-found happiness amounted to rank ingratitude.

73. THE SEARCH NARROWS

As winter yielded to spring Hamid and Mervyn continued their search for the mystery computer and the Hugh Jones files. But there were other calls on their time. They were obliged to spend many days over at Fallowfields, where they were helping to fit the bright new lecture rooms with a complex state-of-the-art audio-visual system that threw up any number of challenges. And Maddening Fiona, who was in any case about to take redundancy, was only one among several peevish academics who seemed to need their help to solve the simplest of computing problems. But whenever they found a moment they resumed their quest. They'd identified an area within which the computer functioned, and thought it almost certain that the person using it was associated with the university. On the other hand, and thanks to the artless testimony of the two Yemenis, the only recognisable name they had was that of Brian, the lumbering ESMO. That he should be behind the scam struck Mervyn as 'about as likely as Mr Bean solving Fermat's last theorem'. But they ruled nothing out and shared their knowledge and suspicions with no one.

After several weeks they'd become convinced that the computer was located on the main university campus, and once they could determine when it was being used they'd be able to narrow the search still further.

'Right, Hamid,' said Mervyn when they arrived at their workshop one morning, 'I'll go up to Fallowfields today. You stay here and track down Mr Jones.'

When he got back, his pal was downcast. 'I thought I'd found the location, but it can't be right. I decided it must be in the basement of this building, so I took a look. There's damn-all down there – just store-rooms, boiler rooms and suchlike. Nobody's going to be working a computer down there.'

'You're probably right,' said Mervyn. 'All the same, we'd better see what's in them so we can rule them out of the search. I'll go and find an ESMO to open them up for us.'

The first ESMO Mervyn encountered was Brian. For a moment he toyed with the idea of dismissing their absurd hypothesis and simply asking Brian to unlock all the basement doors for him, but instead he made small talk which yielded some useful information. Complaining about the problems the AV system was causing up at Fallowfields, he learned that Brian was on duty there tomorrow. 'Not that I could help you there, Merv. All this technology's over my head.'

The following day the first ESMO they found was Kev, which was a stroke of luck because he and Hamid were on good terms. Hamid had not only fixed a minor problem with Kev's lap-top but installed a couple of computer games on it, acts of generosity which, Kev assured Hamid, he wouldn't forget in a hurry. So they invited him into their workshop for a cup of coffee, and by appealing to his sense of importance on the one hand and his mercenary impulses on the other, set out to win him to their cause. Because of their expertise in technology, they said, they'd been tasked by the university's top brass to investigate a major concern about its security system. They were unable to give details, but they assured him that the matter was of vital importance to the uni. As it happened, Kev enjoyed cloak-and-dagger matters. The more he was kept in the dark, the more convinced he became of their importance. and the more thrilled to be a player in them. So with many nose-tappings and winks, Mervyn and Hamid told him that if he could be absolutely trusted, Kev would become a key figure in the investigation by giving them access to certain rooms and assisting them in any counter-measures they might be obliged to take. But he was to breathe no word to anyone, not even his closest colleagues among the ESMOs. They also hinted that if the investigation was successful, there'd be 'a drink' in it for him, not to mention the download of the latest version of 'Grand Theft Auto'.

The deal was clinched, and jingling the large bunch of keys that was attached by a chain to his belt, Kev led them straight down to the basement. At first, all was plain sailing. Most of the store-room doors opened on repositories of junk – broken office furniture, unwanted filing cabinets, knackered printers, old desk lamps. But when they reached the electrical room, Kev could find no key for it. For some time he was baffled. The label on the key was unmistakable, as indeed was the sign on the door: ELECTRICAL APPARATUS. HIGH VOLTAGE. DANGER. DO NOT ENTER, but the marriage of lock and key could not be consummated. Kev stared at the door, a half-muttered exclamation escaping him from time to time.

'Sure you've got the right key, Kev?' Hamid asked.

'Wait a minute,' he said at length, 'if I remember right, this isn't the electrical room at all. That's two doors down.' And sure enough, a nearby door labelled STORE ROOM 4 yielded to Kev's key and revealed racks of electrical equipment. 'Some knobhead's labelled the rooms wrongly.' Kev gaped back along the corridor. 'What they're calling the electrics room is Dr Cunliffe's old office. But I haven't got the key for that one. The only one likely to have a key is Brian 'cos he's got keys to everywhere.'

'Don't ask Brian!' Hamid and Mervyn blurted in unison.

'Kev, my good friend,' said Hamid. 'Go back to the ESMO office and when no one's around make us a copy of the ESMO rosters for the next month. And swear on your child's life that you'll breathe no word of this to Brian or anyone else.'

Relishing his new role, Kev swore.

'So where do we go from here?' Back at the workshop Mervyn dropped into his chair.

'We need to know who's accessing that locked room. And improbable as it seems, Brian remains our number one suspect. When we get the rosters we'll find out when he's on shift and when he's off, when he's on duty here and when he's working up at Fallowfields. Then when we know he's out of our way, we'll rig up a spycam that's trained on the door of the mystery room.'

Later in the day Kev brought the rosters, and with them some important caveats.

'Thing with Brian is that when he's off, he's sometimes on.'

'What do you mean?'

'He often pops into the uni even when he's off duty. Basically he's got nothing else to do except take his mum to the supermarket. Sad, innit? Your best bet would be to set up the kit while he's on duty at Fallowfields.'

'And how often is that?'

'Only about one shift in four or five. If you like, I could fiddle the rosters so he's up there more often.'

'No,' said Hamid, 'don't do anything to arouse his suspicions. We'll just have to work round the problem.'

And so the matter was arranged. Kev would keep his eyes peeled. If the rosters were changed, or if Brian decided to make a visit to the main uni buildings even when he was supposed to be on duty up at Fallowfields – something that was not totally unknown – Kev would text them a warning.

They ordered the smallest spycam they could find and by the quickest mode of delivery. They decided they'd try a wireless connection but it might need hard wiring, and they'd certainly want a motion sensor. Work on installing the system was tormentingly slow. The days when Brian was working at Fallowfields didn't always coincide with quiet days in their regular work. And once or twice, when they were about to continue with the installation, Kev sent them alerts that Brian had turned up at places he wasn't expected.

'We mustn't let him catch us with our pants down,' said Hamid.

'And our ladders up,' added Mervyn.

They quickly made a significant discovery. Another tiny spycam already existed in the corridor. It wasn't part of the university's official security system but was located in the ceiling above the door of the mystery room and trained along the corridor. 'Whoever occupies this room clearly wants to see who might be outside it,' observed Hamid, as they set up their ladders. Their biggest challenge was to make sure that their work was not readily detectable while still in progress. Whatever his identity, the occupant of the mystery room was clearly observant. If he noticed a wire left dangling from the ceiling or a scattering of plaster dust on the floor, their whole operation would be in jeopardy.

At last the spycam was installed, though not without a hitch. Mervyn spent a long time looking at the image of an empty corridor before exclaiming that if he watched any more he'd go barmy.

'It could rank as video art and carry off the Turner Prize,' laughed Hamid.

What was now clear was that the motion sensor had failed to operate. Moreover, the wireless connection seemed erratic, but they had to wait several days for their next opportunity to return to the corridor, fix the sensor and run a length of cable up through the ceiling to a signal enhancer. There followed two image-less days, but then a development. Triggered by the sensor, their screen showed one person entering the corridor, and one person only. After carefully looking in both directions, he unlocked the door and entered the mystery room. The person was Brian.

The next day Mervyn got a call from Bill Castles to ask if he and Hamid would care to drop by Castles' office and give him a report on their progress.

'We think we know the whereabouts of the computer that holds the Hugh Jones files,' said Mervyn, as Castles' secretary brought them tea and biscuits. 'We also think we know who's operating them.'

Castles smiled wrily. 'I hope you're not going to tell me . . .'

'We'd prefer not to say at this stage,' interposed Hamid. 'We won't name names till we have all the evidence. But we've hit a major problem. The room where we think the computer's located is locked and the only one who has a key is our suspect. There doesn't seem to be a duplicate.'

'What kind of lock is it?'

'Five-lever Chubb.'

'None of your rubbish, then. All the same, I might be able to get you some assistance. In my business you need to get to know all sorts of people. People with cameras. People with microphones. People with keys. One of my contacts has a 3D laser scanner – a box of tricks that takes three-dimensional images of the inside of a lock. Then you can make the exact shape of key to fit it.'

'That's just what we need,' said Mervyn. 'But how long would it take to scan it?'

'Half an hour or so, I'd say.'

'Trouble is, we can only use him when the coast's clear. And that would be at pretty short notice.'

'No problem. That's exactly how my contacts are used to working.'

Hamid sat up. 'But wouldn't it cost a lot of money, Mr Castles?'

Castles was beaming into the distance. 'Money's no object,' he said.

74. INSPECTOR FOREMAN IS BAFFLED

'You've done quite well so far. Better than my last two interns. They were about as useful as an ash-tray on a motor bike. You got the dirt on Learn and Earn. And I'm sure if you sniff around the university you'll find other kinds of dirt. That place has got too big for its boots.'

Bill Castles was winding up his mentoring session with Leighton Rogers. There was a knock on the door and he was told that Inspector Foreman would like a word. 'Show him in, show him in. Always pleased to welcome the constabulary.' He raised his eyebrows to Rogers, who backed his chair into a corner, pulled out his iPhone and said he'd just check his emails.

'Hello, Bill, hope I'm not interrupting. Spare a moment?'

'Absolutely. What can I do to help?' Castles introduced his student intern, but Foreman was too preoccupied to give Rogers more than a cursory nod. 'It's this spate of burglaries, Bill. They haven't stopped. We get the occasional lull and think they either know we're on to them or they've pushed off to some other town. Next thing, the calls start coming in again. It's not so long since we nicked the Green Gorillas. Now this lot. It's doing my head in.'

'Has the hot-line number we've advertised been any use?'

'Yes and no. We think it's possible a couple of break-ins may have been averted. Against that, we get a lot of time-wasting calls from people who think they're Sherlock Fucking Holmes. Claim they can see the burglars' van right outside their front door.'

'And can they?'

'What they've usually spotted is a drop-off from one of the supermarkets. You'd think that a van with OCADO written on it might give them pause for thought.'

'Is there a pattern developing?' asked Castles. 'Are they hitting particular post-codes, or similar types of property? Always choosing the same time or the same day of the week?'

'Good questions. The answer to each is no. I've got a list of the latest half-dozen places that have been done over. They're here, there and everywhere.' He read out some of the addresses. Castles turned to his computer and pulled up a map of the town to see exactly where they were. 'I can find a clearer pattern in the dog droppings in the park,' added Foreman bitterly.

'What sort of stuff are they taking? Any clue there? Is it electronic or arty stuff or fine tableware? Or is it cash left lying about, or car keys followed by the car?'

Foreman looked at the sheet of paper in front of him and then up in the air. 'The only common theme is that they always hit places with something worth nicking – which in Mixton isn't totally straightforward, as you'll appreciate. They seem to know exactly what they're looking for and where to find it. A lot of valuable stuff has been lifted.'

'So what do you want me to do?'

'I'd appreciate it if you could put out a further "Neighbourhood Watch" alert, Bill. At the same time, if you could go easy on the "Why are the plod dragging their feet?" line and build up the suggestion that we're hot on their trail and just need that little extra assist to make the arrests, that'd be very helpful.'

Castles grinned. 'OK, Derek. But remember, one good turn . . . '

'Course. If we get to feel any collars you'll be the first to hear.'

When Foreman had left, Castles looked at his intern. 'Any ideas, young Rogers? Are you going to be our Detective Boy Wonder?'

Rogers smiled deprecatingly. 'Not sure, Boss.' While Foreman had been talking he'd pulled out his notebook and jotted down some of the addresses that had been read out. And he now had a hunch, but he would presently keep it to himself.

75. KATE'S PARTING GIFTS

Hands on hips and hair tied up in a scarf, Kate Huckerby surveyed the disorder of her flat. The baby grand had just gone to the home of a music teacher, and the sitting room carpet was all but invisible under half-filled cartons and packing cases, piles of books and framed pictures propped on end against the walls. Unsentimental though she was, she'd miss this flat more than anything else in Mixton, perhaps a strange feeling for a woman who was also leaving behind not one but two lovers. Prendergast was no great loss. Their relationship was highly rationed, and she'd been attracted to him only in a physical way. They hadn't once discussed anything of any significance: she'd never shared with him her suspicions or discoveries about Loren Lafayette. Loren herself was a more complex matter. Though they'd been lovers Kate had never been 'in love' with her, and they'd parted in the Coffee Mill on civil terms. But as she picked up a file that was lying on a tea chest, Kate was reminded that she had unfinished business with both. She planned to expose Loren as a criminal and cause Prendergast public embarrassment.

The truth of the matter was that her vanity had been wounded by Loren Lafayette. It was always of great importance to Kate that she should be in control of all aspects of her life, and she'd believed she controlled her affair with Loren. But Loren had turned out to be less enamoured than Kate had assumed. It irked Kate that unbeknown to herself Loren had taken up with someone else and dumped her before she'd had the chance to dump Loren. Loren had not only failed to be upset when Kate announced she was leaving: she was positively relieved.

This was not, of course, how Kate represented the matter to herself. She told herself instead that Loren Lafayette had masterminded the Green Gorillas and must be made to answer for it. Ridiculous though they were at one level, the Gorillas' activities had posed a real threat to public safety, and she believed that the evidence of Loren's involvement was compelling. In the States she'd been on demos and had skirmishes with the law, and at one of them her child had been killed. She'd then become radicalised and got involved with 4DK, which was known to have links with eco-jihadists. She'd been obliged to leave the University of Wyoming, yet her record was whitewashed. Before she arrived at Mixton, the students had shown not the slightest interest in ecological matters: after her arrival an eco society had swiftly been formed, and not long after that the Green Gorillas were on the rampage. Yet when they were arrested she was never implicated. The Gorillas, it seemed, kept quiet, and the police hadn't got the gumption to look higher than the small fry they'd caught.

This was all very well while the Gorillas were unable to cause further harm and Kate was close enough to Loren to keep an eye on her. But now that she was leaving and Loren had taken up with this other eco-warrior – Sue? – the acts of terrorism might well start up again. In a glow of self-righteousness Kate told herself that it would be only too easy for her to ignore the danger, to walk away and let matters take their course. But how would she feel if more vehicles got blown up? Could anything guarantee that such actions would harm only property? What would she feel if a child, this time not Loren's, got killed?

So what should she do? The obvious thing was to hand over her file on Loren to Ed Prendergast, but here too she was a victim of wounded vanity. At the job interview Prendergast had dismissed her reservations about Loren – reservations which in Kate's view had now been thoroughly vindicated – and for this he should pay a price. But, again, this was not how she put the matter to herself. She perceived it as a public safety issue which the university should not be allowed to sweep under the carpet. Instead, and under the cloak of anonymity, she would send the file to the local police. Just in case they were too obtuse to grasp its significance, she'd print a covering note suggesting they look closely at Lafayette's involvement with the Green Gorillas. When the police brought charges against her it would cause Prendergast and his senior colleagues much public embarrassment. But that was just too bad.

Sending the file was the last thing she did before leaving. The spring term had just ended. On the final day her few remaining colleagues in media had thrown a slightly awkward drinks party for her and presented her with a gift token. And yesterday she'd enjoyed a pleasantly typical evening with Prendergast, in which they'd shared the bottle of champagne she'd promised and ended up on a mattress in the middle of what was otherwise a bare bedroom. All her belongings had now been packed up, containerised, sold off or loaded into the Volvo. About to let herself out of the flat and hand the keys to the estate agent, she once again checked the contents of the package she would send to the police. Then, with a malicious frisson – a sign, so she told herself, that she was doing the right thing – she licked the big buff envelope. Holding the pen awkwardly in her left hand she addressed it in block capitals to Mixton Central police station. And finally, feeling a bit foolish, she removed the latex gloves she was wearing and threw them away.

76. FIT IS A FIDDLE

It was an early evening in May and summer term at the university. Bill Castles was still in his office at the Chronicle and pottering at his computer until his daughter arrived. Astrid was presently spending long days at the uni completing work on her project for the end-of-year art show. The plan this evening was that when she finished she'd come to his office so that he could give her a lift home. Mervyn and Chloe were calling round later, and the three of them were going out to the pub. While he waited Castles was considering what letters to publish on the correspondence page of the next issue of the paper. Most of the time it was a job he delegated, but occasionally he took a closer look at readers' letters. He liked to check if his editorials succeeded in provoking reactions and debate, and, conversely, if there was any issue raised by the letters that might give him fodder for an editorial. What caused him particular satisfaction was that several months after his mischief-making piece on the Feed-In Tariff, there was still an occasional argument among the readers about the pros and cons of the scheme.

There came a knock at his door and without waiting for a reply, Astrid breezed into his office, kissed his cheek and dropped into a chair. 'Come on, daddy. Ready to go? My friends'll be coming round shortly.'

'OK, love. Be with you in a moment. But I've been waiting for you for a while. You can't expect me just to drop everything. How's your project going?'

Astrid pouted. 'OK.'

'Your mum tells me your bedroom's what passes for a work of art nowadays. Couldn't you submit that?' Astrid smiled wearily at the old jibe, and Castles closed some files prior to shutting down his computer. 'Some of this correspondence about the Feed-In Tariff makes me laugh,' he said, more to himself than his daughter. 'There's a letter here from someone living on the Compton Farm

Estate making the most ridiculous claims about how much she saves on FIT.'

'That's 'cos it's a fiddle,' pronounced Astrid, getting to her feet. 'Ask my friend, Chloe.'

'Really? How would she know?'

'She's got an internship at Central Energy. Says they've launched an investigation. She'll be calling for me in an hour. You can ask her yourself.'

As they went down to the car-park Castles reflected that this was the most intriguing thing he'd heard from his daughter in a very long time. When Chloe Stark arrived at Astrid's house, Castles made sure it was he who let her in. 'Come in, Chloe, sit down. Get you a drink? Astrid'll be down in a moment, she's just drying her hair. She was telling me your bosses at Central have found something amiss with the Feed-In Tariff.'

Chloe stiffened. Fond as she was of her exuberant pal, she was only too aware that discretion wasn't Astrid's strongest point. But it was her own stupid fault for mentioning it – and to the daughter of the local newspaper editor, of all people. Castles poured himself a drink and sat down next to her on the sofa, giving her that appraising look that so unsettled her. He seemed to exert an intangible pressure, create the feeling that if you didn't tell him what he wanted to know he could introduce another topic that was even more discomforting. She parried as best she could. 'I wouldn't want to drop Central in it. They've given me an internship. They're very good to me.'

'You wouldn't be dropping them in it,' said Castles softly. 'If there's a fiddle going on, it doesn't reflect badly on them. They're merely the power suppliers. People try to fiddle their meters every day but that's not the fault of the suppliers.'

'It's not a lot of people. Just in the new Fallowfields development.'

'Fallowfields?' Castles seemed to be sitting more closely to her.

'Only about half a dozen houses on the Compton Farm Estate. And they're not the main offenders, anyway.' The words had left her almost before she was aware of them.

'Who is the main offender?' Castles was now sensing the truth. She cursed herself. In trying to minimise the crimes of Compton Farm, she'd all but implicated the uni.

'Loyalty's all very well,' continued Castles quietly, 'but not to people who break the law. This is a matter of public interest. In fact, it's already in the public domain, it's not a state secret. I could get the details by making a demand under the Freedom of Information Act. So if you were to tell me about it now, you wouldn't be implicated.'

Chloe hesitated. She felt wretched. But she couldn't argue with what he said. There was now no point in withholding anything. 'The university seems to have done much better out of FIT than it should've. But only on the Fallowfields campus,' she added pointlessly, 'it doesn't benefit anywhere else.'

'Of course not,' agreed Castles, leaning back on the sofa.

At that moment, a buzzer sounded. 'That'll be Merv,' Astrid sang out as she descended the stairs and went straight to the front door. Castles took a sip of his drink and his eye ran over Chloe from top to toe, and back again. 'You're quite a photogenic young lady,' he observed. With an inward shudder she felt as if she'd been bared – twice.

77. DARLING, I'LL NEVER LET YOU GO

Derek Foreman and Marian Bussell were spending a May afternoon together – in bed. They'd recently been forced to rearrange their trysts. Foreman's wife Jenny had begun to complain about all the evening shifts and night-time surveillance he was required to do. She suggested to him that she phone the superintendent's wife to have a woman-to-woman chat about the loneliness of her nights, and ask her to drop a word in her husband's ear about giving Derek a short break from unsocial duties. Derek had had to think quickly to avert the call. He told his wife he'd already spoken to the super, who'd been sympathetic and would spare him late duties for the next few months.

But the solution of one problem begat another: if he and Marian were to continue their trysts, Marian, at short notice, would have to take afternoons off which coincided with those that Foreman could wangle. Turpin was in the office irregularly, but since she kept his engagements diary she had a fair idea of his movements and could sometimes leave early when she knew he was away. But on other days she could absent herself only by feigning illness, a ploy that vexed her for two reasons. First, Turpin always believed what she told him and was unfailingly kind to her, telling her to take great care of herself and go home to rest at once. Second, she liked to pull her weight. She'd no wish to acquire a reputation for taking frequent sick leave.

For Derek, then, some of their trysts had been marred by Marian's slight irritability. This afternoon Turpin was away at a conference, and he and Marian were sitting in bed side by side, sipping glasses of *vinho verde* and eating handfuls of nibbles from a bowl. Foreman thought he knew why Marian was grumpy. He believed she was annoyed with Grumble Guts for posing an obstacle to their enjoyment. In truth, she was annoyed with Foreman himself for so readily putting his wife's wishes ahead of her own. Acting on his mistaken hunch, he now sought to cheer her up with some information that would embarrass Turpin in particular and the university in general.

'Do you remember those Green Gorillas I nicked last autumn?' he said casually, as he refilled their glasses.

'I don't remember you nicking them. I thought it was one of our porters and an elderly lecturer.'

'Any fool can feel collars. But I was the one who got them all charged.' He cracked his knuckles at the memory and helped himself to another handful of Bombay mix. 'Anyway, I've received a very credible tip-off that someone else was involved – someone who was masterminding them from high up in the university.'

'So you didn't get them *all* charged, did you?'

He persevered. 'If the information checks out, this someone will shortly be arrested and charged. It won't look good for the uni, and it won't look good for old Grumble Guts.'

This had the opposite effect on Marian from what he'd intended. In her view, the Green Gorillas were a bunch of stupid kids who'd been caught before they managed to harm anyone. And the fact that there'd been no trouble since made her certain that none of them were still at large. Moreover, she hadn't the slightest wish to see

Turpin embarrassed. Insensitive as Foreman was, it seemed not to have occurred to him that giving Turpin a hard time would not make her own job any easier. Turpin could be peevish but he was a kindly man. She was fond of him and felt protective of him, and winced at the thought of Derek Foreman's huge boots trampling over the smooth carpet of university affairs. Noting her lack of interest in what he'd told her, Foreman was somewhat dashed. Perhaps she needs time to digest it, he thought. And talking of digestion, he'd had rather more than his share of the *vinho verde*, and that bloody Bombay mix was giving him heartburn. He turned on to his side and was soon fast asleep.

He was awoken by Marian's voice. 'Wake up and smile.' She'd cuddled up behind him, turned down the coverlet and was now taking a selfie of them on her iPhone.

Foreman grinned sleepily. 'This is a bit kinky, isn't it? Can I take a few while we're, you know . . .'

'Naughty boy. But after pleasure comes work.' She jumped out of bed and pulled on her jeans.

'Where you going?'

'Sainsbury's. Do some shopping. Won't be long.'

'OK, I'll get on with some stuff.' He made to get up off the bed, only to discover that his left wrist had been attached to the wrought-iron headpiece by his own handcuffs. 'Hey, what's going on? I didn't know this kind of stuff was on the agenda. Unlock me, love.'

Marian patted some pockets and peered in her handbag before declaring she couldn't find the key.

'Oh now come on, love, stop messing about . . .'

'Don't worry, I'll find it when I get back. Shan't be long. Have a nice rest while I'm out.'

Foreman lay back and stared at the ceiling. Marian's attitude to the loss of the key was a bit offhand. She was almost certainly playing a game. He wouldn't put it past her. She was a lady who enjoyed this kind of thing. But as time went by, uncertainty niggled at him. How long was she going to be? And suppose she'd really lost the key? He sat up and looked round her bedroom but couldn't see it anywhere. Still, in these circumstances it could only be mislaid, not lost. But at the very thought that the key might actually be lost, he felt a twinge of panic, a suffocating feeling of entrapment.

323

God, it was hot in this bedroom! He kicked off the coverlet and sprawled naked on the mattress.

It was nearly an hour before she returned, going straight into the kitchen to unload her shopping. Foreman felt a surge of relief, but was determined not to show it. At last she came up to the bedroom, sat down on the bed and began to complain about the queues in the supermarket. He could stand it no more.

'Marian, find the bloody key and let me off this bed. I should be home by now.'

Marian gave a little start, as if she'd forgotten all about his predicament. 'Now let me see … No, can't find it.' She got out her iPhone. 'I think we'd better ring the police station and see if they've got a duplicate.' And she tapped the screen and put the phone to her ear.

'For Christ's sake, Marian, what are you playing at?' Joke or serious, this had gone too far. Panic now flamed through him. If the lads came up from the nick and found him bollock-naked and chained to the bedstead by his own handcuffs he'd become a laughing stock throughout the force. '*Marian!*'

She seemed oblivious to him. 'Strange, they're not picking up.'

'Marian, this is no longer funny. Find the key and unlock me, I promised Jenny I'd be home soon after five.'

'I told you, I've lost it. So we'd better warn her you're going to be late,' and she tapped the screen once more.

'Marian, I don't know what your game is but – '

'Oh dear, she doesn't seem to be at home, either. But we can text the reason you'll be late,' she fingered the screen once more. 'Even better, we can *show* her what the problem is', and she held the selfie before Foreman's eyes. It showed them both naked from the waist up, Marian pressed voluptuously into Foreman's back, Foreman grinning sleepily at the camera, and behind him his wrist handcuffed to the bed-head. She swiped and tapped the screen as if sending off the photo to Mrs Foreman.

'Marian! Why are you doing this? For God's sake, find the bloody key and let me out of here.'

Marian knelt astride him and held the key before his eyes with one hand while she undid her belt with the other. 'Two things before I set you free. First, do what you have to do as a copper. Arrest who you want, charge who you like. But stop slagging off my boss Turpin. He's not perfect, but that's something he shares with a lot of people,' and she prodded him sharply in the chest with the key.

'Ouch! OK, OK. What's the second thing?'

Marian kicked off her jeans. 'Need you ask?'

Later that week Foreman was on his way home at the end of another stressful shift, and decided to drop into the Carpenters Arms for a quick one. Standing at the bar was Bill Castles. 'I'll have a pint, Bill. It's been a nightmare of a week.'

'I bet it has,' said Castles as he set the drink in front of him. 'Wasn't that about the seventh place that's been done over – or was it the seventeenth?' He was referring to yet another house that had been burgled. The crime had taken place in broad daylight – at about the time, Foreman reflected ruefully, that he'd been chained to Marian's bed by his own handcuffs. 'Thing is, Derek, I can't hold back the dogs for much longer. I'm getting irate letters from our readers asking why you can't get a result. If you don't give me some encouraging news pretty shortly, I'm going to have to write an editorial slamming the plod. Not nice, I know, but if I don't express the public mood I'll lose my readers.'

'I know, Bill, I know. Give us a bit longer. We'll get a breakthrough very shortly. They can't go on doing places under our very noses.'

'They've been very successful so far.'

'Look, I appreciate the fact that you haven't been as, er, negative about us as you might've been. So I've got a little reward for you. Remember that bunch of kids called the Green Gorillas?'

'Yeah, but you potted them several months ago. They're water under the bridge.'

'Not entirely.' He looked round the bar, checked that nobody was in earshot and leant forward. 'It looks as though their ringleader is still at large – and she's a high-up at the university.'

'Did you say "she"?'

'American lady, name of Dr Lafayette. We've received some very interesting information about what she got up to in the States before she got a job here. Seems she might've had links with eco-terrorists. Links the uni should've known about before they hired her. We're getting people over there to check the allegations. Then we'll pull her in for interview and expect to charge her. So I should have a nice exclusive for you very shortly, Bill.' He drained his glass and looked at his watch.

Castles fought down a smile. His vendetta against the university was, in his own mind, a moral crusade against an institution that was a hotbed of fraud and a haven for criminals. And he barely had to search for the evidence: it was dropping into his lap. Suddenly expansive, he laid a hand on Foreman's arm and nodded at his empty glass. 'You need a chaser for that. Whisky?'

Foreman pondered. Castles could be an awkward sod, but he had his decent side. They could still do business together. Above all, it had been one hell of a week.

'Just the one,' he replied. 'But make it a double.'

78. GARY GROPES FOR THE RIP-CORD

One Saturday morning Gary was woken by the imperious ringing of his door bell. Cursing the bright May sunshine, he staggered to the front door to discover his neighbour. 'Hello, Gary, sorry to get you out of bed but the postman's put these through our letter box and they're all for you.'

'Why the hell can't they put stuff through the right box?'

'Probably one of your students, Gary. Just learning the ropes and confused by numbers with two digits.'

He went into the kitchen, put on some coffee and started to open the mail. There were five letters. The first was a demand from the Child Support Agency, no doubt egged on by Cynthia and that ball-grinding woman lawyer she'd hired. He tossed it aside and hoping for something better, picked up the next one. The writing on the envelope was familiar – Rebecca's. Rebecca was the postgrad student with whom he'd been sharing the flat and having a kind of off-on relationship for more than two years. When they'd got together she told him she was just finishing her PhD, but soon began to complain that the difficulties in their relationship were ruining her concentration. There was a lot of moping and weeping, punctuated by tumultuous rows. She and his ex-wife hated each other, and wherever they met, on the doorstep or in the flat or in Mixton High Street, they often ended up screaming at each other. Rebecca also claimed to suffer from psychological and physical problems whose nature she declined to specify. Submission deadlines for her thesis came and went. Sometimes they lived as lovers (usually when Gary was going through a lean spell in his relationships with other women) and sometimes they lived as mere flat-mates. He'd always found her company a mixed blessing – a consolation when other women weren't around, an obstacle when they were.

One good thing was that she went away quite often, usually to stay with her parents, and last Wednesday she'd told him she was going home for a long weekend. He reminded her that they'd arranged to go out the following evening and was he supposed to hire an escort instead. She replied that this wouldn't be necessary since she'd just put the phone down on a woman who'd asked her who she was ('I said I was your sister') and what time Gary was picking her up tomorrow evening. Had he muddled up his dates? Gary claimed he was pestered by quite a few women, but Rebecca said it was clear who did the pestering. A row quickly developed until a tearful Rebecca told him she was leaving until he could straighten his head out and learn to treat her with a scrap of decency.

Inside the envelope there was only a lined sheet which had been torn out of a cheap note-pad. It read, 'Deal done! Am changing uni's and changing my life. Be back for my stuff on Wed. If you're out will drop key back through letter box. Love and kisses, R.' But 'Love and kisses' was struck through and replaced by 'Go fuck yourself'.

Gary tossed the note on to the kitchen table and stared at it for a few moments. Her departure would at least help him in the steps he was taking to de-clutter his life. Then he turned to the third letter. This was from the owners of *La Jonquille*, again demanding payment for the damage to the restaurant, and informing him that if it was not forthcoming by the end of the month the matter would be placed in the hands of their solicitors. The fourth was a notice from the council giving details of a parking infringement and demanding fifty pounds within seven days or one hundred pounds thereafter. With a sigh, he pushed these aside, took a sip of coffee and opened the last.

This was a letter from Lucinda Murchison, his commissioning editor at Wessex University Press, and was a typical blend of breathy enthusiasm and covert threat. She couldn't wait to read the draft of *Culture, Identity and the Postgendered Imaginary*, with respect to which, she need hardly remind him, the latest deadline had now passed. This was regrettable because she was hoping to package the book as part of the publisher's flag-ship series, 'New Thinking in Feminism'. His contribution would be all the more valued for being among the very few in the series to be authored by a male scholar. She was therefore dismayed that he'd failed to respond to the texts and emails she'd sent him and asked him to make early contact 'to determine the future of our collaboration'.

Hung over from his solitary bout with the whisky bottle the previous evening, and with the belt of his dressing gown trailing behind him, he padded into the sitting room and slumped in front of his computer. Life was closing in on him, and ever since his disastrous evening with Holly he'd been taking steps to break free. Virtually every woman in his life had been giving him hell, and it was they who'd largely inflicted on him the mountain of debt he was also facing. He needed a way out of Mixton and the chance to get clear of both women and debts. For the past couple of months he'd therefore been applying for the few university jobs that were advertised, but with no success. He was never even short-listed for interview.

But now, as he was checking his emails, there came, at last, a gleam in the gloom. Among his applications he'd made one of a different and slightly quirkish nature – to a college of technical and further education in Sydney, Australia. His thought was that Australia was a very long way from his problems in the UK. If a fresh start was possible, it'd be possible there. And wasn't life Down Under just a beach – a life of sand, surf and perpetual sunshine? Moreover, the fact that the job was in further rather than higher education was part of the appeal. The lower-level work – teaching basic theory to kids training to work in media production – would give him more time to finish his book. In academia, feminism was all the rage ('rage' struck him as an apt word), and if his book allowed him to pose as that rare thing, a feminist academic who was male, he might then be able to get a good job back in the university sector. The college in Sydney had now emailed to say that it had short-listed him and wished to arrange an interview on skype. It was also about to contact his referees.

This seemed like the only ticket out of the mess that was engulfing him, and he determined to grab it with both hands. Among those he'd cited, the referee who would count most was the one with the highest status – and that, of course, was Prendergast. It's payback time, thought Gary, and pleading urgency he gained an interview early on Monday morning.

'A couple of years ago, Ed, you asked me to take charge of two big tasks. One was to sell the idea of 2-4-3 to staff inside the uni. The other was to roll out Learn and Earn. I think you'll agree that I've made a success of both.'

'Yes, you have,' Prendergast agreed, but without much enthusiasm. 'But you got a lot of help with 2-4-3 from Kate Huckerby, didn't you?'

Since Kate had now left for the States Gary felt he could offer his own perspective without risk of contradiction. 'Kate certainly helped from time to time, but she didn't seem able to give it quite the commitment that I did.'

Prendergast knew the precise extent of Gary's commitment, but to say what he knew might suggest that he'd been more intimate with Kate than he was even now willing to reveal. So instead he said, 'And then, of course, Ben and Gemma took on the main burden of Learn and Earn.'

'Except that a few problems developed, and it took me to sort them out. Some of the students had a rather naïve view of the placements. I think they expected to start at the top. Ben and Gemma hadn't properly briefed them, so I had to step in and bang a few heads together. Help the students make the right mental adjustment.'

'Excellent,' replied Prendergast, still without conviction, 'so why have you come to see me?'

'I think it's time for me to move on, and I'm sure you'll agree. I like a fresh challenge and I think I've found one. And no doubt the uni will be keen to get me off its pay-roll as soon as possible.'

'Quite so.'

'As you know, jobs are scarce but I'm shortlisted for a post at a college in Sydney. A good reference from you and I'd have a very strong chance of getting it.'

Prendergast stared at him and flipped his gold pencil through his fingers. Gary had suggested to him that he'd like to get rid of Gary in order to save money. In fact, thought Prendergast, I'd like to get rid of you not only in order to save money but because you're useless and unpleasant. And through a familiar miracle these sordid considerations mutated into a written encomium on Gary's probity, diligence and scholarship that would have the effect they both desired. Within a few short weeks, Gary would find himself in the departure lounge at Heathrow and looking forward to a life Down Under.

79. OPEN SESAME!

Hamid and Mervyn were simmering with impatience. They were unable to sit still for more than five minutes. They snapped at each other and they snapped at their friends, most of whom wondered what on earth had got into them. Courtesy of Bill Castles, the duplicate key to Brian's secret room had been delivered by courier, and they were just a turn of the wrist away from what might be a momentous discovery. Yet the opportunity to use it remained teasingly elusive. Kev was adamant that it wasn't safe to attempt an entry on Brian's days off because he often appeared suddenly at different parts of the uni, and at any hour. The only safe time was when he was on duty at Fallowfields – and even then he sometimes made trips down to the Mixton campus. The agony was that at the time the key was delivered it would be more than a week before Brian was again rostered for duty at Fallowfields. In the meantime he was due to take a couple of days off, and Mervyn's feelings finally got the better of him.

'Come on, Hamid, Brian's off tomorrow. Why don't we take a chance and try his room.'

'No, Merv, no! We haven't gone through all this just to screw up at the very end.'

They had, indeed, gone through a lot. The most nerve-racking experience had been a few weeks before, when Brian was on duty at Fallowfields and they'd summoned Bill Castles' friend, the locksmith with the laser scanner. Although they impressed on him that his job must be done unobtrusively and with the utmost speed, he showed an alarming lack of urgency, gazing at the lock, blowing out his cheeks, shaking and scratching his head and telling them how difficult it was. When he finally got down to work, Mervyn and Hamid felt so edgy that Mervyn went up to the car park to watch for any unscheduled appearance by Brian's Cavalier. It was only when he got there that it occurred to him that if Brian did appear he'd have to find a means of waylaying him, and on this his mind was a complete blank. For what purpose could he possibly accost Brian in a university car-park? If he could even think of one, would it not at once arouse Brian's suspicions? In any event, luck was on his side. Brian didn't appear, and after fifty minutes or so the locksmith had completed his laborious scan of the lock and noted every measurement he'd need. By the time they'd shown him out of the building their nerves were in tatters.

Now, at last, the day had come. The shiny new key was in their possession and Brian was up at Fallowfields. Fortunately, Kev was on duty at the Mixton campus and promised to keep a sharp eye on the comings and goings in the car-park. Any glimpse of the Cavalier and he'd warn them on their phones. They locked their workshop, leaving a 'Back shortly' notice pinned to the door, and walked down to the basement in silence. Mervyn looked up and down the corridor, Hamid produced the key, inserted it and gave it half a turn. It would turn no further. 'Damn!' He turned it back and turned it forward once more – again, there was resistance, but perhaps a resistance that would yield. He turned it back and forward a third time, exerted a little more pressure – and the lock gave. He gripped the handle, pushed the door open and switched on the light.

They'd both speculated for weeks about what the room might contain, but the sight before them confounded all their imaginings. For a moment, they stood and stared. 'Strewth,' said Mervyn at last. On the table before them was a desktop computer with two large screens, and surrounding it a profusion of equipment: a radio mouse, two or three phones, a collection of high-end USBs, thickets of

331

cables and wires, memory sticks, Blu-Ray discs, a variety of audio recording equipment and a number of miniature security cameras. On the edge of the table there was also a pile of pages that had been torn from computing magazines and had partly fallen to the floor. But if IT was the occupant's main obsession, food and drink came a close second. Coffee mugs and paper plates occupied the remaining spaces on the table. The discarded wrappings of toffees, chocolate bars, crisps, marshmallows and boiled sweets were everywhere. On a desk near the door sat two lap-tops, one with its lid open, along with old pizza boxes and the remains of several other ready meals. The benches, shelving and cupboards that ran along the walls were equally disordered. On the benches was more hardware – some discarded speakers and a collection of cables draped over a multi-meter – together with a grimy microwave, an electric kettle, a giant box of tea-bags, a carton of milk and a collection of mugs, none of which had recently been washed. In the middle of the benches was an ancient laboratory sink with a central tap. It was half-filled with more dirty mugs and plates, but to save the occupant the trouble of washing up there were numerous plastic and polystyrene cups and containers, some half filled with discarded food. Next to the table stood an overflowing waste bin. A broken chair leant against the wall like a recovering drunk. Every cupboard door was open, every surface covered. On a shelf were what looked like an oil-can and two nasal inhalers, but which were actually disguised cameras and recorders. The windowless room was musty. Over everything hung a smell of stale food and old dirt.

'I've never seen anything quite like this,' said Mervyn, moving cautiously into the room and peering closely at some of the hardware. 'There could be a few other things to interest Bill Castles here.'

'Don't get carried away,' Hamid was settling himself gingerly into the chair in front of the desktop computer. 'We're in here to find the Hugh Jones files, and there are at least three computers lying around. So we may have to search all three.'

'My guess is they're in that desktop.'

'Mine too, but we haven't got time to explore all the other stuff that's in here.'

'Bloody hell, look at these!' Mervyn had picked up the oil-can and one of the inhalers.

'Put them back where you found them and don't touch a thing,' warned Hamid. 'This place may look like the mother of all rubbish tips, but he could be just the sort of guy who notices if there's a thing out of place. And remember, he could turn up at any minute. We need to get a move on.'

He turned on the desktop and Mervyn stood behind him while it powered up. The left-hand screen lit up and invited them to enter their password. Anticipating this, they were able to bypass it by putting the computer into a mode that enabled them to create an account of their own. Then they'd be able to access Brian's files. No more words were spoken. From time to time Hamid clattered furiously on the keyboard or wiggled the mouse at his elbow. Moments passed. At last, tense jubilation: Mervyn gripped Hamid's shoulders and shook them. Spreading out before them in a visual fanfare were the rows and columns of Hugh Jones folders. Hamid plugged a pen-drive into one of the USB ports. They'd copy the folders and take them away for decryption. Glancing at their watches and praying for a speedy transfer, they were startled by a distraction. Something happened to make the right-hand screen spring into life, and through twelve partitioned images show an assortment of university locations.

'Holy Moses,' said Mervyn, 'he's got spycams all over the place. He's got more viewing options than Sky TV.'

'Big Brian is watching you,' murmured Hamid.

At that moment Mervyn's phone chirped. 'Shit and corruption! Text from Kev. He's just seen Brian turning into the car-park. We've got to get out of here.'

'Go and head him off!'

'How? What can I say?'

'Anything! Talk about the weather. Ask him how his mother is. Wait, the download's finished. Let's get out of here.'

Mervyn raced to the doorway and looked up and down the corridor while Hamid yanked out the pen-drive and switched off the computer. With a final glance round, and confident that the chaos had been left intact, they switched off the light and closed the door.

'Come on. Quick! If we bump into him anywhere round here, it'll look fishy.'

'The key! The key!' yelled Hamid. 'It won't turn. I can't lock the sodding door.'

Mervyn pushed him aside and twisted the key once, twice – and finally it turned. Like kids laden with fruit after a scrumping expedition, they raced along the corridor laughing uncontrollably.

80. ALL IS DECRYPTED

Mervyn pushed his backside against the door and sidled into the workshop carrying two plastic cups of tea and a packet of biscuits. He put one cup beside Hamid and another on his own desk and the biscuits between them. 'How's it going?'

Staring at the screen, Hamid grimaced and shook his head. It had been more than twenty-four hours since they'd captured the files. Every now and then he waggled the mouse at his wrist or rattled on the keyboard and hit the return button. 'Nicking files is one thing. Finding out what's inside them's quite another. Our friend Brian's done a first-class encryption on these. We could be in for a long haul.'

Meanwhile, down in Lecture Theatre 014 Victor Margolis, Director of Learning Applications, was drumming his fingers on the lectern. He was about to hold a top secret meeting. He looked anxiously at the carefully invited members of staff as they entered in their twos and threes, most of them trying to continue conversations while carrying phones and lap-tops in one hand and drinks in the other. Brian stood at the door ticking the arrivals off the list that Margolis had given him. Margolis looked at his watch. 'How many still to come, Brian?'

'Just Dr Dorn now. Ah, here he is.' Dressed in a T-shirt bearing the image of a fashionable band, Gary banged through the swing doors, and thinking 'out of the way, you fat sod' spilt some of his coffee over Brian. After his recent meeting with Prendergast, he was in a bullish mood. He took up his favourite place at the back of the tiered auditorium. There he could both eyeball the speaker at the lectern and talk loftily over the heads of those sitting below him.

'Right, Brian, can you shut the door now, please. Check the gallery's empty, then shut and lock the door up there. Thank you.'

Brian left the lecture theatre, closing the doors carefully behind him, which Margolis then secured from the inside. Brian went up the stairs and round to the projection room at the back of the lecture theatre. It was empty, and through its window he gave Margolis a theatrical thumbs-up, went out and locked the door behind him. As Margolis began to speak, he paused outside the lecture theatre. He could hear the voice but not make out the words. It was evident that Margolis was warming quickly to his theme. But then, thought Brian, university people grew warm about the strangest and most trivial things. Better just check what it was about. He took a Bluetooth device from his pocket and pressed a button. Inside the projection room, and discreetly located on a shelf between an old video-cassette entitled 'Mixton University – Building on Our Heritage' and a DVD entitled 'Mixton University – Forging the Future', a recording device silently went into action.

'Ladies and gentlemen, with the exam season almost upon us I regret to be the bearer of bad news. Some of the question papers have been leaked. We're not sure how many. So I'm afraid we have no alternative but to draft an entirely new set – in all subjects that involve unseen exams, and across the entire university.'

There was uproar. 'This is outrageous!' 'What the hell's going on?' 'Finals are due to begin in less than two weeks.'

'I know, I know,' Margolis raised his voice. 'Highly regrettable but it can't be helped. The IT system seems to have been hacked. So till further notice, nothing – nothing! – must be put on the intranet. All the new papers will have to be typed or written, and passed round as hard copy. They'll need to be sent to the external examiners by snail-mail and circulated to admin staff by internal post. And, yes, the time-scale's ridiculously tight, but the exam papers have to be your number one priority. If colleagues can collaborate face to face and the externals be consulted by phone or skype, so much the better. Yes, Ms Allerdyce?' he addressed a woman who had got to her feet.

Marjorie Allerdyce had gone down in the world – at least, the world of Mixton University. She'd been appointed as a lecturer in mathematics in the distant days when the university still boasted a maths department. When it closed she became a teacher of statistics in the Department of Business and Marketing, and lasted there until the rigours of her subject proved too much for most of the students. Now, on the brink of retirement, she was teaching a module entitled 'Brush Up Your Numeracy' for those students on the BA Leisure and Hospitality degree who wished to have a stab at book-keeping. Like most people who are about to be put to extra work, she was keen to be sure it was really necessary. 'How do we know that exam papers have been leaked?'

'It'd be a good thing if yours had,' chortled Eric Uggles, who was sitting just behind her. 'Then the pass rate might be higher than the usual twenty per cent.'

'But a leak doesn't matter in your case, Eric,' another voice interjected, 'because you set pretty much the same paper over and over again.'

'Gentlemen, please,' resumed Margolis. 'Ms Allerdyce, I'm sorry to say that the matter's beyond doubt. The leaks have come to light due to the fortunate – or unfortunate – accident that the Department of Engineering and Technology holds its final exams a month or so before the other departments. Dr Mike Williams teaches there, and he'd like to show you how the leaks were discovered.'

Mike Williams replaced him at the lectern. He was young and spare, clad in a denim shirt and jeans. He looked like the president of a global software corporation. 'We were alerted by some answers to three out of four questions on the exam paper in Computer Architecture.' He pressed a button and threw up an image on the screen behind him. 'Here are parts of the exam scripts of three different students. Look at the second paragraph of the answer to Question 2 on the script of Student One. Now look at the third paragraph of Student Two's answer to the same question. Finally, look at the opening sentences of Student Three's answer to that question.'

'Ah, they were copying from each other,' someone shouted. 'Doesn't mean the paper was leaked.'

'No indeed,' agreed Williams. 'Except that one was in a different room from the other two, and the two in the same room were a long way apart.'

'Thought transference or walkie-talkies,' came a waggish suggestion.

'Did the students know each another?' someone asked.

'Yes, they did. As well as studying the same course they all lived in the same house.'

'So they could've been working and revising together. Perhaps there was a similar question in the past, and they all recognised it as an old friend and answered it in the same way.'

'You have a charitable disposition. But this was a new module with no previous papers containing similar or related questions. Now look at this extract from the confidential model answer we prepared and deposited in our departmental database.' Williams threw up the next image. There was silence as the audience recognised that the three students' answers were close copies of the model answer, except for minor variations in spelling, wording and punctuation. None of these were an improvement on the original.

'This made us pretty suspicious, but we still felt we could give them the benefit of the doubt. Until we looked at their answers to the numerical part of Question 5.' Up went another image. 'You can see that all three candidates did well in this part of the paper. They successfully solved the problem.'

'Nothing wrong there,' said somebody.

'Numerical calculations are nearly always going to be similar, if not identical – though I agree these are more identical than most,' observed Bob Harding, a Psychology lecturer.

'Quite so,' said Dr Williams. 'But now alongside the model answer, I'm highlighting those parts of the calculation that use the bandwidth provided. You'll see that everyone reached the same answer.'

'Congratulations on your excellent teaching!' shouted Gary.

'Kind of you. Except that the bandwidth in the first draft of the model answer was in error. A revised number appeared in the final exam paper, as shown here.'

337

'Then how did they . . . ?' started Marjorie Allerdyce, but then the penny dropped. 'You mean they committed the answer to memory and failed to notice the change in the bandwidth value.'

'Exactly. None of the three used the bandwidth figure given in the final exam paper, but they all used the figure that appeared in the first draft of the secret model answer.'

There was a silence. Victor Margolis had rejoined him at the lectern and took up the story. 'We called the three students in for questioning. First they denied any wrongdoing, but then in the face of the evidence they had to admit it. Claimed that in return for paying a fairly hefty fee they'd been given the details of the exam paper by a Mr Hugh Jones.'

'Who is Hugh Jones?' asked someone in the audience.

'It's clearly an alias,' said Dr Williams. 'We've checked, and no one of that name works at the university. But the students claim they were given his contact details by one of the ESMOs. They can't remember which one.'

'What makes you think this Hugh Jones has access to exam papers across the whole university?' asked Bob Harding. 'Perhaps he's only got inside the Eng and Tech database.'

'That's possible,' agreed Margolis. 'Our Mr Jones clearly terrified the students by threatening them with failure and expulsion if they spilled the beans. It was only when we pointed out that they'd nothing to lose by being as frank with us as possible that they started to talk. But he was smart enough to tell them very little. They don't know for sure, but they got the impression he was offering a university-wide service. So, ladies and gentlemen, we simply can't take the risk. We'll have to re-write all the other papers.'

There was a chorus of groans and a babble of conversation.

Still feeling aggressively cheerful, Gary decided to annoy a few people with a show of intellectual superiority. 'Sorry folks, but this is a classic case of chickens coming home to roost. If you make a fetish of unseen exams, this is what can happen. But a lot of us moved away from the "sit down, be quiet, turn over the paper" routine a long time ago. It's formulaic, artificial, steeped in a discredited history and should be discarded altogether. If there are a few remaining dinosaurs – no disrespect to you, Marjorie, that's a metaphor not a physical description – who insist on parking students for hours in front of a blank piece of paper, they can issue questions in advance and make it an open-book exam. That'd assess the personal and intellectual qualities we should be seeking to develop.'

This received a mixture of jeers and endorsements. Someone was heard to mutter, 'So that's how he passed his driving test.'

Eric Uggles rose ponderously from his seat. 'We should be about standards, about ensuring a degree is worth something. About ensuring that a student at the end of three years is in some way different from that same person at the beginning of his or her university course.'

'Of course they're different,' shouted Bob Harding. 'They're taller, hairier and have had more sex.'

'And we know who with, Bob.' The remark caused much knowing mirth.

'Ladies and gentlemen!' Margolis broke in firmly. 'This is not a forum for debating the merits of exams and the broader benefits of higher education. It's to solve a practical problem. For better or worse, exams are due to take place in a couple of weeks, and we need to provide papers that haven't been leaked.' Amid much grumbling the meeting broke up.

Brian had hoped to return to the lecture theatre just as the staff were leaving, for he knew from experience that they'd be discussing what had just taken place. However, he was called away to deal with a visitor to the university who'd returned to the car-park and found that her car had been clamped, and by the time he got back the meeting was over. He'd just have to go down to his den and listen to the recording, not something he was looking forward to. The agenda probably contained some or all of the usual moans – about workloads or redundancies or pay. But the stress on secrecy was a bit unusual, so he felt he should check it out.

Down in his office he made himself a mug of tea, pulled a Twix out of his pocket, cleared a space in the debris on his table and sat down to play the recording. When he heard what was being discussed, he got a shock. He always knew the scam might one day be discovered. What shocked him more was the manner of the discovery. He'd assumed that his undoing would be technology:

what he hadn't appreciated was that the crassness of the students posed a far greater threat. He just despaired of them. You do your best to help them but they haven't got the brains to help themselves. What were they always told? *Read the bloody question!* And they clearly had not. It broke your heart.

But as he slurped and chewed he reflected that the exam business was not such a great loss. In the years that he'd been at the uni, the number of exams had steadily gone down and the income with it. It wasn't like his day, when you were given a blank answer book, a set of unseen questions and a time limit, and someone like Miss Watts wandered up and down the aisles to make sure you hadn't smuggled anything in or written times-tables on the palm of your hand. Nowadays, it was all about not stressing the students too much, and giving them opportunities to be creative and express themselves. Brian didn't know what it was all coming to.

Still, it was time to cover his tracks. He wasn't worried about being fingered as the ESMO who'd supplied Hugh Jones's contact details. If questioned, he'd admit that the name rang a faint bell. But being well known in the town and in a uniform bearing the university's logo, he was being stopped all the time by people giving him leaflets and business cards offering student services – pizzas, kebabs and burgers for the hungry, counselling for the depressed, babyminding for mature students with kids. Yes, he did vaguely recall a bloke called Hugh Jones but thought he was offering extra tuition services to struggling students. Knew nothing more about him and had long since lost his particulars. Nevertheless, all the Hugh Jones files would have to go. His name was now known to university staff and the scam had become too risky. Draining his mug, he swung his chair round to face the computer. He pressed some keys and the folders popped up before him. 'Party's over, Hugh old mate. A fond farewell', and within seconds Hugh Jones and all his works and pomps were vaporised.

Yet at the very moment that he died in Brian's den, Hugh Jones was born again in the technicians' workshop. After hours of silent, patient concentration, Hamid and Mervyn had at last cracked the files. Following the shouts, high-fives and fist-bumps came a longer and astonishing discovery, the extent and scale of the fraud that Brian had been operating. Exam papers went back over six years and covered a range of disciplines. The number of students taking advantage of the service went up, and then, especially in non-scientific courses where exams became more the exception than the rule, started to decline – a problem Hugh Jones tried to solve by raising his fees and offering special deals such as 'buy one, get one free'. The threat that accompanied the provision of the question papers – if the students breached confidentiality they'd be reported to the authorities, failed and expelled – had evidently worked. As far as Mervyn and Hamid were aware, nobody but the two Yemenis had revealed the scam, and even then with some trepidation and only because they thought they'd been swindled.

So what now?' asked Mervyn, when they'd spent an hour or two marvelling at what they'd found. Their day was ending and they were getting ready to leave. 'Go back to Prendergast with the hard evidence and rub his nose in it?'

'Not sure that'd get us anywhere. Remember how dismissive he was? He isn't the type to admit an error and apologise. He'd tell us to keep quiet if we knew what's good for us, and come on heavy if we didn't. Not only that, but you'll remember he didn't even take it very seriously. Told us not to get too fixated on exams.'

'So do we go with Plan A – take it down to Bill Castles at the Chronic?'

'I think we do. It's an issue you and I both feel strongly about. Let's see if the public feel the same. Castles clearly thinks they do because he paid for the key that got us the evidence.'

'Not only that but the fraud's even bigger than we thought it was. Bill promised he wouldn't reveal the whistle-blowers. Since I'm dating his daughter he'd better make sure he doesn't.'

Duly resolved, they spent the next two days poring over the Hugh Jones folders and compiling a very fat file. Then they took it down to the Editor of *The Mixton Chronicle*, who, needless to say, was more than grateful.

81. RAINING ON THE PARADE

'"The time has come," the Walrus said, "To talk of many things." '

Bill Castles spoke Lewis Carroll's words aloud as he stood looking through the glass wall that separated his office from the editorial suite of *The Mixton Chronicle*. Jingling the coins in his pocket, he couldn't keep the smile from his face, and had any of his subordinates in the suite looked over at him instead of staring at their computers they might have thought he'd gone a bit mad. He now had a mass of highly damaging information about Mixton University – information which would destroy its newly-acquired prestige and pretensions to be the blueprint for the university of the future. He would reveal it to be nothing more than a factory of fraud and deception. What it had not originated it had at the very least condoned, and a key element in it – the exam racket – had destroyed its academic integrity. On top of all this, its students had committed acts of terrorism in which they'd almost certainly been directed by a senior member of staff.

So, as the Walrus said, the time had indeed come. It was now late June, and as one of Mixton University's VIP guests Castles was about to go to a buffet lunch in Fallowfields to celebrate its various achievements. There was the completion of the fine new campus. There was the launch of a new academic era – the success of Learn and Earn and the new two-year degrees in 'relevant' subjects. And as embodied in the integration of the Fallowfields campus and the Compton Farm Estate, there was the triumph of the green project and the Connected Community. It was arranged that just before the lunch Betty Attwood, who was the guest of honour, would unveil a window in the main Fallowfields building in memory of her late husband and name it the Cyril Attwood Building. Castles knew very well why he'd been invited: the university was looking for a front-page splash on all its dazzling feats. 'Think again, you silly sods,' he said, also aloud. His plan was that as the occasion was reaching its happy end he'd request a short meeting with Turpin, Unthank and Prendergast, inform them of his discoveries, and warn them of his intention to run them as a series of exclusives in the Chronic.

The timing was good for another reason: Astrid had completed her degree, and was no longer subject to the whims of Tom Burley. Castles was someone who operated in parallel worlds and seldom made any connection between them. On the one hand, he was fond of his daughter and wanted her to get a respectable degree, even if he had no high opinion of her artistic ability. On the other, he was nursing information which would discredit, perhaps even destroy, the university she'd been studying at. It didn't occur to him to use this information as a bargaining tool to win her a better degree, though it did occur to him that if he released the information prematurely she might get an even worse one. So it was just as well that the results had now been published and that Astrid was on the pass-list, albeit as the holder of a mere third. What neither she nor her father knew was that even this was awarded only after an ill-tempered exchange at the exam board between Barry Powell and the external examiners on one side and Tom Burley on the other.

'If we give Astrid Castles a degree,' said Burley, 'we should also award them to window cleaners for making patterns on glass and road sweepers for piling dirt into pretty pyramids.'

Powell and the externals felt that Astrid was being picked on. They accepted that she was no Michaelangelo, but then neither were the other students, all of whom would be permitted to graduate. The debate rumbled on until Burley announced that he'd better things to do with his time, and that while he thought his opponents were wrong he would yield, provided she was awarded nothing higher than a third. And so the matter was concluded. All that Astrid and her father knew was that she'd indeed gained a degree, even if not a very distinguished one. He was now free to launch his attack, and he'd decided that the end of the buffet would be the ideal time to do it. In giving the senior management notice of his intention to reveal the scams, he would create an impression of honesty and fairmindedness. At the same time, it'd be too late for them to adopt defensive measures, and above all, it would ruin their entire day. No wonder he could hardly stop smiling.

There was a tap at the door, and Leighton Rogers looked round it. 'Got a minute, boss?'

'Not much of one,' said Castles, fiddling with his bow-tie. 'I'm going to a swanky do at your alma mater. What do you want?'

'Remember when Inspector Foreman dropped in to see you a few months ago? About those burglaries? Gave me an idea. I got very, er, friendly with a secretary at the uni. In DoCTOC – you know, Community Therapy and Outreach Care. Nice girl by the name of Leanne Heggarty. I took her out and bought her a few drinks.'

'Have you come in here to boast about your conquests, son? Or have you got something interesting to tell me?'

'She was really chatty and helpful. Told me DoCTOC keeps a register of all those patients who get mediskype consultations. The students have to record the patients' names and addresses, plus their ailments and treatments. There's also a diary where they have to enter future appointments. I managed to get a look at both.' ('They're supposed to be confidential,' Leanne had told him, 'so if I leave them up on the screen while I nip out to the loo, let's hope *nobody will see them.*' Acting on this heaviest of hints, Rogers had copied them down as fast as he could.)

'So what are you telling me?'

'I checked the patients' addresses in the register against those Mr Foreman told us had been burgled. In the richer neighbourhoods, there's an almost exact match.'

'I'll be damned! Do you mean to say the students are using mediskype to case people's houses before doing them over?'

'Looks very much like it, boss. I also copied the appointments from the diary so we could give Mr Foreman some addresses that'd be likely targets in the future.'

'You've got a bit more nous than the local plod, that's for sure. Well done, son.'

'There's more. A few months ago, you asked me to find out about the local drug scene, remember? The big drug round here's called hip-hop-high – 3H for short. It's huge among youngsters. You can easily get it at parties and nightclubs. You could say that for most of the time Mixton's off its face on it. Our Leanne was a little bit indiscreet,' Leighton tapped the side of his nose. 'Told me that the source of manufacture and supply was someone *very* close to . . . in fact, someone very possibly *indistinguishable* from, the Head of Department, a man called Clive Wilkinson.'

Castles stared at Rogers. 'Are you telling me that the head of a department at Mixton University is making and dealing illegal drugs?'

Rogers made a deprecating gesture. Castles continued to stare at him. You had to hand it to this kid, he was worth more than Castles' entire news staff. Rogers pulled his notebook out of his pocket. 'I've got all the chapter and verse, boss. I know where he makes the stuff. He's got a lock-up on Glabthorpe Road, I've seen him going in and out of it. And I know where he deals from.' Rogers gave Castles some more information before the latter concluded the interview. 'Right, now sod off and put it all in writing 'cos I've got a party to go to. I want it all on my desk by 5 pm. Oh, and Leighton,' he shouted at the retreating figure, 'good work, son. We'll make a journalist of you yet.'

Castles sat quite motionless. Inside, he felt so elated he thought he might burst. All this dirt on the uni was beyond his wildest hopes. He felt like a small boy who has been invited to plunge the handle of a detonator and destroy a massive architectural eyesore. It was the kind of thing you both hastened – and, savouring the sheer thrill of it, hesitated – to do. After a few moments he picked up the phone and called Foreman, briefing him on Rogers' discoveries about mediskype and promising to send him the evidence by the end of the day. As he did so, he was slightly irked by the feeling that he was throwing a pearl at a swine, for it was quite clear that Rogers had grasped in a few minutes what had never once occurred to Foreman in several months of investigation. Feeling that not all the fruits of other people's endeavours should fall into the lap of someone who was so dense, Castles decided he wouldn't tell Foreman about the 3Hs or the other scandals he'd unearthed. Let him learn about them instead, like the ordinary members of the public and indeed the national media, from the series of exclusives that the Chronic would run over the coming days. For the 3H scandal Castles had already thought of his headline: UNIVERSITY PROF FUELS DRUG-CRAZED MIXTON.

Ed Prendergast was feeling mellow. The buffet lunch was a huge success. The Vice had elegantly summarised all that the university had achieved over the last couple of years, but since Brenda Hodges was among the guests Prendergast had many opportunities to remind her who could take much of the credit for it. Even the Toff had done a useful job. He spoke a few words that people evidently found witty and charming, and, more important, took gentle charge of Betty Attwood, who seemed frailer and madder than ever. Prendergast had heard that she'd been a victim of one of the burglaries that were presently plaguing the town, and robbed of almost everything but the clothes on her back. When she unveiled the window and named the building after her husband, she got almost everyone's name wrong except Cyril's. But with a murmur or two and some tactful reminders, Unthank steered her through the business very adroitly. Harry Hunter was present, as always, glad-handing people to left and right and hungrier than ever. Few were the troughs into which Hunter failed to get his snout, but it was always prudent to keep the local MP happy.

Most satisfying of all was the presence of Bill Castles from the Chronic. Among the first to arrive, he was dressed rather raffishly in a check jacket and pink and green bow-tie, and with a leather document case tucked under one arm. You never quite knew where you were with Castles, but today he was all smiles and evidently enjoying himself. When Prendergast arrived at the uni he'd set out to make a good relationship with Castles, buying him lunch and giving the Chronic a campus distribution deal. But his refusal to grant Castles an exclusive on the sit-in marked a turning-point in their relationship. The Chronic declined to join the rest of the press in their later praises of the university, and its editorials – notably the piece on the Feed-In Tariff – became faintly disparaging. Today, however, all seemed sweetness and light, perhaps because Prendergast told a waitress to make sure that Castles' glass was kept filled.

Soon after the unveiling of the window, Castles approached Prendergast and asked if, after the buffet, he might have a brief private word with the senior management. Prendergast hesitated. Poor old Mrs Attwood was already making her departure, but the other VIP guests, Brenda Hodges and Harry Hunter, might wish to remain a fair bit longer. No problem, said Castles. In fact he'd like it if they, too, could hear what he had to say. So Prendergast relayed the request to his colleagues and their two guests, and, perhaps because he also hinted at what he thought Castles was going to say, all were happy to stay behind for a while. Castles probably wished to give the uni a big promotional splash in the Chronic. Asking for a special meeting with the top brass in order to announce it was, Prendergast felt, overdoing things a bit. The Chronic was, after all, only a local rag, and these days Mixton University was a national, even a global, player. But it was a nice gesture, their response would be gracious, and for everyone, not least Brenda, it would round the day off neatly.

So at about three thirty, when the last of the other guests had shaken Turpin's hand, thanked him for a delightful lunch and congratulated him on what the university had achieved, the remaining party – Turpin, Unthank, Prendergast, Bill Castles, Brenda Hodges and Harry Hunter – made their jovial way, amid much back-slapping, joshing and mutual ushering, to Committee Room 3. Castles allowed the others to take seats, into which they all slumped happily, but placed his document case on the table and remained standing. Prendergast hadn't previously thought him the type to make such a formality out of something so trivial.

He cast a brief smile round his listeners.

'Lady and Gentlemen: I should begin by thanking you, Dr Turpin, and your colleagues for your splendid hospitality. In this context, it's hard to keep in mind that an editor's job is to make sure his newspaper tells the truth without fear or favour. The best I can do, as a mark of my gratitude, is give you advanced warning of the disclosures about the university I'm going to be making in the Chronicle. I've received so much information, from so many different but very credible sources, and quite a lot of it unsolicited, that I'm going to have to report that all these achievements you've been boasting of are nothing less than a sham.'

The monosyllable was tossed – and exploded – like a grenade. His listeners stared at him. Was this the preamble to some elaborate joke? He continued.

'Let's begin with 2-4-3. There's been much public debate about whether two-year degrees would lower academic standards. But Mixton University's standards were corrupted some time ago. I know for a fact that, in return for payment and over the past six years, exam papers have been leaked across the entire university.

347

Leaked, I may add, by a mere estates officer,' and here he named Brian. 'Moreover, when the leaks were brought to the attention of higher management they declined to do anything about it.'

Prendergast flushed deeply. He was as shocked as his colleagues. The treacherous bastard! But ever ready for a fight, he recovered more quickly than they did. If Castles was about to name him as the culprit, he'd pre-empt him with some lofty extenuation.

'Hold on a moment, Bill. I don't for a moment accept that any such thing has happened, but from time to time all universities have to face the problem of exam fraud. And what you don't seem to understand, Bill, is that here at Mixton exams are only one element in the, er, complex process of academic appraisal. Another one, and every bit as important, is Learn and Earn. This university's great achievement is the way it's using its internships to integrate work and study.'

'Ah yes, the wonderful internships,' returned Castles. 'I was coming to those. They were supposed to enrich the students' learning experience. But, for many, Learn and Earn is a con. They've been placed in menial jobs that are unrelated to their degrees and career ambitions. And when they complain, they're threatened. They're told to shut up or they'll be thrown out of the university.'

'I think we've heard quite enough of this.' Turpin had at last recovered himself, and could scarce contain his fury. 'How dare you, Mr Castles, turn up on an occasion such as this, accept our hospitality, and then make these outrageous allegations.'

'I admit that, stated in this bald way, the allegations do seem outrageous. But I'm outlining them only, as I said just now, to give you fair notice of what you can expect. Because – believe me, Dr Turpin – I can support every one of them. An old newsman never prints anything he can't substantiate.'

'I can't presently pronounce on their veracity, Mr Castles,' said Unthank, 'but while you make much of your duty to tell the truth, the editor of a local paper surely has another duty – to defend cherished institutions and report the good things about them as well as the bad.'

'What good things were you thinking of, Dr Unthank?'

'I'd have hoped they'd spring readily to your mind. Our degrees in ecology and therapy. They're highly innovative, they've recruited lots of students and they've attracted plaudits from the national media.'

'But, alas, the national media don't know things about those degrees that I know. Or the departments that are running them.'

'What's that supposed to mean?' snapped Prendergast, now looking for a way to fight Castles toe-to-toe.

'That the ecology department was a hotbed of eco-terrorism whose ringleader was none other than its head.'

'That's a preposterous suggestion! And you'd better be careful who you're naming.'

'I am, Dr Turpin. As I said, a newsman doesn't name names till he's very sure of his facts. This lady was well-known to the police in the States. Yet the university failed to check her out properly. It's now clear she was the guiding light of the Green Gorillas. Remember them? Went round Mixton blowing up cars and damaging property. If they hadn't by a lucky chance been caught they might've killed someone by now.'

His audience took a moment to digest this. Harry Hunter mopped his brow with a large polka-dot handkerchief. Brenda Hodges maintained her silence. She sat perfectly still. Her mouth was set in a tight rouged line, her hands were clasped. Only her small, bright eyes flicked back and forth between the protagonists.

It was Castles who spoke again. 'Of course, you might want to claim that the uni's green agenda has been rather more successful. That's what Central Energy thought when it looked at the latest Feed-In Tariff figures for Fallowfields. But now it's looked again and realised the uni's been fiddling its meter readings. On a grand scale.'

'What a damnable insult!' spluttered Turpin. 'Are you saying that the university would stoop to tampering with its own electricity meters?'

'All I can say is, the meters have indeed been tampered with. And the only explanation, particularly after the bad publicity you got from the autumn figures, is that the uni – or someone inside it – has been hell-bent on making the latest figures look a whole lot better.'

The next voice to be heard was Brenda's. 'Well, Mr Castles, since you're determined to show us what a fine poker player you are,

I'm sure you have a royal flush in your fist. So what are you going to allege against DoCTOC and Complementary Therapy?'

'You're right, Ms Hodges. And I always like to save the best till last. It seems that one of the therapies DoCTOC likes to prescribe – or should I say, *deal in* – is what are technically known as new psychoactive substances. Drugs, to you and me. Illegal, recreational drugs. DoCTOC is in effect what the youngsters call "a head shop", a place they can buy narcotic substances. The drug it peddles is known as a hip-hop-high, or 3H for short, and you can easily find it at parties, pubs, discos and the like. In fact, 3Hs are everywhere. Half of Mixton's high on them.'

Good God, thought Brenda. Would that explain the bizarre phone call she'd received from Turpin? Surely not. And yet . . .She looked across at him, but he seemed oblivious.

'Once again,' continued Castles, 'I have it on good authority that these drugs are being made and supplied from high up within the department – from as high as one can go. Names will be published.'

'Even if all this is true,' said Unthank, 'the illegality of these substances has yet to be tested. And it's fairly trivial when set against the enormous good DoCTOC's done through its home diagnosis scheme.'

'Hmm, mediskype,' mused Castles. 'Another brave new experiment that has gone so sadly wrong . . .'

'And what dirt do you propose to fling at that?' snapped Turpin.

'You'll all be aware of the recent spate of burglaries in the town. It's mediskype that seems to have made them possible.'

'What the devil do you mean?'

'DoCTOC students have been using the mediskype consultations to get a good look at what people have got in their houses – and then stealing it. There's a clear match between the consultations and the break-ins. The police are about to make arrests and the Chronicle will splash that story, too. So it seems the head of your dazzling new university department is a drug dealer and his students are house-breakers.'

Castles straightened up and looked at his watch. Making a supreme effort to swallow his anger, Turpin hoped that a rational tone might persuade him to stay his hand. 'I can promise you, Mr Castles, that these matters will be promptly and thoroughly investigated. Any wrongs will be righted and those responsible will be rigorously dealt with. But it'd be really helpful if your newspaper could hold off until we've concluded our investigation. It'll do nobody any good, least of all you, if these matters turn out to be quite different from the way you've represented them.'

Castles shook his head and patted the document case in front of him. 'Sorry, Dr Turpin, but I've already done my own investigation and I intend to publish. And I'm telling you in advance not as a threat, not in order to demand money or favours in return for keeping quiet, but simply as a matter of courtesy. We've had a friendly relationship in the past, so I'm letting you know that I'll be running these revelations from the day after tomorrow. Not out of rancour, I assure you, but simply because I'm a journalist – by profession and by instinct. I report what I find, and I'm sorry that in this case it doesn't reflect well on the university. But look, don't take my word for it.' He unzipped the document case and pulled out a thick folder. 'Here's a copy of some of the information I've acquired. I'll leave it with you. You'll find it's particularly revealing on the exam scam. Good afternoon. Oh, and thank you again for your hospitality.'

Castles turned and left the room.

For some time nobody spoke. In their different postures, all five figures gazed into space. The number and gravity of Castles' allegations, and the clinical manner in which he delivered them at the end of what was meant to be a joyous occasion, had devastated them. Feeling a tightness in his chest, Turpin half-wished he could be carried out in an ambulance and no longer held responsible for what might have happened.

Brenda suddenly rose and glanced round at them all. 'Well, gentlemen, this isn't looking good, is it? For you in Mixton or us in government. We chose you, over all other universities, as our partners in devising a bold new form of higher education – one that'd serve the needs of the modern world. But it seems to have gone pear-shaped. If just half of what he's alleging turns out to be true, I can't see this university surviving in its present form. Perhaps, Ed, you'll be good enough to call my car.'

'I'll show you out,' Prendergast leapt to his feet, and escorted her out of the room and down the staircase of the atrium. The silence between them was a wall. They walked out into the June sunshine.

He opened his mouth to say something but gazing straight ahead Brenda spoke first. 'I normally back winners, Ed, so I do hope I haven't made a mistake.' An electric car was waiting at the entrance. Prendergast opened the door for her, and as she stepped inside said, 'Leave it to me, Brenda. I'll sort it'.

She looked at him through the window, then lowered the glass. 'I very much hope you will. Because it could be a case of sort – or *be* sorted.' Up went the glass, and Prendergast saw his own stricken reflection as the car pulled away.

82. SPIN WHILE YOU'RE LOSING

On his way back to the committee room he met Harry Hunter, who was coming down the stairs and patting his forehead with his handkerchief. 'Very nice buffet, Ed, but must be off. Constituents.'

'What the devil's got into Bill, Harry? We've never done the dirty on him.'

As they were talking, Prendergast noticed from the corner of his eye a tall, striking lady descending the stairs. She stopped at Hunter's side, a good half a head taller than he, and gazed coolly at Prendergast.

Hunter half turned to her and back again. 'Oh, Ed, don't think you've met my new research assistant, Ms er – '

'Yes, I have,' said Prendergast, looking straight at her and suddenly remembering. 'We shared a lift a year or two ago. But then you were dressed, er, differently.'

The lady said nothing, merely acknowledging him with her frank, dazzling smile.

Prendergast turned back to Hunter. 'Harry, can't you get Castles to pull all this stuff about the uni?'

Hunter looked like someone who was fearing this question. 'Bill's not a man to cross. If you ask him to even reconsider his opinions, he seems to bear you a grudge. Sorry, Ed, can't help you with this one. You know how it is. My majority's not huge, and if I get on the wrong side of the Chronic, that's me shafted. But, er, good luck with it. Perhaps he'll change his mind.'

Prendergast continued up the stairs. Now that the university was in trouble, Hunter was starting to distance himself before he'd even digested the lunch it'd given him. You lily-livered bastard, thought Prendergast, go off and screw your so-called research assistant. We should've saved ourselves the cost of courting you.

The mood in the committee room was desolate. Turpin sat, grey-faced and slumped. He'd spent his entire professional life in academia, much of it in senior management. Latterly he'd been in charge of a university whose daring innovations were about to make it the benchmark of all other universities, and he'd allowed himself to hope, with some encouragement from the great and the good, that with retirement not far away he might receive a public honour for his work. That was in grave doubt: now he must aspire not to gain an accolade but avoid ignominy. On the far side of the room, hands in trouser pockets, Unthank was staring out of the window and having thoughts of a different kind.

Castles' file lay on the table, as yet unopened. With scarcely a word to the others Prendergast picked it up, walked to Badgers Lane to collect his car, and drove slowly back to the main campus in Mixton. Could he think of any way of persuading Castles to pull his revelations? The university would deny everything and threaten injunctions and legal action. He'd call their lawyers first thing in the morning to see what could be done. Lawyers could finesse matters. They could mitigate the university's failings, claim that the misdeeds of its employees took place without its knowledge. But aside from the fact that a friendlier, more diplomatic solution would be better, these measures would buy the university nothing more than time. Unless Castles could be persuaded to suppress them altogether, the revelations would sooner or later embarrass it; and if he, Turpin and Unthank didn't emerge as crooks, they'd look no better than fools on whose watch all kinds of villainy had occurred.

Back at his office he opened the folder. Most of the material was about the exam scam. As he read it, Prendergast felt his scalp prickling. Year after year, question papers had been leaked in virtually every subject the university taught. Throughout the country, and indeed scattered across the globe, were graduates of the

353

University of Mixton whose qualifications were to some extent bogus. Why the devil had the staff taken so long to suspect it?

Prendergast tossed the file on to the table and walked round to his office window. No point in crying over spilt milk, the main thing now was to protect himself and the university. He couldn't yet decide how they'd deal with the other scandals, but the exam scam, at least, might be successfully spun. It was true that the two IT managers, Mervyn and Hamid, had reported their suspicions to him, but as he'd told them at the time, how could he act without firm evidence? (And when those rat-bags had acquired the evidence, why the hell didn't they bring it to him instead of running off to Castles?) He'd encouraged them as well as Victor Margolis to continue their investigations, and the existence of a scam was soon established. Margolis had reported that the exam papers had been re-written and disaster averted, and he, Ed Prendergast, would be able to assure the outside world that the culprit had been discovered and instantly dismissed, and that legal advice was being taken to see if he could be made the subject of a criminal prosecution.

At that very moment, Prendergast's eye fell on the culprit himself. Shuffling across the car-park was Brian, dressed as usual in his ESMO uniform but perspiring copiously in the summer heat and carrying a plastic carrier bag. No time like the present, thought Prendergast. It's been a bitch of a day, and I owe myself one small pleasure. He'd call him in straightaway and sack him on the spot. He phoned down to the porters' lodge. 'I've just seen Brian in the car-park. Would you please ask him to come up to my office at once.' The meeting would be as brief and brutal as he could make it: in order to dominate the proceedings more effectively he would remain standing on his side of the desk. Brian's arrival was presaged by a great deal of coughing and shuffling, and finally there came a knock at the door.

83. SHADES OF THE PRISON-HOUSE

Prendergast stared down at the ESMO's lowered head and spoke in quiet and measured tones.

'I've just come from a meeting with the other senior managers. We've been given details of an exam fraud that's been running for the last six years. It's done massive damage to this university. The fraud was conducted in the name of "Hugh Jones", but we have overwhelming evidence that that person was you.'

Now at last, thought Brian, the axe has fallen. He felt a stab of fear, but a hint, too, of something like relief. It wasn't an absolute surprise. There'd been straws in the wind – the removal of George Abbott's computer, the discoveries of Victor Margolis. What had happened was bound to happen, sooner or later.

'So, Mr . . .' Having decided on strict formality Prendergast suddenly realised he'd no idea what Brian's surname was. 'You were a trusted employee and you've been guilty of gross misconduct. You're dismissed from your post with immediate effect. The two other duty ESMOs will escort you to the places you keep any personal possessions. But you won't be allowed to take with you any university property or anything that'd be relevant to our investigations. We intend to pass your file to the police, and it's more than likely they'll bring criminal proceedings against you.'

There was a pause. Brian rested his forehead on the tips of his thick, white fingers and looked down at the desk. His shoulders rose and fell. That he could lose his job at the university was unthinkable: it was his whole life. He straightened up, cleared his throat noisily and began to speak.

'Mr Prendergast, you and I have had a good working relationship in the past, so I wonder if you could see your way to – '

'I don't know what you're going to ask, but the answer's no,' Prendergast broke in. 'You've done no end of harm to this university, so you can expect no favours from me or anyone else.'

He felt a sudden hatred for the creature now fidgeting and sweating in front of him, this fat, lumbering oaf who'd so thoroughly hoodwinked them all. Brian shook his head almost imperceptibly. Then, with the hangdog air of a schoolboy who has been asked to empty his pockets, he leaned ponderously to one side, unhooked a huge bunch of keys from his waistband, and laid it on Prendergast's desk. Attached to the ring, and giving the gesture a certain pathos, was a grubby figurine of Mickey Mouse.

'Please wait outside for the ESMOs to come and collect you.'

Brian got slowly to his feet and traipsed to the door. Still standing, Prendergast picked up the phone to call down to the lodge.

'Mr Prendergast . . .'

What was it now? He seemed to be taking an age to leave the room. He'd opened the door and was standing with his hand on the knob. Was he going to have another try at begging? Couldn't he just take his medicine and leave with some dignity?

'If the police do get involved, I'll obviously try and get the best deal I can. I'd be as helpful as possible.'

'I'm sure that'd be wise of you.'

'So I'd have to tell them the sad story of how Fallowfields was destroyed.'

Prendergast put the phone down.

'Oh dear, yes,' Brian tutted and shook his head wistfully. 'They'd find that *very* interesting.'

Prendergast stared at him. He was evidently trying some desperate bluff, but Prendergast would have no truck with it.

'I fail to see how Fallowfields relates to your exam leaking activities, but I'm sure it'd be a good idea to tell the police anything you know.'

'You quite sure, Mr Prendergast? But then I might get banged up. You might get banged up. We might get banged up together.'

Prendergast had heard enough.

'You know as well as I do that Fallowfields was an accident. If you're suggesting something else, if you're implying I was in some way mixed up in it, I'd like you to repeat that suggestion outside this room. And if you do I'll take legal action. Then when you come out of prison you can spend the rest of your life paying libel damages.'

Brian held up his hands appeasingly. 'Far be it from me to tell porkie pies, Mr Prendergast. Only, you may recall that when you first came to the uni, you was late for one of your presentations and asked me to park up your Beamer for you.'

'So what?'

'When I did, I stuck one of these' – and here, with what was almost a conjuror's flourish, he produced a small electronic device from his pocket – 'under the front seat. Some time later it relayed a *very* interesting conversation you had with somebody about Fallowfields. Just after I told you Fallowfields had no alarms above the ground floor, you was telling this person the very same thing. Then you instructed him to approach the building at half past one in the morning. From an angle where there was no cameras. At a time when, as I also told you, the night staff'd be watching videos. Then you said that if you had to change the date the code phrase would be "Guy Fawkes cancelled". Just a few days later, Fallowfields burns to the ground. An astonishing coincidence, wouldn't you agree, Mr P? But if you wouldn't, I'm sure the police would.'

There was a silence. It was not absolute. From the pathway below came a snatch of laughter, and in the distance a car horn sounded. The silence may not even have been lengthy, though it seemed so. But it was a silence that was certainly profound.

'Close the door,' said Prendergast. 'Sit down.'

84. IT'S NOT OVER TILL IT'S OVER

'What people don't understand, Brian, is that although we've cut a few corners, everything we've tried to do has been for the good of this university.'

Without breaking stride, Prendergast had switched from a moral denunciation of Brian to a non-moral justification of them both.

'You're right there, Mr Prendergast.'

'Mrs Attwood had promised us the Fallowfields estate, which we were going to re-develop anyway. Make into the campus we needed for the uni's expansion. We got bogged down in planning laws, so my aim was just to cut through the red tape.'

'Course it was.'

'Obviously, we can put a negative interpretation on what you were doing. But I can see that you were probably trying to act with the uni's best interests at heart. Improve its academic record, enhance the well-being of the students.'

'That's exactly it, Mr Prendergast.'

'In effect, Brian, we're going to be punished for our own idealism. We're victims of our aim to make Mixton the university of the future.'

'You have a way with words, Mr Prendergast, that I couldn't hope to emulsificate.'

There was a silence which Brian broke. 'Can't we keep this between you and me, Mr P? You know, since people might misunderstand things.'

'Not a hope, Brian,' Prendergast was sunk in his chair and endlessly rolling the gold pencil between his fingers. 'Castles is going to publish the exam sca-, er issue, along with several other very damaging allegations about us. Starting the day after tomorrow and running for God knows how long. It could mean the end of us as a university."

'What's his price for keeping quiet?'

'Hasn't got one. Aims to splash the lot. Think he warned us only so he could pile on the agony. Didn't just want to execute us but put us on death row for a day or two first. I'll call our lawyers tomorrow and see if we can get an injunction. But even if we can delay him, we can't gag him. Sooner or later it'll all come out. The national media'll pick it up and run with it, too. However you look at it, we're in deep shit.'

'Bill Castles, eh?' Brian sucked his teeth thoughtfully. 'Might be able to help you there, Mr Prendergast.'

85. ASK ME NO QUESTIONS

'Ed, it's always a pleasure to see you but if I'd known you were calling in about this I'd have told you not to waste your time.'

'You seem to be waging some kind of vendetta against the university, Bill. And I don't understand why.'

It was early the following morning and they were sitting in Castles' office in Tribune House. Castles sighed. 'There are some reasons I could give. Like the fact that my daughter spent three years being victimised by Tom Burley before coming out with a third and a debt of 30K. Or my discovery that Mixton Uni's up to its neck in frauds, fiddles and crimes just as it starts posing as the future of British academia.'

Prendergast tried to think of a reply.

'But as I said yesterday, Ed. It's just business – nothing personal. These revelations will be huge for the Chronicle, and I simply can't pass them up. Sooner or later the other media'll get hold of them, and if Mixton's own paper doesn't splash them first we're going to look pretty stupid. Yes, I'll admit I was a bit miffed when you denied me an exclusive on the sit-in, because I'd always thought we had a good relationship. But not to worry. This story's far bigger.'

'So you won't hold them – at least for a while.'

Castles sighed again. 'What more can I say?'

It was Prendergast's turn to sigh. He picked up his attaché case from the floor beside him and placed it on his lap. Then he opened it and took out a large manila envelope before returning the case to the floor. He opened the envelope and took out four sheets of A4 printing paper which he laid in a row, face-down, on the desk in front of Castles. Finally, like a magician concluding his trick, he turned them over one by one so that the photographs on the other side were facing Castles. Castles' eyes dropped to them but otherwise he remained rigidly still. He looked at each of them in turn and grew very pale.

'Where did you get these?'

'Never you mind. You seem to be a bit of an exhibitionist, Bill. But then again, you've got plenty to exhibit. However, it's the ladies that concern me. I know that in this day and age, girls of fourteen can look like eighteen-year-olds and vice versa. It doesn't bother me, but the police may take a different view. And whatever their age, I don't suppose Mrs Castles would be totally enraptured by your personal, er, enthusiasms.'

There was a silence.

'So this is blackmail, is it?'

'Come, come. Just a close cousin of pure, investigative journalism. Like you said, Bill, nothing personal.'

'So what do you want?'

'I want you to drop all these damaging stories about the university.'

'Some of this is already out of my hands. Like the mediskype burglaries. The plod have been staking out houses they think'll be targeted. If they make arrests, we can't fail to report them in the Chronic.'

'But you needn't associate the burglaries with mediskype, or the DoCTOC degree, or the university. If you do,' Prendergast gathered up the photos and put them back in the envelope, 'the police might be making a further arrest.'

Castles gave him a look of pure, impotent loathing. 'OK, but you'll have to make it easier for me. Derek Foreman's the man in charge of the case. If you don't want him to drag the uni into it, he'll have to be convinced it can't happen again.'

'No problem. From now on we'll make sure the patients are skyped against a blank background.'

'You've had a lucky escape,' muttered Castles.

'No, Bill. *You've* had a lucky escape. But your secret's safe with me – as safe as ours are with you.' Never had Prendergast seen a man look so thwarted as Castles. He offered some words of comfort.

'Look on the bright side, Bill. As long as you're careful how you report it, the arrest of the burglars'll give you your big story. And isn't it great that we've managed to mend our relationship! I'll look forward to seeing you at the uni's next big social event.'

Before he visited Castles, Prendergast had asked Brian where he'd got the images.

'Ask me no questions, Mr P.'

They'd come into his possession more than two years ago, awaiting, as so many of Brian's illegal acquisitions did, an occasion on which they could be turned to good use. It was just after he'd helped out Gary Dorn and contrived an end to the student sit-in. Before driving Holly home, he'd taken her to the offices of *The Mixton Chronicle* for the exclusive interview that Bill Castles had asked him for. At the beginning of the subsequent photo session

360

he'd been told to wait behind in Castles' office, where he regaled himself with a packet of Starbursts. So enjoyable were these that he felt in his pockets to see if he had any more and, instead, came across a pen-drive. Noticing that Castles' computer was switched on, and being instinctively interested in other people's business, he plugged in the pen-drive and, with a shrewdness that shaped his own computing habits, made a bee-line for those files with workaday titles. Sure enough, under 'Overtime payments for cleaning staff', he found a pornographic cornucopia. It consisted entirely of images of Castles himself disporting with females of an indeterminate age – indeterminate between the years of twelve and twenty. Suspecting that, life being what it is, they might one day come in handy, Brian promptly downloaded them.

86. MIXTON REDUX

Later that day Turpin, Prendergast and Unthank managed to arrange a teleconference with Brenda Hodges, who was back at her office in Whitehall. It was Turpin's happy duty to inform her that Bill Castles had agreed to withdraw his allegations, but thereafter most of the talking was done by Prendergast. He was eager to convince her that the credit for this change of heart was entirely his, and that it had been achieved only with consummate skill.

'For the most part I used persuasion,' he smiled coyly, 'with only the odd reference to the costs and uncertainty of legal action. I stressed that this was a very difficult time for the uni – a time of transition. We were changing almost overnight from a third-rate institution . . . ' This description annoyed Turpin, who, since he had presided over the university for many years before Prendergast arrived, wouldn't normally have allowed it to pass. But so relieved was he at the turn events had taken that his tolerance was almost indestructible. '. . from a third-rate institution to being a trailblazer and a benchmark for all the other universities. And I pointed out that there were bound to be oversights and setbacks along the way. But this was very far from admitting some of the things he was alleging, and if he published them we'd seek a legal remedy.'

'And what did he say to that?' The tone of Brenda's question was flat rather than curious.

'He had to accept that some of the allegations were based on pretty thin evidence. And others were totally unfounded and came from nameless people who probably had a grudge. We agreed that concerns about the burglaries were already in the public domain, but he promised his coverage of them would stick to the known facts. And we reminded each other that the uni and the Chronic have a lot in common. We've both got the local community at heart. A university that's a world leader puts Mixton on the map and the Chronicle with it. To put all this at risk by making a mountain out of a few minor teething troubles only causes problems for everyone.'

'And?'

'I'm glad to say he took the force of these arguments. He agreed that in the cause of honesty and fairness he wouldn't proceed with the allegations.'

As Turpin listened to this account for the second time, smiling all the while at the camera, he found it no more convincing than he did when he first heard it. He knew Castles to be an implacable individual who wouldn't wheel out his guns unless he was certain he'd win the battle, and Turpin didn't believe for a moment that he would've been persuaded by any of the arguments Prendergast was now vaunting. Why Castles had decided to back down was unfathomable. But Turpin was too canny an operator to be over-curious. The point was that the university had been saved, and his own reputation along with it, and though not a religious man he was ready to fall to his knees and offer thanks to the deity. So while Prendergast gave his account, Turpin nodded in sage endorsement of his colleague's words.

As Brenda listened, she wasn't convinced, either. From the little she'd seen of Castles she believed he was more than a match for Prendergast, and that he would not have backed down under anything less than threats to his good name or his life. But she, too, knew better than to hint at any scepticism. Returning from the lunch at Fallowfields, she'd all but accepted that the Mixton Experiment would have to be abandoned. But a lot of government capital, not to mention government rhetoric, had been sunk in it. She herself had persuaded many of its ministers that the experiment was worthwhile and achievable, and she'd backed her own judgement by choosing Prendergast as the person to manage it. So yesterday, when it all fell apart so dramatically, she feared she'd be among those who were in for some very testing times. Now a gift-horse had appeared, into whose mouth she would not look.

What occurred at the teleconference, then, was a little ritual in which, for the sake of decorum, Turpin and Brenda pretended to believe what Prendergast pretended was the truth. The only person who actually believed it, merely because he had no reason not to, was Robert Unthank. But Unthank had other things on his mind.

87. NOT RESIGNED, SO RESIGNING

Unthank was the only member of the teleconference who failed to share the feeling of relief. He accepted Prendergast's claim that he'd appealed to Castles' better instincts in order to get him to drop his allegations, but he also believed that they were mostly true. Moreover, he couldn't ignore the fact that the things Castles alleged were extremely grave and that they'd happened while he was part of the management. It wasn't for him to tell Turpin and Prendergast what they should or shouldn't do. He'd seen enough of the world to know that in moral matters logic didn't fully apply, that what pricked one person's conscience gave no unease to another's. What caused him the greatest torment was the mediskype affair, for it was he, in his culpable naivety, who'd been the author of Betty Attwood's misfortunes. He'd persuaded her to submit to a home diagnosis that seemed to have cost her all her most precious possessions, including her dog. Yet worse, he'd persuaded her to recruit her elderly friends from the bowls club, many of whom had no doubt suffered a similar fate. He didn't know how to begin to tell her or what comfort or compensation he could offer.

For these reasons alone, he believed he should resign. But in addition, he'd never quite managed to suppress his doubts about the direction in which higher education in general, and Mixton University in particular, was travelling. He was an enthusiastic supporter of a system which strove to raise the largest number of students to the highest realms of knowledge and thought, whether of a pure or applied nature. But even though he berated himself for being an intellectual snob he couldn't rid himself of a belief that the reverse was happening – that in Mixton at least, knowledge and thought were being debased to accommodate the largest number of students. The rationale for two-year degrees stared every student in the wallet. But while the students gained financially, he had no doubt that they lost out academically. Learn and Earn, which had been presented as the perfect synthesis of theory and practice, seemed to have turned into a squalidly utilitarian farce in which much of the practice offered about as much intellectual challenge as the tying of a shoelace. So Unthank resolved on an act of retreat, if not downright cowardice. Let others who could more fully believe in it take up the cause of mass higher education. In the short term he'd withdraw to his ivory tower and, in a place where no one would question its usefulness, resume his struggle with Empedocles. And in the long term he'd find other and more honest ways of improving the lot of his fellow humans.

At their weekly meeting, which took place the very next day, he announced his resignation to Turpin and Prendergast. He made no mention of his philosophical misgivings, feeling that it was expedient – even, perhaps, more honest – to dwell on his own shortcomings rather than on what he perceived as those of the university. He told them that he felt unfitted in both experience and temperament to do justice to his job. He took particular responsibility for the disastrous consequences of mediskype, believing that a shrewder individual would have foreseen and prevented them, but he also felt that the university's attempts at outreach and enterprise, those areas for which he'd been primarily responsible, could be much more effective if directed by someone with a better knowledge of the business world. Neither Turpin nor Prendergast heard him with surprise, but in other respects their reactions were very different. Turpin was saddened. Having known Unthank as boy and man, he'd always been fond of him, and had to admit to himself that he'd appointed him primarily for this reason and because he wished to acquire a civilising counterweight to what he foresaw would be the pushy and vulgarian Prendergast. But inventing the post of Director of Outreach and Enterprise was the only way he would ever have got

Unthank's appointment past the board of governors, and he had to admit that it was a post to which the talents of his young protégé were not well suited. So guilt at the slightly underhand way in which Turpin had acquired him now combined with regret at losing him. Still, the battle to secure Mixton's future had been won, his own career was culminating in conspicuous achievement, and as far as Turpin was concerned the field could now be left to Ed Prendergast and the rest of the Philistines.

Prendergast's reaction was a mixture of delight and disbelief. He'd always made sure that Brenda knew that credit for the Mixton success story lay primarily with himself. Nevertheless, as part of the management team who presided over that success Unthank could assume some credit for it in the eyes of the world. Why, then, quit while he was winning? Prendergast suspected that Unthank's problem was a combination of paralysing intellectualism and sheer envy at what he himself had achieved. The Toff's attempts at outreach and enterprise had hardly been distinguished, but then he made matters worse by beating himself up over mediskype and Betty Attwood. With all his brains he couldn't understand that power politics is a game of hardball: there's no place for moral nicety. A successful outcome is the only moral yardstick, and he, Ed Prendergast, had won success for them all, even if he'd had to throttle it out of Bill Castles. So, deep down, Unthank probably envied what Prendergast had achieved and, realising he could never emulate it, was now withdrawing gracefully. Ed had seen him arrive and was now seeing him off. In today's university there was no place for people like Robert Unthank.

88. UNFINISHED BUSINESS

Before Mixton's future as a benchmark university was assured, a number of matters needed to be resolved, and Prendergast had a hand in most of them. The first was the mediskype burglaries. Using the list of future appointments that Leighton Rogers had copied from the DoCTOC diary, Inspector Foreman and his colleagues staked out one or two houses in smart neighbourhoods, and managed to catch the burglars red-handed. Under questioning they admitted that they encouraged the 'patients' to be interviewed in their sitting rooms, ostensibly to put them at their ease but in fact because that was where they kept most of their valuables.

'We got them to sit back a bit from the camera. Explained that rather than just focusing on their ailment we needed to get a more rounded view of them. In fact, we wanted to have a better look at what they had in their sitting rooms.'

'So all these jobs were carefully planned,' observed Inspector Foreman.

'Well, we had to, didn't we? You should see some of the stuff in people's houses. I mean they'd have had to pay us to take it away. But in others– '

The duty solicitor laid a hand on his client's arm. 'It's not necessary to burden the officer with too much detail.'

As thanks for his tip-off and to tell the public that the burglars'd been caught, Foreman took the news to Bill Castles, but was mildly surprised to hear that the paper wouldn't make too much of the burglars' connection with the uni. Nor would it refer to DoCTOC or mediskype.

'Didn't think you were keen to do the university any favours, Bill.'

'I'm not. Trouble is, all this outreach care and mediskype caper have given Mixton Uni a big national reputation. If I run a negative story on it, the whole town'll suffer.'

'I see what you mean.'

'Not only that but the government wouldn't thank you lot for ruining a medical experiment it's publicly backed.'

'That's all very well, Bill, but if the students are using mediskype to case people's houses, how we going to stop future crimes?'

'So happens I've had a word with Ed Prendergast at the uni,' Castles took a piece of paper out of his desk. 'He's drawn up some safeguards to ensure the mediskype sessions can't be abused in the future.'

Foreman glanced down the list. 'Looks like you've been doing my job for me, Bill.'

'Always like to do an old mate a favour, Derek. See, what I was thinking was, if we report that the burglars've been caught but say nothing about my lad's tip-off, the credit for it would be all yours. Sherlock Foreman, a sleuth of deductive brilliance! And a hot candidate for promotion, I'd say.'

So dazzled was Foreman by this prospect that he forgot to speculate any further about Castles' motives. If the public learnt that the villains had been nicked and that the credit for it was his, he didn't much care how the Chronic reported it. And when Castles added, 'I can see the headline now: FOREMAN FINDS THE FELONS', he was ready to hug himself. At the back of his mind, too, were some dire words from Marian: if he did any unnecessary harm to the uni, there'd be more bedroom sessions in which the handcuffs wouldn't come off, the pain would outweigh the pleasure, and all their trysts would be faithfully reported to Mrs Foreman. She'd also be supplied with helpful photographic illustrations.

There were two other issues on which Prendergast moved quickly. Central Energy's inquiry into the Feed-In Tariff had discovered that the six houses on the Compton Farm Estate whose meters had been 'readjusted' had each been visited by someone who made a point of flourishing his ID and declaring himself to be Doug Schmeltzer. Despite vehemently denying any involvement in the scam, the real Doug Schmeltzer was sacked and Brian's revenge over his old adversary completed. But the uni's much greater involvement was another matter. Under threat from Prendergast, Castles made no mention of it in the Chronic, and as it happened the silence suited Central Energy. In return for the university's readiness to settle its outstanding debt, Central was happy to avoid any publicity that would've made it look foolish, though it swiftly made its meters much more tamper-proof. Since whoever had doctored the Fallowfield meters could not have been Schmeltzer, Prendergast could think of only one other person who might be the culprit. But mindful of the old adage that those who are curious shall be rewarded only with lies, he asked no questions of Brian.

Finally, there was the little matter of the 3Hs – the hip-hop-highs which were being made and sold from within DoCTOC. Soon after the teleconference with Brenda Hodges, Prendergast summoned Clive Wilkinson to his office and got a shock. He'd not seen Wilkinson for some weeks, and although he'd noticed that Wilkinson had been growing somewhat more hirsute he now gave the appearance of utter dereliction. His face had almost disappeared behind unkempt hair and a beard, and he was wearing a baggy T-shirt, track-suit bottoms tucked into his socks, and a pair of trainers that seemed to have been scavenged from a recycle bin. Nor did he improve matters by responding to Prendergast's curt greeting with a 'Hi' and a limp, distant wave of the hand.

Prendergast at once put the accusation: that Wilkinson was making and selling drugs from his own department. Wilkinson smiled sleepily, as if receiving a compliment. He didn't deny it. It was no big deal, he said, and when Prendergast affirmed that the tablets were illegal, Wilkinson replied that they shouldn't be and that they put many of the world's wrongs to rights. Prendergast disagreed and sacked him on the spot. Showing neither surprise nor distress, Wilkinson got to his feet, gave Prendergast another wave, and with the exhortation, 'Keep it real', shuffled out of his office. It was evident that Wilkinson was an assiduous sampler of his own merchandise, but there was no reason to trouble the police or the media with details of the matter, a new and more responsible head of department was appointed, and DoCTOC then thrived on less addictive forms of medication.

In Westminster, too, there were signs that the tide was turning. Mixton's MP, Harry Hunter, was summoned to the office of the chief whip.

'Just a reconnoitre, Harry. Looks like you've played a good hand up there in, er, um, yes, Mixton. The PM likes what your university's done.Got rid of pointless courses, cut costs, made the students job-ready in two-thirds the time. An example for all the other uni's to follow.'

'Glad to hear that, Sidney. The local rag hasn't always been kind to the uni. But I and the vice chancellor have stood up to the editor and told him what-for.'

'There isn't any aspect of the government's agenda that gives you concerns? No? Good. In that case, the PM's minded to offer you the job of Parliamentary Under Secretary for Higher Education. New post. New challenge. Ready for it?'

Hunter was. He didn't know much about higher education, but if he could make a research assistant out of a life model he felt he was equal to anything. Had he not just eaten a large lunch he would've bitten Sidney's hand off.

89. CRESTING THE WAVE

Mixton University is now sailing full-steam ahead. Since his ennoblement for outstanding services to higher education, Lord Turpin of Barford St Michael has retired to his beautiful old tudor mansion in Oxfordshire. His friends acknowledge that he keeps a good table and an excellent cellar, and during the long summer months hosts some very pleasant games of croquet. But since Turpin's departure, the new vice-chancellor and chief executive officer, Professor Ed Prendergast OBE, has dispensed with assistant directors and adopted a more streamlined, hands-on style of management. During his time at Mixton the university has been transformed, and there are rumours that he's been short-listed for a VC's post at one of the universities in the Russell Group. Mixton's two-year degrees are hugely successful, if success be judged by the number of students it attracts, and it's believed that Prendergast enjoys a particularly close working relationship with Professor Lafayette in what used to be the Department, but is now the School, of Environmental and Ecological Studies. Soon after Castles' revelations, Lafayette was interviewed by Derek Foreman in connection with the Green Gorillas, but no charges were brought and she now lives a placid life with her daughter, Forest, and partner, Sioux. The age gap between Loren and Sioux is considerable, yet nullified by their shared commitment to saving the planet.

The School of Art and Design continues to flourish, thanks not so much to the mediocre leadership of Barry Powell as the notional presence of its internationally renowned artist, Professor Tom Burley. Burley is hardly ever to be seen on the premises, but when Powell complains to Prendergast the latter wisely ignores him, believing that the mere association of Burley's name with the university will benefit the latter enormously.

Thanks also to Prendergast, many of the old, drily academic degrees have been discontinued, their staff pensioned off or put to more useful purposes. But Eric Uggles is busier than ever. His timetable is divided between teaching letter- and report-writing to the Business and Marketing students, native as well as foreign, and English as a foreign language to vast numbers of Chinese students. Many of these arrive with only the most rudimentary English, but in the modern British university money speaks louder than words, and conscious of the high fees they pay Mixton takes a humane view of the problem. Uggles is still trying to get his articles published in academic journals, but has at least become the darling of the town's literary appreciation society, where he's in regular demand to give talks.

Much excited gossip attended Gary Dorn's hasty departure for Australia. Behind him, he left several angry women and a trail of unpaid bills. He loves the life Down Under, and his book is now in production at Wessex University Press for their flagship series, 'New Thinking in Feminism'. So impressed were the two leading academics who refereed the manuscript that Gary has been invited as keynote speaker to the forthcoming international conference in Barcelona on sexuality and gender studies. The only cloud in his sky is that after a liaison with the wife of a lifeguard on Bondi Beach, he has been obliged to take some leave of absence from his college. The lifeguard has been vowing to all and sundry that should they ever meet he intends to make sure that Gary will never again trouble his wife – or, indeed, any other woman. This has brought a connotation to the term 'postgendered' that Gary hadn't previously considered.

Someone whom Prendergast has gratefully elevated within the university yet who is not wholly contented is Brian. The new post of Director of Security and Internal Communications was created especially for him, and has brought with it a handsome increase to his salary. But now installed in a spacious office he yearns for the secret den he once occupied down in the basement. He has also been obliged to swap his beloved ESMO uniform for a suit that is just 'not him' and already feels too tight. And finally, whenever he meets Tosh, Mitch or Bomber and they put their hands together and bow down before him, he finds it hard to enjoy the joke.

Perhaps the ultimate sign of the university's newly acquired glamour is the growing number of pop stars and professional footballers who are eager to accept its honorary degrees. But it retains its intellectual gravitas by conferring them on other, worthier figures too. Bill Castles, for instance, has received a doctorate in recognition of *The Mixton Chronicle*'s work in binding the university and the local community more closely together. He likes to give his friends an occasional jokey reminder that they should call him '*Doctor* Castles', but he can't help noticing the discrepancy that often exists between fancy academic titles and the jobs they command. With her third-class BA in Fine Art, his daughter Astrid is now working as a flight attendant on a low-budget airline. It was a job she could've walked into when she left school, thus saving him the thick end of thirty grand in undergraduate fees. Castles sometimes feels rueful about the massive, multiple scoop he was forced to renounce – a story that would've had earth-shaking consequences and ensured that Provincial News Editor of the Year would've been the least of his honours! But he also feels rueful about what forced him to spike it – his trivial and wholly artistic predilection for the younger female form. Iris is still by his side, the Range-Rover is parked in the drive, and all-in-all his present life isn't a bad one.

90. A CHILLY AUTUMN

It seemed a strange place in which to find himself. The back of beyond. He felt as if he were clinging to the rim of the world. All along the coast were relics of industry's ebb. To the north, Workington, Maryport, Aspatria; to the south, Cleator Moor, the nuclear behemoth of Sellafield, Barrow-in-Furness. Narrowing his eyes against the rain, he looked out at the turbid sea and scudding clouds, with their angry, orange edges. Waves heaved and spilled over the harbour wall. The rising spume looked like ghostly locks of hair. To the right, a whirling wind-farm, with hills not sky behind the turbines, seemed cluttered rather than elegant. The town centre was half-empty. Streets of low terraced houses were painted in defiantly bright colours, but it seemed like a place where the clocks had stopped more than half a century ago. Now, after hours of driving rain, came some weak, apologetic sunshine.

He'd just come from the Lake District, where the charity of which he was a trustee had organised a conference on outdoor activities for the disadvantaged and delinquent youngsters in its care. One of the other trustees had given him a lift thus far, the first leg of his long journey home. But Whitehaven was a hard place to get out of. The west coast main line could be joined at Carlisle, but Carlisle lay some forty miles to the north and the local trains were infrequent and took more than an hour to reach it. How would he kill the time?

Standing in the main street with a small suitcase in his hand, he looked at the supermarkets, charity shops and snack bars on the opposite side, and his eye fell on 'Heads Up Unisex Hair Stylist'. This reminded him of Clare's remark that if he found himself with a spare moment he could do with a haircut. He crossed the street and pushed open the door. A bell tinkled. The shop was empty, but a woman's voice from the back shouted, 'Coming. Just choose a chair.' The choice was easy. There were only two, each facing a wash-basin and mirror, and one of them was obstructed by a huge hair-dryer on castors. He took off his coat and sat in the other, looked at the array of shampoos, lotions and hairdressing instruments on the ledge above the basin, and then regarded himself blankly in the mirror. Along the wall behind him was a row of empty plastic seats for those waiting to be served. Business was evidently slow. The hairdresser had yet to appear, and since the conference had been lengthy, he yielded to an impulse to shut his eyes.

'Bloody hell! It can't be. Robert Unthank?' He stared at the reflection in the mirror. In accent and appearance the woman was unmistakable: Holly.

'Good God,' he muttered and leapt out of his chair to kiss her on both cheeks. 'What a marvellous surprise. And you haven't changed a jot.' The compliment was true enough. Her beauty had thickened, but there was the same broad, ingenuous smile, the dark-blonde hair precariously pinned with a comb. She pressed him back into the chair, and as she fetched him coffee and a biscuit he quickly explained his reason for being in the area. 'But how the devil did you end up here?'

372

As she washed and cut his hair she told the story. 'After I finished with Gary Dorn at the uni . . .'

'You were in a relationship with Gary Dorn? I had no idea.'

'Wasted most of my time at Mixton going out with that two-timing bastard. But in the end I got wise to him and cut my losses. For the last few months I put my head down and did some work. Ended up with a lousy degree but I s'pose it were better than nowt. Must make me the best qualified hair-dresser in Whitehaven,' and she chuckled throatily.

'So what did you do then?'

'Shaun were still hanging round Mixton. Remember him?'

'Of course. He used to take you out for rides in his souped-up Ferrari that was a clapped-out Fiat.'

'I think he'd always had a bit of a crush on me. He were a tower of strength after I finished with Dorn. Said he couldn't offer much in the way of glamour but he'd stick with me through thick and thin.' She snipped busily. 'And I decided that's what I preferred. By the time I left Mixton I were pregnant. We're still together. And we've got a little boy, Jasper, who is my own true sweetheart.'

'Do you miss it – the glamour? When you were at Mixton the media hardly left you alone.'

'Naah! Even at the time, I knew it were bullshit and wouldn't last five minutes. I don't want to do this for the rest of my life,' and as she cut and combed his hair she glanced round the shop, 'but I'm sure I'll find summat different before long. How's the dear old uni these days?'

'I believe it's thriving, but I'm no longer there. I resigned about the time you left. But you still haven't told me how you ended up in Whitehaven.'

'Yeah, well Shaun . . . and speak of the devil, here he is. With my little darling!'

Shaun had entered the shop with their child in his arms. Holly took the child and he and Unthank shook hands. He seemed as skinny and awkward as ever, and after an exchange of social niceties stood silently, hands in the back pockets of his jeans and watching Holly and Jasper with the gaze of a happy man.

'I think he needs changing,' he told Holly. 'I'll take him out the back while you finish Robert's hair.' And off went father and son.

'Shaun comes from this part of the world,' she explained as she plied the hair-drier. 'And when his auntie died she left us this shop. It hardly covers itself, but Shaun's also a jobbing carpenter. He gets lots of work 'cos he's really good with his hands. We get by.'

When Unthank got to his feet she flatly refused payment, so as she turned to take his overcoat from the hanger he left notes on the ledge under the mirror. 'But you haven't told me something,' she said, as she helped him into his coat. 'Why did *you* leave Mixton?'

Unthank hadn't expected the question and thought for a moment. 'I suppose I felt that I didn't really fit in.'

Her answer surprised him. 'That were always obvious.'

She turned him round and swept his shoulders with a clothes brush – 'Mrs Unthank won't be too ashamed of you now' – and he turned back to give her a farewell embrace. As he did so she held him for a moment and, with her cheek pressed to his, murmured fiercely in his ear, 'You're a good man, Robert Unthank. A good man.'

Outside it had come on to rain again. He pulled the coat collar round his newly bare neck and looked up at the sky. If he stepped out, he might just catch that Carlisle train. There was a gust of wind. Leaves skittered along the gutter. It was going to be a chilly autumn.

Printed in Great Britain
by Amazon